Zoophysiology   Volume 31

Zoophysiology

M. S. Kaulenas

Insect Accessory Reproductive Structures

Function, Structure, and Development

With 30 Figures

Springer-Verlag
Berlin Heidelberg New York London
Paris Tokyo Hong Kong Barcelona
Budapest

Professor Dr. M. S. KAULENAS

University of Massachusetts at Amherst
Zoology Department
348 Morrill Science Center
Amherst, MA 01003, USA

ISBN 3-540-52111-9 Springer-Verlag Berlin Heidelberg New York
ISBN 0-387-52111-9 Springer-Verlag New York Berlin Heidelberg

Library of Congress Cataloging-in-Publication Data. Kaulenas, M.S. Insect accessory re-
productive structures: function, structures, and development / M.S. Kaulenas. p. cm. —
(Zoophysiology; v. 31) Includes bibliographycal references and index. ISBN 0-387-52111-9
(U.S.) 1. Insects — Generative organs. 2. Insects — Reproduction. I. Title. II. Series.
QL494.K38 1992 91-27958 595.7'016—dc20

© Springer-Verlag Berlin Heidelberg 1992
Printed in the United States of America

Typesetting: International Typesetters Inc., Makati, Philippines
31/3145-543210 — Printed on acid-free paper

Preface

In retrospect, the range of topics covered in this monograph, although forming a coherent ensemble, is so extensive that a detailed discussion could easily extend to three or four times the current length. My approach has been to identify the critical issues, summarize the major accomplishments, and to suggest promising avenues for future research. To facilitate this summary presentation, I have limited the literature review largely to material published after 1970, extending to material appearing late in 1990.

I gratefully acknowledge the advice of many colleagues, particularly the valuable criticisms of Drs. Warren Burggren, Joseph Kunkel, Randall Phillis, and John Stoffolano. I also wish to thank Mrs. Elizabeth Brooks for secretarial assistance. Finally, thanks are due to Dr. D. Czeschlik and his staff at Springer Verlag for their patience and support.

Amherst, MA, October 1991   M. S. KAULENAS

Contents

1 Introduction

The last decade has been a very exciting one in developmental biology, as a combination of new approaches in cell biology, embryology, genetics, and molecular biology has allowed progress on a number of long-standing questions. Before this recent explosion of information, it could be plausibly maintained that studies of development largely reformulated, in more up-to-date terms, questions originally posed by workers of the late nineteenth and early twentieth centuries. Such reformulations need not imply a deeper understanding of the problems. In fact, many developmental biologists were pessimistic about the utility of adopting molecular approaches to problems in cell differentiation. From this point of view, analyses of systems at more detailed levels of structure do not contribute to the solution of problems, but rather, as Davenport (1979) stated, lead to "a disappearance of the phenomena we are concerned with and the reappearance of new problems of form in association with new structural levels. Properties appear and disappear as each new structural level is reached, but the formal problems associated with the emergence of physical systems remain." Development, viewed as the successive emergence of progressively higher levels of order, would be unanalyzable by reductionist approaches if there were no possibility for interconnecting the different levels of complexity.

It seems now likely that such views are too pessimistic. For instance, analysis of the genes which control early events of embryogenesis has revealed a cascade of interactions between transcriptional regulators, leading to the positional specification of cells (Ingham 1988). Molecular mechanisms behind pattern formation, embryonic induction, and cell-cell interactions in general, as well as the nature of the "determined" state are emerging (Dressler and Gruss 1988; Yarden and Ullrich 1988; Harrison and Aggarwal 1990; Takeichi 1990). Such definitions begin to provide the basis for interconnections between the various structural levels encountered in development.

In these emerging molecular and genetic definitions of developmental problems, such as the establishment of the embryonic axis and the specification of segmental identity, insect systems, especially that of the fruit fly *Drosophila*, are playing a leading role. While the focus is on the events taking place during actual development, a number of accessory reproductive structures play vital roles in establishing the background against which the differentiative processes take place. For example, none of the dramatic events of embryogenesis would be possible without the provision of adequate energy resources to the egg, or the supply of most of the components of the protein synthetic machinery. Equally, systems that ensure the physical survival of the egg, as well as those designed to deliver viable sperm, are essential. Accessory reproductive systems which play out their roles away from the oocyte itself therefore perform vital functions in enabling the complicated interplay of development to occur. Such accessory systems also provide outstanding models for the analysis of a

1

variety of questions in cell biology, endocrinology, and genetics. These accessory systems and their contribution to insect development are the subjects of the present volume.

The scope of the coverage is illustrated and summarized in Fig. 1. From a developmental perspective, the central site of action is the ovary. As documented in Section 3.2, three basic types of ovary organization are found in insects: (1) the panoistic ovary, in which most of the informational/instructive resources of the oocyte are provided by the synthetic activity of the oocyte nucleus itself; (2) the meroistic polytrophic ovary, in which a number of cells derived from the germinal tissue, termed nurse cells, form a part of the egg chamber and supply the bulk of the nonyolk cytoplasmic content of the mature oocyte; and (3) the meroistic telotrophic ovary, in which a syncytium of trophocyte cells provides informational and other components to growing oocytes via specialized organelles called trophic cords. In the vast majority of species, in all three types of ovary, the nutritive, or yolk, contribution is supplied largely by the fat body, a metabolically versatile and multifunctional tissue (Sect. 3.5). In some cases, the follicle cells can serve as additional sources of yolk (Sect. 3.2.2). Another follicle cell function is the formation of the protective layers of the egg. These include the vitelline membrane and the chorion (Sects. 3.2.3, 3.2.4). Ovary and oviduct-associated secretory cells can have important contributions to various aspects of egg production. Possibly the most significant of such structures are the spermathecal accessory glands (Sect. 3.4.1), and the female accessory glands, such as the collaterial glands (Sect. 3.4.2). Lastly, various secretory functions of the vagina may play a role in egg production.

With regard to male accessory reproductive structures, the accessory glands are of major significance; such glands enable the transfer of the sperm to the female (Sect. 4.3). In many cases this involves the production of a spermatophore, a packaging device for sperm, which facilitates sperm transfer. Various ancillary functions, which affect sperm survival or impinge on postmating female behavior, are often associated with spermatophore production. Other secretory activities of the male efferent reproductive ducts, such as the products of the vas deferens or the ejaculatory duct, also facilitate the mating process (Sects. 4.2, 4.3). The synthetic activities and the definitive morphological characteristics of most of these structures are influenced by either juvenile hormone and/or ecdysteroids, at some stage, and provide important experimental systems for the investigation of the effects of hormones on developmental processes. Together, these various systems make important contributions, whether direct or indirect, to the analysis of embryonic development.

2

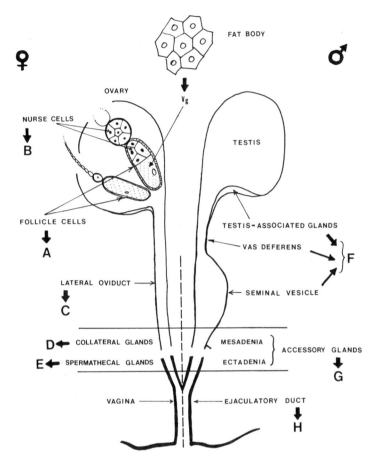

Fig. 1. Diagrammatic representation of the female (*left*) and male reproductive systems and associated structures. The full range of complexity for the oviducts, accessory glands and vagina for the female and the accessory glands for the male are not illustrated, but are discussed in detail under the appropriate sections in the text. *Thick lines* ectodermally derived structures. *Thin lines* mesodermally derived structures. *A-H* The major products or activities of reproductive system-associated structures. *A* Yolk protein, vitelline membrane, chorion. *B* rRNAs, mRNAs and other cytoplasmic components. *C* Variable secretory contribution to egg-laying. *D* Trophic secretions; egg cases; glues. *E* Sperm storage and maintenance. *F* Generally various nutritive secretions. *G* Formation of spermatophore and various fecundity-enhancing and female receptivity limiting factors. *H* In cases where the duct is secretory, generally the production of materials which influence the female's physiology; *Vg* vitellogenin

3

The Reproductive Efferent Duct Systems and Associated Structures. Development and Genetic Control of Differentiation

As in almost all other aspects of their structure and ecology, insects exhibit an almost bewildering array of patterns for the differentiation of the germ cells and the formation of the gonads and associated secondary structures, such as the efferent ducts and appendages. Various aspects of these topics have been described and reviewed by Snodgrass (1935), Imms (1957) and Matsuda (1976), among others. Even reviews that are nearly a century old (Graber 1891; Heymons 1895) contain relevant information, and provide some flavor of the full range of variation. From the perspective of this monograph, the embryonic origin and further development and differentiation of the reproductive efferent ducts and their associated structures are of greatest interest. The situation in the orthopteroid insects (the grasshoppers, crickets, cockroaches, and mantids) and in the Diptera will be discussed in greatest detail, since the bulk of the published information is on these systems; other examples will be considered to highlight common features or to stress differences in development. Whether the structures formed are male or female is under genetic control. Rather intense recent effort, using genetic and molecular approaches, has begun to yield substantial insights on the control of sexual differentiation in insects. This work is discussed in some detail in Section 2.3).

2.1 Origin of the Germ Cells and Associated Cells and Tissues

The apparent origin of the germ cells in the exopterygotes depends to a large extent on how early in development they can be distinguished. Among the orthopteroid insects, in species where the germ cells appear relatively early in development, such as the house cricket, *Acheta domesticus* (Hemons 1895; Echard 1968), and the grasshopper, *Melanoplus* (Nelsen 1934), the germ cells appear to be of ectodermal origin, forming at the posterior pole of the egg at the time of mesoderm segregation. Later in development in *Acheta*, they become associated with the mesoderm of the second and third abdominal segments; in *Melanoplus* they migrate into the coelomic cavities of the first to eighth abdominal segments, where they associate with the splanchnic wall and form a genital strand, from which the gonad differentiates later in embryogenesis. In species where the germ cells are first recognizable slightly later in development, they are usually associated with the median walls of the dorsal coelomic cavities; in abdominal segments 1–6 for *Xiphidium* (Wheeler 1893), segments 2–5 for *Locusta* (Roonwal 1937) and segments 1–7 for the Stenopelmatid, *Tachycines* (Ibrahim 1958). A similar situation is found for the cockroaches, *Blattella* (Heymons 1890, 1892) and *Periplaneta* (Heymons 1895) and for the mantid,

Hierodula (Görg 1959). In each of these species a genital ridge containing the germ cells is formed on each side of the embryo, extending from abdominal segment 2–5 in the cockroaches and segments 2–8 in the mantid. A similar progression in germ cell derivation is noted for the Heteroptera. In *Rhodnius* (Mellanby 1936), *Oncopeltus* (Butt 1949) and *Blissus* (Choban and Gupta 1972) the germ cells appear at the posterior pole at or just after the establishment of the germ band. In other bugs, however, germ cell differentiation is delayed and they appear in the mesodermal areas of abdominal segments 2–8 (e.g., *Pyrrhocoris*; Seidel 1924).

The typical genital rudiment in most of the above insects, during or just after the involution of the germ band (anatrepsis), consists of the following components: (1) a terminal filament membrane; (2) a mesodermal dorsal cell mass, immediately ventral to (1); (3) a central cell mass, composed of primoridal germ cells and mesodermal cells; (4) a ventral cell strand of mesodermal cells which are the primordia of the gonadal portion of the genital ducts; and (5) a surrounding epithelial membrane which envelops all of the above (see Fig. 2B,E).

Among the endopterygotes, germ cell formation is best understood in the Diptera. The germ cells are formed from pole cells, which are established very early in development at the posterior pole of the embryo. In *Drosophila*, at about the eighth or ninth nuclear division, a variable number (about 18) of energids (cleavage nuclei) enter the posterior pole plasm and are pinched off as pole cells (Bownes 1982a). They can be seen in a posterior space between the vitelline membrane and the egg surface which is created by the posterior contraction of the egg (Imaizumi 1958). In this location the pole cells continue to divide, but no longer synchronously with the rest of the potential blastoderm nuclei, to produce eventually between 37 and 71 cells (Huettner 1923; Sonnenblick 1941). This scenario, with a small and sometimes variable number of cells entering the pole plasm and eventually generating the definitive pole cell number by further divisions, is found throughout the Nematocera and the Cyclorrhapha (Table 1). Only some of the pole cells eventually migrate to the presumptive gonads, which lie on either side of the gut and are mesodermally derived (Bownes and Dale 1982). About eight pole cells enter the female gonad to become germ cells (Wieschaus and Szabad 1979). The pole cells which fail to reach the gonad have a variety of destinations, but all of such cells probably later degenerate rather than differentiating into other tissue types (Underwood et al. 1980).

Up to the blastoderm stage, and possibly until gastrulation, *Drosophila* nuclei are totipotent (Zalokar 1971, 1973; Illmensee 1973). The determination of the pole cells as presumptive germ cells, therefore, depends upon the interaction of the entering energids with the pole cells cytoplasm. The polar plasm has a characteristic signature in the presence of RNA containing polar granules (Mahowald 1962, 1971). UV-irradiation of the posterior pole of the embryo, before the entry of the energids, leads to the formation of sterile adults (Geigy 1931). This phenotype can be rescued by the implantation of untreated cytoplasm into irradiated embryos (Warn 1975). A series of decisive experiments by Illmensee and Mahowald (1974, 1976) confirmed the essential role of the posterior pole cytoplasm in germ cell determination. In these experiments they transplanted posterior pole plasm to the anterior end of another egg. Nuclei entering this chimeric region acquired cytological characteristics of pole cells. Moreover, if such cells were implanted among normal pole cells of another embryo, carrying different genetic markers, they formed germ cells capable of giving

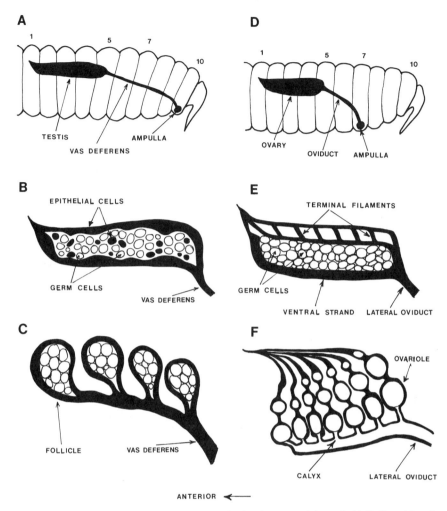

Fig. 2A-F. Diagrammatic representation of the early development of the male (**A,B,C**) and female (**D,E,F**) reproductive systems in a hypothetical "typical orthopteroid" insect. **A,B,D,E** Late embryonic; **C,F** first instar nymph (After Heymons 1891, quoted by Korschelt and Heiden 1890)

rise to progeny. The germ cell "determinants" specifiying the developmental fate of any energids which interact with them seem to make their appearance during the latter (stage 13) stages of oogenesis (Illmensee et al. 1976). Only rather preliminary experiments have been carried out to characterize at the molecular level what such "determinants" could be (Waring et al. 1978).

In other Diptera, e.g., the fungus gnat *Bradysia*, a conspicuous cytoplasmic area, the oosome, is present at the posterior pole of the egg. Cleavage nuclei entering this area eventually form germ cells. As for the polar plasm of *Drosophila*, synthesis of the ooplasm components starts well before the end of vitellogenesis. While no more

Table 1. Pole cell formation in the Diptera

Species	Cells entering polar plasm	Final number of pole cells	Reference
Nematocera			
Anopheles	4	20–30	Ivanova-Kazas (1949)
Chironomus	1	8	Balbiani (1882)
			Ritter (1890)
			Yajima (1960)
Culex	Variable	12–16	Idris (1960)
			Davis (1967)
Miastor	1	8	Metschnikow (1866)
			Hegner (1912)
Sciara	2	22–28	DuBois (1924)
Cyclorrhapha			
Calliphora	Variable	19–37	van der Starre-
			van der Molen (1972)
Dacus	4	32	Anderson (1962)
Drosophila	Variable	36–71	Huettner (1923)
Lucilia	Variable	26–30	Davis (1967)
Phormia	Variable	5–20	Auten (1934)

detail than in *Drosophila* is available on the nature of the morphogenetic materials stored in the ooplasm, it is of interest that maintaining the posterior localization of this activity in *Bradysia* is dependent on cytoskeletal elements (Gutzeit 1985). It is possible that the microtubular network serves to anchor the morphogens at specific cytoplasmic locations.

Functionally similar, but not quite as well-characterized, posterior pole plasms, which determine germ cell differentiation, occur in the Coleoptera and the Hymenoptera. In the Coleoptera, a posterior ooplasm or polar disc is distinguishable in many species (e.g., *Donacia*, Hirschler 1909; *Leptinotarsa*, Hegner 1909; *Corynodes*, Paterson 1935). In these forms the germ cells become distinguishable, at the time of blastoderm formation, at the posterior end of the egg. Beyond establishing that the oosomal materials are important in the determination of the germ cells, very little information on the nature of the active components is available. In the Hymenoptera, some species (e.g., *Pimpla*, Bronskill 1959) contain a distinctive region called the oosome. The structure migrates to the posterior end of the egg, where the cytoplasm disperses. Germ cells are formed from the cleavage nuclei which enter the posterior germinal cytoplasmic region during blastoderm formation. Later, further mitoses by these cells generate a mass of germ cells at the posterior pole. In other Hymenoptera, as in most of the Exopterygotes, germ cell formation is delayed and they become first recognizable during gastrulation (*Pteronidea*, Shafiq 1954) or later, forming from the mesodermal tube (*Chalicodoma*, Carrière and Bürger 1897).

In many of the Lepidoptera germ cells appear at the posterior pole just after blastoderm formation (e.g., *Ephestia*, Sehl 1931). In some cases, germ cell differentiation is delayed; when it is, they appear in association with the mesoderm at the time of coelomic cavity formation (*Antheraea*, Saito 1937). A similar situation has been described for another silkmoth, *Bombyx*, although in this case experiments in which specific egg regions were killed at different times in development by cauterization show that germ cell determination occurs during blastoderm formation, while the cells become distinguishable morphologically only at later stages (Miya 1958).

In summary, insect germ-cell determination may depend on the interaction of totipotent nuclei with maternally derived "determinants" localized at specific regions of the egg, or the differentiative decisions may be postponed for varying intervals and depend on later cell-cell interactions. Almost the full range of variations are encountered in all groups, with possibly the majority of the endopterygotes opting for the former approach, with the reverse situation encountered in the Exopterygota. In all cases, the presumptive germ cells become associated with mesoderm-derived components to produce the rudimentary gonad.

2.2 Differentiation of the Efferent Duct System and Associated Structures

2.2.1 The Male System

The structure of the "typical" orthopteroid male reproductive system during the embryonic and immediate postembryonic stages is shown in Fig. 2A,B,C. The testis rudiment is usually confined to a limited number of more anterior or medial abdominal segments. The germ cells form a series of follicles of varying complexities in which the spermatogonia differentiate. No further discussion of this aspect will be persued in any detail since spermatogenesis is outside the scope of this Volume. The ventral mesodermal strand gives rise to the vas deferens. This structure is usually extended to the tenth abdominal segment, where terminal ampullae are formed by association with the mesodermal coelomic cavities of the tenth abdominal segment. The definitive terminal ampullae are ventually localized in the ninth segment (Fig. 3A). Figure 3 illustrates the situation found in *Acheta*, where in the first instar nymph the paired vasa deferentia end in the terminal ampullae in the posterior portion of the ninth abdominal segment. A single, rudimentary ejaculatory duct invagination is located between the primary phallic lobes. At this stage the mesodermal and ectodermal components remain separate (Quadri 1940). Later, in the last instar, the mesodermal terminal ampullae fuse and their distal ends join the ectodermal ejaculatory duct. The accessory gland is formed from a portion of the fused terminal ampullae, while paired terminal dilations, also derived from the terminal ampullae, form the seminal vesicles.

In other exopterygotes the details may differ. For example, in the Ephemeroptera, the vasa deferentia remain separate and eventually join paired ejaculatory ducts (Fig. 4A). In most cases the terminal ampullae fuse (Fig. 4B), and the seminal vesicles and accessory glands may differentiate from the fused structure as distinct organs (Fig. 4C); or only the accessory glands may be derived from the fused structure, while the seminal vesicles are the dilated ends of the vasa deferentia (Fig. 4D). In any event, all of the efferent ducts, with the exception of the ejaculatory duct, are mesodermally derived in most exopterygotes.

9

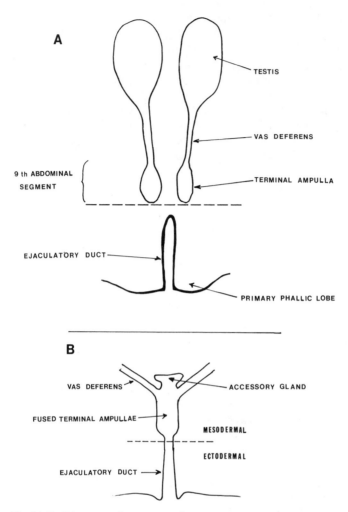

Fig. 3A,B. Diagrammatic representation of the male reproductive system in the first (**A**) and last (**B**) instar nymphs of *Acheta domesticus*

In many endopterygotes, on the other hand, derivatives of ectodermal invaginations replace, to varying degrees, many of the primitively mesodermal efferent structures (Fig. 4E). In those cases, e.g., some Coleoptera and some Lepidoptera, the seminal vesicles and the accessory glands are derived from the anterior portions of the ejaculatory duct, and even part of the vasa deferentia may be ectodermal (Matsuda 1976). While these systems generally develop as ectodermal invaginations, parts of them may form from genital imaginal discs (Kroeger 1959b; Dewes 1979). The most extreme condition is found in the Diptera, where the whole of the efferent system is derived from one or more imaginal discs (Laugé 1982).

10

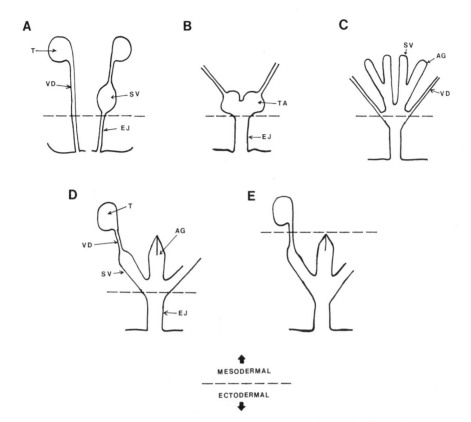

Fig. 4A-E. Diagrams illustrating the relationships and derivation of the male efferent duct system. *AG* Accessory gland; *EJ* ejaculatory duct; *SV* seminal vesicle; *T* testis; *VD* vas deferens

Drosophila provides the example in which a single genital imaginal disc gives rise to a variety of adult structures during the pupal stage. In the male, these include: (1) the adult analia (the anal plates and hindgut); (2) the external genitalia; and (3) the duct system (vas deferens, seminal vesicles, anterior ejaculatory duct and the ejaculatory bulb), as well as the accessory glands or paragonia. Comparative studies and clonal analysis suggest that the genital disc may have evolved through the fusion of the imaginal primordia of at least three or possibly four abdominal segments (Dübendorfer and Nöthiger 1982). The genital disc rudiment first becomes detectable as a group of about 60 cells in the late embryo, and in the newly hatched larva the rudiment is detectable as a clump of cells in front of the anal opening (Madhavan and Schneiderman 1977). Clonal analysis (Schüpbach et al. 1978) indicates that about 11 cells becomes committed as male genital disc cells at the blastoderm stage. Analysis of gynandromorph data strongly suggests that the portion of the disc giving rise to the analia is common to both male and female discs, but that the remaining structures (external genitalia, the duct systems, etc.) are derived from separate primordia for male and female (Nöthiger et al. 1977). For the development of the male genital disc, the male primordium and the primordium for the analia develop together in the larva as a single disc, while the female primordium is suppressed (Epper and Nöthiger 1982). During the larval period, the genital disc grows by cell division and probably by recruitment of cells from outside the disc (Laugé 1975), and eventually forms a hollow, saddle-shaped structure. A fate map of the disc can be constructed (Bryant and Hsei 1977).

During the larval stages the testis is surrounded by fat body, but otherwise lies free in the abdominal cavity. The junction between the genital ducts and the gonad is formed during metamorphosis. After attachment, the testes supply an outer sheath to the vasa deferentia (Stern and Hadorn 1939). The remaining structures are formed as a result of the eversion of the imaginal disc. Very similar events take place in other Diptera, except that usually three distinct genital imaginal discs are present (*Musca,* Dübendorfer 1971; *Calliphora,* Emmert 1972a,b); together they give rise to an equivalent set of structures produced by the single disc in *Drosophila.*

The origin and developmental relationships of the accessory glands is known in considerable detail. Three conditions can be documented (Table 2). In the Thysanura, Ephemeroptera, Plecoptera, Dermaptera and most of the Odonata, accessory glands are absent altogether, arguing for the possibility that this is the primitive condition. The Strepsiptera, and most Isoptera, where accessory glands are lacking also, probably represent a condition in which a secondary loss of these structures has occurred, since rudiments are detectable during development. The remaining accessory glands are classified either as mesadenia or ectadenia, depending upon their development derivation, with the mesadenia predominating among the exopterygotes, while ectadenia are of common occurrence in many of the endopterygotes.

Table 2. Accessory gland occurrence in some of the major insect groups[a]

Absent	Mesadenia	Ectadenia
Thysanura	Phasmida[b]	Diptera
Ephemeroptera	Blattaria[b]	Coleoptera (most)[e]
Plecoptera	Mantodea[b]	Homoptera (some)
Dermaptera	Orthoptera[b]	Lepidoptera (some
Odonata (most)		Mallophaga
	Thysanoptera	
Strepsiptera[c]		
Isoptera (most)[d]	Coleoptera (some)	
	Homoptera (some)	
	Heteroptera	
	Mecoptera	
	Lepidoptera (some)	
	Hymenoptera	

[a]Data based largely on Matsuda (1976).
[b]From terminal ampullae.
[c]Secondary loss.
[d]Neoteny.
[e]From swollen anterior ends of ejaculatory ducts.

2.2.2 The Female System

The structure of the "typical" orthopteroid female reproductive organs during the embryonic and immediate postembryonic stages is illustrated in Fig. 2D,E,F. The ovary rudiment is usually confined to a number of more anterior abdominal segments. The germ cells, in collaboration with mesodermal cells, form a variable number of follicles. Part of the dorsal mesodermal covering differentiates into the terminal filaments of the individual follicles. Sections of the ventral mesodermal covering differentiate into the pedicels at the base of each follicle. The follicle cells around the initial, terminal oocyte form from the mesoderm at the upper ends of the pedicels (Seidel 1924; Lautenschlager 1932). The follicle cells, the pedicels, as well as the terminal filaments and the tunica propria around the whole gonad, form therefore from portions of the mesodermal sheath around the primitive gonad.

In contrast to the male system, the lateral oviducts (derived from the ventral mesodermal strand around the ovary) generally extend only to the seventh abdominal segment, where they end in terminal ampullae derived from the coelomic cavities of this segment (Heymons 1895). In *Acheta domesticus* the ectodermal common oviduct rudiment appears in the third instar nymph (Quadri 1940) on the anterior portion of the eighth abdominal sternum (Nel 1929). A similar site for the common oviduct invagination, between the seventh and eighth sternae, ranging in timing from the freshly hatched nymph to the sixth instar, is found in other gryllids, as well as in grasshoppers and in Blatteria and Dermaptera (Nel 1929; Gupta 1948; Rakshpal 1961). The generalized "orthopteroid" conditions are illustrated in Fig. 5C. The paired mesodermal lateral oviducts generally are each dilated into an anterior calyx, which communicates with the pedicels of the individual follicles. The common oviduct is an ectodermal invagination on the eighth sternum, which develops between the third and sixth nymphal instars and opens into the germinal chamber. In *Gryllodes sigillatus* (Gupta 1948), an accessory gland invagination forms in the second instar nymph in the ninth sternum, but soon degenerates; in other Orthoptera, a female accessory gland either does not form, or exists in rudimentary form only for a short period. For the Blattidae, however, the accessory gland is an important organ, and generally forms as an invagination of the ninth sternum. The general physical relationship of all these invaginations, when they are present, for "orthopteroid" insects is illustrated in Fig. 5.

The "orthopteroid" condition diagrammed in Fig. 5C probably represents an intermediary condition. Possibly more primitive arrangements are illustrated in Fig. 5A and B. In the Ephemeroptera, paired, mesodermal lateral oviducts open separately at two gonopores at the back edge of the seventh sternum. The spermatheca is an ectodermal invagination of the eighth sternum (Fig. 5A). A somewhat different condition is found in many Odonata. In this case, the efferent ducts are mesodermal, but the terminal ampullae fuse to form a short median oviduct, which opens at a single gonopore. The spermatheca, again, is of ectodermal origin (Fig. 5B). In many other insects, especially among the Holometabola, evolutionary change has been by the addition of parts. In many cases, another ectodermal derivative, the vagina, is interposed between the common oviduct and the vulva. The duct systems become largely ectodermal, either by more vigorous assertion of the ectodermal invaginations or by the development of the duct and accessory structures from imaginal discs (as

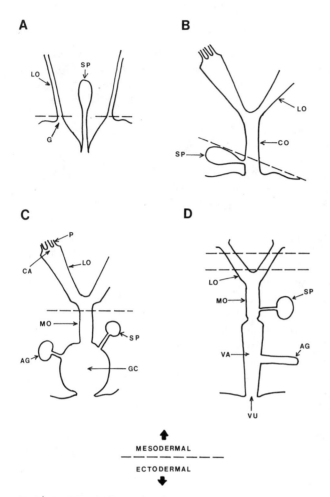

Fig. 5A-D. Diagram illustrating the relationships and derivation of the female efferent duct system. *AG* Accessory gland; *CA* calyx; *CO* common oviduct; *G* gonopore; *GC* genital chamber; *LO* lateral oviduct; *MO* median oviduct; *P* pedicel; *SP* spermatheca; *VA* vagina; *VU* vulva

in some Lepidoptera, Coleoptera, and Diptera; Matsuda 1976). The spermathecae and the accessory glands develop either from the imaginal discs or as separate invaginations in segments posterior to the common oviduct invagination. The relationship and derivation of the various components in these systems is illustrated in Fig. 5D. Snodgrass (1935) has diagrammed the segmental derivation of the various invaginations; a liberal interpretation of these observations, illustrating how the multiple invaginations could yield a single structure, is presented in Fig. 6.

As is the case for the male system, *Drosophila* represents what could be considered as an extreme development of the trend found in the endopterygotes. The anal plate, hindgut, ovipositor, and all of the internal genitalia are derived from a

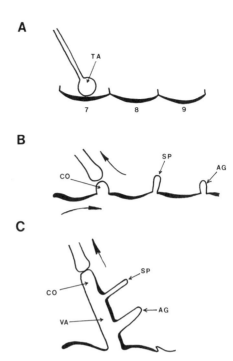

Fig. 6A-C. Diagrams illustrating sequential stages in the formation of the female efferent ducts and accessory structures. *AG* Accessory gland; *CO* common oviduct; *SP* spermatheca; *TA* terminal ampulla; *VA* vagina; *7,8,9* seventh, eighth, and ninth abdominal segments

single genital imaginal disc during the pupal stage. While there are differences in detail between the male and female genital discs [for example, clonal analysis suggests that only five blastoderm cells are involved in establishing the initial primordium; (Schüpbach et al. 1978)], many of the observations made in the previous section on male genital discs apply in broad outline. Development involves the incorporation of the primordium for the analia and the suppression of the male primordium to give the definitive female imaginal disc. As for the male disc, detailed fate maps have been constructed (Littlefield and Bryant 1979).

The culmination of disc development is the evagination of the disc during the pupal stage. Early in the process, about 6 h after the onset of puparium formation (APF), the disc elongates along the anteroposterior axis. The development of the internal structures consists of the protrusion of parts. At the beginning, the spermathecase are arranged in tandem, and not as two lateral organs. The lateral oviducts form the ovaries by 36 h APF and fusion is complete by 42 h. The ovaries exist as independent entities during the larval stages. They are round bodies consisting of large and small cells; the former are the germ cells, while the latter are the presumptive follicle cells and other mesodermal cells, which later form the ovarian sheath and the terminal filaments. The latter begin to form at about the middle of the third larval instar. Few other changes take place during the larval stages, and the complex cellular interactions which result in the adult ovary take place during the pupal stage.

At about 2 h APF, a basal lamina is secreted around the forming ovarioles (King et al. 1968). Some of the mesodermal cells differentiate into the ovarian epithelial sheaths and the oogonia in each ovariole form the stem cells. Eventual stem-cell

15

division produces one daughter cell which remains as a stem cell, and another daughter cell (the cystoblast), which goes on to produce cystocytes. The latter divide to give clusters of interconnected germ-line cells. The maximum cell number per cluster is 16 in *Drosophila*. Cystocyte division is discussed in detail in Section 3.2.1.

Part of the organization of the developing follicle is the acquisition of anteroposterior axial polarity. The first signs of anteroposterior polarity become apparent in the germarium when one of the 16 interconnected cystocytes, the prospective oocyte, migrates to the posterior pole of the follicle (King 1970). At about the time of oocyte migration, the germ cell cluster becomes enveloped by somatic follicle cells. A number of observations suggest that continuing cellular interactions between germ-line cells and follicle cells are essential for establishing and maintaining polarity. For example, the *dicephalic* (*dic*) mutant, which produces an aberrant nurse-cell distribution pattern, which in turn leads to the formation of a "double-headed" embryo (Lohs-Schardin 1982), has been analyzed using genetic chimeras (Frey and Gutzeit 1986). The results show that *dic* gene activity is required in both the follicle cells and their germ-line cells. If any of the two cell types is *dic⁻*, the mutant phenotype may result. Intercellular communication and cooperation between these two cell types is also evident from the experiments of Schüpbach (1987), who produced chimeras of the genes *gurken* (*grk*) and *torpedo* (*top*), respectively. Both genes affect the formation of the dorsolateral axis in the follicle as well as the embryo, with the expression of *top* essential in the follicle cells. On the other hand, some aspects of normal polarity of the follicular epithelium may be established in the absence of morphologically differentiating germ-line cells. In the tumor mutant *benign gonial cell neoplasm* (*bgcn*), the follicle cells differentiate to some extent even though the germ-line cells remain undifferentiated. Such follicle cells can synthesize vitelline membrane material, and in some cases, a columnar epithelium which resembles that of wild-type stage-9 follicles formed around the folliclés posterior end (Gutzeit and Strauß 1989). These observations indicate that the follicle cells have a certain autonomy with regard to the timing of their developmental program.

2.3 Genetic Control of Sexual Differentiation

There has been a substantial amount of work on the genetic control of sexual differentiation in insects. The vast bulk of this work has been on *Drosophila*. From one point of view this is unfortunate, since a comparative approach is often informative. On the other hand, the *Drosophila* system is well understood at a number of levels as a result of intense effort, which seems to be accelerating, over the last 80 years.

In *Drosophila*, somatic-cell and germ-line sexual differentiation and dosage compensation (a process which equalizes the amount of product derived from the single X chromosome present in males and the two X chromosomes present in females) is regulated by a cascade of interacting genes. The various participants in this cascade and their interactions are summarized in Fig. 7. This topic has been extensively reviewed (Baker and Belote 1983; Cline 1985; McKeown et al. 1986;

Baker 1989). The primary controlling agent in sex determination and dosage compensation is the ratio between the X chromosomes to sets of autosomes (the X:A ratio). The ratio is "read" by the products of a number of genes; some of which function as numerator elements, while others as denominator elements. Two of the numerator genes have been identified [*sisterless a* (*sis a*) and *sisterless b* (*sis b*)] and others probably exist. The denominator elements are less clearly defined. The end result of this "reading" is probably the production of DNA-binding proteins, which, with the cooperation of the *daughterless* (*da*) gene product (and possibly other components) activate the *Sex lethal* (*sxl*) gene. This gene is the key element in regulating female differentiation. One early function is autoregulation, which sets the gene in the functional mode. Once functional, it controls the proper expression of the *transformer* (*tra*) gene. The latter, in collaboration with *transformer-2* (*tra-2*) gene product regulates the expression of the *doublesex* (*dsx*) gene. The function of *dsx* in female somatic cell differentiation is to suppress male differentiation genes. *Dsx* needs the action of the *intersex* (*ix*) gene for this function. Female differentiation genes are not repressed, and female development ensues.

Sxl is also involved in the regulation of dosage compensation. When *Sxl* is active, it represses the activity of the *male-specific lethal* (*msl*) and the *male lethal* (*mle*) loci. The activity of the *msl/mle* genes is necessary to get hypertranscription of the male's X chromosome. In the absence of *msl/mle* activity, the lower, female-specific transcription rate ensues. *Sxl* activity is also involved in regulating the female germ line differentiation.

In males, the *Sxl* gene is turned on, but does not produce a functional product. In this case, the expression of the *msl/mle* loci is not repressed, and a male transcription rate of the X chromosome genes results. Moreover, *tra* also produces a nonfunctional product in the absence of *Sxl* function. In this case, *tra-2* gene activity alone selects a male mode of expression in the *dsx* gene; repression of the female differentiation genes occurs, while male differentiation is not repressed and male development takes place. The *tra-2* gene also has a role in the male germ-line differentiation.

The interacting regulatory cascade is rather complex, but the genetic evidence for this scheme seems to be solid. Genetics defines the activities and requirements, but in some cases has a feel of the "black box" approach, in which the participants in the action are defined, but not their mode of functioning. The application of molecular biological techniques has provided a way to look into the "black boxes". In fact, genetics and molecular biology have interacted synergistically in the analysis of the sex determination problem in *Drosophila*; so much so that many of the fine details of the process are emerging, as discussed below.

2.3.1 Daughterless

The gene *daughterless* is named for an unusual maternal effect shown by a leaky mutant allele, da^1 (Cline 1980). At intermediate growth temperatures, all of the daughters of homozygous mutant mothers fail to develop properly and die, while all of the male offspring survive. The daughters die even if they are genetically wild type for *da*, demonstrating a maternal requirement for da^+ expression (Cline 1980). At higher temperatures, however, nearly all of the sons die as well, regardless of their

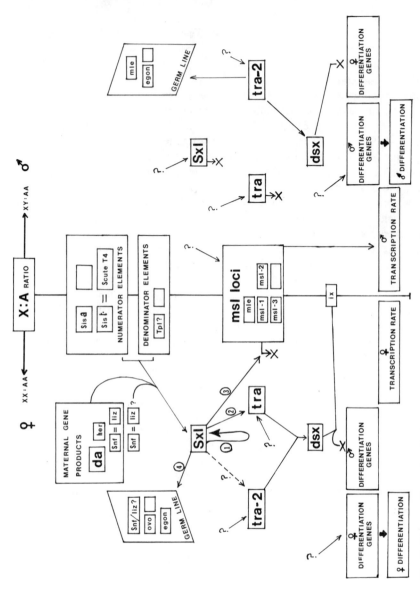

Fig. 7. Diagram illustrating the interrelationships of the genes involved in the control of sexual differentiation and dosage compensation in *Drosophila*. See text for the gene abbreviations

da genotype, indicating that *da*⁺ expression is necessary in both sexes. The latter observation is probably related to an essential zygotic role for *da* in both sexes (Cronmiller and Cline 1987). Its maternal activity is essential for correct sex determination, while zygotic activity is necessary for the formation of the peripheral nervous system, and probably other functions (Caudy et al. 1988a).

The effect of *da* is via an interaction with the genes of the *achaete-scute* complex [(AS-C) (Dambly-Chaudière et al. 1988)]. The AS-C, which is located at the tip of the X chromosome, plays an important role in the development of the embryonic central nervous system and the peripheral system of larvae and adult flies (Garcia-Bellido 1979; Dambly-Chaudière and Ghysen 1987). The AS-C complex covers about 90 kb of DNA and contains at least seven transcription units (Campuzano et al. 1985; Alonso and Cabrera 1988). Only four of them, T5, T4, T3 and Tla, all encoding proteins with extensive homologous domains, seem responsible for the neurogenic functions of the complex. The fours genes are involved in similar genetic operations. Loss of function mutations or deletions cause the loss of different, but overlapping subsets of sensory organs (Garcia-Bellido 1979); each gene is required for the differentiation of at least some neural state and in promoting the early stages of neural differentiation (Romani et al. 1987). Both AS-C and *da* appear to play a positive role since loss of either activity results in a lack of sensory organ development; genetic analysis predicts a very close interaction between them. The gene *extramacrohaetae* (*emc*) is a negative regulator of the AS-C genes (Ellis et al. 1990).

The *da* gene has been cloned by means of a chromosome walk (Caudy et al. 1988b). A number of new *da* alleles were used to characterize the cloned region. Five of the mutants, associated with chromosome rearrangements, cluster within a 6-kb region of DNA. The gene contains a single intron, and a coding sequence indicating a protein of 710 amino acids, with an approximate molecular weight of 72 kD. The predicted protein sequence has a number of interesting similarities to other proteins. The one of major interest is the-so called *myc* similarity region of about 60 amino acids. The *da* protein in this region has the complete conservation of ten residues, and other similarities, when compared to three *myc* proteins (*c-myc*, *N-myc*, *L-myc*); the *myc* proteins are nuclear oncogenes, which in normal development probably control cellular growth and differentiation. A similar degree of relatedness, in the same region, is found between *da* and three genes (T3, T4 and T5) of the AS-C and *Myo Dl*, a gene involved in myoblast determination in vertebrate cells (Robertson 1990). Other proteins belonging to this apparent superfamily include the E12 and E47 proteins, which bind to a specific control sequence located in the immunoglobulin kappa chain enhancer (Murre et al. 1989a), and another *Drosophila* regulatory protein, *Enhancer of split* (Klaembt et al. 1989). All of these appear to be DNA binding proteins which are involved in the regulation of differentiative decisions.

The homologous regions in this group of proteins have the potential to form two amphipathic helices separated by an intervening loop. There is a stringent conservation of hydrophobic residues in both helices. These proteins have been termed HLH proteins because of the helix-loop-helix motif (Murre et al. 1989b), or the bHLH group when the HLH motif is present near a basic amino acid domain (Jones 1990). The bHLH proteins are capable of forming homo- and heterodimers. Dimerization is mediated by the helix-loop-helix structure. Mutagenesis experiments on the *MyoD*

19

protein indicate that the basic region, which precedes the first amphipathic helix, is the region that contacts DNA (Davis et al. 1990).

A direct demonstration that *da* functions as a DNA binding protein when it is present in a heterodimer has been made by the in vitro experiments of Murre et al. (1989b). Using the specific DNA motif of the kappa chain enhancers (the KE2 site), they showed that *da* protein alone did not bind to this DNA motif. In the presence of the AS-C T3 protein, however, the heterodimer bound in a sequence specific manner. The *da* protein, apparently, is a striking homologue of E12, the natural DNA binding component in this system. E12, E47 or *da* constitute a class of proteins (class A) which can associate in heterodimeric form with any of a second group of proteins (class B), e.g., AS-C T3 or *MyoD*, to give dimers of very high affinity for specific DNA motifs. The class B proteins would be responsible for conferring different enhancer sequence specificities to the heterodimeric complexes and would confer target specificity on the class A transcription factors.

It is of interest that *emc*, which acts as a negative regulator of the AS-C, also contains an HLH motif, but lacks an adjacent basic domain (Garrell and Modolell 1990; Ellis et al. 1990). It seems probable that dimers containing the *emc* protein are incapable of binding DNA. In fact, negative regulation by this method could be quite general. For instance, the negative regulation of *MyoD* action is effected by a protein named *Id* (Benezra et al. 1990), which also lacks a basic region but contains an HLH motif, and, as *emc*, it may not be capable of binding DNA efficiently.

The maternal and zygotic *da* transcripts differ in size (3.2 kb for maternal; 3.7 kb for zygotic; Caudy et al. 1988b). However, the functional sections of both appear to be identical, and at present there is no evidence that the *da* products which interact with AS-C and *Sxl* are different. In both cases, it is highly likely that the *da* protein acts as a positive DNA-binding transcriptional regulator, using different partners in the functional heterodimers to confer appropriate target gene specificity. In fact, the case of *da* appears to be typical for the way transcription factors function in general. The theme seems to be one of combinatorial diversity of transcription factor proteins and control sequences. Control sequences can interact with multiple distinct factors, which themselves may be multimers in which different combinations of subunits produce different functions. Thus, combinations of control sequences often produce expression patterns that differ markedly from the summed effects of the individual control elements (Berk and Schmidt 1990).

2.3.2 Sex Determination: Measurement of the X:A Ratio

As noted briefly above, the ratio of the X chromosomes to sets of autosomes (X:A) is the primary genetic signal which triggers sex determination in *Drosophila* by defining the state of activity for the *Sxl* gene (Cline 1978). There are no known hormonal components, and, unlike the situation in vertebrates (Mardon and Page 1989; Mardon et al. 1989), genes on the Y chromosome play no role in sex determination. Once the state of activity for *Sxl* is set, at about the blastoderm stage (Sánchez and Nöthiger 1983), the X:A ratio is no longer needed as a genetic signal (Baker and Belote 1983). The genetic basis of the X:A signal is unclear. It is thought that it results from the interactions between X-linked components (numerator elements) and autosomal-linked components (denominator elements; Cline 1986).

A numerator element should possess several properties, the major ones being: (1) a reduction of its zygotic dose(s) should kill females as a consequence of a failure to activate *Sxl*; (2) an increase in its zygotic dose(s) should kill males because *Sxl* is inappropriately activated; (3) the female lethality should be suppressed by the constitutive *Sxl* M1 mutation (Cline 1978), while the male lethality should be suppressed by loss-of-function *Sxl* mutations. A number of subsidiary predictions must be satisfied as well (Cline 1986, 1988). So far, two numerator elements of the X:A signal, which satisfy the above criteria, have been identified. They are *sisterless a* (*sisa*; Cline 1986), an X-linked element (at *1*–34.3; 10B4), and *sisterless b* (*sisb*; Cline 1988), a region in the *achaete-scute* complex. Both function as positive regulators of *Sxl*. Torres and Sánchez (1989) have presented evidence that *sisb* is the AS-C gene *scute* (*T4*). Cline (1988) suggests that the T4 products which affect *Sxl* activation and neurogenesis are not totally overlapping. However, Torres and Sánchez (1989) indicate that there is no evidence to support the existence of two different T4 products, and it is possible that the T4 specificity may depend on the developmental stage at which the gene is expressed.

The nature of *sisa* is somewhat in the realm of a "black box", an activity delineated by genetic experiments. *Sisterless b*, however, if it is equivalent to or the same as *scute* (*T4*), appears to be a DNA binding protein. Since among its functions would be triggering *Sxl* to establish dosage compensation, which appears to be in action at the blastoderm stage (Gergen 1987), it must be among the earliest genes transcribed in *Drosophila* embryogenesis. This requirement would be consistent with the demonstration that T4 undergoes a preblastodermal transient expression (Romani et al. 1987; Villares and Cabrera 1987), leading to a homogeneous distribution of T4 RNA, which coincides with the first zygotic activation of many genes (Anderson and Lengyel 1980).

The demonstration that at least a part of the X:A nominator signal involves transcribed genes argues against the proposal that the X:A signal is composed of noncoding sequences able to bind with high affinity a *Sxl* repressor of autosomal origin (Chandra 1985). This observation also argues against a role in the X:A ratio signal for the moderately repeated sequence that is found almost exclusively on the X chromosome (Waring and Pollack 1987). This contrasts with the situation found in *Caenorhabditis elegans*, where sex determination is also controlled by the X:A ratio. For *C. elegans*, a feminizing element of about 131 bp is found within introns of many of the X-linked genes (McCoubrey et al. 1988), and such results would be consistent with the Chandra (1985) model for sex determination. However, sex determination mechanisms seem to be variable and rapidly evolving features of many animal groups (Jaffe and Laird 1986), and it would not be surprising if *C. elegans* and *Drosophila* have adopted different solutions to this problem. In any event, it is highly likely that *sisa* and *sisb* are not the only X:A numerator elements (Cline 1988). Identification of these components and their analysis will be needed to further progress in understanding the nature of the X:A numerator signal.

Very little is known about the denominator portion of the X:A signal. It has been suggested that the *triplo-lethal* (*Tpl+*) locus is in some way involved (Lucchesi and Manning 1987). Clearly, more work is necessary in this area.

2.3.3 Sex Lethal

As illustrated in Fig. 7, the gene *Sxl* is the key element in the initiation, maintenance and expression of sex differentiation pathways, in both somatic cells and the germ line, and in controlling dosage compensation. Cline (1988) has described *Sxl* as a binary switch gene in the establishment of sexual dimorphism, and most of the experimental evidence indicates that it has only two stable activity stages, feminizing and nonfeminizing, that are accurately maintained from early embryogenesis to adult differentiation (Cline 1978, 1984, 1988). The decision whether or not to express *Sxl* in its feminizing mode is cell autonomous, that is, it is made independently by individual embryonic cells (Lakhotia and Mukherjee 1969). The decision is maintained, also, in a cell independent manner, by the mitotic progeny of these embryonic cells (Sánchez and Nöthiger 1983).

The *Sxl* gene is activated early in the blastoderm stage (Gergen 1987) in both females and males. Despite the fact that *Sxl* has no essential function in males, and can be eliminated by mutation with no effect on phenotype (Maine et al. 1985; Salz et al. 1987), the frequently made statement that *Sxl* is off in males (Baker 1989) is not strictly correct. The gene is transcribed, since male specific RNAs can be detected (Bell et al. 1988); however, as discussed below, these transcripts do not produce a functional product. Gene activation in both males and females clearly occurs, since *Sxl* zygotic transcripts appear only at about 2 h postfertilization (Salz et al. 1989). Presumably the *da* gene product is involved in switching *Sxl* on, and the X:A signal transducing elements (such as *sisa, sisb* and probably other gene products) serve to set the female mode of expression. It might be noted, however, that direct biochemical evidence for this mode of activation is currently lacking. Once on, *Sxl* activity is required continuously to maintain its differentiative effects (Sánchez and Nöthiger 1982).

The *Sxl* gene is located in the 6F5-7A1 cytogenetic interval of the X chromosome (Nicklas and Cline 1983). Using P-element transposon tagging to recover lambda phage recombinants from this cytogenetic region, the *Sxl* chromosomal DNA has been cloned (Maine et al. 1985) and sequenced (Bell et al. 1988). The most interesting observation to emerge from the sequence analysis is the presence of a domain clearly related to that found in a variety of RNA binding proteins (Mattaj 1989; Bandziulis et al. 1989). The presence of the RNA binding domain and the characteristics of the genes controlled by *Sxl* strongly suggest that *Sxl* gene products are involved in regulating pre-mRNA splicing.

It is important to emphasize that, in eukaryotic cells, the formation of functional mRNAs often requires the removal of intervening RNA sequences (introns) from precursor mRNAs (pre-mRNAs, often referred to as HnRNAs) and the rejoining of coding sequences (exons) by a process called RNA splicing. The biochemical mechanism of this process is quite well understood (Padgett et al. 1986). The first step in splicing involves cleavage at the conserved 5'-splice site sequence with the concomitant covalent joining of a conserved guanosine residue at the 5'-end of the intron, via a 2',5'-phosphodiester bond, to a site within the intron known as the branch point sequence. This process yields the 5'-exon and intron-3'-exon intermediates. In the next step of splicing, cleavage at the conserved 3'-splice site takes place, and the two exons are joined by ligation, creating the mature mRNA and leaving the excised intron. Splicing occurs in large ribonucleoprotein complexes known as spliceosomes, which are assembled from abundant small nuclear ribonucleoprotein particles (snRNPs; Guthrie and Patterson 1988) in an ordered, ATP-dependent pathway. In addition to snRNPs, other protein factors can facilitate spliceosome formation, possibly by stabilizing interactions between the various components of the activity.

Messenger RNA precursor splicing can serve as an important mechanism for the posttranscriptional control of eukaryotic gene expression. Numerous examples of alternative splicing, where different mRNAs can be obtained from a single transcript by combining different exons, illustrate that regulation can occur in a temporal, tissue-specific, or developmental fashion (Breitbart et al. 1987; Mattay 1989; Helfman et al. 1990; Siebel and Rio 1990). *Sxl*, and as noted below, other genes in the somatic cell determination cascade, seem to be involved in splicing regulation. Recently, this prediction has been confirmed directly. Inoue et al. (1990) have performed cotransfection experiments in which *Sxl* complementary DNA (cDNA) and the *tra* gene are expressed in *Drosophila* K_c cells. They find that female *Sxl*-encoded protein binds specifically to the *tra* transcript at or near the non-sex-specific acceptor site, strongly implying that the female *Sxl* gene product is the *trans*-acting factor that regulates the alternative splicing.

Analysis of the transcripts produced by the *Sxl* gene shows a surprising complexity (Salz et al. 1989; Fig. 8). The *Sxl* transcription unit, of about 20 kb, encodes at least ten distinct, but overlapping RNA species. These RNAs range in size from 4.4 to 1.7 kb and show sex, stage and tissue specificity. Three of the ten transcripts comprise an early set found only at the blastoderm stage. Bell et al. (1988) propose that these early transcripts function in the autoregulation of splicing, thus establishing a stable "memory" of the initial, female-specific mode of gene expression. While this interpretation, indeed, may be correct, it should be noted that a distinct gene product, that of the *fl(2)d* gene, located on the second chromosome, is also required for the sex-specific splicing pattern of *Sxl* RNA in females (Granadino et al. 1990). Both the early *Sxl* and the *fl(2)d* functions may be needed to block the male specific splicing route. The precise mechanism of interaction has to be worked out. Equally, just what activates *fl(2)d* remains to be defined. The latter question is intriguing: *fl(2)d* is not simply a universal component of the splicing machinery, but appears to be specifically related to *Sxl*, since loss of function mutations in both genes are equivalent. Do the same regulatory mechanisms for turning on the genes apply in both cases?

A later set of transcripts from the *Sxl* locus appear after the blastoderm stage and persist throughout the remainder of development and into adult life. These transcripts are present in both males and females. The three female late transcripts overlap extensively, and share most exons, but differ in their 3'-ends. The overall evidence is very strong that they participate in the control of splicing of the gene products further along in the cascade of female somatic-cell sexual determination (Hodgkin 1989). The three male transcripts are similar to their female counterparts, except for the presence of an additional internal exon (exon 3). This exon contains a translation stop codon (Bell et al. 1988), and therefore the translational products of these transcripts are presumably inactive, truncated proteins. In the light of this, male differentiation could be regarded as a "default state" (Baker et al. 1987), since a female develops only when an active signal from the X:A ratio causes the expression of additional regulatory genes, supervised by the splicing activity of *Sxl*.

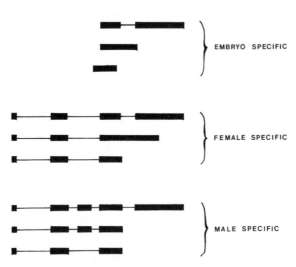

Fig. 8. RNAs derived from the *Sxl* transcription unit. *Thick lines* represent exons; *thin lines* represent introns. Direction of transcription is from *left* to *right* in all *Sxl* RNAs. Homologous regions in the RNAs are aligned *vertically* (After data of Salz et al. 1989)

At least one more *Sxl* transcript appears in adult females associated specifically with the development of the germ line (Salz et al. 1989). While germ-line differentiation is not the main subject of this Volume, it may be noted that a number of genes in addition to *Sxl* (Salz et al. 1987) are involved in sex cell and gonad development (e.g., *egon*; Rothe et al. 1989). In addition, the gene *fs(1)1621* (*Snf* Oliver et al. 1988; = *liz*, Steinmann-Zwicky 1988) has germ-line as well as somatic functions, one of which may well be the correct splicing of the germ-line *Sxl* transcript.

Some elegant experiments by Steinmann-Zwicky et al. (1989) have revaled an additional complication. These authors analyzed the fate of XY germ cells in ovaries, and that of XX germ cells in testes. Their results show that in ovaries, germ cells develop according to their X:A ratio; that is, XX cells go through oogenesis, XY cells form spermatocytes. In the testis, however, XY and XX germ cells entered the spermatogenic pathway. Therefore, not only the X:A ratio, but inductive signals from somatic cells can play a role in differentiation. However, both routes act through *Sxl* to achieve sex determination in germ cells.

2.3.4 Genes Controlling Somatic Sexual Differentiation

In *Drosophila*, four autosomal loci [*transformer* (*tra*); *transformer-2* (*tra-2*); *doublesex* (*dsx*) and *intersex* (*ix*)] govern the sex-specific gene expression responsible for sexual dimorphism (Baker and Belote 1983). Mutations at these loci do not affect dosage compensation, suggesting that the genes act after the control of sex and dosage compensation diverges. In addition, these genes do not control sex determination in the germ line (Marsh and Wieschaus 1978; Schüpbach 1982), and are essential only for normal somatic sexual differentiation. Recent molecular work has confirmed genetic evidence that these genes function as regulatory elements interposed between *Sxl* and various somatic genes which directly define the differentiated sexual phenotype (e.g., yolk protein expression, Belote et al. 1985; development of the genitalia and analia, Wieschaus and Nöthiger 1982; establishment of sex specific courtship behavior patterns, Baker and Belote 1983).

The *tra* gene is directly below *Sxl* in the epistatic hierarchy; *tra* has been cloned (Butler et al. 1986; Boggs et al. 1987) and sequenced (Boggs et al. 1987). Analysis of the transcripts shows that it gives rise to two sizes of RNA, one female-specific, the other present in both sexes. Both types of RNA are present throughout the life cycle. Expression or lack of expression of the gene has no effect on viability in XX or XY flies, and the gene has no known essential functions in males (McKeown et al. 1988). In females, however, a number of experiments suggest that *tra* may be needed continuously to allow expression of the genes under its control (Epper and Nöthiger 1982). The two types of RNA product are generated by alternative splicing of the pre-mRNA. In males, splicing of the first intron removes only 73 nucleotides from the primary transcript and produces an RNA without a long open reading frame, i.e., the presence of termination or stop codons precludes the synthesis of a functional protein. In females, about half of the *tra* RNA is spliced as in males, while most of the other transcripts are processed by using a female-specific, alternative 3'-splice site. In this case, 248 nucleotides are removed as part of the first intron. The female-specific splicing mode removes stop codons present in the longer RNA and yields a single long open reading frame. Substitution of a heat-shock gene promoter for the *tra* promoter still leads to female-specific differentiation of otherwise *tra⁻* females, strongly suggesting that the significant control level of this gene is not transcriptional, but rather involves the processing of the transcript.

Sosnowski et al. (1989) have investigated in greater detail the question of alternative splicing of the *tra* RNA. They have shown that the process involves competition between two 3'-splice sites. In the absence of *Sxl* activity, only one site is functional; with *Sxl* functional, both sites are active. The information for sex-specific splice-site selection is contained within the intron. Deletions of the splice site used in males lead to *Sxl*-independent expression of the otherwise female-specific site. The results of a number of deletion experiments are consistent with a model in which female-specific factors (the *Sxl* protein) block the function of the non-sex specific 3'-splice site. This prediction has been confirmed by a number of elegant experiments. Miyake et al. (1987) have investigated what happens when the *tra* gene is allowed to function in an artificial environment. In order to do so, they constructed a chimeric plasmid, a combination of plasmid DNA (which functions as a vehicle for the genes under investigation), the *tra* gene, and a promoter from a different gene (the *copia*-element long terminal repeat, which is known to be functional in all *Drosophila* cell types), to permit the transcription of the *tra* gene. They transfected K_C cells in cell culture with this construct and inspected the type of *tra* mRNA formed. The plasmid-borne *tra* gene was transcribed and spliced. The product was exclusively the non-sex-specific mRNA. It is clear that the molecular processing machinery of the K_C cells could transcribe and splice the *tra* gene product, and that this basic machinery produced a single type of mRNA (the non-sex-specific type). The experimental strategy and results are illustrated in Fig. 9A. If, in addition to the plasmid-*copia* promoter-*tra* gene construct, the K_C cells were also transfected with a chimeric plasmid containing *Sxl* cDNA [together with a heat-shock-protein (*hsp* 70) gene promoter to allow the transcription of the *Sxl* cDNA; Inoue et al. 1990); Fig. 9B,] the processing (splicing) pattern was dependent on the type of *Sxl* cDNA used. Only non-sex-specific splicing of *tra* transcripts was found when the *copia-tra* DNA was cotransfected with the *hsp* vector or with the male specific *Sxl* cDNA. On the other hand, female-specific processing of *tra* transcripts was found when the *copia-tra* plasmid was cotransfected with the female-specific *Sxl* DNA, or with a mixture of male- and female-specific cDNAs. The latter result showed that the *Sxl* male product did not interfere with the function of the female-specific RNA, and confirmed the previous interpretation that the male-specific *Sxl* transcript is nonfunctional. The results are totally consistent with the action of the female *Sxl* gene product as a *trans* factor regulating alternative splicing.

The splicing of *tra* clearly depends on *Sxl* function; the events controlling the activation of *tra* are not anywhere near as clear. One alternative would be for *Sxl* to turn on *tra* as well as regulate its splicing. The fact that *Sxl* appears to have its main function as an RNA-binding protein seems to argue against this dual role. Other possibilities include an alternative, so far undefined, mode of activation or a stage-dependent constitutive mode of expression for *tra*. The enthusiasm in following up the various splicing functions seems to have, so far, precluded a detailed analysis of the mechanisms involved in the activation of this gene.

The other interesting observation is that the *tra* product itself seems to be an RNA-binding protein (Baker 1989). The sequence from *Sxl* to *tra*, therefore, seems to be one splice-control agent regulating the splicing pattern of another splice control gene. As noted below, this sequence is the initial one in a cascade of regulated splicing which is associated with somatic sex differentiation in *Drosophila* (Hodgkin 1989).

The function of *tra* is to impose a female-specific splicing pattern on the *doublesex* (*dsx*) gene product; it does so with the collaboration of the *transformer-2* (*tra-2*) gene. Mutations in the *tra-2* locus cause chromosomally female (XX) animals to develop as males, but have no effect on the somatic development of chromosomally male (XY) animals (Epper and Bryant 1983). This morphological phenotype is identical to that found for *tra* mutations so it has been difficult, on the basis of genetics alone, to establish how the two genes interact. With the cloning and sequencing of *tra-2*, a clearer picture of the mechanism of gene interaction has emerged (Amrein et al. 1988, 1990; Goralski et al. 1989).

It should be noted that *tra-2* does not control *tra* expression (Nagoshi et al. 1988). The pattern of gene expression makes it likely that the two genes act in parallel to influence *dsx*. The protein coded by *tra-2*, identified by the conceptual translation of the gene sequence, is homologous to RNA-binding proteins (Amrein et al. 1988), strongly suggesting that the *tra-2* product may be directly involved in the processing of the *dsx* pre-mRNA. This suggestion is strengthened by sequence analysis of temperature-sensitive mutations in *tra-2*, which shows that the RNP motif is an essential functional domain in this protein (Amrein et al. 1990). So, in all probability, this is yet another gene in the somatic cell sex-specific differentiative pathway which

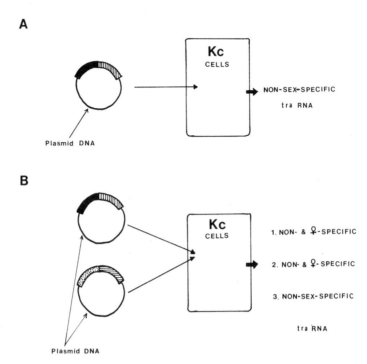

Fig. 9A,B. Diagrammatic representation of the experiments of Miyake et al. (1987) demonstrating the effect of *Sxl* transcripts on the splicing of *tra* RNA. **A** A chimeric plasmid, containing an inserted *copia* promoter (*solid box*), and the *tra* gene (*vertical striped box*), functions in K_c cells to produce non-sex-specific *tra* RNA. **B** When the K_c cells are cotransfected with the plasmid used in **A** and a second chimeric plasmid, containing a heat-shock-protein gene promoter (*stippled box*) and *Sxl* cDNA (*horizontally striped box*), the following results are obtained. *1* when the *Sxl* cDNA is of the female-specific type, the *tra* RNAs detected include non-sex-specific and female-specific types. *2* When the *Sxl* cDNA is a mixture of male and female specific types, the *tra* RNA detected include non-sex-specific and female-specific types. *3* When the *Sxl* cDNA is of the male-specific type, the *tra* RNA detected is only of the non-sex-specific type

is involved in some way in RNA splicing. The *tra-2* gene product is itself differentially spliced, to give two transcripts, one major and one minor (differing in the absence or presence of one exon), which are detectable in both males and females. Two other transcripts are present in male germ cells only (Amrein et al. 1990). It is interesting that transformation studies suggest that the major common transcript is sufficient for all functions in female sex determination and male fertility. The situation is complex and still not fully understood; for example, what controls the differential splicing of the products of this gene, and, of course, what precise roles do these differentially spliced products play? In any case, to produce the female specific processing pattern in the downstream, *dsx* gene, for somatic cells, the additional presence of the *tra* product is essential (Goralski et al. 1989).

In the germ line, the situation is somewhat different. The wild-type function of *tra-2* is required for normal spermatogenesis in XY males (Belote and Baker 1983).

27

The production or activity of the *tra-2* protein in the testes of XY animals cannot be dependent on the female-specific function of *tra*, since functional transcripts of the *tra* gene are not detected in males (Butler et al. 1986). In addition, XY animals homozygous for a null allele of *tra* are fertile males. In fact, in both sexes, the *tra-2* expression level is high in the germ line, and low in the soma (Amrein et al. 1988). The transcriptional regulation of this gene appears to be tissue- rather than sex-specific, and high expression of *tra-2* is found in cells which have entered the gametogenetic pathway; with low expression occuring in somatic cells. Some observations implicate different *cis*-regulatory sequences in the control of tissue-specific levels of expression. Some alleles of *tra-2*, which cause almost complete transformation of XX animals into pseudomales, do not affect the male germ line (Fujihara et al. 1978). Mapping of these mutants indicates that they have an insertion in the 5'-flanking region of the gene, which may exclusively affect the regulation of expression in somatic cells (Amrein et al. 1988).

The least clearly defined gene in the somatic sex differentiation pathway is *intersex* (*ix*). Mutations at this locus cause diplo-X individuals to develop as intersexes but have no effect in XY males (Kroeger 1959b). The product of this gene appears to be required in females, in conjunction with the *dsx* gene product, for the repression of male differentiation (Baker 1989).

In some respects *doublesex* (*dsx*) is the most interesting gene in the somatic sexual differentiation pathway. As pointed out by Nöthiger and Steinmann-Zwicky (1985) the products of the *dsx* locus are the final (and possibly the only signals) needed for sex determination in the soma. This locus, therefore, is the penultimate recipient of the X:A ratio signal. It has functions in both male and female flies. Analysis of mutagenized *dsx* flies shows that the locus contains two genetic functions, dsx^m to implement the male program, and dsx^f in control of the female program (Nöthiger et al. 1987). Dominant mutations correspond to constitutive expression of the male determining function, with a simultaneous abolishment of the female-determining function. When the effects of dsx^m and dsx^f are combined in the same cell, they appear to neutralize each other, leading to a null phenotype. This is in contrast to the mosaic pattern of male and female tissues found in triploid intersexes; the intersexes resulting from *dsx* mutants are morphologically intermediate between males and females, and the null phenotype appears to result from a combined expression of both male and female differentiation genes (Baker and Ridge 1980).

The *dsx* DNA region has been cloned (Baker and Wolfner 1988). The cloning was accomplished by means of two sequential chromosomal walks of nearly 200 kb. The walks were bridged by jumping via a deficiency that brought sequences from these two regions close together. It appears that all sequences necessary for *dsx* expression are found within a region of from 40–73 kb. This is a fairly large gene, even for *Drosophila*. The DNA is unique and is organized in the same way in males and females. Transcription from this locus is developmentally and sexually regulated. During the larval period, two non-sex-specific transcripts are produced. At the end of the larval stage, these transcripts disappear and are replaced by a set of male-specific and female-specific transcripts. In adults, an additional ·male-specific transcript appears (Baker and Wolfner 1988). The timing of the sex-specific expression does not quite correlate with the presence of the elements that are involved in regulating the differential splicing of *dsx*. *Sxl* and *tra* transcripts are present substantially before the appearance of sex-specific *dsx* products. It seems likely that there is an additional regulatory signal (possibly *ix*?) which is necessary for the switch in the pattern of *dsx* expression.

The various products of the *dsx* locus are due to differential splicing (Burtis and Baker 1989). As in *Sxl* and *tra*, there is a "default" pattern found in males, which appears to require only the basic cellular splicing machinery, and an alternative splicing pattern found in females. At the sequence level, the male acceptor splice sites are good matches to the *Drosophila* consensus, but the female 3'-splice site is a poor match. It is reasonable to suppose that modified or additional components may be necessary to achieve the female splice. Analysis of mutations which disrupt the regulation of *dsx* RNA processing indicate that sequences in the female specific exon are important for the regulation of sex-specific RNA splicing (Nagoshi and Baker 1990). It is possible that these sites interact with *trans*-acting regulators.

While the *dsx* transcript is differentially spliced, as are *Sxl, tra* and *tra-2*, the situation is different in several respects. In *dsx*, both male and female splicing patterns yield full-length products. In addition, the control of splicing is much more precise. These observations are consistent with genetic evidence, which indicates that *dsx* has important functions in both males and females. To some extent these functions are antagonistic, because, as noted above, expression of both yields intersexual differentiation. The proper functioning of *dsx* requires a precise distinction between the male and female patterns of expression. The protein products are identical in their amino termini, so it is possible that they might compete for the same targets. The way they do so is not clear at present, since the putative protein products do not resemble any other regulatory molecules.

The exact biochemical mechanism by which alternative splicing takes place in these regulatory genes of *Drosophila* has not been defined in great detail. Molecular genetic approaches suggest that *Sxl* and *tra* may use what has been called the "blockage" model (Helfman et al. 1990). In such cases, *trans*-acting factors could regulate splicing by binding to and preventing the use of one site, with a consequent use of the other site. Alternatively, RNA secondary structure or *trans*-acting factors may make one site the preferred one. This mode of regulation may be used in *dsx* (Nagoshi and Baker 1990). Further analysis of these systems by the use of in vitro reaction systems will be required to define the biochemistry in more detail.

Hodgkin (1989) presents an interesting speculation as to why regulation of splicing, rather than transcription, is used to control the sexual differentiation pathway. He proposes that the splicing machinery may be more easily maintained at high fidelity through successive mitoses than transcription complexes, which must be reestablished after every replication of the chromosome. Since the correct sexual state is crucial for cell viability, any mistakes in the transmission of the determined state could be fatal.

2.3.5 Dosage Compensation

In addition to its key role in the specification of germ-line and somatic sexual differentiation, *Sxl* is also the key controlling element in establishing dosage compensation. The relevant literature in this field is reviewed by Jaffe and Laird (1986) and Lucchesi and Manning (1987). In *Drosophila*, dosage compensation is accomplished by the transcriptional hyperactivation of most X-linked genes in males, in contrast to the case in Hymenoptera, where there is an extra round of DNA replication in haploid males (Rasch et al. 1977) or in Lepidoptera, where there appears to be no compensation at all (Johnson and Turner 1979). The fact that *Sxl* functions as a link between sex determination and dosage compensation is, perhaps, not surprising. As pointed out by Cline "the latter process is required only as a consequence of the particular signal that *Drosophila* has evolved to control the former" (Cline 1985). This signal is the X:A chromosome ratio, and *Sxl* is the key mediator in the transduction process.

Sxl functions by controlling the expression, presumably by regulating differential splicing, of a number of control genes, which function after *Sxl* expression. So far, four male-specific lethals of this type have been identified, namely *msl 1, msl 2, msl 3* and *mle*. These mutations are all autosomal recessive lethals for males; they do not affect female viability (Belote 1983). The genes *msl 1, msl 2* and *mle* appear to function in the same pathway, since a triple mutant for null alleles of all three genes has the same phenotype as each single mutant. The lethality appears to be due to a reduction in transcription level (Belote and Lucchesi 1980). It seems clear that additional genes are probably involved in interpreting dosage compensation signals; it is difficult to say how many of these there may be (Jaffe and Laird 1986).

In *Drosophila*, both X chromosomes are active in females (in contrast to the mammalian situation; Gartler and Riggs 1983), and most X-linked genes, but not all, are doage compensated in males (Lucchesi 1983). The hyperactivation of the male X-linked genes is accomplished at the transcriptional level. It is clear, therefore, that there should be *cis*-acting regulatory elements, associated with individual genes or chromosomal domains, which are responsible for dosage compensation. Evidence for such *cis*-acting elements has been obtained from a number of experiments: (1) translocation of X-chromosome fragments to an autosome shows that the X-chromosome genes exhibit dosage compensation regardless of their location in the genome (e.g., Tobler et al. 1971); (2) translocation of autosomal chromosomal fragments to the X chromosome generally results in unaltered levels of transcription (e.g., Roehrdanz et al. 1977); (3) in most cases, insertion of specific autosomal genes into the X chromosome by P-element mediated transformation failed to enhance activity (e.g., Goldberg et al. 1983); (4) X-chromosome genes transduced to an autosome are generally dosage compensated (e.g., Levis et al. 1985b). The potential regulatory sequences have been located to sites which precede transcriptional start areas and appear to be enhancerlike elements.

The *cis* regulatory elements respond to the signal generated by *Sxl*, which sets the activity mode or level of the *msl*-loci and associated genes. The function of *Sxl* appears to be to shut down these loci in females, in which case the female specific transcription rate is established, or to allow full "*msl-gene*" function, in which case hyperactivation of most X-chromosome loci ensues. The details of this interaction sequence are still reasonably obscure. A number of complicating observations, such as the essential function of the *mle* gene in spermatogenesis (Bachiller and Sánchez 1986), have still to be integrated into the overall scheme. It will probably require the cloning and characterization of the "*msl*-genes" to advance this problem further.

The target genes at which any of the control elements function, whether they are the "*msl*"-complex, *dsx* and/or *ix*, or *Sxl*, are very poorly defined. Clearly, they include various genes associated with terminal differentiation programs, such as those involved in the differentiation of specific sex-distinguishing features (Wieschaus and Nöthiger 1982; van Breugel and Huizing 1985; Schäfer 1986b), or the production of yolk proteins (Belote et al. 1985). The connecting lines between these various components presumably will emerge in the next few years.

Chapter 3

Structure and Function
of the Female Accessory Reproductive Systems

Various aspects of insect oogenesis have been the subjects of a number of reviews (e.g., Mahowald 1972b; Dorn 1977; King and Büning 1985). The aim of this Chapter is not to examine the phenomena or factors that are concerned with oocyte differentiation and are mediated by the oocyte itself, but rather to look at the role of various adjunct cells and structures that contribute to the full development of the oocyte. The discussion will center on the functions of the follicle cells and the various types of trophic cells associated with oocytes. In order to facilitate this, a brief overview of the types of ovary structure encountered in insects is necessary.

3.1 General Overview

Insects have adopted one of two basic solutions to the problem of provisioning the growing oocyte with developmental information and other structural components necessary for embryonic differentiation. One approach, which is adopted by most other animals, is the case in which the informational resources of the oocyte are largely furnished by the transcriptional activity of the oocyte nucleus itself. The characteristic ovary organization in cases of this type is termed panoistic.

The more specialized type of ovary arrangement is the meroistic one, in which cells in addition to the oocyte contribute to the accumulation of developmental information and the protein synthetic apparatus. Such cells, termed nurse cells or trophocytes, are derived from the germ line but do not directly form a part of the mature egg. In both panoistic and meroistic ovaries the yolk is usually obtained from extraovarian sources.

The meroistic ovary may be divided into two major classes:

1. Meroistic polytrophic, in which a number of nurse cells, derived from germinal tissue, form a part of the egg chamber and contribute much of the eventual non-yolk cytoplasmic content of the mature oocyte.
2. Meroistic telotrophic, in which anteriorly located trophocyte cells, connected to the growing oocytes by nutritive or trophic cords, provide substances essential for oocyte growth.

King and Büning (1985) have reviewed the probable evolutionary relationships of the various ovary types. They illustrate their conclusions with a phylogenetic tree, highlighted by cartoons of typical representatives of the various insect orders. The standard interpretation is that the panoistic ovary type is most probably the primitive condition, as it is found in the apterygotes, the Ephemeroptera, Odonata and the vast majority of the Polyneoptera. Telfer (1975) has pointed out, however, that this question is not definitively settled, and more detailed analysis may reveal that this ovary type may be of very mixed derivation. Nevertheless, if the panoistic type is assumed to be primitive, the polytrophic meroistic ovary seems to have arisen in two lines of descent, once in the Dermaptera and once in the common ancestor of the Paraneoptera and the Holometabola. The telotrophic meroistic ovary seems to have arisen independently from the polytrophic type in three separate lines: once in the ancestors of the Hemiptera and twice in the Holometabola, in the ancestors of the polyphagous Coleoptera and in those of the Megaloptera and Raphidioptera. The occurrence of panoistic ovary types in the Thysanaptera, some Megaloptera, some Neuroptera, as well as some Mecoptera and Siphanaptera, is explained by a reversal to the ancestral condition in these groups.

The structure of the three major ovary types is illustrated in Fig. 10. The panoistic ovary is made up of a number of ovarioles, each of which is composed of a terminal filament, the germarium, a series of oocytes at the previtellogenic phase of development, one or more oocytes in the process of vitellogenesis, and lastly, the mature egg. The terminal filament is made up of a group of flattened cells, surrounded by a basement lamina and an ovarian sheath. The latter two structures in fact surround the entire ovariole. Oogonia are located in the most anterior region of the germarium, followed by a zone of oocytes in the early stages of meiosis. At the posterior of the germarium, the oocytes are beginning to be surrounded by follicle cells. The oocytes continue to increase in size; by the time they have grown to stretch right across the ovariole, they have become completely surrounded by a monolayer of follicle cells. Oocytes at this stage are considered to be at the previtellogenic stage of development. A long string of oocytes of increasing size is typical of this region of the ovarioile. The size increase is accomplished by expansion of the cytoplasmic volume. A single layer of follicle cells continues to surround each oocyte, while in many cases a multilayered pad of interfollicular tissue is located between successive oocytes.

The changes taking place during the vitellogenic phase are typified by those described for *Melanoplus sanguinipes* (McCaffery and McCaffery 1983). By day 3 after ecdysis the terminal previtellogenic oocyte has reached a length of about 1.0 mm with a volume of 0.05 mm^3. In the next 24 h, yolk deposition commences and proceeds rather slowly to give a terminal oocyte of 1.2 mm in length and 0.2 mm^3 in volume. This is followed between days 4 and 6 by a rapid phase of vitellogenic growth, with an increase in oocyte length to 3.5 mm and in volume to about 1.3 mm^3. A final phase of vitellogenic development of the terminal oocyte takes place over the next 3 days, achieving a final volume of over 2.5 mm^3. At the end of vitellogenesis, the follicle cells secrete the vitelline membrane, followed by the formation of the chorion. The mature egg is then expelled into the oviduct, with oviposition taking place soon thereafter.

The number of ovarioles in panoistic ovaries is quite variable. In just the Orthoptera, the number can range from 4 (2 per ovary) to close to 400 (Waloff, 1954). In the Acrididae, the common number is 5, for the Tettigonioidea, 15–30, while in the Gryllidae it is much higher (150–170; Voy 1949). The large intergeneric differences in ovariole number among the grasshoppers demonstrates that this is a highly variable feature (Rubtzov 1934; Phipps 1968). Many insects with panoistic ovaries support just a single vitellogenic oocyte per ovariole; vitellogenesis commences in the penultimate oocyte only after ovulation of the first (e.g., *Locusta*, Phipps 1950, Singh 1958; *Schistocerca*, Tobe 1977), or, in the case of ovoviviparous cockroaches (Buschor et al. 1984), after the loss of the egg case. In other species, two (*Periplaneta*, Weaver and Pratt 1977; *Melanoplus*, Gillott and Elliott 1975) or more (*Melanoplus*, Mc-Caffery and McCaffery 1983) may be vitellogenic at the same time, although at different stages of the yolk deposition cycle. All of the above-mentioned insects produce eggs in batches, and in all these cases, there is evidence that juvenile hormone regulates the vitellogenic cycles. In some, e.g., *Nauphoeta* (Buschor et al. 1984), there may be additional complexities, in that the penultimate oocytes may show a period of refractoriness to juvenile hormone even after the loss or release of the mature eggs; however, hormonal regulation of yolk uptake seems to be of primary importance. In some insects which do not lay eggs in batches, but rather produce a few eggs every day, the oocytes of the different ovarioles can mature asynchronously and maturation need not depend solely on the female's endocrine medium. For example, in the stick insect, *Clitumnus extradentatus*, the fertilized female lays about five to seven eggs per day from the third week of imaginal life up to the sixth month. Each of the 40 ovarioles functions asynchronously and each ovariole matures only a single oocyte at a time. It has been shown that growth of the sub terminal oocyte is hindered by the terminal oocyte itself during maturation until its ovulation (Mesnier 1980). The effect is twofold and mediated by the interfollicular cells which occur between adjacent oocytes. These cells appear to pass an inhibitory substance from the anterior to the more posterior oocyte. However, secretions from such cells located proximal to the oocyte are required for the stimulation of vitellogenesis.

A terminal filament and a germarium are also found in polytrophic meroistic ovaries (Fig. 10B). In this case, the anterior region of the germarium contains one or more stem-line oogonia and a number of daughter cells or cystoblasts. The latter divide to give a cluster of cells that remain interconnected by structures called ring canals. This type of cell cluster contains the oocyte and a number of nurse cells. Nurse cell number varies in different species between 1 and 63. In *Drosophila*, where the final number of cells in the cluster is 16, the clustering of the cells as well as the formation of the ring canals, is mediated by structures called fusomes. These structures have been described as tube-shaped, gelatinous masses (Telfer 1975), which when examined by electron microscopy contain a random array of membranous vesicles and fibrils (Storto and King 1989). Mitochrondria are excluded from the fusomes, as, to a large extent, are ribosomes and microtubules. The initial function of the fusome appears to be to arrest the progress of the contractile ring during the first cystoblast mitosis, resulting in incomplete cytokinesis. A ring canal is then constructed in the center of the arrested cleavage furrow. The fusome material then functions to align the mitotic spindles of the ensuing division so that one pole of the spindles touches the fusome and the other points away from it. Assembly of additional fusomes in the ensuing cleavage furrows again results in incomplete cytokinesis, followed by the construction of additional ring canals. The fusome material then fuses to form a continuous polyfusome, and contraction of this material pulls the ring canals towards one another. The spindles of the next division are again aligned with reference to the polyfusome. This positioning ensures that one cell of each dividing pair retains all previously formed ring canals while the other receives none. Contraction of the polyfusomal system at the end of each incomplete cell division results in

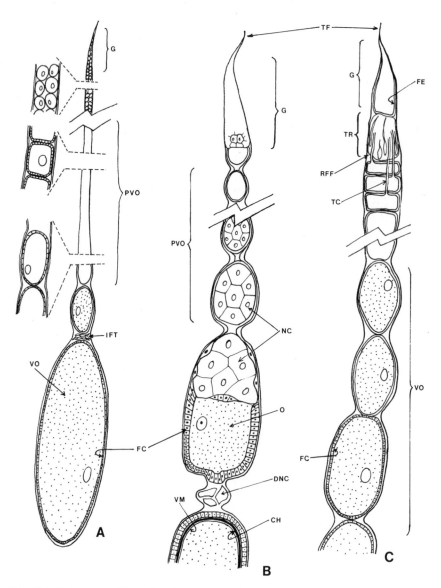

Fig. 10A-C. Diagrams illustrating the structure of **A** panoistic **B** meroistic-polytrophic and **B** meroistic-telotrophic ovaries. *CH* Chorion; *DNC* degenerating nurse cells; *FC* follicle cells; *FE* follicular epithelium; *G* germarium; *IFT* interfollicular tissue; *NC* nurse cells; *O* oocyte; *PVO* previtellogenic oocytes; *RFF* region of follicle formation; *TC* trophic cord; *TF* terminal filament; *TR* tropharium/trophic syncytium; *VM* vitelline membrane; *VO* vitellogenic oocytes

a centripetal gathering together of new canals, and the formation of a tight cell cluster. The cystocytes divide synchronously four times, and the completed clone displays a multiply branched chain of 16 interconnected cells, with two cells possessing four ring canals, two cells having three canals, four cells with two canals and eight cells with one canal. One of the four-canal cells eventually becomes the oocyte, while the remaining 15 become nurse cells. The mechanism by which the two four-canal cells chose such different developmental pathways is obscure (Koch and Spitzer 1983). In the central region of the germarium, prefollicular cells begin to grow around the oocyte-nurse cell clusters, while in the posterior section of the germarium, typical egg chambers are detectable, with the oocyte-nurse cell complex completely surrounded by a unilayer of follicle cells. Further pre-vitellogenic development of the egg chambers includes the enlargement of the oocyte, an increase in the number of follicle cells, followed by the polyploidization of the follicle cells and nurse cells. As in the case of panoistic ovaries, an epithelial sheath surrounds each ovariole. In the region of the vitellogenic oocytes, the epithelial sheath consists of a thin, acellular, inner membrane, a median cellular network of muscle and tracheal cells, an on outer epithelial membrane. The inner membrane lies against the tunica propria, an acellular layer which serves as a basement membrane for the follicle cells (Cummings 1974).

Commonly in polytrophic ovaries, a single oocyte may be vitellogenic per ovariole at one time. In those cases, as in the panoistic examples, juvenile hormone levels appear to regulate late vitellogenic onset and previtellogenic development (Readio and Meola 1985), although in some cases this may be by the indirect action of an oostatic hormone (Adams 1970, 1976). The number of ovarioles in polytrophic ovaries can be quite variable, as in the Diptera, where 10–30 are found in *Drosophila*, and 70–100 in *Musca* or *Lucilia* (King 1970). In the Lepidoptera the number is usually rather constant, and four ovarioles per ovary are found throughout most of the order (Gross 1903); exceptions include *Nematois metallicus*, with 12–20 (Cholodkowsky 1885) and *Nemophora* with about 12 (Petersen 1900).

A germinal region is also found in telotrophic meroistic ovaries (Fig. 10C). In *Geris* and *Oncopeltus* (Bonhag 1958) the number of oogonia increases by mitosis through the nymphal stages. The oogonia form a ball of cells surrounded by an epithelial sheath of mesodermal origin. After the transition into the last instar, the oogonia divide into two cells, one the prospective oocyte and the other the future trophocyte. As the oocytes move posteriorly towards the region of follicle formation they become surrounded by prefollicular cells; they also retain their connection to the trophocyte via a cytoplasmic strand (nurse strand or trophic cord). In aphids, this constitutes the final morphological condition, since a single oocyte is connected to a single trophocyte via trophic cords (Couchman and King 1979). The oocyte is extruded posteriorly from the germarium and becomes temporarily surrounded by follicle cells, which occupy a small region at the base of the germarium. In *Oncopeltus*, however, a number of previtellogenic follicles are formed. In each, the oocyte is surrounded by a follicular epithelium and sends a trophic cord to the trophocyte. The latter contributes its nucleus to a growing syncytium composed of the nuclei of trophocytes and other cells; the syncytium constitutes a distinct region, the tropharium. A somewhat different scheme is used to generate the previtellogenic oocytes and the syncytial tropharium in other examples of the telotrophic ovary. For example, in *Sialis flavilatera* (King and Büning 1985), germ-cell clusters, connected by cytoplasmic bridges, form in the ovariole anlage. In the central regions, the intercellular bridges and all cell membranes disappear, giving rise to a syncytium. Cell membranes and intercellular bridges survive at the periphery and these cells form the germ-cell tapetum. The cell nuclei of the central region are restrained by their position from entering the oocyte developmental pathway but constitute the tropharium. Some of the tapetum cells at the base of the tropharium differentiate into definitive oocytes, which retain a cytoplasmic bridge with the synctial tropharium and gradually become surrounded by a follicular epithelium.

Another, and rather interesting, variant is found in the polyphagous Coleoptera. In *Geophilus* (Kloc and Matuszewski 1977) the differentiation of trophocytes (nurse cells) and oocytes occurs within linear chains of sibling cells. These configurations result from a series of mitoses in which the orientation of the spindle is parallel to the long axis of the germarium. Only one member of the sibling cluster, the most basal (posterior), develops into an oocyte; the others differentiate into nurse cells. Matuszewski et al. (1985) have surveyed other polyphage Coleoptera and have found the linear chain model to occur widely. In *Philonthus, Adalia,* and *Dermestes*, as in *Creophilus*, as a result of incomplete cytokinesis, the oogonial cells in each sibling cluster are linked to each other by intercellular bridges, which are filled with fusomes. The authors suggest that failure of the fusomes of linearly adjacent cells to fuse into a polyfusome allows the spindles to orientate with their long axes parallel to the long axis of the cluster. This would explain why the oogonial divisions in coleopteran telotrophic ovaries generate linear chains of cells rather than the cystlike arrangement found in polytrophic sibling clusters. Dividing sibling clusters within ovarioles are arranged in bundles, and intercellular bridges occur between cells of adjacent clusters. These transverse connections also contain fusomes, which, in contrast to the linear fusomes, do fuse to form continuous polyfusomes. Evidently, these transverse structures do not participate in aligning mitotic spindles. With so many variants to the telotrophic developmental pattern, it is entirely reasonable to assume multiple, independent evolutionary origins (Büning 1972).

A variable number of vitellogenic oocytes may be present; up to eight at once may be found in *Dysdercus intermedium* (Dittman et al. 1981). In such cases as *Rhodnius*, where a single vitellogenic oocyte is present, that oocyte is believed to produce an antigonadotropin which acts on the follicle cells of the succeeding oocyte (Huebner and Davey 1973). The action appears to alter follicle receptivity to juvenile hormone and prevent the development of patency, a condition in which gaps appear between follicle cells to allow ease of access of vitellogenin to the oocyte surface.

3.2 Accessory Systems Associated with the Ovary

3.2.1 Follicle Cells: General Observations

General follicle cell morphology is well exemplified by Anderson's (1964) description for *Periplaneta*. The earliest follicle cells are of the squamous type, with the apical ends of the cells applied closely to the oolemma. As the oocyte grows, the follicle cells rapidly increase in number and gradually become cuboidal. The follicle cells send out slender, blunt processes which interdigitate, in very close association, with the microvilli of the oocyte. The cuboidal cell shape is maintained until just prior to vitellogenesis when the follicular epithelium becomes columnar. The transition from cuboidal to columnar epithelium at an equivalent developmental stage, and the maintenance of an elaborate microvillar contact area between the follicle cells and the oocyte, are characteristics commonly encountered in other species (*Locusta*, Bassemir 1977; *Galloisiana*, Matsuzaki et al. 1979; *Formica*, Billen 1985). In *Periplaneta*, the lateral plasma membranes of the follicle cells are extensively folded and closely applied, and numerous septate desmosomes and adhesion plaques are present. At the start of the vitellogenic phase, the cell shape changes to assume a somewhat spherical (*Periplaneta*) or flattened character (*Locusta*, Bassemir 1977).

Ultrastructural studies show that the cytoplasm of the follicle cells at the late previtellogenic and vitellogenic stages is characteristic of a highly active tissue (Anderson 1964; Bassemir 1977; Matsuzaki et al. 1979). Typically, large numbers of mitochondria are present and multivesiculate bodies and Golgi complexes are prominent. The columnar cells are well supplied with rough endoplasmic reticulum and large amounts of ribonucleoproteins. As in *Campodea* (Bilinski 1983), the cells accumulate numerous electron-dense secretory vacuoles. Most of these features are correlated with the production of the materials for the vitelline membrane and the chorion; the synthesis of these components can start before the oocyte achieves its maximum size (Matsuzaki 1971).

In some insects, in addition to septate junctions and adhesion plaques, intercellular bridges interconnect adjacent follicle cells. In the honey bee, *Apis mellifica* (Ramamurty and Engels 1977) each follicle cell has two to three intercellular bridges to adjacent cells, with the result that an extensive series of interconnections are established. The bridges appear to result from incomplete cytokinesis, and may serve to synchronize the differentiation and function of the follicular epithelium. Similar intercellular connections have been described in dipterans (*Culex*, fiil 1978; *Aedes* and *Stomoxys*, Meola et al. 1977). In *Culex*, syncytial groups of up to 32 cells have been described. The cells in the syncytium divide asynchronously, giving rise to an irregular, branched organization. In *Drosophila* (Giorgi 1978), the intercellular bridges are restricted to the columnar portion of the follicular epithelium: that is, to those cells which are capable of elaborating the various egg-covering precursors. The cytoplasmic continuity could be interpreted as ensuring a synchronous secretory activity for the columnar follicle cells all around the oocyte. The interpretation is certainly plausible, though currently there is no direct experimental evidence. It has been noted that the intercellular bridges form in the immediate vicinity of desmosomes, and there could be a causal relationship implied in this observation. However, it must be noted that the exact mechanisms involved in the process of bridge formation remain to be worked out.

In addition to the lateral associations between follicle cells, there is a close association between oocyte microvilli and follicle cell processes during the pre- and vitellogenic phases. A number of authors have described the occurrence of gap junctions between the oocyte and follicle cells (e.g., *Rhodnius*, Huebner 1981a; *Tribolium*, Bilinski et al. 1985; *Drosophila*, Mahowald 1972b, Giorgi and Postlethwait 1985), as well as between adjacent follicle cells (*Locusta*; Wollberg et al. 1976). The junctions disappear during the chorion formation phase and during atresia. In

Rhodnius, Huebner (1981a) has shown that fluorescent dyes, such as Procion yellow and Lucifer yellow, pass from injected oocytes into follicle cells at all stages prior to chorion formation. Most of the authors speculate that the gap junctions function in the coordination of oocyte-follicle cell differentiation. The gap junctions generally become reduced in number after the onset of vitellogenesis, and Mazzini and Giorgi (1985) suggest that an interaction between the follicle cells and the oocyte in the previtellogenic phase may serve as a signal for the assembly of the coated pits, which function in the uptake of yolk proteins by the oocyte. The coincidence of follicular epithelial changes with the differentiation of the oolemma and oocyte cortex becoming competent to incorporate yolk precursors implies an integration between oocyte and follicle cell differentiation. Again, the interpretation is plausible, but direct evidence is currently lacking.

The typical transition of follicle cell morphology from cuboidal to columnar and finally to more or less flattened, with large intercellular spaces, suggests that cytoskeletal changes are responsible for the cell shape transformations. The role of microtubules and microfilaments in follicular cell shape changes has been studied in *Rhodnius* by Watson and Huebner (1986). In this insect, the tall, columnar, tightly aposed cells present during previtellogenesis show a decrease in cell height, a change to an irregular shape, and a marked reduction in cell to cell contact during the vitellogenic phase (Huebner and Anderson 1972). The transformation from a tightly packed epithelium to one with large extracellular spaces has been termed patency; this condition provides a pathway for yolk precursors to the oocyte (Huebner and Injeyan 1980). Antitubulin immunofluorescence and transmission electron microscopy have been used to assess the relative abundance, orientation and dynamics of microtubules in follicle cells from the previtellogenic to the post-vitellogenic stages. A role for the cytoskeleton in the development of patency was first indicated by the work of Huebner (1976) and Abu-Hakima and Davey (1977), which showed that colchicine, an inhibitor of microtubule polymerization, and cytochalasin B, which interferes with microfilaments, inhibited the juvenile hormone-stimulated development of patency. The electron microscopical and immunofluorescent studies both demonstrate that the initiation of patency is correlated with a reorganization of the microtubules in the follicle cells. The change is from a highly organized cylindrical array of microtubules in previtellogenic cells to a random pattern of microtubule arrangement by midvitellogenesis. These results suggest that the maintenance of the columnar shape for the follicle cells is associated with a well-organized, cylindrical orientation of the microtubular cytoskeleton. A random redistribution of the microtubules would facilitate the transtion to a new, more flattened morphology for the follicle cells. This new microtubular distribution would allow the assumption of a different cell shape as a result of overall cell shrinkage, promoted by the (Na^+-K^+)-ATPase-mediated pumping of fluid out of the cell (Davey 1981). Watson and Huebner (1986) suggest that the microtubular cytoskeleton restrains juvenile hormone-stimulated cell shape changes, and it is possible that as one of the effects, the hormone alters microtubular associations. The details of such action remain to be worked out.

Follicle cells of the columnar type do not exhibit the dense microfilament arrays which become a prominent feature of patent lateral follicle cells. Thus, microfilaments as well as microtubules are involved in the modulation of cell shape. The production of subplasmalemmal band of microfilaments within the lateral follicle cells may produce an inward contractile force that contributes to the achievement of the eventual irregular cell shape. Overall, cell shrinkage, the rearrangement of the cytoskeleton, and the disassembly and rearrangement of cell junctions (Huebner and Injeyan 1981) all contribute to the change in follicle cell shape during the development of patency.

The total number of follicle cells associated with a single oocyte varies with the developmental stage and, not surprisingly, with the size of the oocytes. A vitellogenic oocyte of *Leucophaea* has approximately 27 000 investing follicle cells (Koeppe et al. 1980). *Drosophila* follicles when first formed have 80 cells, increasing to about 1200 in mature follicles (King 1970). Total cells per follicle in *Aedes aegypti* number 18 immediately after adult emergence, increasing to about 200 after 48 h, remaining at this level unless the mosquito manages to obtain a blood meal. By 4 h after a blood meal, the follicle cell number is 278 and by 10 h, 472 per follicle. In *Culex pipiens*, follicle cell number starts at 29 immediately after emergence and peaks at 510 per follicle at 40 h. A similar range of values has been obtained for *Aedes togoi* and *Mansonia uniformis* (Laurence and Simpson 1974).

While most insects show an increase in follicle cell number before and during vitellogenesis, a rather interesting additional feature is found in *Drosophila*. Once the maximum follicle cell number of approximately 1200 is reached, the cells go through a period when they increase their surface area. Then some of the follicle cells undergo a series of migrations (King and Vanoucek 1960; King 1970). The sequence of the migrations is illustrated in Fig. 11. In the first series, which starts with the earliest signs of yolk accumulation by the oocyte, a migration of cells takes place over the surface of the nurse cell portion of the follicle towards posterior end. As a result, the number of follicle cells above the nurse cells is drastically reduced and the number above the oocyte increases (Fig. 11, *1*). Eventually, a 15-fold difference in cell abundance develops between the two regions. As yolk deposition continues the follicle cells above the oocyte become columnar, while those above the nurse cells become very thin. A second migration of cells takes place during the early stages of yolk accumulation, when a small group of cells moves from the anterior of the egg chamber, between the nurse cells of the central region, to the surface of the oocyte (Fig. 11; *2*); these "border cells" eventually move dorsally (Fig. 11, *3*) and come to reside above the oocyte nucleus. The cells first secrete the vitelline membrane and later are responsible for the formation of the micropylar complex. Just after the mid-portion of the yolk accumulation period, a number of anterior cells of the columnar layer migrate centripetally between the nurse cells and the oocyte (Fig. 11, *4*). These cells are responsible for the formation of the anterior vitelline membrane; they also form the dorsal appendages. Later, some of these cells migrate anteriorly and ensure the elongation of the dorsal appendages (Cummings and King 1969). Mutants such as *Fc(3)Apc*, which cause incomplete migration of the follicle cells between the oocyte and the nurse cells, lead to an eventual leakage of anterior egg cytoplasm and degeneration of the egg or the deposition of aberrant, flaccid eggs (Szabad and Hoffmann 1989).

The various cell migrations are microtubule dependent. The border cells and the cells migrating centripetally between the oocyte and nurse cells stain prominently with antitubulin. In the presence of colchicine, these cells showed a number of

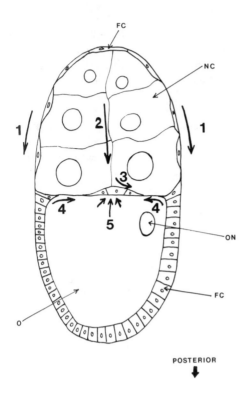

FC

NC

1

2

1

3

4

4

5

ON

O

FC

POSTERIOR

Fig. 11. Diagram of a *Drosophila* mid-vitellogenic follicle indicating follicle cell migration pathways (*1–5*). *FC* Follicle cells; *NC* nurse cells; *O* oocyte; *ON* oocyte nucleus.

abnormalities, and centripetal migration was prevented (Gutzeit 1986c). In addition to the involvement of the microtubules, a role in guiding the cell migrations has been proposed for the large, steady electrical currents, which have been shown to traverse the *Drosophila* follicles (Overall and Jaffe 1985). Similar currents have been noted in *Hyalophora* ovaries (Woodruff et al. 1986). Overall and Jaffe (1985) propose that the currents help to direct the follicle cell migrations. All of the intracellular spaces through which the follicle cells move might be sufficiently restricted to maintain fields or voltage gradients that are large enough to direct cell movement. In addition, all of these migrations appear to be against the current: against the direction of the flow for positive ions and towards the positive anodal pole. Ion asymmetries within the follicle, which may be directly associated with the electrical phenomena, have been confirmed in *Drosophila* by an analysis of cation distribution, visualized by precipitating cations with pyroantimonate (Heinrich and Gutzeit 1985).

The follicular epithelial cells typically become polyploid before or during the vitellogenic stages (*Carausius*, Pijnacker and Godeke 1984; *Leucophaea*, Koeppe and Wellman 1980, LaPointe et al. 1985; *Pyrrhocoris*, Mays 1972). It seems that in panoistic ovaries an exact doubling of DNA during polyploidization is typical. For example, in *Leuocophaea* follicle cells the final ploidy levels are generally 32C or 64C (LaPointe et al. 1985). In meroistic ovaries polyploidization is generally not exact, and there is an underreplication of some of the DNA sequences (*Drosophila virilis*, Renkawitz-Pohl 1975; *D. melanogaster*, Mahowald et al. 1979; *Dysdercus*, Dittmann and Maier 1987). For example, in *D. hydei*, DNA sequences for the ribosomal RNAs are severely underreplicated (Renkawitz and Kunz 1975), and it has been suggested that polyploidization increases the concentration of those genes which play important roles in follicle cell function. Experiments with *Dysdercus* (Dittmann and Maier 1987) clearly show that tissue polyploidization, although occurring concurrently, is not causally related to yolk protein uptake. The implication is that the increased DNA levels in late follicle cells are related to vitelline membrane and/or chorion production.

It has been shown in *Leucophaea* that the uptake of thymidine into follicle cells (Koeppe and Wellman 1980), the levels of thymidine kinase (LaPointe and Koeppe 1984), DNA synthesis (Koeppe et al. 1980), and polyploidy levels (LaPointe et al. 1985) are all regulated by juvenile hormone. This effect of the hormone is independent and in addition to the membrane level action, such as the stimulation of Na^+/K^+-ATPase activity and the development of patency in the epithelium (Ilenchuk and Davey 1987a, b). Juvenile hormone effects on the ovary are pleiotropic and affect many, if not all, of the major functions of the follicle cells.

Once the follicle cells secrete the vitelline membrane and the chorion, in most insects the mature oocyte ruptures an epithelial plug, which closes the ovariole posteriorly, and passes into the ovariolar duct. The follicle then collapses and the follicular cells undergo autolysis and gradually disappear. The degenerating follicular cells are generally referred to as a corpus luteum and structures of this type have been described in several species (*Periplaneta*, Bhide and Sahai 1981; *Musca*, Kulshrestha 1969; *Calpodes*, Griffith and Lai-Fook 1986b). The study on *Calpodes* notes that in the early stages of degeneration, lysosomal activity and autophagy are the predominant activities. After lysosomal digestion, materials from dying cells are taken up by neighboring follicular cells. In advanced stages, hemocytes come in to clear up the debris.

Following this general overview of follicle cell structure and function, some of the major secretory functions will be examined in greater detail.

3.2.2 Yolk Protein Synthesis by Follicle Cells

The fat body is the major, and in many cases, the only site of vitellogenin synthesis in insects (Kunkel and Nordin 1985). Among some of the Holometabola (Diptera, Lepidoptera, Coleoptera), however, the ovarian follicle cells are involved in yolk protein production as well. In the Diptera the same structural genes, synthesizing identical proteins, are active in both the fat body and in the follicle cells. It has been shown for *Drosophila* that two different *cis*-acting DNA elements in the same gene control the tissue specificity of yolk protein expression. One is necessary for expression in ovarian follicle cells, while the other controls expression in fat body (Shepherd et al. 1985). These DNA elements are distinct from those controlling sex and time specificity of expression (see Sect. 3.5.3). Ovarian and fat-body yolk proteins appear to be the products of distinct genes in the Lepidoptera. The situation is less clear for the Coleoptera.

Not surprisingly, the details of ovarian yolk protein production are best understood for *Drosophila*. The capacity of *Drosophila* ovaries for autonomous yolk protein synthesis was clearly demonstrated by a series of transplantation experiments (Srdic et al. 1979). Immature ovaries of *Drosophila mercatorum* were injected into young larvae and into adult males of *D. mercatorum, D. melanogaster, D. hydei, D. virilis,* and *Zaprionius vittiger.* All of these homo- and heteroplastic transplantations allow normal vitellogenesis to take place in the donor ovary. SDS-polyacrylamide gel electrophoretic analysis of the yolk proteins, which makes it possible to distinguish species-specific differences, confirmed that mature eggs contained yolk proteins exclusively of donor-specific origin. When females were used as hosts, host specific yolk proteins also became incorporated into the donor eggs. Other transplantation and in vitro labeling experiments have confirmed ovarian autonomous yolk protein synthesis (Postlethwait et al. 1980a).

While the above experiments conclusively established that the ovary does independently synthesize vitellogenins, the cells in which this synthesis occurred were not defined. Gutzeit (1980), on the basis of an analysis of ^{35}S-methionine in vitro-labeled proteins, concluded that the nurse cells are the source of vitellogenin. Further research has failed to confirm these findings. Brennan et al. (1982), using a radioactively labeled probe containing the coding regions of two of the three yolk protein genes, and in situ hybridization techniques, have shown that the follicular epithelium is the specific site of vitellogenin synthesis. This conclusion confirms ultrastructural and autoradiographic studies on other dipterans that implicate follicle cells as the site of yolk protein synthesis (Chia and Morrison 1972; Huebner et al. 1975). In addition, analysis of proteins isolated from briefly pulse-labeled follicles, which were then manually separated into nurse cell, follicle cell, and oocyte components, shows that the follicle cells produce at least the majority, if not all, of the yolk proteins. These results, together with in situ hybridizations, which show that the oocyte itself does not synthesize yolk proteins, lead to the firm conclusion that, in the ovary, follicle cells alone produce yolk proteins (Brennan et al. 1982).

The maximum level of yolk protein synthesis by the follicle cells occurs in early vitellogenic stages (stages 8 to 10b; King 1970; Isaac and Bownes 1982; Brennan et al. 1982). Cell-free translations of isolated mRNAs and dot-blot hybridizations, using cloned DNA probes of the three vitellogenin genes, show that the level of mRNA for yolk protein 3 is much reduced in comparison to the mRNAs for the other vitellogenins. This contrasts to the situation in the fat body, where all three yolk protein mRNAs are present in comparable amounts. Comparisons of the relative contributions of fat body and follicle cells to the yolk content of the oocyte indicate that, under normal conditions, the follicular epithelium contributes roughly 35% of the yolk proteins 1 and 2 to the total oocyte content, but only about 10% of the smaller, yolk protein 3 polypeptide. This differential is not controlled at the level of gene number, since none of the yolk protein genes is amplified in the fat body or the follicle cells. Detailed experiments by Williams and Bownes (1986) have demonstrated that all three yolk protein genes are transcribed at similar rates. It is concluded, therefore, that yolk protein 3 mRNA is destabilized in the ovarian follicle cells, accounting for the reduction in its steady-state level. The basis for the selective mRNA stability has not been determined as yet.

The nature of the control of ovarian yolk protein synthesis has been addressed in a series of experiments by Bownes (1982d). When the developmental capacity of ovaries was tested by transplantation into an adult male host, it was found that the ovaries become competent to mature very early after metamorphosis, and synthesis of yolk proteins begins in a time-dependent manner related to the age of the ovary at the time of transplantation. Maturation of the ovaries seems to be intrinsic to the ovary, since transplantation to earlier developmental stages shows that neither eclosion itself not the adult "milieu" is essential for the initiation of yolk protein synthesis. The actual time when ovaries become competent to mature appears to be 25–30 h after puparium formation. The ovaries first acquire the ability to complete metamorphosis, without a concomitant competence for vitellogenesis; only later is the competence for yolk protein production achieved. Once the ovaries pass a transition period in metamorphosis, their maturation seems to become independent of the sex or developmental stage of the host environment. It appears, therefore, that the onset of the expression of the vitellogenin genes is not triggered by a hormone external to the ovary, but rather that ovarian maturation becomes autonomous early in metamorphosis. The regulation of the yolk protein genes in the ovary may well be different to the control of these genes in the fat body (see Sect. 3.5). The role of the control elements in the yolk protein genes which determine the tissue specificity of expression is discussed in Section 3.2.4.

The actual mechanism for the export of the yolk proteins from the follicle cells involves the usual route through the Golgi and exocytosis at the apical plasma membrane. The normal export mechanism can be disrupted by colchicine and other microtubule inhibitors, suggesting an important role for these cytoskeletal components (Gutzeit 1986c). The secreted yolk proteins are not normally liberated into the hemolymph at large, but possibly are presented directly to the oocyte surface (Srdic et al. 1979; Postlethwait et al. 1980b). Brennan et al. (1982) suggest that some component of the extracellular matrix may function in sequestering ovarian-produced yolk proteins prior to their uptake by the oocyte.

Results very similar to those reported for *Drosophila* have been found for a variety of other dipterans. Using a specific antiserum to the yolk proteins, Geysen et al. (1987) have demonstrated the presence of these proteins in the follicle cells of *Sarcophaga bullata*. At the start of vitellogenesis, all follicle cells contain yolk proteins. The squamous cells covering the nurse cells and the border cells lose their yolk protein content before mid-vitellogenesis; the columnar cells over the oocyte continue to react to yolk protein antiserum until late vitellogenesis. All follicle cells are immunonegative after this point in development. In vitro translation of isolated mRNA shows that mRNA content correlates well with immunopositivity for yolk proteins in the follicle cells. In *Musca domestica*, at the start of vitellogenesis, the fat body appears to be the main site of yolk protein synthesis; later the dominant role is taken over by the ovaries (De Bianchi et al. 1985). Overall, the follicle cell contribution of yolk proteins to the oocyte exceeds that of the fat body (DeBianchi and Pereira 1987). In *Ceratitis*, as in *Drosophila*, the ratios of the various yolk protein species synthesized by the fat body and the follicle cells are not identical. In the case of *Ceratitis*, however, there is a higher expression of the vitellogenin 2 gene in the ovaries than the fat body, rather than decreased vitellogenin 3 expression (Rina and Mintzas 1988). Whether this variation is at the transcriptional or other levels of regulation has not yet been determined.

A differential screen of a genomic DNA library of *Calliphora erythrocephala*, designed to identify genes actively expressed only in the previtellogenic and early vitellogenic stages, has yielded two clones which are homologous to the yolk protein 1 gene of *Drosophila*. Genes identified by these two clones are expressed in the columnar follicle cells and in the border cells as well (Rubacha et al. 1988). This result is similar to the one obtained for *Sarcophaga* (Geysen et al. 1987), and suggests that the vitellogenin genes may be turned on in all follicle cells before later events modulate their expression in different regions of the follicle.

As in the Diptera, the yolk proteins of the Lepidoptera are synthesized in two separate tissues, the fat body and the ovarian follicle cells. In the case of the Lepidoptera, however, the follicle cell yolk proteins are the products of genes different from those responsible for vitellogenin synthesis in the fat body. For example, in *Bombyx mori*, the follicle cell product has been termed the egg-specific protein, a trimer (225 kD) of two large subunits (72 kD) and one small subunit (64 kD); the vitellin in this species, synthesized in the fat body, is a tetramer of 420 kD, consisting of two subunits of 178 kD and two subunits of 43 kD. The egg-specific protein constitutes 25% of the weight of newly laid eggs, and is rapidly and completely utilized in early embryogenesis (Zhu et al. 1986). The early and complete use of the egg-specific protein, in contrast to vitellin, suggests that it serves as the most important source for embryonic growth. The presence of a highly specific protease for the egg-specific protein has been shown to be responsible for the targeted use of this protein during embryogenesis (Yamashita 1986). In the moth, *Plodia interpunctella*, two of the four major yolk polypeptides are produced by the follicle cells (Shirk et al. 1984). The fat body and the follicle cell yolk proteins show no immunological cross-reactivity, either as native proteins or as individual subunits (Bean et al. 1988). The paravitellogenins described for *Hyalophora cecropia* (Bast and Telfer 1976) are another example of follicle-cell synthesized yolk proteins, and they may account for approximately 20% of the total yolk protein of the oocyte. It would appear that the nutritional requirements of the embryo can be satisfied in a number of ways. The Diptera and the Lepidoptera have adopted different approaches to the solution of a common problem.

There is some evidence that follicle cells contribute secretory proteins to the yolk of coleopteran eggs (Ullmann 1973; Chaminade and Laverdure 1980; Zhai et al. 1984), and it has been suggested that gap junctions play some role in the transfer of these proteins to the oocyte (Bilinski et al. 1985). These preliminary results will have to be expanded considerably to evaluate fully their significance.

3.2.3 The Vitelline Membrane

The role of the follicle cells in the formation of the vitelline membrane has been described at the ultrastructural level for a large number of insects. Differences in a number of details of the process have been encountered; in all of the systems, however, vitelline membrane production is preceded by an extensive hypertrophy of rought endoplasmic reticulum and formation of Golgi complexes, followed by an accumulation of secretory granules in the apical zones of the follicle cells (e.g., Beams and Kessel 1969; Favard-Sereno 1971; Liu et al. 1975).

What seems to be almost the canonical model for vitelline membrane formation is found in the Diptera. In *Simulium* (Liu et al. 1975), the build up of the endoplasmic reticulum and Golgi vesicles occurs at mid-vitellogenesis. Golgi vesicles containing dense material are observed and dense droplets become abundant in the cytoplasm adjacent to the microvilli. By the time that vitellogenesis is almost complete, the Golgi complexes, containing both dense and fibrous materials, become even more prominent and the previtelline membrane secretory substance begins to be deposited between the follicle cells and the oocyte. The secreted material then begins to coalesce and gradually forms the vitelline membrane. Similarly, in *Aedes* (Mathew and Rai 1975), the presecretory phase is characterized by the hypertrophy of the endoplasmic reticulum and the Golgi complexes. Synthesis of vitelline membrane precursors begins immediately after the start of yolk protein uptake by the oocyte. Secretory droplets are budded off Golgi cisternae and released into the follicle cell-oocyte interface by exocytosis. The vitelline membrane first appears as dense plaques which eventually fuse to form a single homogeneous layer. In *Drosophila*, the follicle cell plasma membrane forms numerous microvilli at the time of vitelline membrane formation. These microvilli interdigitate with similar structures produced by the oocyte plasma membrane. Sudanophilic secretory vesicles, produced by the follicle cells, are extruded into the intercellular space and form numerous vitelline bodies, which eventually fuse to form the vitelline membrane (King and Koch 1963). In all these cases, it seems clear that the follicle cells are solely responsible for the formation of the vitelline membrane, producing and secreting the precursors at a very specific developmental time.

Most of the ultrastructural observations of vitelline membrane formation in exopterygotes support the above outline for the process. In *Aeschna*, the rough endoplasmic reticulum produces granules, which are transported to the Golgi. With the onset of vitelline membrane formation, the Golgi complexes secrete previtelline membrane components into the follicle cell/oocyte intercellular space (Beams and Kessel 1969). Favard-Sereno (1971) describes three waves of endoplasmic reticulum and Golgi activity in *Gryllus* follicle cells, the first one correlated with vitelline membrane synthesis. An equivalent account of vitelline membrane formation is presented for the grylloblatid, *Galloisiana nipponensis* (Matsuzaki et al. 1979). Bassemir's (1977) electron microscopical study on vitelline membrane formation in *Locusta* shows that this structure is composed of two ultrastructurally distinguishable components: (1) vitelline membrane bodies (VMBs) and, in addition, (2) a fine granular material, which eventually cements the VMBs together to give the complete vitelline membrane. The VMB-precursor substance is secreted into the intercellular space between the follicle cells and the oocyte and subsequently condenses to form globular vitelline membrane precursors. In Bassemir's (1977) opinion, there is no clear evidence which demonstrates that the VMB-substance is produced by the follicle cells rather than the oocyte. In fact, the observation that the first globular condensations appear in the vicinity of the oocyte membrane might indicate that the oocyte is the source of this secretion. On the other hand, the second vitelline membrane component, which cements the VMBs to the definitive vitelline membrane, is clearly the product of the follicle cells. It is secreted via the apical protrusions of the follicle cells. The possibility that, at least in some cases, the vitelline membrane has a dual origin must be considered.

The case for an oocyte contribution to the vitelline membrane has been made most frequently in studies on the Lepidoptera. Griffith and Lai-Fook (1986a) describe the process of vitelline membrane formation in the butterfly, *Calpodes*. During vitellogenesis in this species, the follicle cells are separated from each other by large intercellular channels. The channels close at the end of the yolk uptake phase by the rejoining of the lateral surfaces of the follicle cells. At this time, some electron-lucent material is found between the follicle cells and the oocyte. Soon thereafter a distinct vitelline membrane is detectable, although it is still somewhat discontinuous. It has an electron-dense layer away from the oocyte and an electron-lucent layer apposing the oocyte. Both the oocyte and the follicle cells contain coated vesicles, which appear to be in the process of exocytosis. The electron-dense material appears to be exocytosed from coated vesicles at the apical surface of the follicle cells. At the oocyte surface, coated vesicles exocytose the electron-lucent granular material. Later, the vitelline membrane thickens and becomes continuous. Initially, the electron-dense layer is considerably thicker than the electron-lucent one. Once fully formed, however, the vitelline membrane is completely electron-dense. It appears, then, that both the follicle cells and the oocyte cortex contribute to vitelline membrane formation.

Some support for the dual origin of the vitelline membrane has come from studies on other Lepidoptera. Cruickshank (1971) has studied the process of vitelline membrane formation in *Anagasta kuhniella* using pulse-chase experiments. In such experiments the tissue is exposed to a brief pulse of labeled ^{3}H-leucine, after which the labeled precursor is flooded out by a large dose of unlabeled amino acid. At varying intervals during the so-called chase the fate of the protein labeled during the pulse can be followed by autoradiography. He finds that the oocyte cortex contains centers of protein synthesis and that the labeled proteins migrate to the oocyte periphery and later play a role in the formation of the vitelline membrane. Membrane-bound organelles, the "accessory yolk nuclei" (Cruickshank 1972), are scattered throughout the cortex of the oocyte, and could be the sites for the synthesis of the vitelline membrane proteins. In *Hyalophora cecropia*, an electron-lucent layer is formed at the beginning of vitelline membrane formation, while an electron-dense layer is added later (Telfer and Smith 1970; Rubenstein 1979). These authors consider that, while the follicle cells are the major contributors to the vitelline membrane, there is credible evidence for an oocyte contribution. In *Korscheltellus lupalinus* (Chauvin and Barbier 1979) the material for the vitelline membrane is said to be secreted by the follicle cells, but it is later modified by substances produced by the oocyte. A definitive decision on the source of the various contributions to the vitelline membrane will not be made until it can be demonstrated, with molecular biological techniques now becoming available, that definitive vitelline membrane proteins are synthesized by the oocyte.

In contrast to the ultrastructural studies on vitelline membrane formation available in a whole range of insects, data on vitelline membrane proteins and their genes is much more limited. Glass and Emmerich (1981a) have isolated a low molecular weight (7.8 kD) protein from *Locusta* follicles, whose time of synthesis and immunofluorescent localization (Glass and Emmerich 1981b) suggest that it may be a vitelline membrane component. Rubacha et al. (1988) have identified, by differential screening, a DNA sequence which is expressed during the middle and early-late stages of oogenesis in *Calliphora*. This clone (GG7K) identifies a transcript which is equivalent in size and abundance to the 17.5 and 24 kD vitelline membrane producing

RNAs found in *Drosophila*. In situ hybridizations show that the GG7K gene is transcribed in the columnar follicle cells surrounding the oocyte, but is not expressed in the border cells.

By far the most information on the vitelline membrane proteins and their genes is available for *Drosophila*. In preliminary studies, four vitelline membrane proteins were identified, based on the amino acid content and stage-specific synthesis during the period of membrane deposition (Petri et al. 1976). In a more detailed study, Fargnoli and Waring (1982) have documented the occurrence of six major size classes of radiolabeled components in purified vitelline membrane preparations. These six types are of 14, 16, 17.5, 23–24, 70, and 130 kD. With the exception of the 16 kD component, all the others are identified as vitelline membrane proteins on the basis of two independent criteria: (1) selective enrichment in purified eggshell fragment preparations; and (2) stage specific synthesis during the period of vitelline membrane deposition. Three of these, the 14, 23–24 and 130 kD components, also selectively bind eggshell specific antisera containing antivitelline membrane activity. The 16 kD entity may be a modified variant. Comparing the results of the two reports, the 17 and the 21 and 22 kD components may be equivalent. However, according to Fargnoli and Waring (1982), the 67 kD fraction of Petri et al. (1976) may represent a heat shock protein.

The vitelline membrane from laid eggs is insoluble in SDS. This feature probably is a result of the formation of tyrosine cross-links catalyzed by a peroxidase at the time of oviposition. Prior to that time the vitelline membrane can be solubilized by SDS under reducing conditions (Petri et al. 1979a). This suggests that the early membrane is cross-linked solely by disulfide bridges. However, there are some indications that cross-links, in addition to disulfide bridges, occur gradually before oviposition, so that the membrane is stabilized in a sequential manner (Fargnoli and Waring 1982).

The mRNAs for the vitelline membrane proteins are polyadenylated and expressed maximally in stage-10 egg chambers. Fargnoli and Waring (1984) have shown the presence of two broad, distinct bands in urea-agarose gels, which they have labeled T_1 and T_2. In vitro translation of these RNAs in reticulocyte lysates, in the presence and absence of microsomal membranes, shows that both of these bands code for proteins that are synthesized in precursor form and are processed to species comigrating with vitelline membrane proteins. The translation products of the T_1 band comigrated with the 14 kD protein, while those of band T_2 comigrated with the 17.5 and the 23–24 kD proteins. The 23 kD in vitro translation product gave a very sharp band, suggesting that the diffuse nature of the in vivo-labeled 23–24 kD band reflects posttranslational modifications of a single protein species.

In situ hybridization to polytene chromosomes, using a variety of probes, has allowed the chromosomal localization of a number of the vitelline membrane genes. So far, all are located on the second chromosome. Using radiolabeled RNAs as probes, Fargnoli and Waring (1984) localized the gene coding for the 14 kD polypeptide at position 39 DE. Their T_2 RNA, which in in vitro translation produced the 17.5 and 23–24 kD proteins, hybridized to the 42A region. These authors noted that the *fs(2)E7* mutant, which may be vitelline membrane defective, also maps in this region. Later work, however, has failed to substantiate the tentative assignment of the gene coding for the 17.5 kD protein to 42A, but rather, places it at 26A (Burke et al. 1987). The 26A region has been pinpointed as a vitelline membrane structural gene site by other groups (Higgins et al. 1984; Mindrinos et al. 1985). Both of these groups locate two genes for vitelline membrane proteins at 26A. Mindrinos et al. (1985) note that the vitelline membrane genes are part of a multigene family, and other members of this family are located at 34C and 32EF. Therefore, like the chorion genes, vitelline membrane genes appear to be clustered; in addition, there is some evolutionary relatedness between the vitelline membrane and chorion gene families (Higgins et al. 1984).

A 12-kb DNA fragment from the 26A region of chromosome 2 has been cloned and characterized (Dopodi et al. 1988). Four follicle cell genes, which are expressed during vitelline membrane formation, were found to be clustered in this area. Three genes, encoding RNAs of approximately 700 nucleotides, are within 4 kb of each other. Two of them are transcribed off the same strand, while the other is transcribed from the opposite strand. The fourth gene of the cluster, encoding a 1.3 kb RNA, is located approximately 2.5 kb away. Unlike the chorion genes, the four 26A region genes appear to lack introns. Temporal and quantitative differences in the RNA accumulation patterns suggest that the genes are independently regulated. In vitro translation products from hybrid-selected RNAs and sequence analysis show that two of the genes code for vitelline membrane proteins; one of them is the previously described 17.5 kD protein. From the overall evidence, it is probable that the other two genes in the cluster, producing less abundant RNAs, also play a role in early eggshell production. Unlike the chorion genes (see Sect. 3.2.4), the genes in the 26A cluster do not appear to undergo tissue-specific amplification prior to the time of their maximal expression; apparently, gene amplification is not essential to meet the burden of vitelline-membrane protein production.

Gigliotti et al. (1989) have isolated and characterized cDNA and genomic clones from the 32E region of the second chromosome which contain a gene for a different vitelline membrane protein. The gene product is a protein of 116 amino acids which has a high proline and alanine content, characteristic of vitelline membrane proteins. The sequences of the cDNAs and of the genomic subclone show homology with other vitelline-membrane protein genes that have been identified so far.

An interesting feature of this family of genes is the presence of a highly conserved region of approximately 110 bases. It codes for a hydrophobic domain of over 30 amino acids (Mindrinos et al. 1985; Petri et al. 1987; Popodi et al. 1988; Gigliotti et al. 1989). The latter authors, using the conserved sequence as a probe, have isolated other cDNA clones which clearly do not participate in the formation of the eggshell layers. They speculate that this common conserved domain must result from a common function, possibly some role in the formation of extracellular membranes. It will be interesting to learn of the significance of this region.

The functional analysis of any regulatory sequences in the genes that code for the vitelline membrane proteins has not been reported so far. It may well be that comparisons between the regulatory elements of the vitelline membrane, chorion, and oothecin genes could be particularly informative.

3.2.4 The Chorion

The final and most dramatic feat of the follicle cells is the synthesis and assembly of the egg shell or chorion; with this flourish the follicle cells complete their duties and then die. Chorion formation has been the subject of intense investigation over the last twenty years or so, with most of the work concentrated on saturniid and bombycid moths and on *Drosophila melanogaster*. The level of effort reflects the usefulness of these systems as models for areas which are of great current interest, such as the control of gene expression in differentiating cells and the evolution and organization of gene families, in addition to them being of great intrinsic interest.

3.2.4.1 Chorion Morphology

The functional morphology of the insect eggshell has been under study for a long time (Leuckart 1855; Korschelt 1887) and there is much literature on the subject (Hinton 1981). In part, this may be explained by the easy accessibility of the structure and its possible contribution to taxonomic problems (Hinton 1961; Plachter 1981), and in part by the fact that numerous physiological studies on gas exchange, permeability, and other aspects of egg metabolism were carried out from the 1930s into the 1950s (e.g., Slifer 1938; Wigglesworth and Beament 1950). The development of techniques for studies at the molecular level and the emergence of these systems as important contributors to the analysis of gene regulation has stimulated more recent work on chorion structure. The recent literature is reviewed by Margaritis (1985a).

Figure 12 presents a hypothetical "consensus" eggshell structure, based on a variety of literature accounts (Kimber 1980, 1981; Margaritis 1985a; Mazzini and Gaino 1985; Griffith and Lai-Fook 1986a; Fehrenbäch et al. 1987; Powell et al. 1988). Numerous variations and permutations on this basic theme exist, but this summary is a useful way of discussing chorion structure. Closest to the oocyte plasma membrane is the vitelline membrane (discussed in the previous section). In some species (e.g., *Rhodnius*, Beament 1946), a wax layer is formed immediately above the vitelline membrane by the coalescence of oil droplets secreted by the follicle cells at the same time or immediately after the formation of the vitelline membrane. Eventually, in most cases, this layer is hard to distinguish from the vitelline membrane proper. Viewed from the perspective of the oocyte, the next structure is the basal or inner chorion layer. In the mature chorion, in many species, this region exhibits a periodic arrangement of components, producing a crystalline structure. The crystalline arrangement has been described in detail for *Acheta,* and in the beetles, *Phaedon* and *Oryctes* (Furneaux and Mackay 1972, 1976), where periodicities of about 42 ° have been documented. Margaritis (1985a) has assembled a list of 18 species, in 6 insect orders, in which the existence of crystalline eggshell layers has been detected; periodicities of between 37–140 ° have been encountered. The crystalline components appear to be stabilized by disulfide bridges and, also, possibly, by dityrosine bonds. The crystalline chorion layer, although flexible, puts a limit to the volume that the oocyte can achieve. Speculations as to its other functions include a role in the confinement or molding of the wax layer, as well as allowing for gas exchange, through plastron respiration or directly.

Distal to the basal chorion is the trabeculate layer; this structure is generally considered to be part of the endochorion. The trabeculate layer is characterized by the presence of cavities or pores. The small pores may be formed by the withdrawal of follicle cell processes during and/or after the deposition of this layer. In the case

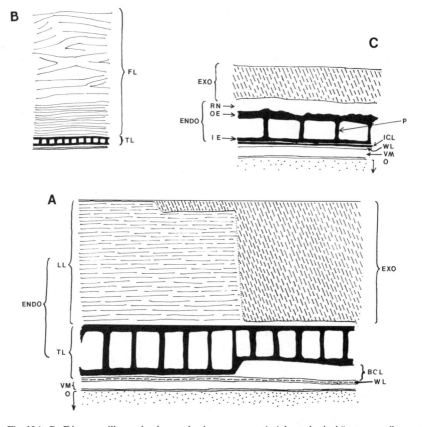

Fig. 12A-C. Diagrams illustrating insect chorion structure. **A** A hypothetical "consensus" structure, showing three variations in exochorion thickness. **B** Chorion structure in silkmoths. **C** Chorion structure in *Drosophila*. *BCL* Basal chorion layer; *ENDO* endochorion; *EXO* exochorion; *FL* fibrillar lamellae; *ICL* inner chorionic layer; *IE* inner endochorion; *LL* lamellar layer; *O* oocyte; *OE* outer endochorion; *P* pillar; *RN* roof network; *TL* trabecular layer; *VM* vitelline membrane; *WL* wax layer

of larger cavities, a flocculent material may serve as a temporary filler for the spaces while the pillars or columns and the overlying roof of this layer are laid down. The cavities may interconnect and form extensive channels. In many insects these may serve as air spaces and open to the exterior via aeropyles; in such cases their main function may be to facilitate gas exchange (Wigglesworth and Salpeter 1962). In other cases the cavities may be filled with a mucuslike substance; possibly the mucus serves as a reserve to surface-localized adhesive material used to attach eggs to the substrate (Mazzini and Gaino 1985).

The outermost layer of the endochorion, if present, is generally characterized by the presence of lamellae, stacked more or less parallel to the egg surface. The lamellar pattern is based on the helicoidal arrangement of stacks of fibrils and oblique sectioning of the lamellae reveals the presence of parabolic patterns (Smith et al.

1981). At the end of choriogenesis the presence of the fibrils can become obscured due to the intercalation of a matrix material and/or to secondary shortening of the fibrils (Mazur et al. 1982). The lamellar layer may be traversed by pores to the exterior. In *Calpodes* (Griffith and Lai-Fook 1986a) these pores are filled with a fibrous material when the egg is ovulated, but at oviposition they become filled with air and act as aeropyles.

In many Lepidoptera, the lamellar layer serves as the outer portion of the shell. In many other insects, however, another layer, the exochorion, is present. In the house cricket, *Acheta domesticus*, the exochorion is a thick structure, consisting largely of mucoprotein (McFarlane 1962). In *Schistocerca* (Kimber 1980) and *Drosophila* (Margaritis 1985a), the layer contains polysaccharides.

Figure 12B,C illustrates chorion structure for silkmoths and *Drosophila*, insects for which the bulk of the molecular information on chorion synthesis is available. The most prominent feature in *Drosophila* is the cavity-rich endochorion; for the moths, the fibrillar lamellate portion of the outer endochorion is the outstanding character, while the exochorion is absent altogether.

Regier et al. (1982) provide a detailed description of the morphogenesis of the silkmoth eggshell. After the formation of the vitelline membrane and the trabecular layer, deposition of a thin sieve layer ensues, followed by that of the thick, lamellate chorion. All of the components which form the lamellae must pass through the sieve layer, since the latter remains attached to the microvilli. Initially, lamella formation occurs in patches; later the patches fuse and new lamellae are added. The final lamellar number is reached before the chorion is completed with respect to thickness and mass. The early lamellae provide a framework which is subsequently modified through expansion and "densification." In *Drosophila*, the silkmoths, as well as other insects (Kimber 1980), the synthesis and secretion of the eggshell precursors by the follicle cells is a continuous process, but the nature of the material synthesized changes in a sequential manner. The molecular explanation for such a sequence of gene activity is of great interest.

While Fig. 12 summarizes the basic architecture of the chorion, it should be noted that in nearly all cases there is a greater or lesser regional differentiation to eggshell structure (Arbogast and vanByrd 1981; Margaritis 1985a). In *Drosophila* the regional differentiation includes the formation of special respiratory appendages and the assembly of an elaborate micropylar apparatus. As illustrated in Fig. 13, the regional differences are due to acquisition of different synthetic capacities by specific groups of follicle cells (Fig. 13). For example, the "border cells", which migrate to their final position from the anterior pole, are responsible for the formation of the micropylar apparatus. These cells construct the paracrystalline component, with cellular proces-ses from some of the cells serving to mold a pocket. Later, the cells are involved in the formation of the "vitelline protrusion", and later still, aided by opercular cells, they construct the endochorion, when some of the cell processes mold a pore canal, forming the micropyle (Margaritis 1985a). The follicle cells display an impressive degree of coordinated temporal and spatial differentiation. It is no surprise, therefore, that these systems have been the focus of a substantial body of work at the cellular and molecular levels.

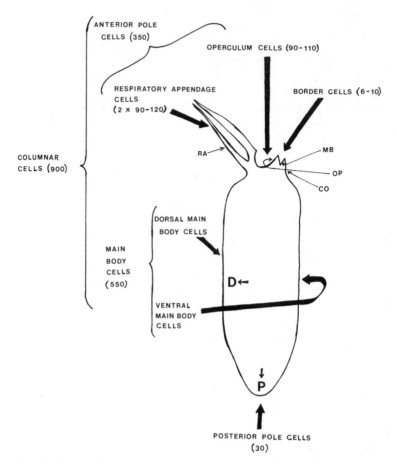

Fig. 13. Diagram illustrating the main features of the *Drosophila* eggshell and the contributions to the eggshell of the various follicle cell types. The data on follicle cell numbers, indicated in *parenthesis*, is from Margaritis (1985a). *CO* Collar; *D* dorsal; *MB* micropyle base; *OP* operculum; *P* posterior; *RA* respiratory appendages

3.2.4.2 Proteins

Information on the chorion proteins from a variety of insect species is available (dragonflies, Kawasaki et al. 1974; beetles, Kawasaki et al. 1975, 1976; a cricket, *Gryllus mitratus*, Kawasaki et al. 1971b), but most of this data is of a preliminary nature. Only the silkmoths and *Drosophila* have been worked on extensively, and most of the following discussion will be based on these two types of organisms.

Initial studies on *Drosophila* documented the presence of six major chorion protein species, named A1, A2, B1, B2 and C1 and C2, in order of increasing molecular weight (Petri et al. 1976). Isoelectric focusing analysis has shown that the six major species are made up of multiple components (Yannoni and Petri 1980);

while two-dimensional electrophoretic analysis of long-term labeled chorion proteins has shown the presence of a number of minor components (Waring and Mahowald 1979). The total number of proteins found in the latter study is about 20, and these are generally accepted as genuine chorion proteins, on the basis of time of synthesis, amino acid composition and copurification with intact chorion (Margaritis et al. 1980). Up to 35 additional minor components can be demonstrated in purified eggshell samples (Regier and Kafatos 1985). The molecular weight range for all these components is from approximately 15–150 kD.

The nomenclature for the proteins varies between laboratories. Waring and Mahowald (1979) specified each form by its position on SDS-gels combined with their migration position on nonequilibrium pH-gradient electrophoretic gels (NEPHGE gels). The protein c15–0 has a molecular weight of 15 kD and migrates at 50% distance on NEPHGE gels. The Kafatos group have adopted a nomenclature based solely on molecular weight, thus s36–1 is the major species at 36 kD. For consistency, the Kafatos terminology will be adopted in the present discussion.

Rapid and substantial changes take place in chorion protein synthesis during the latter stages of vitellogenesis and thereafter. Early in choriogenesis, the s36 and s38 major proteins are the predominant products. A little later (stage 13) most of the chorion proteins are being synthesized, some in greater amounts than others. By the end of the synthetic period, production of s15 and s18 dominates, while many of the other proteins are no longer formed (Waring and Mahowald 1979). The sizes and times of synthesis are closely matched by the concentration of appropriately sized poly(A+)RNAs in the follicle cells (Spradling and Mahowald 1979).

Analysis of the amino acid composition of total eggshell proteins shows that they are, at 0.6 mol%, surprisingly low in cysteine. This is only one-third of the next lowest value so far recorded for chorion proteins (*Gryllus*, Kawasaki et al. 1971b). Silkmoth chorion proteins have at least an order of magnitude greater content of cysteine (Kafatos et al. 1977). The *Drosophila* proteins are rich in Gly, Ala, Pro, Glx, and Ser, which together make up about 60% of the amino acid residues. Also reasonably abundant are Tyr residues. As data on the gene sequences have accumulated, other characteristics of the chorion proteins have become evident. For three of these proteins, s15–1, s18–1, and s19-1, calculated amino acid composition shows 14.4, 10.9, and 12.2 mol% Tyr, much higher that that determined for total chorion proteins. Methionine is absent from all three proteins; Cys is absent from two of them. Calculated isoelectric points are basic and range from 11.1–12.0 (Wong et al. 1985). The predicted molecular weights for these proteins, minus the signal sequences, are 9.9, 15.5 and 16.7 kD, in good agreement with the estimates of Petri et al. (1976), though somewhat smaller than those indicated by the electrophoretic system of Waring and Mahowald (1979).

A most strikign feature of the s15–1, s18–1, and s19–1 amino acid sequences is the presence, in all three proteins, of alternating, multiple hydrophilic and hydrophobic segments. It has been proposed, for some of the silkmoth chorion proteins, that the hydrophobic region may function in intermolecular associations between adjacent proteins and contribute to the three-dimensional structure of the chorion (Regier 1986). The hydrophilic sections would serve as spacers between the hydrophobic regions. Other striking features of the sequences are some extremely Ala-rich segments and the presence of Gly- and Tyr-rich repeats. In fact, the Gly-Gly-Tyr-Gly or related sequences are the principal elements which provide a suggestion of relatedness to silkmoth chorion proteins (Wong et al. 1985). Lastly, the presence of long segments with almost evenly spaced Tyr residues is of interest, given the major type of cross-linking proposed for the *Drosophila* chorion proteins.

In oviposited eggs of *Drosophila*, the chorion components are insoluble in denaturing solutions (e.g., 2% SDS, 8 M urea or 6 M guanidine hydrochloride) which do not disrupt covalent bonds (Petri et al. 1976). The insoluble character of the chorion develops during the last stage of oogenesis and has been correlated with the appearance of di- and trityrosine residues in shell proteins. The use of tyrosyl cross-links as a mechanism for insolubilizing the chorion proteins makes sense, given the fact that Cys residues are low or nonexistent and the possibility for disulfide linkages proportionately reduced or eliminated. The occurrence of tyrosyl cross-links has been documented in a number of other proteinaceous extracellular structures (e.g., resilin, Anderson 1966), including other chorions (Kawasaki et al. 1974). Using an in vitro system, which allows the development of *Drosophila* eggshells in isolated follicles cultured in a defined medium (Petri et al. 1979b), Mindrinos et al. (1980) have shown the presence of a peroxidase among the secreted chorion proteins. This enzyme remains inactive until the terminal stage of oogenesis, when it catalyzes the cross-linking of the chorion proteins. Using the in vitro cultured follicles, it can be demonstrated that premature, but otherwise normal, cross-linking can be induced by hydrogen peroxide and that the cross-linking can be prevented by peroxidase inhibitors, such as phloroglucinol. This report confirmed the earlier observations of Giorgi and Deri (1976) that peroxidase is involved in stabilizing the endochorion.

Margaritis (1985b) has used two cytochemical methods, one, a diaminobenzide assay for peroxidases, and the other, a cerium (III) chloride procedure for the localization of hydrogen peroxide, to investigate chorion protein cross-linking in more detail. He finds that the peroxidase can be demonstrated in the inner chorion layer and in the endochorion as part of the chorion structure. Hydrogen peroxide, which acts as a substrate for the enzyme, enabling it to catalyze the formation of covalent bonding between eggshell proteins, can be shown to be present at the follicle cell plasma membrane during the last stage of oogenesis. Margaritis (1985b) concludes that the hydrogen peroxide is a specific, programmed product of the follicle cells and is responsible for initiating the action of peroxidase. This action results in the oxidation of the tyrosyl residues and the formation of di-tyrosine and tri-tyrosine bonds between chorion proteins.

The chorion proteins of silkmoths (especially *Antheraea polyphemus*, *A. pernyi*, and *Bombyx mori*) are the best described among insect eggshell components (see review by Regier and Kafatos 1985). Over 150 distinct proteins make up the silkmoth chorion. The quantitatively major proteins have been divided into three classes, A, B, and C, based largely on their molecular weights, with molecular weight ranges of 9–12, 12–14, and 16–20 kD, respectively. A quantitatively minor group, the D class, has molecular weights of over 20 kD. A further class, E, has been distinguished on the basis of distinctive solubility properties. In *Bombyx*, another class of proteins, with unusually high cysteine content, is distinguishable. These Hc-class proteins are of variable molecular weight. Regier et al. (1983) have resolved about 75 proteins in the C-class alone; clearly silkmoth chorion proteins form a large and complex group.

Protein and nucleic acid sequencing studies show that most of the complexity is due to the presence of multiple genes rather than to secondary modification.

The A and B classes of proteins together constitute about 85% of the chorion mass (Kafatos et al. 1977; Kafatos 1981). Both types of protein have a similar organization. For the A proteins, a central region of 42–48% of the total protein length is distinguishable. This region is evolutionarily conserved, being very similar in the various members of the A family. The amino- and carboxyl regions, or arms, are highly variable, showing extensive evidence of insertions, deletions, duplications, and replacements. However, both arms are rich in cysteine and glycine and/or variants of the pentapeptide, Gly-Tyr-Gly-Gly-Leu. A similar tripartite structure is found in the B protein group, although the central region and the carboxyl arms are significantly larger. The Hc group is made up of high cysteine proteins that have been found only in *Bombyx*. Together they account for about a quarter of the chorion mass (Kawasaki et al. 1971a). Judging from an inspection of cDNA and genomic clones, two distinct Hc multigene families are present, one related to the A and the other to the B family of genes. Again, the tripartite structure is encountered in the Hc proteins. Available data strongly suggest that all of the chorion proteins belong to a single superfamily of related genes. This point is considered in more detail in the discussion of chorion gene structure.

There is a distinct timing and regional specificity to the production of the chorion proteins. The early formation of the lamellar framework is correlated with the synthesis of many of the C-type proteins. Lamellar expansion and densification is associated with the production of the majority of the A and B class proteins; even finer distinctions with respect to protein types and chorion formation stages are possible. The late developmental period, when regionally specific surface features of the chorion and specialized structures, such as the aeropyle crown, form is associated with specific components of the A, B, C, and E classes.

In attempting to correlate features of protein structure and the overall architecture of the chorion, two major topics need to be considered: (1) the fibrils, which in highly ordered, helicoidal arrays make up the lamellae; and (2) the spongelike network, or filler, which functions to create channels through the lamellar chorion, particularly in the aeropyle crowns. With regard to the fibril formation, much of the evidence suggests that the central domains of the proteins play a key role. For example, in the A and HcA proteins, the central domains show strong sixfold periodicities with respect to the occurrence of glycine and large nonpolar residues. The periodicities and their phase relationships support a model for secondary structure in which short β-sheet strands alternate with β-turns. The final structure is a compact antiparallel β-sheet (Hamodrakas et al. 1985). This finding is consistent with the demonstration by laser Raman analyses (Hamodrakas et al. 1982) and X-ray diffraction (Hamodrakas et al. 1983) of the presence of substantial amounts of antiparallel β-sheet in intact chorion, and places much, if not all of it, in the conserved central domain. Both faces of the proposed β-sheets would include large hydrophobic residues, which may mediate interactions with other central domains and/or with other sections of the chorion proteins. A significant possibility is that the proposed β-sheets may be twisted; this feature could be related to the helicoidal architecture of the chorion (Regier et al. 1980, 1982).

The arms of the tripartite structure may serve to cross-link the proteins through the action of the cysteine residues. They may also function in determining the pitch of the helicoidal array or regulate the thickness or spacing of the fibrils. The differences in the length of the arms among the chorion protein families may be significant in this latter regard (Regier and Kafatos 1985). It should be noted that all of these possibilities for specific function are in the theoretical category and further work will be necessary to establish precise roles for the various components.

Towards the end of oogenesis, a few new lamellae, made up largely of the C-type proteins, form in the aeropyle crown regions (Mazur et al. 1982; Regier et al. 1982). The remaining space in this region becomes occupied by what have been termed as filler proteins. Filler accounts for about 5% of the chorion mass and consists of two proteins, E1 and E2. These proteins cross-link shortly after synthesis and continue to be deposited until the end of choriogenesis. As pointed out above, filler proteins function in the formation of air channels through the lamellar chorion and, in addition, serve to mold a small number of outer surface lamellae into structures called aeropyle crowns.

Genomic and cDNA clones for E1 (Regier and Pacholski 1985) and E2 (Regier 1986) have been sequenced. For E1 a hydropathy plot, which illustrates the relative degree of hydrophobicity at each amino acid residue shows periodically alternating stretches of hydrophobic and hydrophilic amino acids. Variations in hydropathy indices are nowhere near as strong or as periodic for lammellar proteins, and, in general, the E1 sequence shows little or no homology with other known non-E chorion sequences. Secondary structure predictions suggest that the hydrophobic regions of E1 are arranged as α-helices and strands of β-sheet. β-turns are predicted in three, and possibly all four, of the hydrophilic sections. The α-helical arrangement is predicted to be slightly more abundant for the overall protein than β-sheet. For protein E2, the amino terminal domain contains four alternating stretches of hydrophobic and hydrophilic residues, with the first three being homologous to about half of the E1 protein. The carboxy terminal 75% of E2 consists almost entirely of hexapeptide repeats, some of which are lysine- and other asparagine-rich. It is suggested that E1 and the amino terminal domain of E2 bond to multiple molecules and form a highly interconnected and ordered core network of filler. The peptides in the hydrophobic areas, which are predicted to form β-sheets and α-helix, are good candidates for being the major components of the core. Separating the hydrophobic regions are hydrophilic sections that could act as spacers and hinges to permit a change of orientation of the hydrophobic regions. The carboxy terminal repeat domains, given their uniformly hydrophilic nature and probable highly ordered structure, appear to be well suited for hydrogen bonding interaction between themselves, to other E2 molecules and/or to water. Regier (1986) concludes that bonding to water may be important for a loosely organized structure such as filler, which collapses on dehydration.

Regier and Wong (1988) have documented the formation of small amounts (5–10%) of low molecular weight, disulfide-bonded chorion protein multimers throughout the choriogenic period. Such multimers are formed intracellularly by the follicle cells within minutes after synthesis and appear to be secreted in the normal way. Regier and Wong (1988) suggest that multimers are normal intermediates in the chorion protein assembly pathway, since the covalent association takes place in only some of the proteins in the rough endoplasmic reticulum, the rate of multimer export is similar to that of monomers, and there is substantial specificity to multimer assembly. E1 and E2 proteins cross-link only with themselves, B proteins cross-link preferentially to themselves and, at a lower rate, to A proteins, while A proteins show only a low level of self-cross-linking. The disulfide-bonded multimers may form parts of larger complexes held together by weak bonds; upon secretion these complexes could serve as nuclei for further noncovalent association. Eventually these nuclei are fixed or cemented (Blau and Kafatos 1979), near the end and after choriogenesis, by further disulfide linkage formation.

Disulfide bond formation in multimers and disulfide bond formation during cementing at the time of ovulation appear to be separate phenomena. The cementing process transforms the bulk of the chorion proteins from a form completely extractable in the absence of reducing agents to a state completely resistant to solubilization. During this process the major portion of the cysteine is converted to cystine. The conversion process is not instantaneous, but proceeds steadily for several days after ovulation. The importance of disulfide bond formation in stabilizing the chorion has long been recognized (Kawasaki et al. 1971a); the actual trigger and the mechanism for bringing this about is yet to be defined.

3.2.4.3 Transcription, Processing, and Translation

There has been comparatively little systematic work on what might be called the mechanics of transcription and translation using the chorion system. Chorion genes and, as discussed in the previous section, their final products, the chorion proteins, have received an extensive amount of investigative attention. The area between the gene and product is relatively neglected. This is probably not very surprising, since in biology each system has different advantages with regard to different specific questions. While the follicle cells are almost ideal for the analysis of specialized gene structure and regulation and the functional definition of the relevant proteins, they certainly are not the first system which might come to mind for RNA polymerase isolation or for the study of ribosome functional dynamics or structure. Nevertheless, a number of observations, of greater or lesser significance, on various aspects of transcription, processing, and translation have been made using the chorion system.

A potentially promising approach was presented by Lecanidou et al. (1980). These authors reported on a procedure for the isolation of transcriptionally active nuclei from developing silkmoth follicles. The ionic conditions for in vitro transcription were optimized in this system, and changes in the absolute and relative rates of α-amanitin-sensitive and resistant radiolabeled precursor incorporation into RNA mirrored those thought to occur in vivo. This nuclear system showed some promise for detailed studies on the mechanisms of specific transcription during follicular development. To date, this potential does not appear to have been realized.

A promising approach to the determination of transcription termination sites in genes which produce polyadenylated products has been reported by Osheim et al. (1986). The electron microscopic method, in which transcription unit lengths are measured in chromatin spreads, supplements the recombinant DNA techniques, such as deletion mapping, for the analysis of this problem. Using the s36–1 and s38–1 *Drosophila* chorion genes, these authors have localized the efficient termination sites to a region of approximately 210 bp for s36–1 and about 365 bp for s38–1. In the former case, the center of this region is about 105 nucleotides downstream from the poly(A) site. For the s38–1 gene, it is about 400 nucleotides downstream from the poly(A) site. The termination site for these genes appears to be closer to the poly(A) addition site than for many other examples for which sufficient data are available. The significance of this observation is not totally clear, and it may be that how close a termination site is to the poly(A) site is determined by the proximity of the next downstream gene. For many genes, termination of transcription occurs with increasing probability over a stretch of DNA sequence. In the case of the s36–1 gene the termination site seems to be more closely defined, with at least 97%, and possibly 100%, of the transcripts ending at the defined site.

The extensively transcribed s36–1 and s38–1 *Drosophila* chorion genes have been used to evaluate the significance of ribonucleoprotein (RNP) particles detected in chromatin spreads using electron microscopy (Osheim et al. 1985). It is well known that nascent hnRNA becomes associated with proteins to form ribonucleoprotein structures (hnRNPs; Malcolm and Sommerville 1974; Zieve and Penman 1981). In dispersed chromatin, the nascent hnRNPs become extended and fibrillar, with some remaining particulate components. Beyer et al. (1980) have suggested that the RNP particle location is nonrandom and sequence-dependent in any given gene. In some descriptions, nearby particles, separated by fibrillar RNP, are said to coalesce, forming a loop in the smooth fibrillar RNP (Beyer 1983). The looped-out portion may be eliminated, and the whole process of particle coalescence and loop formation may represent the lariat structure correlated with the splicing out of introns during eukaryote hnRNA processing (Keller 1984). The stable RNPs detected in the chromatin spreads possibly represent complexes of hnRNPs and snRNPs (associations of small nuclear RNAs and proteins, such as U1 and U2, which are thought to be part of the hnRNA splicing mechanism: Padgett et al. 1983; Black et al. 1985). Osheim et al. (1985) have sought to determine if the sequences bound by the RNPs detected in chromatin spreads play a role in RNA processing by carefully plotting the location of such particles with reference to the s36–1 and s38–1 chorion genes, which are of known sequence. Both genes have a single, small intron near their 5'-ends. RNP particles of about 25 nm diameter are found consistently only at the potential splice junctions in these two transcripts. These particles are seen to coalesce into a single, larger (40 nm) particle in some cases. The results support the conclusion that the RNPs are involved in bringing splice junctions together and in maintaining them in close proximity during the splicing intermediate stage.

A number of workers have reported that the chorion mRNAs in both silkmoths and *Drosophila* have a typical and expected structure for RNAs concerned with the synthesis of export proteins (Kaulenas 1985). The 5'-ends of the mRNAs are capped, the major cap structure in silkmoth mRNAs is $m^7G(5')ppp(5')A^m$ (Morrow et al. 1981), and polyadenylated (*Drosophila*, Vournakis et al. 1975; silkmoths, Morrow et al. 1981). The mRNAs contain a sequence for a signal peptide (Thireos et al. 1979), as expected for export protein messengers. While currently the presence of this signal is easily detected from gene sequence data, at the time of this work the results contributed to the development of the signal peptide hypothesis.

A number of studies have explored the correlation between mRNA concentration and the production of the chorion proteins (*Drosophila*, Spradling and Mahowald 1979; silkmoths, Gelinas and Kafatos 1973), including stage specific changes (Thireos and Kafatos 1980). While there are some indications of possible translational level control (Thireos et al. 1980), the results show that alterations in chorion protein synthesis are normally based on changes in concentrations of the corresponding mRNAs, and strongly imply that the regulation of chorion protein production is largely at the level of transcription.

Other than electron microscope observations, the actual mechanism of protein export has not been explored extensively. A protein secretion deficient mutant in *Bombyx mori* has been reported (Nadel et al. 1980). When homozygous, the G_r^{col} mutation results in the production of an eggshell in which most proteins are underrepresented to varying degrees; protein loss being maximal at early and middle stages of choriogenesis. The presence of mutant-specific cytoplasmic vesicles can be demonstrated, but the exact cause for any deficiency has not been defined. Lastly, some data which are possibly relevant to the regulation of ribosome concentration in follicle cells have been reported (Fragoulis and Traub 1984).

3.2.4.4 Chorion Genes in Drosophila

As noted above, the chorion of *Drosophila* is constructed from 20–30 different proteins, six of which are major components. All of the major protein genes have been localized, by in situ hybridization or genetic analysis, to two gene clusters, one on the X and the other on chromosome III. Genes s36 and s38 are near the site of the *ocelliless* mutation (Spradling et al. 1979) and have been localized to between 7E11 and 7F 1–2 region of the X chromosome (Spradling and Mahowald 1979; Spradling et al. 1980). As discussed below, 80–100 kb of DNA becomes amplified before the expression of these genes. In addition to the s36 and s38 genes, the central 18 kb region of this area has been shown to contain a number of genes coding for minor chorion proteins. These include the A, B, and E genes, upstream from s36, and gene product C, which partially overlaps B, and may be the result of differential splicing. The minor components have not been characterized in detail. Ethylmethane-sulfonate (EMS) mutagenesis (e.g., Komitopoulou et al. 1983) has turned up a number of genes which affect chorion formation. Among these are alleles of a large complementation group (*fs*(1) 410, Bauer and Waring 1987; *fs*(1) 384, Komitopoulou et al. 1988; *fs*(1) 1501, Lineruth and Lambertsson 1986; *dec-1*, Hawley and Waring 1988), which map at 7C on the X chromosome. This gene produces a large, 130 kD protein during stage 10 of oogenesis. It appears to be essential for endochorion formation (Bauer and Waring 1987). A second transcript from this gene, of 5.8 kb, generated by alternative splicing, accumulates during stages 11–12 (Hawley and Waring 1988). In addition, the s70 minor chorion component maps near the *yellow* locus at the tip of the X chromosome (Hawley and Waring 1988). Other X-chromosome mutants which influence eggshell structure appear largely to affect amplification and other processes rather than representing chorion protein genes (Komitopoulou et al. 1983, 1988).

61

The major chorion genes s18, s15, s19, and s16 have been located near the *sepia* locus, and have been shown to map at 66 D 11–15 region of the third chromosome (Spradling et al. 1980; Griffin-Shea et al. 1980). All four genes are arranged in a cluster within 6 kb of each other (Griffin-Sea et al. 1982) (see Fig. 14). As discussed below, this DNA region is also one which becomes amplified before the expression of the genes. A minor (s16–35) chorion protein gene has been localized to 54 C-D on the second chromosome (Griffin-Shea et al. 1980).

The sequences of five of the major chorion genes have been determined: s18–1, s15–1 and s19–1 (Wong et al. 1985); s18–1, s15–1 (Levine and Spradling 1985); s36 and s38 (Spradling et al. 1987). In addition to these genes of *D. melanogaster*, sequences for s15–1 and s19–1 for *D. subobscura* and *D. grimshawi*, and for s15–1 in *D. virilis* have been published (Martinez-Cruzado et al. 1988). All of the genes have very similar general features. In all there is a short, 5'-exon (coding for five, four, and five amino acids in s18–1, s15–1, and s19–1, respectively, and 16 and 15 amino acids for s36 and s38), followed by a single intron, which ranges from 71–226 nucleotides in length, followed by a large exon. The coding regions have sufficient hints of homology to suggest a rather distant common ancestral sequence. Most of the noncoding areas have diverged even further. In each gene, a Goldberg-Hogness TATA box (the transcriptional selector sequence) is found upstream from the potential cap sites, and in all five genes a chorion specific hexamer, TCACGT, is located 23–32 nucleotides upstream from the TATA box.

Comparison of the gene structure between different *Drosophila* species shows that the intergenic and the 3'-untranslated sequences are poorly conserved. The coding regions are somewhat more conservative, but show internal inhomogeneities in sequence divergence. The most interesting finding is that some of the 5'-untranslated regions are highly conserved. In particular, the highly conserved regions are concentrated in a number of short elements, among which is the chorion specific hexamer mentioned above (Martinez-Cruzado et al. 1988). Such elements may represent regions involved in gene regulation as will be discussed below.

Chorion protein synthesis involves the production of massive amounts of protein in a very short time period. In most systems the problem of producing large quantities of specialized product is solved by the accumulation of stable mRNAs over an extended period (Kafatos 1972). This does not happen in the chorion system, since the endo- and exochorion is laid down over a period of about 5 h and prior accumulation of mRNAs has not been detected. Even given the fact that follicle cells undergo several rounds of DNA replication in the absence of cell division (Mahowald et al. 1979), calculations show that at maximal rates of transcription, mRNA levels which could be produced on the basis of standard gene content are about an order of magnitude less than actually found (Spradling and Mahowald 1980). An explanation for this discrepancy emerged from studies of these latter authors on the female-sterile mutation *ocelliless*. This mutation maps near the s-36 and s-38 chorion protein genes on the X chromosome, and results in a *cis*-acting reduction in the amounts of the corresponding proteins that are accumulated in late-stage egg chambers. *Ocelliless* does not affect the level of s-18 chorion protein, whose gene is located on chromosome III. Using a ^{32}P-labeled, cloned section of the s-36 cDNA as a probe, and appropriate controls, it was demonstrated that DNA from wild-type females had significantly greater concentrations of sequences complementary to the probe than DNA isolated from embryonic nuclei and wild-type or *ocelliless* males. Moreover, the increased labeling was not found with DNA from *ocelliless* females. Hybridization of the probe to DNA purified from the ovaries and from nonovarian tissues of wild-type flies showed that the increased s36 gene concentrations were found only in the ovary. The observation that DNA from the tissue expressing the s36 gene showed increased hybridization with a probe complementary to this sequence suggested strongly that a differential replication of this gene is found in the ovary. The amplification level appears to be more than tenfold.

Later work by Spradling (1981) has shown that both the X-chromosome chorion gene cluster and the third chromosome cluster undergo amplification prior to their expression in late oogenesis. Amplification involves the transcribed sequences and the intervening spacer sequences equally. Sequences more distal from the chorion genes also replicate differentially but to a lower extent, producing gradients of decreasing amplification. The total amplification domain on both chromosomes is about 80 kb of DNA. The overall data are best explained by assuming that successive rounds of replication are initiated within the central gene-containing regions, followed by bidirectional replication in the absence of discrete termination sites.

The amplified regions on both the X and the third chromosome have been visualized in chromatin spreads from appropriately staged follicle cells by electron microscopy (Osheim and Miller 1983). The regions can be identified by the presence of complex, multiforked chromosomal structures, in which one chromatin strand undergoes repeated subbranching, and by the topology and molecular anatomy of the transcription units. Occasionally, the active genes can be observed within or contiguous with intact replicons and replication forks (Osheim et al. 1988). The micrographs suggest that forks at either end of a replicon frequently progress to different extents, possibly due to different initiation times or different rates of movement. The molecular biology and electron microscopic data are summarized in Fig. 14. Chorion gene amplification on the X chromosome progresses from a central region containing the transcription units and spreads for about 40 kb to each side. The maximum level of amplification is about 16 copies per genome equivalent. A similar situation exists in chromosome III, but with a maximum copy number per genome reaching to approximately 60. In Fig. 14C, a model for amplification is presented, which visualizes the process occurring via multiple rounds of bidirectional DNA synthesis, initiating from a central region. Each successive round of replication terminates closer to the origin. The replication forks can be at diverse positions on the homologous strands.

The electron microscopic evidence is totally consistent with the hypothesis that the central regions of both chorion domains contain replication origins used during the amplification event (Osheim et al. 1988). These observations confirm the suggestion emerging from a detailed analysis of the *ocelliless* mutation which indicate that a specific chromosomal region is required in *cis* for amplification (Spradling and Mahowald 1981). The mutation is associated with a small chromosome inversion whose distal breakpoint is located 1–3 kb upstream from the s36 and s38 chorion protein genes. The inversion changes the sequences that are amplified and affects the level of amplification. Normally unamplified sequences adjacent to the breakpoint

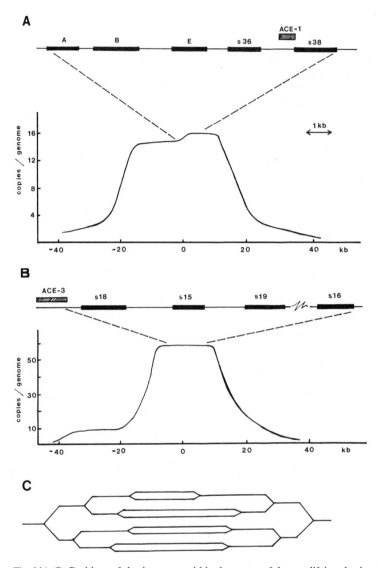

Fig. 14A-C. Positions of chorion genes within the center of the amplifying chorion domains. **A** The X-chromosomal domain at cytogenetic region 7F1,2. The *top* of the figure shows the relative positions of the two major chorion genes, *s36* and *s38*, and three of the minor genes, *A, B, E,* in the central 13-kb region. All of these genes are follicle-cell specific and are active during the early stages of choriogenesis. The location of the 467-bp sequence essential in *cis* for amplification is indicated by the *hatched box* labelled *ACE-1*. The *lower* region shows the 80-kb gradient of X-chromosomal aplification observed in stage 13 and 14 egg chamber DNA. The position of the central region containing the genes is indicated. **B** Chromosome III domain in cytogenetic region 66D. The *upper* portion of the figure displays the four major chorion genes at the locus. The 510-bp region essential in *cis* for amplification and located just upstream of s18 is denoted by the *hatched box* labelled *ACE-3*. The 80-kb amplification gradient observed at the third chromosomal locus in stage 13 egg chambers is also presented. **C** Model of chorion locus amplification. Multiple rounds of bidirectional DNA

differentially replicate in *ocelliless* follicle cells. The pattern of amplification in this mutation is explained best by a repositioning of a control sequence due to the inversion.

Amplification control elements (ACEs) occur on both the X and the third chromosome. Their positions have been mapped by a series of experiments using P-element mediated germ-line transformation (de Cicco and Spradling 1984; Kafatos et al. 1985; Kalfayan et al. 1985; Wakimoto et al. 1986; Spradling et al. 1987), and their locations are indicated in Fig. 14A,B.

A general approach to germ-line transformation experiments is to insert cloned chorion genes or sections of chromosomal DNA adjacent to a copy of a wild-type *ry* (rosy) gene and to place the chimeric construct between the inverted repeats of the transposable P element. The cloned genes can be modified prior to transformation by inserting heterologous DNA (e.g., M13 phage) into transcribed regions or by fusing chorion sequences to the *lacZ* gene from *E. coli*. The modifications allow the transcripts of the cloned constructs to be distinguished from those of normal genes. The chimeric transposon plasmid is then injected into early *ry⁻* embryos. The sequences found between the P element inverted repeats can transpose into germ line chromosomes (Rubin and Spradling 1982, 1983; Spradling and Rubin 1982). Cases where the transposon has integrated can be recovered in the next generation by scoring for individuals with *ry⁺* eye color. The transformation procedure is reasonably efficient since some 10% of fertile recipients give rise to *ry⁺* transformants. Unfortunately, expression of the transformed genes is dependent upon integration position, and in some cases it is necessary to utilize the technique of mobilizing or "jumping" the transposon to new chromosomal locations (Levis et al. 1985a) to fully check their functional capacity. Amplification levels or transcriptional efficiency can be monitored by assaying separated DNA or RNA samples with appropriate probes (e.g. ³²P-labeled *rosy* or M13 sequences hybridized to Southern (DNA) or Northern (RNA) blots). The functional significance of various sequences can be checked by deletion analysis. For example, 5'-flanking regions can be progressively removed from the constructs and the resulting functional properties of the shorter constructs assayed. Internal deletions can be created by removing sequences starting from some internal, restriction nuclease generated, section.

For the X-chromosome gene cluster, using the above procedures, Wakimoto et al. (1986) have identified a DNA fragment (contained in the chorion-*rosy* gene transposon S38M) which alone accounts for amplification in transformed strains, albeit at a low level. This region confers the appropriate time and tissue-specificity as well as the capacity for gene amplification. Spradling et al. (1987) have refined this analysis by inspecting the properties vis-à-vis amplification of the chorion genes, in

◄───

and located just upstream of s18 is denoted by the *hatched box* labelled *ACE-3*. The 80-kb amplification gradient observed at the third chromosomal locus in stage 13 egg chambers is also presented. **C** Model of chorion locus amplification. Multiple rounds of bidirectional DNA synthesis initiate from the central gene region, each successive round of replication terminating nearer the origin. The replication forks can be at diverse position (Redrawn from Osheim et al. 1988)

a total of 129 transposons in 126 separate lines. Their initial analysis localized the ACE (ACE-1) element for the X-chromosome gene cluster to a region including and surrounding the s38 gene. Additional deletion studies have pinpointed the ACE-1 element to a 467 bp section upstream from the s38 transcription start site. Moreover, at least some of the elements essential for amplification are not required for the developmentally regulated chorion gene transcription. DNA sequences which regulate transcription and gene amplification may or may not overlap, but they are not identical.

The location and identity of the DNA sequences essential for the amplification of the chorion gene cluster on chromosome 3 (ACE-3) have been investigated in even greater detail. ACE-3 is located near the 5'-proximal gene, in contrast to the 3'-proximal location for ACE-1 (Kalfayan et al. 1985). While the functional significance of the divergent locations for the ACE elements is unclear, the sites do correspond to the locale of the most abundantly expressed genes in each cluster. Using P-element mediated transformation the ACE-3 function was localized to a 3.8 kb fragment located near the 5'-end of the gene cluster (de Cicco and Spradling 1984). Sequencing of this fragment (Levine and Spradling 1985) showed that it included the genes for s18 and s15 proteins as well as sequences upstream from s18. Orr-Weaver et al. (1989) have narrowed down the position of ACE-3 to between 120 and 630 bp upstream from the s18 gene; deletion of this 510 bp segment abolished the ability of a specific transposon containing three of the four chorion genes of this cluster to amplify. Although ACE-3 is absolutely essential for amplification, it is not equally clear that it is sufficient, since small ACE-3 containing fragments fail to amplify (de Cicco and Spradling 1984). The latter result could be due to position effects or the presence of additional elements.

The experiments of Delidakis and Kafatos (1987) make it clear that, in addition to the essential ACE element, a number of amplification-enhancing elements or regions (AEEs/AERs) can be identified within the chorion locus (Fig. 15). Some of these may be as far as 6 kb away from ACE-3. AERs are required for high amplification levels; however, they are accessory to ACE since they do not function in its absence.

More recent work from the Spradling and Kafatos groups has clarified some additional aspects of ACE-3 and AER function. For example, there have been a

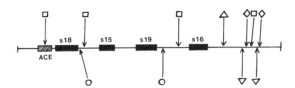

Fig. 15. Diagram showing the distribution of various DNA repeats (□ α; ○ β; Δ γ; ∇ δ; ◊ Σ) relative to other features of the chromosome II chorion locus in *Drosophila*. The ACE region is hatched and the chorion genes are indicated by the thick filled segments. With the exception of γ, δ and Σ, which are found exclusively downstream from s16, other repeats are found in three segments; one overlaps ACE and the other two are found in regions that reduce amplification when deleted. Direction of transcription is from *left* to *right* (After data of Delidakis and Kafatos 1987)

number of speculations that ACE-3 might contain a transcription enhancer which also regulates replication, analogous to the situation found in a number of eukaryotic viruses (De-Pamphilis 1988). However, the experiments of Orr-Weaver et al. (1989) suggest that there is no essential connection between control of amplification and transcription. Amplification control can be shown to be confined to a 320 bp region which excludes the section necessary for transcriptional control of the s28 gene. Addition of heterologous enhancers, such as those for the *hsp70* or the *Sgs-4* genes, failed to influence amplification. While there are several potential caveats to these results, it does appear that ACE-3 is not analogous in any direct way to a transcriptional enhancer. Other results of deletion experiments indicate that ACE-3 may consist of multiple functional domains. In particular the regions between –368 and –310 and between –410 and –370 appear to play important roles, while the –480 to –420 section is dispensable. In addition, ACE-3 has been shown to function independently of orientation.

Suggestions that ACE-3 represents a replication origin have not been borne out. Delidakis and Kafatos (1989) and Heck and Spradling (1990) have shown that at least one, and possibly two, of the AERs close to the ACE region actually function as replication origins. Heck and Spradling (1990) note the presence of elements related to the yeast core autonomously replicating sequences (ARS: Stinchcomb et al. 1979) of ATTTATGTTT in the β AERS (see Fig. 15). It should be noted that numerous conserved repeated elements have been detected in the chorion locus by computer searches (e.g., Delidakis and Kafatos 1987; Kalfayan et al. 1985). Whether or not, or how, these specific sequence motifs contribute to replication origins or other functions remains to be established by more direct experiments. The overall results suggest that ACE-3 and other *cis*-regulatory elements (AERs) interact to influence the occurrence and level of amplification. The presence of ACE-3 is necessary to trigger initiation at one or more downstream sites.

In contrast to the progress in defining the nature of the *cis*-regulatory elements in chorion gene amplification, the analysis of any potential *trans*-acting factors is less advanced. Preliminary descriptions of two X-linked recessive female-sterile mutants (K451, K1214; Orr et al. 1984) and three third chromosome mutations (Snyder et al. 1986) have been reported. These mutations are at sites away from the structural chorion genes and disrupt chorion formation by causing the underproduction of all major chorion proteins. They do so by reducing the level of chorion gene amplification. While there is some evidence that the K451 mutant may act in a nonspecific way, by influencing the general replication machinery, the other mutants may be tissue specific. Further analysis of their roles will be of interest.

A number of studies, mainly by the Kafatos group, and to a somewhat lesser extent by the Spradling group, have begun the dissection of the chorion-gene transcriptional control elements. This aspect is of particular interest, since it involves a number of interrelated facets. The expression of the genes for chorion proteins is sex-, tissue- and stage-specific. These genes are expressed only in females, and only in the later stages of oogenesis in the ovarian follicle cells. In addition, the quantitative level of expression is regulated at the level of the individual gene, as is the spatial or regional specificity. Some of these aspects are illustrated in Fig. 16, based mainly on the data of Griffin-Shea et al. (1982) and of Parks and Spradling (1987). The time and quantitative aspects are particularly strongly demonstrated in this figure. Genes in the same chromosome cluster are expressed at different times in oogenesis and at different final product concentrations. The genes for s36 and s38 are expressed maximally at about stage 12, while genes E and B are expressed earlier but only achieve 5–20% of the maximal quantitative levels. The genes located on chromosome II are the last to be expressed, with the exception of s15–1, which has a biphasic pattern, with an early product accumulation period in stage 11 (paralleling the maximal expression of gene E of the X chromosome cluster), and a later, more intense expression, more or less in synchrony with the other late chorion genes of chromosome III.

A number of studies have shown that the regulation of gene expression is at the level of the individual gene and is independent of gene amplification, which only determines the level at which the gene products accumulate (Parks et al. 1986). There are solid indications that control of the quantitative and developmental aspects of

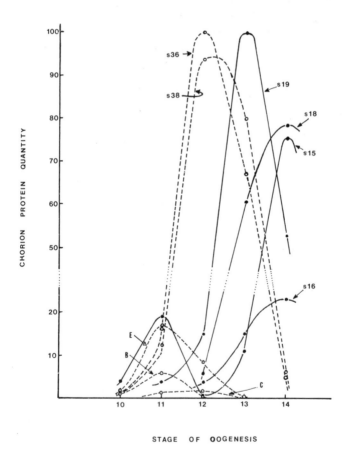

STAGE OF OOGENESIS

Fig. 16. Variation in the timing of synthesis and quantity of chorion proteins during the later stages of oogenesis in *Drosophila*. Protein quantities are estimated relative to the maximum abundance of s15. The *lines* are based on the data of Griffin-Shea et al. (1982) and Parks and Spradling (1987)

gene expression are mediated by different elements in the 5'-upstream gene regions (Kafatos et al. 1985); elimination of sequences upstream from –386 of the s-15 gene depresses the level of expression but does not affect the developmental specificity (i.e., sex, tissue, and stage specificity). The sequences downstream from the –386 site must regulate these aspects as well as the general transcriptional competency of the gene. These results have been largely confirmed by the use of fusion constructs of chorion DNA and the alcohol dehydrogenase (Adh) structural gene (Romano et al. 1988). The results indicate that, almost entirely, the 5'-flanking DNA sequences of the early (s36) and late (s15) chorion genes are sufficient for conferring the normal sex, stage, and tissue specificity on the reporter gene. Control of the quantity of expression, however, must reside within other elements, either upstream of the transcription initiation site, or possibly downstream, within or beyond the coding sections of the genes investigated (s36/s15). In the absence of such elements, the expression level of the fusion construct is more than an order of magnitude lower. Arguments by analogy to the yolk protein-2 gene, which is also expressed in follicle cells, prior to chorion gene transcription (Brennan et al. 1982), suggest that a transcriptional "booster" may be found in the translated region of the gene rather than, or in addition to, distant 5'-sequences.

The temporal regulatory elements have been characterized further in a series of decisive experiments by Mariani et al. (1988). These workers have used detailed germline transformation experiments to dissect the *cis* regulatory components necessary for the transcriptional control of the s-15 gene. The work shows clearly that multiple regulatory elements are localized within a 73-bp region (–46 to –118 with reference to the s15 gene transcription starting point). While other interpretations are possible, the results of the deletion and substitution experiments strongly suggest the existence of a minimum of three regulatory elements:

1. The TCACGT motif (at –60 to –55) appears to be an essential positively acting element (evolutionarily conserved between Diptera and Lepidoptera; Mitsialis et al. 1987). Its removal eliminates the activity of the s15 promoter. However, this element is not alone responsible for temporal specificity, since it is present in both early- and late-acting genes.
2. An element which specifies late activation lies between –80 and –70. This positive element cannot function without the presence of the TCACGT region. Presumably, two factors, binding to two separate regions, or a single factor binding to two domains, determine(s) the temporal specificity of this gene's expression.
3. A region between –118 and –81 appears to prevent precocious expression. If this region is eliminated the s15 gene is revealed as primed for expression even during the early choriogenic stages. This negative *cis* regulator can be dissected into three domains: (1) –89 to –81 of the downstream DNA functions to inhibit expression at stage 11; (2) –98 to –90 is necessary to extend the inhibition to stage 12; and (3) –118 to –99 is necessary to inhibit expression up to stage 13. In an interesting experiment, a substitute DNA segment from the s36 gene, derived from an equivalent location, imparted the early temporal regulation characteristic of s36 to the chimeric s15 gene. Presumably a factor or factors binding to these regions influence(s) transcription initiation. Details of such possible reactions and their participants remain to be defined. The temporal specificity of s15, and probably

69

the other chorion genes, is brought about by the interplay of positive and negative DNA elements and the action of *trans*-acting factors; such a control scheme would not be unique to the chorion system (e.g., Kuhl et al. 1987).

The constructs used by Romano et al. (1988) and Mariani et al. (1988) clearly show tissue-specific expression. The question of which sequences in the genes confer tissue specificity has not been explicitly addressed in these experiments but has been investigated for the yolk protein genes of the follicle cells and for the S36 chorion gene. Logan and Wensink (1990) have shown for the yp1 and yp2 genes that tissue specificity is conferred by two enhancers. Ovarian enhancer 1 (oe1) is located between the two yolk protein genes, while oe2 is found within the first exon of yp2. A core sequence of nine nucleotides is characteristic of both enhancers, for oe1 it is GAAT-CAATG and for oe2 it is GATTCATTG (Table 3). An element identical to oe1 is found in the 5'-upstream region of yp3. Closely related sequences can be located in the s15 chorion gene. Element 1, identical to oe1 in 7 of 9 positions, is found at −575 to −567 in the *D. melanogaster* gene; it is listed as part of a long inverted repeat suggested by computer manipulation of the s15 gene-sequence data (Wong et al. 1985). Very similar motifs are present, in slightly different locations in the 5'-upstream region of s15 in *D. grimshowi*, *D. virilis* and *D. subsobscura* (Martínez-Cruzado et al. 1988). Element 2, which is identical for all four *Drosophila* species, is part of a longer, identical segment in the first exon of the gene. It is of interest that element 1 of *D. virilis* is identical to the oe2 sequence. All of the P-element constructs used by Romano et al. (1988) and Mariani et al. (1988) contain one or the other or both of these elements. It seems possible that regulation of tissue specific expression could involve these DNA segments. On the other hand, based on the sequence data of Spradling et al. (1987), these sequence motifs are absent from the 84 bp upstream region which is sufficient for normal follicular expression of the *D. melanogaster* s36 chorion gene (Tolias and Kafatos 1990). It will be interesting to see this question explored in greater detail experimentally.

The experiments of Tolias and Kafatos (1990) have exposed a very interesting regulatory mechanism for the control of temporal and regional expression of the s36 gene. They have used a construct containing various DNA segments from upstream of the s36 gene TATA box fused to a heterologous basal promoter and a reporter gene (*has70/lacZ*). β-galactosidase activity was assayed in ovaries histologically after

Table 3. Comparison of the *Drosophila* DNA elements in yolk protein and chorion genes which may be involved in conferring tissue specific expression[a]

	Element 1	Element 2
Yolk proteins 1 and 2	GAATCAATG	GATTCATTG
Yolk protein 3	GAATCAATG	
D. melanogaster s15 gene	GAATCTATT	GATTGATTA
D. grimshawi s15 gene	GATTCATTG	GATTGATTA
D. virilis s15 gene	GATTCATTG	GATTGATTA
D. subobscura s15 gene	GAAACATTG	GATTGATTA

[a]Data from Logan and Wensink (1990); Wong et al. (1985); Martinez-Cruzado et al. (1988).

P-element-mediated germline transformation. Their results suggest that multiple, spatially specific *cis*-regulatory elements are present. The downstream half of the 84 bp control segment allows expression in follicle cells found at both poles of the oocyte, but most strongly at the anterior tip; the upstream section allowed expression only at the posterior pole. The upstream regulatory elements are position independent, the downstream elements are position sensitive. An additional distal regulatory element contains redundant control for expression at the anterior pole. This result is somewhat unexpected since s36 transcripts are present throughout the follicular epithelium and a single control element might be forecast. However, the initial transcription of this gene starts at stage 10 in a limited subset of dorsally located follicle cells near the oocyte-nurse cell boundary (Parks and Spradling 1987). Similarly, other transcripts from the X-chromosome linked cluster are initially regionally localized, and some, e.g. B and E transcripts, may have nonoverlapping regions of expression. Parks and Spradling (1987) suggest that initial chorion gene expression is coordinated with the follicle cell migrations described earlier (see Fig. 11). These authors also suggest that cell-cell interactions, between adjacent follicle cells and between follicle cells and the oocyte, may play important roles in regulating the precise pattern and timing of chorion gene expression. If this is the case then genes which determine the spatial organization of the egg chamber, such as *gurken* (Schüpbach 1987) and *torpedo* (Price et al. 1989) may control indirectly chorion gene activity. Tolias and Kafatos (1990) visualize a scenario in which genes specifying oocyte organizational patterns, such as the ventralizing *gurken* and the dorsalizing *fs(1)K10* (Wieschaus et al. 1978) transmit their spatial cues to the follicle cells by the action of genes such as *torpedo*. In the follicle cells, the interaction would result in the production or alteration of transcription factors, which then would regulate the activity of the chorion genes.

The definition of the multiple, sometimes redundant, DNA sequence elements which determine the tissue specificity and the time and place of expression is beginning to emerge. Information on potential nuclear proteins or other *trans*-acting factors (e.g. Müller and Schaffner 1990), which may bind to these control regions is rather limited. Two third chromosome mutations described by Snyder et al. (1986) may be potential candidates in this regard, but no additional information on them has been published as yet. In other experiments, using a follicular nuclear extracts, Shea et al. (1989) have found a number of binding factors which recognize *cis*-acting regulatory sequences. They have identified an early stage repressor, a late stage activator, and an essential activator binding to the chorion-specific TCACGT hexamer. Further characterization of these factors will be of interest.

3.2.4.5 Silkmoth Chorion Genes

Much of the early work on the characterization of silkmoth chorion genes concentrated on *Antheraea polyphemus* (Sim et al. 1979; Jones et al. 1979); the later work has concentrated more on *Bombyx mori*. In *Bombyx*, genetic and cloning evidence permits a rough estimate of the chorion gene number. Over 70 structural genes have been identified in a 270 kb chromosomal "walk" and Eickbush and Kafatos (1982) suggest that about 230 chorion genes are present in toto. All of the genes appear to be evolutionarily related to a lesser or greater extent; the whole group is thought to constitute a gene superfamily, with two major branches, α and β (Goldsmith and Kafatos 1984; Lecanidou et al. 1986). Each branch is composed of a number of multigene families. For the α branch, the families are labeled CA (or ErA), A, and HcA; in the β branch, they are CB (or ErB), B, and HcB. Each family can be subdivided into subfamilies; and these into gene types; each gene type can be made up of several, non-identical genes.

The chorion genes have been mapped near the proximal end of chromosome 2 in *Bombyx* (Goldsmith and Clermont-Rattner 1980). They are localized in two tightly linked clusters, Ch 1–2 and Ch 3, separated by approximately 2400 kb of intervening DNA (Goldsmith 1989). The Ch 1–2 cluster contains the 270 kb chromosomal "walk" of Eickbush and Kafatos (1982), including all of the later acting Hc genes as well as the Gr^B deletion (Iatrou et al. 1980). The remaining genes appear to be predominantly middle As and Bs. The Ch 3 cluster contains all of the early acting genes, some groups of which have been cloned (Hibner et al. 1988), as well as many of the early-middle genes. This partial segregation of the genes with respect to their temporal specificity may have significant functional consequences. Goldsmith (1989) speculates that the gene clusters may correspond to distinct regulatory domains, possibly on the level of chromatin loops. Such loops could affect the global accessibility of the genes to transcription factors, which otherwise function at the level of the individual promoters.

Definitions of which genes are expressed "early", "early-middle", "middle" and "late" in chorion formation have been made by analysis of the proteins (Bock et al. 1986), as well as by using cloned genes. The functional clustering described above by Goldsmith (1989) has been confirmed for the early and early-middle genes (Eickbush et al. 1985; Lecanidou et al. 1986; Hibner et al. 1988) and the late genes, all 15 pairs of which (Burke and Eickbush 1986) are located in a 130 kb contiguous DNA region (Eickbush and Kafatos 1982). Many of the middle genes are located on either side of the late gene cluster (Eickbush and Kafatos 1982); although different A, B gene pairs with different times of expression can be interspersed within a particular section (Spoerel et al. 1989).

Most of the chorion genes, including all examples of the A, B, and HcA/HcB families, are found paired on the chromosome. In fact, the gene pair may be considered as the fundamental unit of organization (Jones and Kafatos 1980a; Iatrou and Tsitilou 1983; Iatrou et al. 1984). Typically, one α and one β gene is located adjacent to each other, and are coordinately expressed. They are divergently transcribed, with a short, intervening sequence of about 300 nucleotides, containing the promoter, located between them. One exception to this arrangement has been described so far. One of the early genes, 5H4, is not divergently paired with any other chorion gene, and appears to be the first characterized example of a chorion gene which is not a member of a multigene family (Hibner et al. 1988); however, other early acting genes are divergently paired.

The individual chorion genes have an exon, intron arrangement which is similar to that found in *Drosophila*. The single intron, found in the signal sequence, separates a short 5'-terminal exon and a long, 3'-terminal exon coding for most of the protein. The coding section has a typical tripartite arrangement, reflecting the protein structure, with an evolutionarily conservative central domain and amino and carboxy terminal arms which are much more diverse (Regier et al. 1983). In fact, analysis of the central domain has given much of the data which suggest that the whole chorion gene superfamily is related (e.g., Rodakis and Kafatos 1982; Lecanidou et al. 1983).

In many ways the silkmoth chorion gene system is very well suited for the analysis of the evolutionary mechanisms involved in the diversification of multigene families, and much of the latter work has addressed various aspects of this problem. While much of the evolution of the chorion gene group can probably be accounted for by postulating gene duplication and subsequent divergence, brought about by drift or selection pressure and facilitated by accumulated mutations, insertions and deletions, a mounting body of evidence suggests the action of an additional process. Analysis of the sequence data for the "late" chorion genes, the Hc group, suggests that the A series has evolved from the A family by extensive modification of the arms, with deletion of most of the sequences and expansion of short cysteine and glycine-rich repeats. Similar modifications occur in the B series. However, the evolution of the HcA and HvB branches does not appear to be entirely independent, since the 3' untranslated regions show evidence of information transfer between the two groups (Iatrou et al. 1984). This information transfer is most likely to be by gene conversion (Rodakis et al. 1984).

A more detailed look at the sequence characteristics of the Hc genes has provided a body of evidence for gene conversion (Eickbush and Burke 1985, 1986; Burke and Eickbush 1986; Xiong et al. 1988). The 15 pairs of Hc-genes have flanking (intergenic) sequences which are highly variable. Using sections of selected reference genes as probes in DNA hybridization experiments, Eickbush and Burke (1985) have demonstrated the occurrence of a "patchwork" distribution of sequence variants. Each gene pair can be shown to contain a unique pattern of regions (patches) that are highly homologous to the reference pair, interspersed with regions showing less homology. The general high level of variation in protein composition and in the intergenic regions indicates an absence of strong selection pressure (Burke and Eickbush 1986); the maintenance of limited regions of high sequence homology must mean that sequence exchange between family members is taking place.

Between gene sequence transfers are highest near the 3'-end of each gene and lowest in the common 5'-region between divergent genes. Eickbush and Burke (1986) have proposed a model to account for these gradients. The model assumes that the predominant 30 bp repeats in the variable C-arms of the genes, which encode copies of Cys-Gly-Cys and Cys-Gly, stimulate local recombination by increasing the probability of initial DNA pairing. In fact, the G-rich sequence has similarities to the generalized recombination signal of *Escherichia coli* (chi; Smith et al. 1981). A number of predictions of this model have been confirmed (Xiong et al. 1988). Gene conversion appears to be the best mechanism to explain the observations of the Hc genes. The long term effect of sequence transfer is the homogenization of the DNA sequences within families. The short-term effect, however, is the rapid generation of sequence variants and the testing of new combinations, providing the potential for rapid evolution.

The analysis of moth chorion gene-regulatory elements has not progressed as rapidly as for *Drosophila*. The obvious candidates for the location of control elements are the 5' untranslated, shared intergenic regions. Detailed comparisons of the sequences of these regions among various chorion genes have revealed the presence, in addition to the expected TATA boxes, of a number of strongly conserved sections (Iatrou and Tsitilou 1983; Kafatos et al. 1987), including the TCACGT motif found in the majority of chorion genes, including those from *Drosophila* (Spoerel et al. 1986). Sequence comparisons of the promoters of genes expressed at different developmental times identify short elements which may be significant in controlling the timing of expression (Spoerel et al. 1989). However, the comparative approach can only provide suggestive evidence, even when coupled to the analysis of natural functional experiments, such as expressed pseudogenes (Fotaki and Iatrou 1988).

Functional analysis of regulatory elements received a boost when it was shown, somewhat surprisingly, that moth chorion genes can be expressed in *Drosophila* after P-element mediated transformation (Mitsialis and Kafatos 1985). In fact, a construct containing most of the 5'-flanking region shared by the divergently transcribed moth genes, of 272 bp in length, and a chloramphenical acetyltransferase (CAT) reporter gene, contains sufficient information to confer chorion genelike developmental specificity on the expression of the CAT gene (Mitsialis et al. 1987). The 272 bp section is strictly intergenic and contains no chorion gene sequences. It seems likely that neither the structural genes nor their 3'-flanking sequences are essential for correct tissue and sex specificity of expression. The reporter gene is not expressed uniformly throughout the chorion formation stages, but accumulates predominantly in the late stages of *Drosophila* choriogenesis, suggesting some element of temporal control. This aspect of control is difficult to dissect further, since the processes of eggshell formation are not easily comparable with respect to timing between these two organisms.

The moth control regions function bidirectionally and various deletion experiments show strong effects on the quantity of expression. In particular, the TCACGT element is absolutely essential. Overall, the experiments indicate that most of the significant control elements are located in the 272 bp promoter region, although strong position effects on the expression of the CAT construct may imply the presence of enhancers in other areas.

Unfortunately, decisive functional assays are not available to evaluate the control elements concerned with regional specificity of expression. For example, as noted earlier, the E1 and E2 genes are expressed only in the aeropyle region late in choriogenesis. Regier et al. (1986) have used the comparative approach in an attempt to identify candidate *cis*-acting regulatory elements for the E1 and E2 genes. Some striking similarities in several short sequence motifs are detected, especially in the first 200 bp of the 5'-untranslated regions. Some of these motifs are not detected in any other chorion gene, and even the TCACGT element is present in its reverse orientation. Whether these common features are due to shared function or common ancestry is difficult to answer categorically without a functional assay.

3.2.4.6 *Juvenile Hormone Control of Choriogenesis*

It is generally assumed that choriogenesis is independent of hormonal control and is initiated at an appropriate late stage of vitellogenesis in response to local signals (Raabe 1986). There have been some suggestions that a brain neurosecretion, a follicle cell trophic hormone, regulates chorion production in locust follicle cells

(Goltzene and Porte 1978; Joly et al. 1978); although, in this case, juvenile hormone appears to play no part. Among the Lepidoptera, some cases have been described where some oocytes in newly emerged adults have completed vitellogenesis but lack chorion (*Manduca sexta*, Nijhout and Riddiford 1974, Proshold et al. 1982; *Heliothis virescens*, Ramaswamy et al. 1990). In such cases it has been claimed that juvenile hormone is essential for choriogenesis (Ramaswamy et al. 1990). It is difficult to evaluate completely these claims, since juvenile hormone may be necessary for the completion of vitellogenesis in subsequent oocytes, which in turn may influence choriogenesis in the mature eggs. Even if juvenile hormone is important to choriogenesis in these moths, it is not clear that this necessarily can be expanded to a generalized statement on the regulation of this process in insects in general. What is clear is that more work on this aspect would be informative.

3.2.5 Other Synthetic Activities of Follicle Cells

While vitelline membrane, chorion and yolk protein syntheses are the major activities of the follicle cells, a number of other components are produced and exported to the oocyte. In *Drosophila*, proteins of 92, 82, and 76 kD, possibly representing different processing stages of the protein (Lineruth et al. 1985), are synthesized by the follicle cells at about stage 10 of oogenesis (Lineruth and Lambertsson 1985). They do not appear to be vitelline membrane or chorion proteins, although their functional significance is currently unknown. In addition, locust follicle cells serve as an example for a source of a synthetic product commonly found in many oocyte types, namely ecdysteroids (Hoffmann and Lagieux 1985). In *Locusta*, the follicular epithelium synthesizes and secretes ecdysteroids (Glass et al. 1978; Kappler et al. 1986), which accumulate in the oocytes (Lanot et al. 1987). Later, their selective release may influence the course of embryogenesis, not only in *Locusta*, but in other species (Bownes 1990; Grau 1990).

3.2.6 Nurse Cells and Trophocytes

A brief outline of the structure and components of the meroistic ovary is given in Section 3.1 and Fig. 10. More detailed treatments of the morphological aspects are given by Huebner (1984) and by King and Büning (1985). Many of the earlier issues in this field, some of which are still current, have been reviewed by Telfer (1975). It has been clear for a long time, from the general structure of meroistic ovaries, that nurse cells and trophocytes have a trophic function (Lubbock 1859). As illustrated in Fig. 17, the structural and functional relationships between the cellular components in polytrophic and telotrophic ovaries are analogous. In both types, the nurse cell-oocyte syncytium is a polarized structure, with the site of "nutrient" formation distinct and separate from the recipient cell, the oocyte. The most significant difference between the ovary types is the greater physical separation between the donor and recipient poles in the telotrophic ovary, making it much more problematical to use diffusion as a principal transport mechanism.

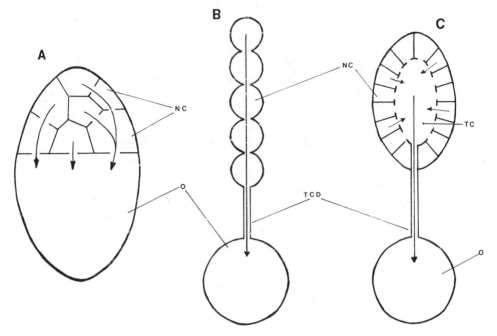

Fig. 17A-C. Diagrams illustrating the principal types of oocyte/nurse cell associations. **A** Follicle of a polytrophic ovariole. **B** Chain of interconnected germ-line cells in a germarium of a polyphage coleopteran. **C** Germarium of a hemipteran, only one of several attached oocytes is shown. *Arrows* indicate the direction of cytoplasmic transport from nurse cells to oocyte. *NC* nurse cells; *O* oocyte; *TC* trophic core; *TCD* trophic cord (After Gutzeit and Huebner 1986)

The trophic function of the nurse cells is facilitated by endoreplication of the DNA. In *Drosophila*, during approximately 60 h of cell growth, most DNA sequences double eight to nine times beyond their copy number in a 4C nucleus. Some differences in the extent of ploidy between different nurse cells have been noted (Jacob and Sirlin 1959). At the 9–10 stage of oogenesis the smaller nurse cells are 765C while the large ones are 1480C (Hammond and Laird 1985). The DNA content between S-phases is not simply a doubling of the diploid number. Hammond and Laird (1985), using probes for specific genes, have noted that some sequences are underreplicated; the ribosomal RNA genes are at 83–90% of their maximal possible levels, histone genes are at 35–37, telomere sequences at 60–63% and satellite sequences at about 5%. The 5S ribosomal RNA genes are at 102–109%, however. Very young nurse cell nuclei have distinct polytene chromosomes (Brun and Chevassu 1958), but chromosomes cannot be distinguished in large nuclei, as different sections are replicated to varying degrees. In the last endoreplication cycle, all sequences, including those previously underreplicated, replicate fully (Hammond and Laird 1985). The polyploidization of nurse cell nuclei is a general feature of polytrophic ovaries; in *Antheraea*, for example, the ploidy level reached is 30 000C (Berry 1985). Similarly, in telotrophic ovaries, trophocyte nuclear DNA undergoes multiple round of duplication; a total of seven in *Dysdercus* (Dittmann et al. 1984). The expansion of germ line gene number by endoreplication of nurse cell or trophocyte DNA means, at least in quantitative terms, that the oocyte nucleus is a minor player in the accumulation of maternal gene products.

There has been considerable discussion on the nature of the materials contributed to the oocyte by the trophic cells. In the case of nurse cells this is clearly a rather broad category, since towards the end of oogenesis, all or most of the nurse-cell cytoplasm is transferred to the oocyte. For telotrophic ovaries the process could be more selective. Among the major products accumulated by oocytes are large quantities of mitochondria; in *Drosophila* about 10^7 mitochondria are found in the mature oocyte (Tourmente et al. 1990). Also produced are massive stores of ribosomes, which are used to stock embryonic cells during the early periods of development, when little or no rRNA synthesis takes place (Hansen-Delkeskamp 1969). The report by Bier (1963) on *Musca* oogenesis probably represents one of the earliest demonstrations of the transfer of ribosomes from the nurse cells to the oocyte. Using autoradiography, Bier (1963) demonstrated a heavy labeling of RNA in the nurse cell nuclei, followed by a transfer of the label to the cytoplasm. The germinal vesicle was unlabeled throughout the oogenic period, but in later stages the oocyte cytoplasm accumulated labeled RNA. Ribosome synthesis and transfer to the oocyte has been demonstrated in other polytrophic (*Antheraea*, Hughes and Gerry 1970; *Calliphora*, Ribbert and Buddendick 1984) and telotrophic ovaries (*Oncopeltus*, Davenport 1974). In *Notonecta*, about 75% of the volume of the trophic cords is packed with ribosomes (Stebbings and Bennett 1976), while in *Oncopeltus*, ligature of the trophic cords prevents labeled ribosome accumulation in the oocyte (Davenport 1976). Transport of rRNA via the trophic cords has been demonstrated in other species as well (*Crynodes*, Ray and Ramamurty 1979).

In most meroistic ovaries, the expanded ribosomal gene numbers in the polyploid nurse cells provide sufficient templates for the massive rRNA synthesis. In a few cases, this is not sufficient and additional rDNA amplification is encountered. In the telotrophic ovary of *Dysdercus* the rDNA quantity is amplified 14 times beyond the gene number provided by seven rounds of endoploidization, producing a 1800-fold amplification of the diploid rRNA gene quantity (Dittmann et al. 1990). In the polytrophic ovaries of *Tipula* (Lima-de-Faria 1962) and *Dytiscus* (Gall et al. 1969) amplified satellite DNA sequences containing rRNA genes are found in the Giardina bodies of the oocyte nucleus. Presumably, the provision of additional rRNA genes is correlated with the occurrence of very rapid oogenesis, in which ribosome production by even highly polyploid tissues is not sufficient.

A large variety of nonribosomal transcripts is synthesized in nurse cells and transferred to the oocyte. Transcription from such genes can be visualized in chromatin spreads (Chooi 1976) by electron microscopy, and demonstrated by hybridization to labeled polyuridylic acid. The latter approach labels poly(A) tails on the HnRNA and mRNA. Using this technique in *Oncopeltus*, label can be detected first in the trophocyte cytoplasm, then in trophic cords, and finally in the oocyte (Capco and Jeffery 1979). The maternal mRNAs are transported and stored as ribonucleoproteins (Winter 1974; Paglia et al. 1976). Measurement of sequence complexity of oocyte maternal mRNAs by DNA-RNA hybridization suggests that 6000 different sequences of 2000 nucleotides in average length are found in *Drosophila* oocytes (Hough-Evans et al. 1980). Twelve thousand different sequences are detectable in *Musca* oocytes. This is a very large number, considering that some reasonably persuasive arguments based on genetic and cytological evidence have been assembled to suggest that the *total* gene number in *Drosophila* could be of the order of 5000 (Garcia-Bellido and Ripoll 1978). While it is likely that not all ovary RNA is made up of functional messages (Thomas et al. 1981), the hybridization data suggest that a very substantial portion of the genome is transcribed and stored in the oocyte.

While the hybridization results indicate that the maternal mRNA stores accumulated by the oocyte are quantitatively large and qualitatively complex, they provide no information on specific mRNAs. In recent years increasingly greater amounts of information on the synthesis and action of specific gene products have begun to accumulate. Among the most interesting and important gene transcripts synthesized in nurse cells and stored in the oocytes are those which specify embryo polarity. Following the pioneering work in insect experimental embryology of Seidel (1926, 1934) and Krause (1934, 1938), the experiments of Sander (1959, 1960, 1961) clearly established the presence of organizing centers, located at each poly of the *Euscelis* egg, which together specify the anterior-posterior polarity of the embryo. Other factors, not regionally confined specify the dorsoventral polarity in insect eggs (Sander 1976).

In *Drosophila*, the anterior localization of a transplantable, head-making activity has been shown to be due to the product of the *bicoid* (*bcd*) gene (Frohnhöfer and Nüsslein-Volhard 1986, 1987). The *bcd* RNA is synthesized in the nurse cells and is passed into the oocyte through the ring canals. As it enters the oocyte, the *bcd* RNA is trapped in the anterior 15% of the wild-type embryo by elements of the cytoskeleton, the latter encoded by the genes *swallow* and *exuperentia* (Berleth et al. 1988; Hazelrigg et al. 1990). Mutations in these two maternal genes result in the distortion of pattern elements along the anteroposterior axis (Schüpbach and Wieschaus 1986; Frohnhöfer and Nüsslein-Volhard 1987). A similar role for the cytoskeleton in the specific containment of nurse cell products at defined localities in the oocyte has been described for *Bradysia tritici* (Gutzeit 1985). The *bcd* gene has been cloned and sequenced. It produces a major transcript of 2.6 kb, which includes a homeobox (a DNA motif found in homeotic and some other developmental control genes) with a low homology to previously characterized homeoboxes. The transcript is localized at the anterior tip of the oocyte and early embryo until the cellular blastoderm stage (Berleth et al. 1988).

Another "spatial coordinate mutant", with gene products found in the nurse cells, which globally influences embryonic patterning is *dicephalic (dic)*. Its extreme phenotype is the "double head" embryo, where a second head and thorax of inverted longitudinal polarity replaces the abdomen (Lohs-Schardin and Sander 1976). In these mutants the 15 nurse cells form two clusters located at opposite poles of the oocyte; with nurse cell distribution among the two clusters ranging from 7:8–1:15 (Lohs-Schardin 1982; Frey et al. 1984). It is possible that nurse cell position influences the localization of some "anterior" signal for the overall patterning system.

At about the same time as the transcription of the *bcd* gene, several other genes which are members of the *oskar* group (Lehmann and Nüsslein-Volhard 1986), are involved in the synthesis, transfer, and deposition of materials at the posterior pole of the egg. *Oskar (osk)* mutants lack pole cells and the specialized pole plasm, including polar granules. In addition, the abdominal region remains unsegmented and eventually dies. Other members of the *osk* group seem to be involved in synthesis and export of the *osk* product from the nurse cell to the oocyte (Lehmann and Nüsslein-Volhard 1987).

The pattern-forming process, initiated by the polarized deposition of the maternal mRNAs, continues after fertilization by the translation of the mRNAs and translocation of the ensuing proteins. After synthesis, the *bcd* protein diffuses away from the anterior pole, and eventually becomes distributed over approximately 50% of the egg length (Driever and Nüsslein-Volhard 1988a,b). Similarly, one member of the *osk* group, *pumilio (pum)*, seems to be involved in the translocation of *osk* material from the posterior pole anteriorly (Lehmann and Nüsllein-Volhard 1987). By the beginning of the blastoderm stage, there is an inhomogeneous distribution of at least these two (*bcd, osk*) maternally encoded products along the anteroposterior axis. As noted above, at least the *bcd* protein has a DNA-binding homeodomain, and it is supposed that the quantitative information available in the distribution of *bcd* and *osk* is transformed into regionally specific qualitative differences in gene expression by the interaction of the maternal products and the zygotic genes. The latter, members of the gap class (Nüsslein-Volhard and Wieschaus 1980), all of which appear to be DNA-binding proteins as well (Tautz et al. 1987), specify the next stage of pattern formation in the *Drosophila* embryo (Ingham 1988).

The genes which specify the dorsal-ventral embryonic pattern are also maternally expressed. A large number of such genes has been described (Anderson 1987), but in contrast to the *bcd* gene product, there is no evidence for an initial localization of the transcripts of the dorsoventral control genes. The most important of these genes appear to be *Toll* and *dorsal (dl)*, the products of both are stored in the egg as polyA+ RNAs. Eventually, the *Toll* activity becomes localized in the presumptive ventral region of the embryo. As in the establishment of the anteroposterior pattern, the maternal dorsoventral specifying gene products are interpreted by the zygotic genome, resulting in the spatially restricted expression of genes around the periphery of the embryo.

Other mRNAs which are transcribed in the nurse cells and are later transferred to the oocyte include those for heat-shock proteins (Ambrosio and Schedl 1984) and transcripts of the *string (stg)* locus (Edgar and O'Farrell 1989). The latter gene product(s) is of particular interest since it is involved in the later control of the timing and location of embryonic cell divisions. Mutations in the *stg* locus cause cell-cycle arrest before interphase 14; later mitotic activity requires zygotic transcription. The *serendipity* delta gene, which codes for a DNA-binding finger protein, is also transcribed in nurse cells (Payre et al. 1988). In this case, translation of the maternal mRNA starts at stage 12 of oogenesis, so both the mRNA and the protein are maternally inherited by the embryo. In other examples, as in the case of the *per* clock gene, transcription and translation takes place in the nurse cells, with the eventual transfer of the *per* protein to the oocyte (Sael and Young 1988). Similarly, a number of other proteins, defined only by monoclonal antibodies, are synthesized in the nurse cells and shifted to the oocyte cytoplasm at a later stage (Maruo and Okada 1987). Clearly, the trophic cells of the meroistic ovary provide a wide range of proteins and mRNAs to the developing oocyte. Other components, such as the nurse cell centrioles, are also accumulated by the oocyte (Mahowald and Strassheim 1970).

The transport of macromolecules from the trophic cells to the oocyte has been clearly established. Despite a very substantial amount of work, the transport mechanism(s) remains to be totally defined. While the polytrophic and telotrophic ovaries are functionally analogous with respect to transport processes, they are sufficiently different in the anatomical details of the components to merit separate discussion.

In polytrophic follicles, for which *Drosophila* is the best investigated example, the nurse cells are connected by ring canals to the oocyte, and eventually contribute their cytoplasm to the growing oocyte. The ring canals are mechanically strengthened by noncontractile rings of F-actin (Warn et al. 1985), and in a variety of polytrophic ovaries in addition to *Drosophila* (*Apis, Pimpla, Bradysia, Ephestia, Protophormia*) a dense network of microfilaments is associated with the nurse cell cytoplasmic membranes (Gutzeit and Huebner 1986). During the final phase of vitellogenesis, the nurse cell cytoplasm flows through the ring canals into the oocyte, where the contents are mixed, by cytoplasmic streaming, with the ooplasm (Gutzeit and Koppa 1982). Clearly, mechanisms for capturing specific regionalized components, such as the *bicoid* mRNAs, must exist, but otherwise the nurse cell cytoplasmic contents become distributed throughout the oocyte (Anderson and Nüsllein-Volhard 1984; Gutzeit 1986a). The nurse-cell cytoplasmic streaming can be reversibly inhibited by cytochalasins, so it is likely that microfilament contraction plays some role in the cytoplasmic streaming phenomenon, possibly by squeezing the nurse cell contents into the oocyte. Alternatively, the microfilament bundles may provide a rigid frame-work which counteracts increasing intracellular pressure, generated by electroos-mosis or other means (Gutzeit 1986b).

Prior to the bulk discharge of the nurse cell cytoplasm into the oocyte, it has been proposed that intercellular electrophoresis may regulate the distribution of charged molecules between the nurse cells and oocyte in polytrophic ovaries. This suggestion is based on the demonstration of Woodruff and Telfer (1973) that microinjected macromolecules are subject to electrically mediated polarized movements in follicles of *Hyalophora cecropia*. Fluorescently labeled proteins were able to cross the inter-cellular bridges in only one direction, dependent upon their ionic charge. The electrophoretic current from nurse cells to oocyte is driven by a voltage gradient produced by the egg chamber. Such a voltage gradient has been reported for *Hyalophora* (Woodruff and Telfer 1973, 1980), for *Sarcophaga* (Verachtert and DeLoof 1989), and for *Drosophila* (Woodruff et al. 1988). In the latter cases the measured potential difference is reported as about 2.3 mV (nurse cell negative). Under improved incubation conditions, a value of 5.2 mV (nurse cell negative) has been found (Woodruff 1989). The resting potentials of nurse cells and oocytes diminished from a range of −50 to −70 mV to an average of −10 mV in the presence of sodium azide, and the transbridge difference was eliminated. Other workers have failed to detect the potential differences or polarized movements in *Drosophila* follicles (Bohrmann et al. 1986a,b; Sun and Wyman 1987; Bohrmann and Gutzeit 1987) and Gutzeit (1986a) has suggested that intercellular electrophoresis plays little or no part in the movement of materials in polytrophic ovaries. Woodruff et al. (1988) suggest that the negative results may be due to failure to use paired data. Since there is substantial variation in the absolute potentials of individual follicles, the averaging of results from a number of follicles may mask a small but significant difference. On the other hand, vibrating probe measurements of extracellular return currents have failed to detect any consistent patterns (Sun and Wyman 1989). If present, the potential differences between nurse cells and oocyte may serve primarily as a regulatory gate effect rather than providing the principal motive force for macromolecular movement.

In the telotrophic ovarioles of Hemipterans the trophic cells generally communicate with an syncytial trophic core from which trophic cords lead to the oocytes. Two structural features are prominent in such ovarioles. Firstly, an elaborate, interconnecting meshwork of F-actin encases the trophic core (Huebner and Gutzeit 1986). Secondly, the trophic core and the trophic tubes show a brilliant form of birefringence along their lengths (MacGregor and Stebbings 1970). The birefringence is due to a massive system of microtubules present in a variety of Hemipterans (*Notonecta, Dysdercus, Corixa, Oncopeltus*; Brunt 1970; Hyams and Stebbings 1977, 1979a,b; Huebner 1981b; Woodruff and Anderson 1984; Huebner and Gutzeit 1986). The microtubule arrays are surrounded by an electron clear sleeve zone; colchicine treatment destroys the microtubules and the sleeve zone (Stebbings and Bennett 1976). Tubulin and microtubule-associated proteins (MAPs) have been isolated and characterized from these systems (Stebbings et al. 1986).

The precise role that these cytoskeleton components play in the transport of materials from the trophocytes to the oocyte remains to be clearly defined. It is possible that transport is largely nonselective and the result of the rapid synthesis of cytoplasmic components by the trophocytes. If the actin meshwork restrains the expansion of the trophic core, and the muscular epithelial sheath around the ovariole serves to maintain a constant volume in the tropharial periphery, then flow of materials through the trophic cords to the oocyte must result. This flow may be assisted by differences in hydrostatic pressure between the trophic areas and the oocyte (Gutzeit 1986a), possibly created by ionic current asymmetries around the ovarioles (Diehl-Jones and Huebner 1989). The electrophoretic movement (DeLoof 1986) of some cellular components may have some role in transport. A small voltage gradient has been demonstrated between the tropharium and the oocyte in *Rhodnius* (–3 mV; Telfer et al. 1981), *Oncopeltus* (–6 mV; Woodruff and Anderson 1984) and *Dysdercus* (–4 mV; Müntz and Dittmann 1987). This voltage gradient is too small to drive electrophoretic transport over the relatively long distance (1+ mm) presented by the trophic cord. However, the potential difference is largely accounted for by a difference between the peripheral cells of the tropharium and the tropharial core. This does produce the movement of negatively charged macromolecules from the periphery to the core (Telfer et al. 1981).

The role of the microtubules in this system has been the subject to debate. It is possible that their major function is in the growth and long-term stabilization of the cords. Over the short term, disassembly of the microtubules does not inhibit at least some forms of transport through the cords (Woodruff and Anderson 1984). No actin, myosin or dynein can be detected in the cords (Hyams and Stebbings 1979b), although dynein can bind to the microtubules in vitro (Stebbings and Hunt 1985). Molecules such as kinesin (Yang et al. 1989) or other translocation motors (e.g., Vale et al. 1985) have not been detected as yet; although studies to date have not been detailed enough to do so even if they were present. In addition, trophic cords in Coleopteran telotrophic ovaries do not have organized microtubule arrays (Stebbings 1981), although they do exhibit macromolecular transport. On the other hand, analysis of mitochondrial motility in the trophic cord of *Dysdercus* by video-enhanced differential interference contrast microscopy strongly suggest microtubule involvement (Dittmann et al. 1987). The observed mitochondrial motility strongly resembles axonal transport. Additional work is required to resolve all the components acting during macromolecular transport in telotrophic ovaries.

3.3 Duct-Associated Structures

Snodgrass (1935) has diagramed a variety of arrangements, both primitive and highly derived, for the main reproductive ducts of female insects. Most insects exhibit some variant of two basic plans. In the orthopteroid orders, the Mecoptera and a few other forms, the lateral oviducts fuse to form the median or common oviduct which opens at the gonopore into a genital chamber. The latter can be of variable complexity and is often associated with an ovipositor. Among other orders, an invaganation of the primitive genital chamber forms a distinct intermediate structure, the vagina, between the external vulva and the gonopore.

The vagina and the common oviduct are generally ectodermally derived and therefore lined with a cuticular intima. The lateral oviducts can be of mesodermal (*Locusta*; Lauverjat 1969) or ectodermal origin (*Lytta*; Gerber et al. 1971a) and appropriately lack or possess a cuticular lining. The epithelium of the ducts is usually one cell thick, with a basement membrane and surrounded by variable amounts of musculature. In many instances at least portions of the ductal system have a secretory function.

The secretory material may serve a number of functions, including acting as a lubricant for egg passage, as protective oothecal coverings, or as glues to attach eggs to various substrates or to hold groups of eggs together. A typical example of the development and functional morphology of the lateral oviducts is shown by the acridids (*Locusta migratoria*, Lauverjat and Girardie 1974; *Schistocerca gregaria*, Szopa 1981a,b, 1982; *Melonoplus sanguinipes*, Elliot and Gillott 1976). In these forms, immediately after the imaginal molt, the epithelial cells of the oviducts and of their anterior extensions, the pseudocollaterial glands, possess a morphology of unspecialized, nonsecretory cells. Over a period of days, this morphology becomes transformed. The cells show a rapid proliferation of organelles associated with protein synthesis and secretion. The cells increase in size, microvilli develop at the luminal plasma membrane, the amount of rough endoplasmic reticulum greatly increases in quantity, and the membrane arrangement changes from the lamellar to the vesicular form. Eventually, secretion droplets are released into the lumen.

Allatectomy (Szopa 1981a; Lauverjat and Girardie 1974) and/or cautery of the median neurosecretory cells (Elliot and Gillott 1976) prevent maturation of the oviduct and the pseudocollaterial glands. The epithelium remains in a juvenile physiological state. The effects can be reversed by the reimplantation of the corpora allata, when the oviducts and their glands quickly complete their development and reach functional maturity. Administration of synthetic juvenile hormone produces the same effect. The juvenile hormone response is dose dependent and a continuous supply of the hormone is necessary for the maintenance of the secretory activity. Szopa (1982 and 1979, the latter work quoted by Gillott 1988) has obtained evidence that juvenile hormone affects the gland cells directly rather than by some indirect route. Glands obtained from immature females and maintained in in vitro culture did not undergo the characteristic differentiation associated with functional maturation. Addition of juvenile hormone to the medium triggered characteristic differentiative changes, including the formation of microvilli, expansion of the apical cytoplasm, and some hypertrophy of the rough endoplasmic reticulum.

Cells of the common oviduct may or may not be secretory (Gerber et al. 1978). In the former case, cell morphology generally resembles that found in the lateral oviducts (Gerber et al. 1971a). Typically, the common oviduct is heavily invested with muscle and the contraction of these visceral muscles contributes to the movement of eggs through the system, or to limit their passage at times inappropriate for egg laying (Thomas 1979). The oviduct contains both octopamine and proctolin (Orchard and Lange 1987). In this muscle, octopamine is released as a neuromodulator. The myotropic pentapeptide proctolin, which has been shown to be a cotransmitter at insect visceral neuromuscular junctions (Orchard et al. 1989), appears to play a role in the contraction of the common oviduct. For example, in *Locusta* the oviducts receive proctolinergic innervation from the VIIth abdominal ganglion (Lange et al. 1986), and proctolin may be involved in the maintenance of sustained contractions by the oviduct, with a resulting occlusion of this structure. Oviducts in other insects have been shown to be sensitive to proctolin (*Tabanus*, Cook 1981; *Periplaneta*, Orchard and Lange 1987; *Leucophaea*, Holman and Cook 1985); low concentrations of this peptide result in an increase in amplitude and frequency of spontaneous phasic contractions. *Rhodnius* oviducts (Lange 1990) also respond to proctolin by an increase in basal tension and in amplitude and frequency of phasic contractions. Such contractions could be important during oviposition. Overall regulation of oviductal contractions and oviposition is complex, involving the brain, the corpora cardiaca and various ganglia (Sefiani 1987; Lange 1987) and the full details remain to be worked out.

Structures associated with postoviduct areas include the vagina and its diverticula (bursa copulatrix; spermatophoral receptacle) or the genital chamber, which in some acridids has associated glandular pouches (Strong 1981). Each pouch consists of a cuticular sac with an epithelium consisting of epidermal cells, secretory cells and duct cells; however, it is unclear what function(s) the overall structure may have.

Generally, the vagina is not secretory and consists of a single layer of epithelial cells, covered by a cuticular intima and surrounded by muscle. A diverticulum or bursa copulatrix, usually associated with the anterior end of the vagina, is found in many species. An important function for this organ is to receive spermatophores or seminal fluid. One example of such a structure is the bursa copulatrix of *Calpodes* (Lai-Fook 1986). The bursal sac has a thin pitted cuticle and an epithelium structure consistent with an absorptive function. A muscular junctional region, with a thick, folded, spinous cuticle may serve to squeeze the contents of the sperm sac out into the seminal duct. A bursal duct with a hardened cuticle appears suited for holding the sperm sac in position. In the bursa copulatrix of some other butterflies (e.g., *Danaus*; Rogers and Wells 1984) toothlike dentata are present and may function in tearing open the spermatophore. Some secretory activity may also be associated with the bursa copulatrix, since empty spermatophores are digested within the bursa of some insects (Khalifa 1950; Gerber et al. 1971b). Presumably, the absorbtive epithelium, such as described for *Calpodes,* serves to take up the products of digestion; and the used spermatophore may contribute to the nutrition of the female.

Studies on the endocrine control of the differentiation of the tissues discussed in this section have not been extensive. The few publications available suggest that both ecdysteroids and juvenile hormone may be involved. For example, during the last larval instar in *Oncopeltus,* the oviducts undergo a drastic morphological transformation from adult to larval form. The thin larval oviducts shorten and become very wide. A number of experiments strongly suggest that this transformation is exdysteroid dependent (Dorn et al. 1986). This hormone may have important effects on the changes in cell shape (Marks and Holman 1979) by affecting the expression and arrangement of microtubules (Lynn and Oberlander 1981). The imaginal development of the bursa copulatrix appears to be under the control of juvenile hormone (Herman 1982).

3.4 The Ectadenia

The ectadenia are ectodermally derived diverticula of the genital chamber or vagina. Typically, they function in sperm storage and/or in facilitating egg deposition. The spermatheca serves as a storage organ for spermatozoa until they are used for the fertilization of the eggs. To maintain the sperm in a functional state, often over extended periods of time, the spermatheca or associated specialized spermathecal accessory glands produce a number of secretions and maintain a correct ion balance in the lumen. Other accessory glands, usually opening more posteriorly than the spermatheca, serve a variety of functions associated with egg deposition. These functions can be quite variable between species. The functional and structural aspects of the ectadenia have been reviewed by Davey (1985), Raabe (1986) and Gillott (1988). Some of the older literature on this subject is covered by de Wilde (1964).

3.4.1 Spermatheca and Spermathecal Accessory Glands

3.4.1.1 General Structure

The overall shape and arrangement, as well as the number, of spermathecae are highly variable characters among insects (Snodgrass 1935; Matsuda 1976). In fact, very substantial intergeneric variation has been described for some forms (Siva-Jothy 1987). Commonly, the organs are spherical or ovoid in form, but they can be tubular or even branched. In most insects the spermatheca is a single organ, although paired (*Bracon*; Gerling and Rotary 1974) and even triplet (*Culex*; Imms 1957) structures are also encountered. The basic structure of the organ includes a duct leading from the vagina or genital chamber into an enlarged lumen. Both duct and lumen are lined with cuticle, which is secreted by a layer of epithelial cells. The epithelial cells are associated with a basement membrane; their basal plasma membranes are often extensively folded, suggesting a transport of materials from the hemolymph into the cells. The overall organ is invested by muscle of variable thickness and complexity, is innervated and receives a tracheal supply.

There are several epithelial cell types. The most numerous are generalized epithelial cells or the "cellules épithéliales banales" (Bitsch 1981a), which are thought to be involved in the formation of the cuticle, but are otherwise nonsecretory. The other major cell types are the glandular or secretory cells and cells closely associated with them. A generalized diagram of the simpler type of spermathecal secretory cell is given in Fig. 18. Such cells generally have a central cavity which communicates with the spermathecal lumen via a cuticle-lined ductule. Generally the duct cell is interposed between the secretory cell and the lumen of the spermatheca; the secretory cell is therefore in direct contact with the basement membrane, but not with the luminal cuticle.

Ultrastructural studies (Ahmed and Gillott 1982b; Happ and Happ 1970, 1975) show that the secretory cells have a phenotype typically associated with cells which are extensively specialized for export protein synthesis. The cytoplasm shows a very

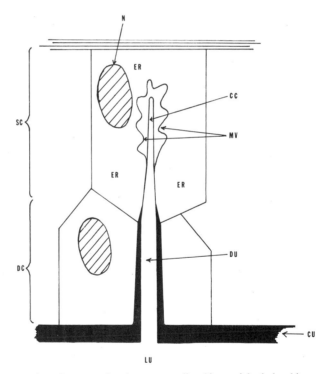

Fig. 18. Diagrammatic representation of a spermathecal secretory cell and its spatial relationship to the duct cell and basement membrane. The *hatched ovals* represent nuclei. *CC* Central cavity; *CU* cuticle; *DC* duct or canal cell; *DU* ductule; *ER* rough endoplasmic reticulum; *LU* Lumen; *MV* microvilli; *N* nucleus; *SC* secretory cell

extensive rough endoplasmic reticulum with packed cisternae and numerous Golgi complexes. The Golgi complexes are involved in the production of secretory vesicles. Exocytosis takes place at the base of microvilli; the latter are generally rather numerous and directed into the central cavity enclosed by the secretory cell. The basic ultrastructure of the secretory cells is very similar in various organisms, although the details of cell arrangement and distribution can vary. In *Thermobia* (Bitsch 1981a,b) the functional glandular unit is mode up of four cells: (1) a central cilium cell, which forms the efferent ducture; (2) the glandular cell itself; and (3) two enveloping cells. The secretory units are separated by the more numerous, nonsecretory epithelial cells. During molting, the apical portion of each glandular unit is eliminated and is reconstructed some time after the molt. The spermathecae of *Rhodnius* lack the cuticular pores and ductules, but do have the tubular apical invaginations in secretory cells. This type of central cavity receives secretion by exocytosis of small vesicles (Huebner 1980). It should be noted that the spermatheca of *Rhodnius* is not homologous to that of other insects; its developmental origin is as a secondary oviductal outpocketing during the fifth larval instar.

The basic arrangement for the structure and distribution of the glandular cells is for each cell to have a single ductule (*Periplaneta*, Gupta and Snith 1969; *Delarouzeei*, Juberthie-Jupeau and Cazals 1985). In other forms several ductules may open at a single pore (*Tenebrio*, Happ and Happ 1970; *Anthonomus*, Grodner 1975). Possibly reflecting the primitive arrangement, the secretory cells or units are often evenly distributed throughout the spermatheca (*Melanoplus*, Ahmed and Gillott 1982a; *Oncopeltus*, Bonhag and Wick 1953). In other insects the glandular cells are restricted to specific regions of the spermathecal wall (*Aedes*, Jones and Fischman 1970; *Drosophila*, Filosi and Perotti 1975). This trend shows its extreme form when the glandular cells are sequestered in a special spermathecal accessory gland (*Tenebrio*, Happ and Happ 1970; *Ips*, Hallberg 1984; *Apis*, Dallai 1975).

3.4.1.2 *Hormonal Control of Differentiation*

In the analysis of the role of hormones in the control of organ differentiation it is important to distinguish two distinct phenomena: (1) a process which may be termed cytodifferentiation, whereby the specific morphological entity is established from a competent or determined anlagen; and (2) the acquisition of definitive levels of differentiated function by the morphological entity. In most cases, including that of spermathecal differentiation, these two processes are separated in time. The spermatheca when first formed usually does not have the eventual full secretory repertoire; it is acquired some time during the adult phase. Information on the role of hormones in either of the two above processes in reference to spermathecae is rather limited. However, some data are available on the characteristics of both.

With respect to the control of cytodifferentiation, the work of Happ and Happ (1977) and Szopa and Happ (1982) on *Tenebrio* is informative. In this beetle the differentiation of the spermatheca occurs in the pupal stage prior to the eclosion to the adult. The differentiative process can be divided into three phases: (1) cellular proliferation, which gives rise to two cell populations, one eventually giving rise to the cuticle producing (axial) cells of the gland lumen and the other yielding the three cell secretory units and the ductules; (2) cellular morphogenesis, including the rearrangement of the cells into the three-cell secretory organules and the formation of the pseudocilium; (3) cuticulogenesis by the axial cells. A natural in vivo peak in ecdysterone concentration occurs at about day 3 of the nine-day pupal stage. Explanted spermathecal accessory glands taken from day 2 pupae and cultured in vitro failed to form the three-cell secretory organules or to secrete cuticle. Treatment of such explants with exogenous ecdysterone failed to produce the secretory organules but did induce cuticle formation. Glands explanted from day -4 pupae differentiated in vitro whether or not exogenous ecdysterone was present. It was concluded (Szopa and Happ 1982) that cuticulogenesis is under ecdysterone control; the hormone is necessary to initiate cuticle deposition. Once started the process does not need the continual presence of hormone and becomes autonomous.

The result on the lack of in vitro differentiation of the secretory organules is more difficult to interpret. It is possible that the culture conditions are incomplete and some additional factor, as well as ecdysterone, is necessary for differentiation of the pseudocilia. On the other hand, it is possible that ecdysterone is not involved in this differentiative process. The organ anlage may have a limited range of possible gene expression patterns, possibly established by the action of a cascade of development regulating genes, such as described for *Drosophila* (Nüsllein-Volhard and Wieschaus 1980; Ingham 1988). For example, in *Drosophila* part of the battery of genes which must be expressed to produce Malphighian tubule differentiation includes the gap gene *Krüppel* (Hoch et al. 1990); lack of *Krüppel* expression in Malpighian tubule precursor cells leads to a homeotic transformation resulting in hindgut development (Harbecke and Janning 1989). Batteries of genes specifying different cellular phenotypes can be controlled by fairly simple genetic switches, and in the case of the spermathecal secretory organule differentiation, such a switch could be activated by positional information following the cell proliferative phase.

With regard to the control of the acquisition of definitive levels of differentiated function by the spermatheca some information is available for a number of Orthopterans. In *Chorthippus* (Hartmann and Loher 1974) spermathecal gland cells degenerate in allatectomized females, while in *Gomphocerus* (Hartmann 1978) allatectomy resulted in the inability of females to dissolve transferred spermatophores, suggesting a failure in the production of spermathecal proteolytic enzymes. The results suggest that juvenile hormone is necessary to initiate and possibly maintain differentiative secretory function in these grasshoppers. On the other hand, in *Locusta* (Lauverjat 1969) and in *Melanoplus* (Gillott and Venkatesh 1985) allatectomy and/or juvenile hormone treatment had no effect on the levels of spermathecal products, suggesting that their synthesis is juvenile hormone independent. It seems possible that in the latter two insects the regulation of secretory product synthesis has become uncoupled from juvenile hormone regulation, and, as in the case of some male accessory glands (see Sect. 4.3.1), may have become a part of an autonomous gene expression sequence initiated by the imaginal molt.

3.4.1.3 Spermathecal Secretory Products

A number of histochemical studies have demonstrated the presence of mucoproteins and mucopolysaccharides in the spermathecal secretions of a variety of insects (reviewed by Davey 1985). Biochemical attempts to characterize and identify the products have been few. Such studies as exist indicate that the secretory material is a complex mixture. For example, an SDS-polyacrylamide gel electrophoretic analysis of spermathecal contents in *Melanoplus* has demonstrated the presence of about 30 major bands, 6 of which are glycoproteins (Gillott and Venkatesh 1985). A mixture of similar complexity (23–27 major bands) can be found on electrophoretic analysis of *Tenebrio* spermathecal products (Happ and Yuncker 1978). Some of these proteins showed increasing levels of radioactive label incorporation up to the sixth day after eclosion. The fact that label accumulation could be demonstrated in most of the bands after in vitro incubation indicates that the majority of the proteins are synthesized endogenously. This is not universally the case; in *Apis mellifera*, where about 20 major proteins can be demonstrated (Lensky and Alumot 1969), at least some are contributed by the male and others appear to be derived from the hemolymph (Galuszka and Kubicz 1970). Twelve protein bands, two of which are PAS-positive, have been demonstrated in *Rhodnius* (Kuster and Davey 1983). In any case, one-dimensional gel elctrophoresis is a rather imprecise level of analysis, since multiple components could be present in any given band and only the major proteins are demonstrable with the staining procedures used.

The demonstration that other components are present in spermathecal secretions relies more on functional assays. For example, in *Gomphocerus* the spermatheca has been shown to possess spermatophore digesting enzymes (Hartmann 1978). Villavaso (1975) has suggested that sperm attractants function in the filling of the spermatheca. In the case of *Anthonomus grandis* this notion has been confirmed by in vitro experiments (Grodner and Steffens 1978). Agar pellets saturated with extracts from a variety of sources show chemotactic qualities only when the material is obtained from spermathecae.

Mating releases oviposition behavior in many insects. In the case of crickets (DeStephano and Brady 1977; Loher 1979) and silkmoths (Yamaja Setty and Ramaiah 1980) it has been shown that prostaglandins are involved in mediating this behavior. In the cricket, *Teleogryllus commodus*, prostaglandin E_2 (PGE_2) has been shown to be present in the spermathecae of mated females, but it is virtually absent from those of virgins, although a large quantity of the prostaglandin precursor, arachidonic acid, is detectable (Loher et al. 1981). During mating the male transfers to the female a spermatopore, the contents of which are emptied into her spermatheca. The spermatophore contents include, in addition to sperm, a variety of fatty acids and a prostaglandin synthetase complex. Esterification of the precursors renders them unavailable to the prostaglandin synthetase action while in the spermatophore (Stanley-Samuelson and Loher 1983); once in the spermatheca, however, an endogenous phospholipase increases the amount of precursor arachidonic acid and provides a large amount of substrate for prostaglandin synthetase action. The major prostaglandins formed are PGE_2 and $PGF_2\alpha$, while PGE_1 and members of the PGF_3 series have also been detected in spermathecae (Loher et al. 1981). PGE_2 seems to be the main active component, and it seems that this spermathecal prostaglandin enters the hemolymph via the genital chamber and from there releases the egg-laying behavior shown by mated females (Ai et al. 1986). As yet, the receptor sites in the central nervous system have not been identified. This interpretation of the mode of prostaglandin action is strengthened by experiments in which injection of PGE_2 into the hemocoel or its application to the genital chamber or common oviduct of virgin females stimulates an effect of mating by promoting egg release. This case provides a very interesting example of the interplay between spermathecal and male-contributed factors in the regulation of egg-laying behavior.

While prostaglandins provide short term regulation of ovipositional behavior, other factors, also associated with the spermatheca, provide for long-term control. In the cricket, *Acheta domesticus*, long periods of ovipositional activity, extending more than 50 days, are stimulated by a single mating. The ovipositional signal appears to be mediated by the spermatheca, since intact neural connections are necessary for oviposition to occur (Murtaugh and Denlinger 1985, 1987). The nature of the factor has not been determined; however, it is derived from the testis and is able to act in the spermatheca for long periods of time and has to be present continually in order to be effective.

3.4.1.4 Function of the Spermatheca and Spermathecal Products

The major function of the spermatheca is as a storage organ for sperm received from the male for later use in the fertilization of eggs. The sperm are transferred to the spermatheca, either from the spermatophore or by direct introduction into the female (Bonhag and Wick 1953). In the former case, a number of processes have been described as playing a role in sperm transfer:

1. By propulsive mechanisms built into the spermatophore (e.g. *Acheta*, Khalifa 1949), in which case the sperm play no direct active part.
2. As a result of contractions by the common oviduct, induced by male accessory gland secretions (commonly found in Hemiptera, Lepidoptera, Neuroptera, Trichoptera and Coleoptera: Davey 1958); again, sperm motility is secondary to the transport mechanism provided by the oviduct contractions.
3. A variation of this theme, in which there is a withdrawal of fluid from the spermatheca, with a resulting aspiration of sperm into this organ (Linley 1981b; Linley and Simmons 1981).
4. In other insects, sperm motility is activated (e.g., *Bombyx, Anthonomus*) and either as a result of chemotactic attraction, or simply by means of enhanced motility, the sperm eventually end up in the spermatheca (Grodner 1975; Villavaso 1974).

There have been a number of speculations that the secretory products of the spermatheca provide appropriate substrates for sperm storage and survival. Certainly, in some instances, for example the honey bee, the sperm retention period may stretch into years. Some mechanism to assure sperm survival must be provided, especially in light of the general observation that the sperm are motile in the spermatheca (Davey 1985). The observation that removal of the spermathecal accessory gland from *Anthonomus* females results in the gradual loss of sperm motility (Villavaso 1975) supports the suggestion the spermathecal secretions are important in sperm maintenance. Whether or not the high molecular-weight glycoproteins, which are described as the major components of the secretions, serve any role in sperm maintenance is debatable. As pointed out by Gillott (1988), there is no evidence of any pinocytotic activity by the sperm, and it is probable that only low molecular-weight substrates are of any significance in this regard.

Other suggestions for a function of the spermatheca in sperm survival include the maintenance of a correct ion balance. A number of authors have noted that the spermathecal nonsecretory epithelial cells have lateral membranes which interdigitate and have conspicuous junctional complexes (Huebner 1980; Happ and Happ 1975). Such specializations could serve to isolate the interior of the spermatheca and impose a role of maintaining correct ionic balance on the epithelium. A number of observations may support this suggestion. The folded membranes and apical concentrations of mitochondria do have the characteristics of ion-transporting epithelia (Happ and Happ 1975; Dallai 1975: Huebner 1980). Although direct evidence is lacking, it would not be at all surprising if the sperm storage organs did possess important responsibilities for the maintenance of optimal ionic balance.

The other major function of the spermatheca is the controlled release of sperm as the eggs pass by the opening of this organ. There is evidence for neural control of sperm release in *Schistocerca vaga* (Okelo 1979); denervated spermathecae cannot initiate the necessary peristaltic contractions. Under normal conditions, the presence of an egg in the genital chamber mechanically stimulates receptors which conduct the stimulus, via a neural loop going through the eighth ganglion, to the receptaculum, there initiating contractions.

The efficiency of sperm usage (sperm lost per egg fertilized) has been assessed in a number of insects. In *Drosophila*, maximal efficiency of utilization is about two sperm per egg (Gilbert 1981), although usually the process is more wasteful. For *Lucilia*, efficiency varies from 15–1.5 sperm per egg fertilized (Smith et al. 1988), while in *Anthonomus* sperm economy is even lower, 1 fertile egg laid per 100 spermatozoa used (Villavaso 1975). In any event, compared to vertebrates, the process seems to be remarkably efficient.

3.4.2 Other Accessory Glands

Included in this category are ectodermally derived glandular diverticula of the vagina or genital chamber that are not associated with the spermatheca and are directly involved in facilitating or enhancing egg production or survival. Matsuda (1976) lists the Ephemeroptera, Orthoptera, Plecoptera, Dermaptera, Heteroptera, Psocoptera, and most Coleoptera as lacking such glands. Most insects belonging to the other orders do have them. They are often paired and generally open to the genital tract behind the spermathecal duct. Examples of such glands are the colleterial glands of cockroaches and mantids that are involved in the production of an ootheca (Brunet 1951; Fuseini and Kumar 1972), the colleterial glands of termites (Soltani-Mazouni and Bordereau 1987), and *Musca* accessory glands, which contribute in aiding in the fertilization process itself by providing secretions which assist in liberating sperm acrosomal contents (Leopold and Degrugillier 1973; Degrugillier 1985). The "milk glands" of tsetse flies have been extensively investigated (Tobe et al. 1973; Tobe and Davey 1974; Tobe and Langley 1978; Hecker and Moloo 1983). These branched, tubular structures open into the uterus and are responsible for the secretion of the nutrients for the developing larva. Other examples include colleterial glands of silkmoths which produce a proteinaceous glue to stick down eggs onto appropriate substrates (Grayson and Berry 1974) and lubricant producing glands in other Lepidoptera (Callahan and Cascio 1963). Only the ootheca-producing structures will be discussed in detail.

3.4.2.1 Colleterial Glands of Cockroaches and Mantids

In cockroaches and mantids the colleterial glands are responsible for the production of the ootheca. In the former case, the structure forms a hardened, discrete case, in the latter, a hardened, frothy secretion around batches of eggs. Ootheca formation has been studied in most detail in *Periplaneta americana*, although data on other cockroaches and some mantids are also available.

In *Periplaneta* the colleterial gland is made up of left and right sections, each composed of a mass of tubules. The left section is much larger than the right. The tubules have a central lumen into which the products of the secretory cells discharge. The tubule products are transported into a vestibular area in which the secretions are mixed. Light and electron microscopic studies of the left colleterial gland (Brunet 1952; Mercer and Brunet 1959) reveal that the secretory cells have many features in common with those of the spermatheca. The cells are attached to a basement membrane and reach almost to the lumen side of the epithelial layer. The apical region is invaginated to give a central cavity, characterized by the presence of numerous microvilli. A ductule, lined with cuticle, leads from the central cavity to the tubule lumen. The apical region of the secretory cells is covered by flattened cells which secrete the intima of the gland. Most of the secretory cells are richly supplied with rough endoplasmic reticulum and generally exhibit an ultrastructural phenotype associated with protein export; the exception are cells from the central region of the tubules, which have a reduced endoplasmic reticulum and are rich in mitochondria.

There is a division of labor in the colleterial gland. The right gland product is exclusively the enzyme β-glucosidase. The left gland produces the structural proteins of the ootheca, the oothecins, as well as the precursor of the tanning agent, the 4-O-β-glucoside of protocatechuic acid (3,4,-dihydroxybenzoic acid), and a phenol oxidase. Calcium oxalate is also produced by the right gland. Based partly on the morphology of the secretory cells, Brunet (1952) has proposed a regional specialization in the synthetic capacity of the tubules. It is suggested that the most anterior region, the most distal from the opening of the tubule into the vestibule, secretes structural proteins and calcium oxalate. Cells in the intermediary region, with columnar secretory cells, are thought to produce the phenol oxidase, but no oothecins, while the most posterior region of the tubule secretes the structural proteins alone. At least for oothecin synthesis, the suggestion of regional specialization does not seem to hold in light of more recent experiments. In this work the gland tubules were subdivided into proximal, central and distal parts, and the different sections were incubated in vitro in the presence of radioactively labeled valine and leucine. Analysis of label distribution after SDS-polyacrylamide electrophoresis shows that the synthetic activity of each of the glandular regions was approximately equal (Weaver and Pau 1987). In addition, all regions are able to produce all of the different oothecin types in the same relative proportions as in the intact left collerial gland. These results suggest that the gland is not regionally specialized for oothecin synthesis, although they do not rule out the possibility that there may be suppression of syntheses in certain regions in vivo, and this suppression is missing in isolated pieces.

The secretory products are moved into the vestibule and there are mixed and molded around a batch of eggs. The glucoside of protocatechuic acid is converted into protocatechuic acid by the action of β-glucosidase supplied by the right collerial gland. The protocatechuic acid is in turn oxidized to the orthoquinone by the action of phenol oxidase; the quinones serve as the protein cross-linking agents to produce the tanned ootheca (Brunet and Kent 1955; Kent and Brunet 1959). The role of the calcium oxalate is not clear, but probably is not critical in ootheca production. The oxalate is not secreted by ovoviviparous and viviparous species (Stay et al. 1960), and possibly represents an excretory product in oviparous forms.

Protocatechuic acid glucoside is not synthesized de novo in the colleterial gland. The precursors to protocatechuic acid are tyrosine (Brunet 1963) or tyramine (Whitehead 1970). The enzymes involved with these substrates, tyrosine decarboxylase and monoamine oxidase, are not found in significant quantities in the colleterial glands; one cell type rich in these enzymes is the hemocyte (Whitehead 1970). The latter author suggests that control of protocatechuic acid biosynthesis is most likely exerted in hemocytes associated with the colleterial glands. In the absence of hemocytes, protocatechuic acid cannot be synthesized from tyrosine by isolated glands. In addition, since in these experiments protocatechuic acid was not detected in the hemolymph, the transport of some precursor and the conversion to the protocatechuic acid glucoside by the colleterial gland is suggested. On the other hand, Shaaya and Sekeris (1970) report the presence of the glucoside in the hemolymph. In their experiments, glucoside-synthesizing activity could be detected not only in the left colleterial gland but also in the integument and fat body. They suggest that the major site of synthesis for the protocatechuic acid glucoside is in the integumental epithelium, from which the glucoside is transported to the colleterial glands. The main function of the latter would be as a storage organ for the glucoside. Apparently, juvenile hormone affects the action of the precursor pathways but does not influence whatever processing of protocatechuic acid that occurs in the colleterial gland.

In mantids, although the general scheme in the cross-linking of the ootheca proteins is very similar, the details of their chemistry show some unique features. This topic has been examined in a number of mantid species (Kawasaki and Yago 1983; Yago et al. 1984; Yago and Kawasaki 1984). The glucosides identified in five mantid species are 3-O-β-glucosides of N-β-alanyldopamine and N-(N-malonyl-β-alanyl)dopamine. The significance of the various N-acyl groups is not entirely clear. It is possible that the glucosides and their esters could be precursors of N-acetyl-dopamine. Pryor (1940) first suggested that, in cuticular sclerotization, N-acetyl-dopamine may be oxidized to a quinone, which then cross links proteins via the aromatic ring. Alternatively, it may be oxidized on the β-carbon, cross-linking proteins at this position (Andersen 1971). Sclerotization by the former process usually results in a dark-colored cuticle; the latter process gives a light or nearly colorless cuticle (Andersen 1976). The light color of the ootheca and the occurrence of phenolic compounds modified particularly at the β-position of the parent compounds suggest that the β-sclerotization found in cuticles occurs also in mantid oothecae (Kawasaki and Yago 1983).

As indicated above, the bulk of the secretory product of the left colleterial gland in *Periplaneta* is made up of the ootheca structural proteins, the oothecins. Pau et al. (1971) isolated and characterized five major secretory proteins, ranging in molecular weight from 13–39 kD. All have rather basic isoelectric points. Two of the proteins, constituting more than 50% of the secretion products, are water insoluble. The 39-kD species has a high valine and proline content, while the other four types are rich in glycine (17–50%) and tyrosene (12–17%). Pau et al. (1986) have revised their original nomenclature for the oothecins and now recognize six size classes, labeled A-F, with molecular weights of 14.5, 15.5, 17–18.5, 23.5–26, 28.0, and 37–39 kD, respectively. In a study by Weaver and Pau (1987) a substantial amount of probably genotypic variation between individual cockroaches has been shown to occur. The protein polymorphism is restricted to the 14–26 kD group; different animals of the same age and stage can show different protein electrophoretic profiles. Both the numbers, and the mobilities of the protein bands are variable, but any given pattern is distinctive for an individual insect. Weaver and Pau (1987) interpret these results as demonstrating that four of the oothecin classes are composed of a number of slightly different isoproteins or iso-oothecins.

Analysis of cloned oothecin cDNA sequences (Pau et al. 1986) confirms the occurrence of the isoprotein forms. Inspection of four different C-type oothecin cDNA clones shows that all the clones contain the 3'-end of the coding region, and three of them show deletions or insertions in one of two regions which code for a highly repetitive pentapeptide sequence of Gly-Tyr-Gly-Gly-Leu. As illustrated in Fig. 19, the primary structure consists of a central region of 17 amino acids flanked on both sides by a number of the pentapeptide repeats. The different cDNA sequences seem to result from the addition or deletion of precisely one or two of these repeat units. Such mutations would account for the presence of difference iso-oothecins in different cockroaches.

Information on the left colleterial gland proteins in cockroaches other than *Periplaneta* is much more limited. In *Nauphoeta cinerea*, Adiyodi (1968) has demonstrated by disc electrophoresis the occurrence of eight fractions with positive charge in left colleterial gland homogenates. Two of these fractions constitute the major structural components of the ootheca. The suggestion that some of these proteins are derived from the hemolymph is hard to evaluate from the published data. In the mantid, *Tenodera sinensis*, structural proteins 43 and 51 kD in molecular weight predominate (Kramer et al. 1973); both contain large amounts of glycine and aspartic and glutamic acids.

Analysis of the *Periplaneta* oothecin cDNA sequences and of the resultant predicted amino-acid sequences, obtained by so-called conceptual translation, allows a number of other observations:

1. There are 11 major glycine-rich oothecins; they all resemble the C-type (16 kD) oothecins in containing amino acid sequences that are variants of the glycine-rich peptapeptide. However, they differ significantly in the central region. This

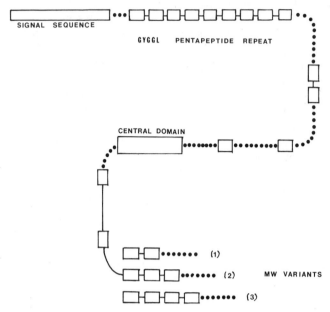

Fig. 19. Schematic representation of the C group iso-oothecins. The figure is based on sequence analysis of cockroach oothecin cDNAs. Each of the smaller blocks represents one of the many "GYGGL" pentapeptide repeats which are characteristic of these colleterial gland proteins. Repetitive units, together with some intervening amino acid residues (●) are arranged as two separate arms which are linked by a short sequence of different amino-acid composition. (*1*), (*2*), (*3*) are molecular weight variants (After Weaver and Pau 1987)

evidence suggests that the glycine-rich oothecin genes belong to different, but related, gene families which may correspond to the major size classes of the oothecins (Pau 1987).

2. Comparison of the oothecin sequences with those of other genes listed in gene databases shows that they have numerous similarities to silkmoth chorion proteins (Sect. 3.2.4). The principal similarities are the tripartite structure, the arms containing tandem repeats of some variant of the common pentapeptide Gly-Tyr-Gly-Gly-Leu, and a hypervariable site near the border of the left arm and the central region (Pau et al. 1986; Pau et al. 1987). The internal repeats are more extensive in the oothecins than in the chorion proteins, while the oothecin central domains are substantially smaller. The current sequence information on the oothecins is insufficient to decide whether the similarities between these two groups of proteins are due to convergence or to a common evolutionary origin, but it seems likely that the chorion and oothecin genes are both members of an ancient gene family, all concerned with some aspect of reproduction. It is possible that the tissue specificity and the mode of regulation may have changed substantially over the last 200 million years.

A 35 kb segment of chromosomal DNA, in four overlapping clones, and containing two complete C-type (16 kD) oothecin genes, has been isolated. Both genes have two introns within the short sequence coding for the signal peptide. The exon at the 5'-end of the gene codes for the first 13 amino acids; the second exon codes for amino acids 14–21. Comparison of the restriction sites around the coding regions for the completed proteins of both genes shows that the two genes are similar but not identical. The oothecin genes do not appear to be identical tandem repeats. In both genes the 5'-end of the coding region appears to be about 6.5 kb upstream from the main coding sequence; the primary transcripts of these genes appear to extend over at least 7 kb (Pau 1987). The large size of the genes, while not unexpected given the large genomes of the orthopteroid insects, is a little disappointing, since it probably makes various in vitro manipulations of the genes more difficult.

Part of the reason for the interest in the oothecin genes is the fact that their expression is hormone regulated. Scharrer (1946) was the first worker to show that the corpus allatum has a role in regulating the development and activity of the colleterial glands. Further studies (Bodenstein and Sprague 1959; Bodenstein and Shaaya 1968; Willis and Brunet 1966) confirmed that the secretion of the oothecal structural proteins by the left colleterial gland is initiated and regulated by the corpus allatum. More current studies, using cDNA probes to oothecin mRNAs and dot-blot hybridization assays, show that, after adult emergence, oothecin mRNA levels progress from very low concentrations immediately after molting to a moderate increase at day 2 and then a much greater rise between days 4 and 6 (Pau 1984). These changes parallel changes in juvenile hormone synthetic rates in the corpora allata (Weaver and Pratt 1977). In fact, studies involving allatectomy and juvenile hormone replacement indicate that juvenile hormone alone is responsible for the induction of synthesis of the structural egg case proteins (Pau et al. 1986).

In most cockroaches, including *Periplaneta* (Weaver et al. 1975), juvenile hormone biosynthesis is highly cyclical in adult females. The peaks of hormone production correlate well with cycles of ovarian maturation (Weaver and Pratt 1977, 1981), and in *Blattella germinica* these juvenile hormone peaks are linked with cyclical activity in RNA and protein synthesis in the colleterial glands (Zalokar 1968). In *Periplaneta*, however, some careful and detailed studies on ^{3}H-leucine incorporation levels strongly suggest that the total rate of synthesis of colleterial gland proteins in general, and at least two oothecin classes in particular, are relatively constant in sexually mature females (Weaver and Pau 1987). Juvenile hormone involvement in oothecal protein synthesis can be demonstrated (Edwards et al. 1985). The difference between the cyclical and noncyclical protein synthetic patterns shown by *Blattella* and *Periplaneta* may have an explanation in a number of factors. *Periplaneta* has a much shorter gonotrophic cycle than *Blattella*, and in the former sufficient juvenile hormone may be present even at lower levels of corpora allata activity to sustain a high level of protein synthesis by the colleterial glands. Additional work will be necessary to substantiate this interpretation. Despite a considerable body of work, the definition of all the parameters in corpora allata activity of this oviparous species remains to be completed (Pipa 1986).

3.5 Fat Body

3.5.1 General Description

3.5.1.1 Function

The most obvious function of the insect fat body is the storage of reserve materials (Wigglesworth 1953). In fact, the term "fat body", or *Fettkörper* in German, while quite graphically reflecting the general appearance of the organ, is a misnomer, since it is equally important as a store for glycogen and progeins. Besides its storage functions, the fat body in many insects has a major role in the regulation of ion balance (Hyatt and Marshall 1985), and, in all insects it is centrally involved in the metabolism of sugars, lipids, amino acids and proteins (Kilby 1963), and detoxification of foreign chemicals (Keeley 1978). The fat body, therefore, is properly viewed as a major hub of insect metabolism.

The main function of the fat body with regard to carbohydrate metabolism is the storage and mobilization of glycogen. Fat body glycogen is the source of hemolymph trehalose. This disaccharide, two glucose molecules joined in an α- 1:1 linkage, is maintained at a constant hemolymph level and is the main immediate energy source in insects. "Consumer" organs, such as muscle, for example, have cell-membrane bound trehalase enzymes (Friedman 1978). The key enzyme in the mobilization of fat body glycogen is glycogen phosphorylase, which is activated, via the cAMP cascade, by a hyperglycemic hormone secreted by the corpora cardiaca (Steele 1964).

Fat body lipids, mostly triacylglycerides, serve as the primary energy reserve. The fats are used as an energy source for "long-term" energy-requiring events, such as sustained flight, metamorphosis, or starvation (Gillott 1980). Large quantities of lipids are transferred to developing oocytes to serve as an energy source for embryonic development. This aspect of lipid metabolism and transport appears to be mediated by juvenile hormone, since allatectomy leads to fat body hypertrophy. General fat body lipid metabolism is controlled by the adipokinetic hormone (AKH: Gade and Beenakkers 1977), a nonapeptide member of a family of structurally related hormones (Gage 1990). AKH is produced largely by the corpora allata (Ziegler et al. 1988), in larvae as well as adults (Schooneveld et al. 1983; Fox and Reynolds 1990). The mobilized lipids are released as diacylglycerides (Chino and Gilbert 1965). Most of the fat-body storage fat is accumulated during the larval stages of the life cycle. Spectacular quantities of fats may be stored; for example, in some endopterygotes at metamorphosis, fat body lipids may make up to 50% of the insect dry weight (Gillott 1980).

Fat body cells are heavily involved in amino acid and protein metabolism. The capacity for a variety of transamination reactions has been documented, establishing the ability of the cells to shunt exogenous and internally produced amino acids, via their keto acid intermediates, into the Krebs cycle (Gillott 1980).

The details of protein metabolism vary between species and stages of development. Larval fat bodies produce and secrete a variety of proteins, including larval serum proteins (LSPs: Duhamel and Kunkel 1978), which belong to the arylphorin family (Telfer et al. 1983; Telfer and Kunkel 1991). The latter, usually hexamers of one or two subunit types with native molecular weights of about 500 kD, occur widely in insects. They contain exceptionally high amounts of the aromatic amino acids phenylalanine and tyrosine, and are massively secreted from the fat body of feeding larvae, only to be reabsorbed by the fat body cells at the end of the feeding period. In some insects storage protein sequestration into the fat body is mediated by 20-hydroxyecdysone, which stimulates the conversion of a membrane receptor protein from an inactive to an active form (e.g., *Sarcophaga*; Ueno et al. 1983; Ueno and Natori 1984). Examples of storage proteins of this type include manducin of *Manduca sexta* (Kramer et al. 1980), the ceratitins of *C. capitata* (Mintzas et al. 1983) and SP_2 in *Bombyx* (Tomino 1985). Other examples of larval fat body secretory proteins include the immune proteins and lysozyme in *H. cecropia* (Trenczek and Faye 1988), diapause-associated proteins of *Diatraea* (Venkatesh and Chippendale 1986) and the lipid transport proteins, the lipophorins (Chino et al. 1981; Kawooya and Law 1983; Kunkel and Nordin 1985).

A list of the major larval proteins produced by the fat body in *Bombyx* illustrate the range of protein types (Tomino 1985):

1. SP1 – a methionine-rich hexameric storage protein whose secretion and reabsorption characteristics parallel those described for the arylphorin. In the native state it exists as a hexamer of about 500 kD in both male and female fat bodies of larvae up to the fourth instar. In the last instar production of SP1 becomes sexually dimorphic, with the amount produced greatly increasing in females but declining in males. Interestingly, in *Bombyx*, sexually dimorphic expression of plasma proteins, including SP1, is primarily dependent on the composition of the sex chromosomes (Mine et al. 1983) which dictates the type of response the cells have to regulatory hormones.

2. SP_2 – a hexameric, aromatic amino acid-rich protein, equivalent to the arylphorins, whose expression is not sex-correlated. It is secreted at the feeding larval stage and reabsorbed at pupation.

3. 30K proteins – the most abundant proteins in late larval and pupal hemolymph. Their expression is not sex correlated. The biological function of this group of proteins is unknown, although, in females they are present in mature oocytes in amounts comparable to vitellin. cDNA analysis indicates that about five types of 30K proteins are produced; however, approximately 15 species are detectable by two-dimensional gel electrophoresis, suggesting secondary modification of the proteins. Three types of 30K proteins have been purified from eggs (Zhu et al. 1986). The expression of the 30K protein genes is regulated negatively by juvenile hormone and positively by ecdysone.

4. Lipophorin – a diacylglycerol-carrying lipoprotein whose expression is also not sex-correlated.

5. Vitellogenin – a glycolipoprotein with a native molecular weight of about 500 kD, consisting of two large (180 kD) and two small (42 kD) subunits. It is a precursor of oocyte vitelline and is detectable in female hemolymph at about the period of the larval-pupal ecdysis. With regard to vitellogenin, the situation in *Bombyx*, and in other lepidopterans which do not feed in the adult stage, differs from that in most insects. Usually vitellogenin production is limited to the adult female fat body. Adult fat body also continues to produce lipophorin. For example, in *Locusta*, protein synthesis in the fat body increases three to four times from

emergence to day 7 in females. Lipophorin makes up 15–30% of the total. Juvenile hormone elevates general protein synthesis, including that of lipophorin; however, there is no specific stimulation as there is for vitellogenin (Gellisen and Wyatt 1981).

3.5.1.2 Cell Types

The insect fat body can contain a number of cell types, including trophocytes or adipocytes, urate cells, mycetocytes, and mesodermal stem cells. The cells are surrounded by connective tissue and supplied with trachae. In some case (Cardoen et al. 1988) oenocytes are also closely associated with the fat body.

The trophocytes function in metabolism and in storage. They are the principal, and often the only cell types present in the fat body (DuPorte 1959). In embryos and early post-embryonic stages, individual trophocytes are clearly distinguishable. They resemble hemocytes, which probably share a common cell-type ancestor (Wigglesworth 1953), in having rounded nuclei and few cytoplasmic inclusions. In later larval stages the trophocytes enlarge, sometimes to such an extent that it is difficult to distinguish individual cells, and become filled with a variety of storage vacuoles. The cells do remain independent, although connected by septate and gap junctions (Hyatt and Marshall 1985), and in starved insects regain their embryonic shapes.

The trophocyte nuclei may remain mononucleate and diploid, as in *Periplaneta* (Guthrie and Tindall 1968); but in many insects enlarge and frequently become elongate and multibranched. In preimaginal stadia of *Rhodnius* (Wigglesworth 1953), for example, the trophocytes become polyploid. In *Locusta*, the trophocyte nuclei become octaploid during the first vitellogenic cycle synthesis in the adult. Ploidy level and cell size is under the control of juvenile hormone (Irvine and Brasch 1981), both characteristics being greater in females than in males. Nair et al. (1981) speculate that there is an incomplete replication of the genome, with a possible selective replication of vitellogenin genes. Allotectomy prevents the increase in ploidy, while juvenile hormone treatment restores it.

The sort of changes which occur in adult fat body trophocyte ultrastructure are illustrated by the events documented for *Aedes* (Raikhel and Lea 1983; Tadkowski and Jones 1979). In previtellogenic trophocytes, in the first three days after eclosion, during which time the cells acquire competence for vitellogenin synthesis, there is an enlargement and activation of the nuclei, proliferation of ribosomes and rough endoplasmic reticulum, development of the Golgi, and extensive invagination of the plasma membrane. The vitellogenic phase is initiated by a blood meal and the ribosome content increases about four times by 18 h after feeding (Hotchkin and Fallon 1987). Vitellogenin becomes detectable 1 h after feeding, reaches a maximum at 24 h and then declines to zero at 48 h. There is an enlargement of the rough endoplasmic reticulum and the formation of dense secretory granules in the Golgi complexes. The granules discharge their contents by exocytosis. Clearly, the coordinate synthesis and assembly of a large number of gene products is required. The termination of vitellogenesis is marked by lysosomal degradation of the remaining vitellogenin (Raikhel 1986), and the autophagic destruction of the vitellogenin synthetic and processing organelles. It may be noted that such trophocyte remodeling is typical of insects with distinct vitellogenin synthetic cycles.

A similar sequence of events has been described for *Calliphora* (Thomsen and Thomsen 1974) and *Sarcophaga* (Stoppie et al. 1981). In *Locusta* (Lauverjat 1977; Couble et al. 1979) and *Gryllus* (Favard-Sereno 1973), the cytoplasm of trophocytes in newly emerged adults is filled with lipid droplets and with fields of glycogen, while ribosomes and rough endoplasmic reticulum are scarce. With the onset of vitellogenin synthesis, the nucleus enlarges, lipid droplets and glycogen decrease, and rough endoplasmic reticulum and Golgi become the most abundant organelles. The changes are prevented by allotectomy and restored by juvenile hormone. Later, the rough endoplasmic reticulum is degraded, and autophagic vacuoles and lysosomes become prominent. In *Leucophaea* (della Cioppa and Engelmann 1980, 1984a,b), juvenile hormone stimulates rough endoplasmic reticulum proliferation, which is temporally coupled with the increase in vitellogenin. A five times stimulation in rough endoplasmic reticulum phospholipid synthesis precedes by 24 h the amplified vitellogenin expression.

Urate cells are found in the fat bodies of insects whose Malpighian tubules are absent or are incapable of uric acid elimination. The accumulation of uric acid in the urate cells is a means of storage excretion. It has been suggested that the uric acid may act as a nitrogen reserve, possibly for purine synthesis, perhaps mediated by symbiotic bacteria (Donnellan and Kilby 1967). Mycetocytes, polyploid (Baudisch 1956) cells containing microorganisms, are found in some insects. In cockroaches these cells appear to be modified trophocytes (Gillott 1980).

In the fat body of *Periplaneta* there is a distinct topology to the various types of cells. The mycetocytes are centrally located, surrounded by urate cells and peripherally by trophocytes (Keeley 1978). Philippe (1982) has shown that, in vitro, mycetocyte survival appears to be dependent upon the presence of trophocytes. These experiments also suggest the presence of mesodermal precursor (or stem) cells; such cells are the only ones which maintain high division rates after 10 months of in vitro culture. Stem cells are extremely important in Diptera and Hymenoptera, for example, where larval and adult fat bodies are distinct organs of separate derivation.

3.5.1.3 General Structure

The fat body occurs in a variety of morphological arrangements, ranging from sheets to strands and ribbons or lobes and spheres, loosely arranged or in compact masses (Buys 1924). Despite the appearance of somewhat indefinite texture, each species has its own particular fat body arrangement. Moreover, in a given insect, the fat body has a specific distribution. Generally, there is a peripheral or parietal layer beneath the epidermis and a central or visceral layer forming a loose sheath around the gut. There also may be distinguishable thoracic and head sections, as well as close investment of other organs such as the ovary.

The subdivision of the fat body in some cases can be shown to have a histological and functional basis. For example, in *Leptinotarsa*, the internal lobe cells contain much rough endoplasmic reticulum and appear specialized for protein synthesis.

These cells are separated by channels, presumably for the export of proteinaceous products during vitellogenesis. The peripheral lobes, on the other hand, consist of an oenocyte surrounded by glycogen cells containing glycogen and lipid deposits (DeLoof and Lagasse 1970). The contents of the internal fat body fluctuate with the physiological status of the insect. The internal fat body was much reduced or undetectable after ovariectomy or allatectomy. Conversely, the glycogen cells show hypertrophy under the same conditions. The different histological types of fat body may also differ in their sensitivities to hormones. The relative stability of the constituents in the peripheral fat body suggests that it serves mainly as a storage tissue and may be less responsive to some hormonal regulation.

Such regional differentiation or specificity in the fat body is possibly a general phenomenon. For example, in *Locusta*, the paragonial fat body, which is closely associated with the ovary, produces a higher proportion of vitellogenin per unit of exported protein than does the more distant perivisceral fat body (Bownes 1986; quoting Wyatt et al. 1984). In *Chironomus*, the subepidermal and not the visceral fat body of larvae (but not adults) is the site of synthesis for hemoglobin (Vafapoulou-Mandalos and Laufer 1984). In the adult, the subepidermal fat body is the main site of vitellogenin and lipovitellin synthesis; the visceral fat body shows much lower levels of immunoreactivity (Laufer et al. 1986).

3.5.2 Development

3.5.2.1 Embryonic Development

The fat body differentiates from the mesodermal walls of the coelomic cavities and therefore has an original metameric arrangement. This segmental arrangement is generally lost with the breakdown of the embryonic coelom and the development of the hemocoele.

In *Acheta* the fat body anlage are first detectable in the mesoderm of a large portion of the outer somatic walls of the dorsolateral coelom diverticula (Fig. 20). This differentiation occurs from the labial to the tenth abdominal segment, as well as from the parts of the lateral walls of the anterior and dorsal diverticula of the antennary coelom which do not provide the mesodermal covering for the corpora allata. The mandibular and maxillary segments do not appear to contribute to fat body formation (Kaulenas 1964). A similar condition is found in *Locusta* (Roonwal 1937) and in *Carausius* (Leuzinger et al. 1926). In *Blatta* (Heymons 1891, quoted by Korschelt and Heider 1890), the fat body is derived from both the splanchnic and somatic walls of the dorsolateral coelom diverticula, but, otherwise, the further development is similar to that of *Acheta*. In all forms, by the end of the embryonic development the fat body is clearly differentiated.

3.5.2.2 Larval to Adult Transition

During metamorphosis and molting, the fat body reserve materials are liberated into the hemolymph, but the fate of the cells differs, depending on the species. The

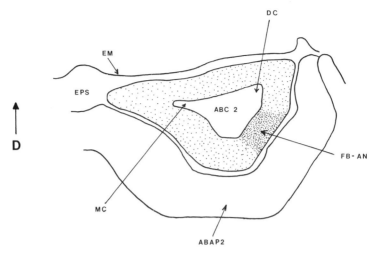

Fig. 20. Diagram of a part of a transverse section across the second abdominal segment, showing the coelomic cavity with the division into dorso-lateral and median coelom diverticula just beginning. 80–84-h embryo of *Acheta domesticus*. *ABAP2* Second abdominal appendage; *ABC 2* second abdominal coelomic cavity; *D* dorsal; *DC* dorsal coelomic cavity; *EM* ental membrane; *EPS* epineural sinus; *FB-AN* fat body rudiment; *MC* median coelomic cavity

exopterygotes show the simplest pattern; the larval fat body cells remain intact and persist into the adult with little change, except for a restructuring of the cytoplasm and the eventual change in the hormonal response capacity of some of the genes.

In other cases, the larval trophocytes undergo cytolysis, and an adult fat body forms anew from precursor cells. In higher Diptera and Hymenoptera, fat body metamorphosis begins as a breakdown of the basement membrane and a freeing of the cells, which may remain in situ, or, as in *Apis*, they may be set free in the hemolymph (Wigglesworth 1953). In the young pupa the trophocytes begin to disintegrate spontaneously, and, eventually, few cells remain intact.

Among the Diptera, larval and adult trophocytes can be shown to have different gene expression patterns in the same environment. In *Calliphora*, where larval fat body cells may persist up to 8 days after metamorphosis, larval cells are involved in arylphorin synthesis but are immunonegative to vitellogenin; adult trophocytes, however, are immunopositive to vitellogenin, and they are the only cells in the adult fat body to be so (Cardoen et al. 1988). In *Drosophila*, histolysis of the remaining larval trophocytes is induced by juvenile hormone (Postlethwait and Jones 1978) and adult cells are immunonegative to larval serum protein. Therefore, the larval and adult sets of cells are distinctive, with different gene expression programs. It is of interest to note that in vitro cultured dipteran embryonic cells will metamorphose into adult fat body cells in response to ecdysone, implicating this hormone in the development of the fat body (Dübendorfer and Eichenberger 1985).

The Lepidoptera include species which exhibit either of the types of fat body metamorphosis discussed above.

3.5.3 Vitellogenesis

3.5.3.1 Vitellogenins and Vitellins

Insect vitellins are female-specific egg-yolk proteins which are accumulated by oocytes. Their vitellogenin precursors are in most cases synthesized in the fat body, released into the hemolymph, and then specifically taken up by the developing oocytes. Some physical and chemical characteristics of a number of insect vitellins and vitellogenins are presented in Table 4. An extensive review of yolk protein chemistry has been presented by Kunkel and Nordin (1985). While there is substantial species-specific variation in the details of composition, it is nevertheless possible to recognize a general vitellogenin type, at least for the exopterygotes and the Lepidoptera and Coleoptera. The relationship of dipteran and hymenopteran vitellogenins and vitellins to the generalized type is somewhat problematical and is discussed in more detail below.

The hemolymph form of the vitellogenin of exopterygotes, Coleoptera and Lepidoptera (Type 1 of Harnish and White 1982b) is a phospholipoglycoprotein which exists as a dimer of 380–550 kD in total molecular weight and sediments between 9 and 19S in glycerol gradients. The monomer consists of a number of protein subunits which are generally derived by proteolytic processing of a larger, provitellogenin. A typical example is that of *Locusta* (Wyatt 1988), where the native protein of 550 kD contains 14% carbohydrate and 8.2% lipid. The protein components separate into subunits of 120, 116, 110, 105, 65, and 56 kD on SDS-polyacrylamide gel electrophoresis. However, there is strong evidence for the occurrence of a primary translation product of 185 kD, both from cell-free translation of fat-body mRNA and the direct demonstration of the presence of appropriately sized mRNAs (Chinzei et al. 1982).

The details for the processing of the initial product of translation are somewhat variable. In *Leucophaea* (della Cioppa and Engelmann 1987), the initial provitellogenin of 200 kD is glycosylated and phosphorylated to give a 215 kD product. While still in the fat body, this is cut down to fragments of 155 and 122 kD, which contain partially overlapping sections. Further processing of the 155 kD subunit occurs in the hemolymph, where it is cut into 95 and 54 kD sections. The 95 kD unit is then clipped to give a final 92 kD piece. The mature vitellogenin, therefore, contains subunits of 112, 92, and 54 kD piece. In *Blatella*, the initial precursor protein is 215 kD. Glycosylation, phosphorylation and lipidation produces a 245 kD species, which contains two subunits of 160 and 95 kD. The 160 kD peptide is further cleaved into 102 and 50 kD sections only after endocytosis of the vitellogenin by the oocyte (Wojchowski et al. 1986; Gochoco et al. 1988). In contrast to the situation for most insects, *Bombyx mori* vitellogenin subunits (180 and 42 kD) are coded for by separate mRNAs and are apparently not derived by extensive processing of a large precursor protein (Tomino 1985).

It seems to be the rule rather than the exception that vitellogenins exist in multiple immunologically and electrophoretically distinct forms. In at least some cases these multiple forms are nonallelic; for example, in *Locusta* (Wyatt 1988), two distinct genes for vitellogenin have been cloned. The biological significance of this variation is not altogether clear, since so far it has not been possible to assign any

Table 4. Physical and chemical properties of insect vitellins (Vt) and vitellogenins (Vg)

Organism	C^a	Native form		Primary translation product M_r (kD)	Subunit M_r (kD)		Comments	References
		M_r	S		Large	Small		
Orthoptera								
Acheta domesticus	1				130,97	49,47	Vt; glycoproteins Multiple antigenic forms	Bradley and Edwards (1978) Nicolaro and Bradley (1980)
Schistocerca gregaria	1				135–100	70–55	Vt contains four large and four small peptides	Harnish and White (1982b)
Locusta migratoria	1	550	17	265,250 235,225	120–53		Vg: 8.2% lipid; Vt: 6.7% lipid 13.3% carbohydr. 5–8 polypeptides 2 distinct genes	Chen et al. (1978) Chen (1980) Chinzei et al. (1981)
Gryllus bimaculatus	1	525			215–50		Two distinct Vgs and Vts. 9 proteins on SDS gels	Kempa-Tomm et al. (1990)
Phasmida								
Carausius morosus	1	287,275			180,120	60,70	Vt: 10% lipid	Giorgi et al. (1982)
Dermaptera								
Forficula auriculata	1	465			162(x3)	84,82,73		Harnish and White (1982a)
Dictyoptera								
Blaberus discoidalis	1		19		190,150,100	50/36	Two types of Vt and Vg. 7–8 unique peptides. Glycolipoproteins	Wojchowski and Kunkel (1987)
Leucophaea maderae	1	2 x 250	14/28	215	115,112, 95, 160,105 105,90,	92,54	5 polypeptide Vt and Vg	della Cioppa and Engelmann (1987) Brookes (1986)
Nauphoeta cinerea	1	Vg:300, 314,32 Vt: 274 293,20	9,4			98,57 85,57	Vg(14S) — Vt(28S) Glycolipoproteins multiple Vgs and Vts	Masler and Ofengand (1982) Imboden et al. (1987)

Table 4 (continued)

Organism	C[a]	Native form		Primary translation product Mr (kD)	Subunit Mr (kD)		Comments	References
		Mr	S		Large	Small		
Periplaneta americana	1	520 440	17	275,266 180	170,105 161,105 140,135	92,78 101,60 63,59	Two Vg types	Storella et al. (1985) Harnish and White (1982a) Clore et al. (1978)
Hemiptera								
Rhodnius prolixus	1	460			180,158	44,38	Vt Vg; glyco-phosphoproteins No consistent stoichiometries for SUs	Masuda and Oliveria (1985)
Oncopeltus fasciatus	1				2x160	60,55		Harnish and White (1982b)
Coleoptera								
Tenebrio molitor	1(?)			240	160	56,45	Vt, Vg Vt: subunits in 1:1:1:2 ratio	Harnish et al. (1982) Zhai et al. (1984)
Coccinella spetempunctata	1				133,130	46,46, Vg		
Leptinotarsa decemlineata	1(?)				280,271, 229 282,271, 48 236,226, 221	50	Vt; 2 types glycolipoproteins	Peferoen et al. (1982)
Lepidoptera								
Bombyx mori	1	440	~200	2x180	2x42		Phosphoglycolipo-proteins, Vt=Vg.	Tomino (1985) Takahashi (1984) Zhu et al. (1986)
Hyalophora cecropia	1	420 516		220	178 180	43 47	9% lipid; 1% CHO	Harnish and White (1982a,b) Harnish et al. (1982)
Manduca sexta	1	~500			177	45	Vg and Vt heterogeneous. Phospho-glycolipoprotein 3% carbohydrate	Mundall and Law (1979) Imboden and Law (1983) Osir et al. (1986a,b)
Pieris rapae	1	380	13.7	200+	153	43	Glycolipoprotein approx. 20% lipid	Shirk et al. (1984) Bean et al. (1988)

Species	No.	MW	%CHO	Subunit MW	Notes	References
Hymenoptera						
Apis mellifica	2	210		2x190		Engels (1972); Harnish and White (1982)
	?	300		180	Phosphoglycolipo-proteins, 7& lipid	Wheeler and Kawooya (1990)
Diptera						
Aedes aegypti	2	350		2x170		Harnish and White (1982); Harnish et al. (1983)
	2			2x200	Vt subject to proteolysis in absence of inhibitors	Hagerdon (1985)
	?	~300		155,120, 200	Two subunits though 202,194,120, 90,56 found. Small subunits due to degradation	Borovsky and Whitney (1987)
	?			62	Vt: 6 subunits Monoclonals recognize small & largesubunits	Rikhel et al. (1986)
				68		
Rhynchsciara americana	1(?)	Vg:506 Vt:386-425	12.5	V_1:70,69 V_5:57,58	Phosphoglycolipo-9.5% CHO	deBianchi et al. (1982); Periera and deBianchi (1983)
Calliphora erythrocephala	3	210		51,49,46	Vt: tetramer of 49 and 46	Fourney et al. (1982); Harnish and White (1982); Huybrechts and DeLoof (1982); Jensen et al. (1981)
Calliphora vicina	3			56,54,51		
Ceratitis capitata	3	~200		52,48		Levedekou and Sekeris (1987)
Dacus oleae	3	~300		49,46 49,47	Vt, Vg: hetero-tetramers	
Drosophila melanogaster	3	190		47.5,46 44.5	Phospholipoglyco-proteins	Bownes and Hames (1978); Brennan and Mahowald (1982); Baeverle et al. (1988)
Lucilia caesar	3	190		54.8,53.7 51.6	Sulfated	Huybrechts and DeLoof (1982)

Table 4 (*continued*)

Organism	C[a]	Native form		Primary translation product M_r (kD)	Subunit M_r (kD)		Comments	References
		M_r	S		Large	Small		
Musca domestica	3	281,283			–	48,45,40	2 Vts and 2 Vgs	Adams and Filipi (1983)
Phormia terrae-novae	3				–	51,43,42		Agui et al. (1985)
					–	56.1,53.7		Huybrechts and DeLoof (1982)
Sarcophaga bullata	3				–	51.6		Huybrechts and DeLoof (1983)
						56.1,53.7		
						50.0		

[a]Classification (Harnish and White 1982).

distinctive functions to the variant vitellogenins. Possibly having to produce large quantities of these proteins may provide part of the explanation for multiple genes, and certainly other oviparous invertebrates (*Caenorhabditis elegans*; Heine and Blumenthal 1986) and vertebrates (*Xenopus*, Schubiger and Wahli 1986; *Gallus*, van het Schip et al. 1987) have multiple vitellogenin genes. Comparisons of such genes (Blumenthal and Zucker-Aprison 1987; Wahli 1988) suggest that the vertebrate and the invertebrate (*C. elegans*, locust) vitellogenins may belong to the same ancient gene family. Although, as would be expected for nonezymatic storage proteins, the coding sequences have greatly diverged, some aspects of the basic gene organization have been conserved and are distinctive. Among such features are the signal sequences and the potential secondary structures of the 5'-ends of the vitellogenin mRNAs. It is of interest that the *Drosophila* yolk protein genes show no similarities to other vitellogenin genes using such criteria.

As indicated in Table 4, the vitellogenins of the Diptera and possibly of the Hymenoptera show some distinctive features which make them harder to relate to other insect vitellogenins. In an attempt to approach this problem Harnish and White (1982b) have proposed an evolutionary scheme by which all of the current vitellogenins are derived from domains of an ancestral gene. The so-called Type 1 vitellogenins, characteristic of most insects, would have retained domains equivalent to the larger as well as the smaller subunits. In the evolution of the Hymenoptera and the lower Diptera, the domain equivalent to the smaller subunit would have been lost, producing a Type 2 vitellogenin, lacking small subunits. In the higher Diptera, only the smaller domain would have been retained, giving a Type 3 vitellogenin, with no large subunits. The evidence for this scheme is not entirely convincing. With regard to the Type 2 class of proteins, the molecular weight of the large subunit is well within the range found for the primary translation product for Type 1 vitellogenins. One interpretation for this could be that the proteolytic processing steps have been omitted or curtailed in Type 2 forms, and that otherwise Types 1 and 2 are equivalent. In addition, there are very substantial variations in molecular weight estimates, depending on the method used. For example, in *Apis mellifera*, gel filtration under reducing and native conditions yields an estimated M_r of about 300 kD; SDS-polyacrylamide gels give an M_r of 180 kD, yet there is reason to suspect that there is only a single apoprotein in this insect, and the 300 kD value is not due to the occurrence of a dimer (Wheeler and Kawooya 1990). More data, especially information on gene sequences, will definitively resolve this question. In the case of the lower Diptera (represented, so far, largely by data on *Aedes*, where a substantial amount of work has been done), it is not even clear that the Type 2 designation applies. The published data (Harnish and White 1982a; Hagedorn 1985) clearly indicates the presence of lower molecular weight peptides in the vitellins; their presence, however, has been interpreted as due to proteolysis during isolation. On the other hand, later work (Raikhel et al. 1986; Borovsky and Whitney 1987), which included the use of protease inhibitors during isolation, has shown the presence of lower molecular weight subunits, placing this vitellogenin in the Type 1 group. Gene sequencing data will presumably resolve this question eventually.

The higher Diptera clearly have distinctive vitellogenins and vitellins. Only subunits of approximately 50 kD are present in the vitellogenins. In *Drosophila*, the native vitellogenins are tetramers of about 200 kD; with the products of the distinct genes potentially contributing to the vitellogenin constitution. The mix of gene products used varies with the species (Srdic et al. 1978). As indicated earlier, there is no evidence that higher dipteran vitellogenins are in any way related to the vitellogenins of other forms (Blumenthal and Zucker-Aprison 1987), and there is a distinct possibility of an independent evolutionary origin. A number of lines of evidence indicate that this could be possible. For example, locust vitellogenin sequences transferred into *Drosophila*, using a P-element vector, were integrated but not expressed (Wyatt et al. 1986), possibly indicating that the *Drosophila* system does not recognize Type 1 regulatory sequences. In contrast, silk-moth chorion genes are expressed in *Drosophila* when transferred by similar procedures (Mitsialis and Kafatos 1985). In addition, in the silkworm, *Bombyx mori*, vitellogenin is only one of a number of protein types stored in the oocyte (Tomino 1985), constituting only about 40% of the total egg proteins. A similar situation exists in *Hyalophora cecropia* (Kulakosky and Telfer 1990), and in the mosquito (Hay and Raikhel 1990). In an interesting report by Yamashita and Irie (1980), it has been shown that vitellogenin-deficient eggs developed in male hosts of the silkworm can give rise to hatched larvae, suggesting that vitellogenin is not absolutely essential in this animal. Possibly related to this observation, sequence data comparisons reported by Bownes et al. (1988b) indicate that a highly significant similarity exists between the three yolk protein genes of *Drosophila* and part of a triacylglycerol lipase sequence. It is entirely feasible that in the evolution of the higher Diptera a different protein type has been coopted as the major storage protein and the use of the original vitellogenin genes has been abandoned.

3.5.3.2 Hormonal Regulation

Insects show a wide variation in life styles. One reflection of this is the variation in the methods for egg production, especially as they are related to feeding (Bownes 1986). In some Lepidoptera, feeding as an adult is not required for vitellogenesis, and egg production appears to be a programmed response to the imaginal molt. In other insects, egg production is dependent on food availability, and can be either continuous, as in *Drosophila* and *Acheta*, or cyclic, as in *Leucophaea* and *Locusta*. An extreme example of the cyclic yolk production method is exhibited by those forms in which feeding is the initial trigger for vitellogenesis, as in *Aedes, Phormia,* or *Rhodnius*. Not surprisingly, therefore, the endocrine pathways which regulate vitellogenesis also vary among insect species. However, a number of generalizations can be made.

In the majority of insects, juvenile hormone appears to be the key element in the control of yolk protein production. This assertion has been most extensively documented for Orthoptera (*Acheta*, Benford and Bradley 1986; *Gryllus*, Kempa-Tomm et al. 1990; *Locusta*, Chen et al. 1979; Wyatt et al. 1987; *Melanoplus*, Elliott and Gillott 1979) and Dictyoptera (*Diploptera*, Mundall et al. 1983; *Leuocophaea*, Engelmann 1969, 1971; Brookes 1976; *Periplaneta*, Bell 1969; Maa and Bell 1977), but also applies to the Coleoptera (*Coccinella*, Zhai et al. 1987; *Leptinotarsa*, Dortland 1979), some Lepidoptera (*Danaus*, Pan and Wyatt 1971) and some Hemiptera (*Dysdercus*, Dittman et al. 1985). The points in the vitellogenic process which are influenced by juvenile hormone in these systems are illustrated in the top portion of Fig. 21. The evidence shows that the primary mode of action for this hormone is at the fat body by initiating vitellogenin synthesis, with a secondary, but important, function in the regulation of yolk uptake by the ovary. In all of these organisms, removal of the juvenile hormone source by allatectomy prevents the initiation or maintenance of vitellogenesis. The effects are reversible by artificial treatment with juvenile hormone or an analog such as methoprene.

Allatectomy experiments clearly cannot by themselves demonstrate that the action of juvenile hormone is directly on the fat body and not by some indirect or secondary route. In *Locusta*, fatbody maintained in in vitro culture has been shown to respond to juvenile hormone and to synthesize vitellogenins (Wyatt et al. 1987). This effect is most easily demonstrable for the secondary response to the hormone. A primary response, by naive fat body, is harder to demonstrate, but has been reported (Abu-Hakima 1981); such reports are probably significant, despite the difficulty of consistently reproducing the results (Wyatt et al. 1987), as optimal in vitro culture conditions are difficult to establish.

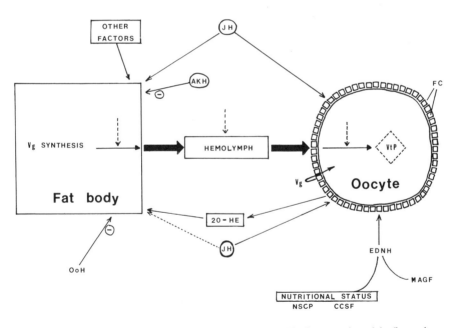

Fig. 21. Diagram illustrating the vitellogenic process in insects. The *lower* section of the figure shows the interacting components in the Diptera; the *top* portion of the figure shows the interaction of components in most other insects. *OTHER FACTORS* refers to the activity of the sex-determining genes, and the nutritional status of the insect, including whether or not feeding is continuous or discontinuous. *AKH* Adipokinetic hormone; *CCSF* corpus cardiacum stimulatory factor; *EDNH* egg development neurosecretory hormone; *FC* follicle cells; *20-HE* 20-hydroxyecdysone; *MAGF* male accessory gland factor; *NSCP* neurosecretory cell peptide; *OoH* oostatic hormone; *Vg* vitellogenin; *VtP* vitellin

Consistent with the notion that the primary site of juvenile hormone action is the fat body is the demonstration, in *Leuocophaea*, of very high affinity (K_d of about 10^{-9} M) binding compounds in both the cytosol and nuclei of adult fat bodies (Engelmann 1984; Engelmann et al. 1987). The putative juvenile hormone receptor showed a higher affinity to the natural enantiomer than to the racemate and the nuclear form could only be detected in vitellogenic fat bodies, either natural or methoprene induced. In addition to the high affinity binders, there are also juvenile hormone III-saturable, low affinity ($K_d = 10^{-8}$ M) binders detectable in the cytosol. Such low affinity binding activities were the only ones found in *Leuocophaea* in other studies (Kovalick and Koeppe 1983; Koeppe et al. 1984) and in *Locusta* (Roberts and Wyatt 1983). Apparently, there are substantial technical difficulties in developing the appropriate methodology for detecting the presence of low concentrations of high affinity receptors in the presence of a large variety of other compounds to which juvenile hormone can bind (Engelmann et al. 1987).

A typical phenomenon is the occurrence of a lag period after the imaginal molt, during which the fat body is refractory to juvenile hormone stimulation. An example of this is encountered in *Acheta* (Fig. 22, curve A) where in the first hours after the molt there is no response to juvenile hormone (Benford and Bradley 1986). A detailed analysis shows that the first of a series of elevations in endogenous juvenile

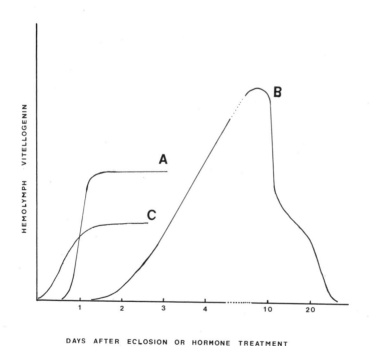

DAYS AFTER ECLOSION OR HORMONE TREATMENT

Fig. 22. Diagrammatic representation of the time course of hemolymph vitellogenin increase. The *curves* are based on the data of: **A** Benford and Bradley (1986) for *Acheta domesticus*; **B** Chinzei et al. (1982) *Locusta migratoria*; **C** Wu and Ma (1986) for *Drosophila melanogaster*

hormone titer occurs at 7 h after the molt (Renucci and Strambi 1983) followed by the first appearance of vitellogenin at 14 h (Benford and Bradley 1986). Therefore, there appear to be two components to the time period before the first detection of vitellogenin: an initial one during which the fat body is refractory to juvenile hormone, and a second period, of about the same duration, that it takes for juvenile hormone to exert its effect in vitellogenin production. A similar situation exists in *Locusta* (Dhadialla and Wyatt 1983); in this case, the response time lag to hormone in competent fat body can be demonstrated more clearly in precocene-treated insects, where the endogenous juvenile hormone source is eliminated. Treatment of such preparations with methoprene leads to the appearance of vitellogenin, but with a delay of approximately 24 h (Wyatt 1988; Fig. 22, curve B). Similarly, it was shown in last instar larvae of *Blattella* that a lag of 16 h preceded the first secretion of vitellogenin, but in pregnant females a secondary response could be obtained in 6 h (Kunkel 1979).

The refractory period in these systems appears to be concerned with the reconstruction of a full hormone-response capacity. Male and female larval fat body is capable of responding to juvenile hormone, but at a lower level than that shown by adult females (Kunkel 1979; Dhadialla and Wyatt 1983). Postmolt, the males lose the response capacity, while the females acquire it at a maximal level. Precisely what events this entails is not understood; it would seem to be of interest to investigate in greater detail the basis for the refractoriness to hormone. Systems of this type may be well suited for the analysis of receptor gene regulation or the relationship of chromatin changes to receptor gene activation.

The extensive delay between hormonal signal reception by competent cells and the appearance of the secreted vitellogenins could simply reflect the fact that juvenile hormone is pleiotropic in its action (Engelmann 1983, 1984), and a large number of cellular and molecular events have to be geared up in a coordinated fashion before the full secretory apparatus is set up. On the other hand, and possibly not even to the exclusion of the above point, it may mean that the initial action of juvenile hormone is the activation of a gene or genes which are required as the direct agents for vitellogenin gene activation. Further analysis of these systems will be of interest.

In the locust the de novo induction of vitellogenin synthesis by the fat body in adults is strictly sex specific. Even very large doses of hormone have no effect in the male. The absence of response does not appear to be due to lack of hormone receptors, since a number of other responses to juvenile hormone, such as a general stimulation of cellular activities related to protein synthesis and secretion, occur in both sexes. There is also some evidence for the presence of juvenile hormone receptors in male and female adult fat bodies (Roberts and Wyatt 1983). In addition, fat body transplanted from females to males in the larval stage and assayed after the imaginal molt had the activity of adult female tissue (Dhadialla and Wyatt 1983; Wyatt et al. 1984). The difference between the sexes appears to be associated with a differential, developmentally related establishment of a specific response capacity in the vitellogenin gene, making this system an exciting candidate for the study of the mechanisms by which specific competence to hormonal induction is acquired.

As illustrated in Fig. 22 (curve B), the production of vitellogenin by the fat body in the locust declines from a peak value at about 10 days postmolt to essentially zero after 25 days. However, this pattern of decline is only evident in vivo. When fat bodies

111

are excised from such females at the end of the ovarian cycle, rinsed, and then incubated in vitro in physiological medium (Harry et al. 1979), only a marginal decrease in the production of vitellogenin is evident. In addition, vitellogenin synthesis stops completely after allatectomy, but fat bodies taken from the allatectomized animals resume vitellogenin production when they are excised and incubated in vitro (Pines et al. 1980). The adipokinetic hormone (AKH-I) is responsible for the negative control of vitellogenesis (Moshitzky and Applebaum 1990). This hormone completely inhibits fat body protein synthesis in vitro when the donor females are at the end of the ovarian cycle, but not when taken from earlier stages. Moreover, during the first ovarian cycle there is no detectable AKH-I in the hemolymph during active vitellogenesis, but the hormone shows a marked increase to about 5 ng per female at the end of egg maturation. A development of responsiveness to AKH-I is also evident in female fat body as vitellogenesis proceeds. The development and cycling of vitellogenin synthetic capacity is due to a complex interaction between fluctuating levels of different hormones and changes in the competence to respond to the hormones.

While the majority of insects conform more or less to the regulatory scheme described above, many display variations on the theme. For example, among the Coleoptera, while juvenile hormone is necessary to set off the initial vitellogenic response, continued yolk protein production then becomes autonomous (Dortland 1979). Many Lepidoptera mature eggs despite allatectomy in the pupae (e.g., silkmoths, *Malacosoma, Galeria*, Sahota 1977) and vitellogenesis appears to be part of a programmed developmental response to the metamorphic molt. However, in Lepidoptera, where the adults feed before egg maturation, juvenile hormone is reqired for vitellogenesis. Among the Hymenoptera, *Apis mellifica* queens show no dependence on juvenile hormone or ecdysone for the production of vitellogenins; although, in this species both workers and drones are capable of some vitellogenin synthesis and this is corpora allata, and therefore, presumably juvenile hormone dependent (Ramamurty and Engels 1977; Trenczed and Engels 1986).

Among the Hemiptera, in *Rhodnius*, vitellogenin is found in minor concentrations in the hemolymph of the female last-larval instar, immediately before the imaginal molt (Chalaye 1979), and in adults both males and females can synthesize vitellogenins; the major controlling factor is the quality of the blood meal (Valle et al. 1987). For *Oncopeltus*, a development of the competence to respond to juvenile hormone has been documented (Kelly and Hunt 1982), but this hormone is essential for the processing of the vitellogenin, but not for the induction of its synthesis (Rankin and Jäckle 1980). Similarly, in *Triatoma*, the main function of juvenile hormone appears to be in the regulation of yolk deposition (Mundall and Engelmann 1977). It would appear that in some Hemiptera a hormone other than juvenile hormone, possibly ecdysone, is responsible for triggering elevated levels of yolk protein production. In these cases, however, the evidence for ecdysone involvement is only circumstantial.

As in the case for vitellogenin genes and vitellin structure, the Diptera handle the hormonal regulation of vitellogenin synthesis somewhat differently than do most other insects. As illustrated in the bottom section of Fig. 21, ecdysone, or more accurately, 20-hydroxyecdysone, appears to be the main hormonal trigger in the activation of the vitellogenin genes. Juvenile hormone is involved in facilitating

20-hydroxyecdysone action in the fat body and in the regulation of yolk protein uptake by the ovary. The mode of hormonal control of vitellogenin synthesis in the Diptera has been the subject of vigorous debate for over 15 years, and has been reviewed several times (Postlethwait and Shirk 1981; Bownes 1982d; Borovsky 1984; Postlethwait and Giorgi 1985; Bownes 1986; Kelly et al. 1987; Klowden 1990). Only recently has a consensus emerged.

The case of the blowfly, *Phormia*, illustrates what may be viewed as the basic situation. Yin et al. (1989a, 1990) have shown that a protein-rich meal leads to an increase in the hemolymph concentration of ecdysteroids several hours prior to the appearance of a significant quantity of vitellogenin. After the appearance of vitellogenin, the corpora allata start to release considerable amounts of juvenile hormone. Precocene treatment, which chemically allatectomizes the animals, does not prevent the appearance of vitellogenin, but does prevent yolk deposition (Yin et al. 1989b). A slight variant of this case has been described for *Musca* (Adams and Filipi 1988) where both juvenile hormone and ecdysteroids are required for vitellogenesis, with juvenile hormone increasing the sensitivity of the vitellogenin-producing tissues to ecdysteroids.

The situations in mosquitos and *Drosophila* vary in detail from the above scheme, but are essentially similar. In most mosquitos a blood meal is a necessary initial stimulus for vitellogenesis (van Handel and Lea 1984). Subsequently, both ecdysteroids and juvenile hormone play roles in yolk protein production, with some conflict in the reports as to precedence and significance. For example, Borovsky et al. (1985) report that an increase in juvenile hormone precedes that of ecdysone; Feinsod and Spielman (1980) observe first an increase in vitellogenin, followed later by an increase in juvenile hormone, while Martinez and Hagedorn (1987) find that both juvenile hormone and ecdysteroids are important after a blood meal. Experiments which indicate that ecdysteroids are the primary vitellogenin trigger and juvenile hormone is the facilitator or primer include the demonstration by Ma et al. (1987) that in vitro, even in non-blood-fed mosquito fat body, 20-hydroxyecdysone alone is sufficient to start a programmed stimulation in yolk protein synthesis, which declines in intensity with time. Using cloned vitellogenin gene probes for the presence of vitellogenin mRNAs, Gemmill et al. (1986) have shown that 20-hydroxyecdysone leads to a stimulation of yolk protein synthesis, which is greater in magnitude in blood-fed insects; and with similar techniques, Racioppi et al. (1986) have demonstrated that ecdysterones lead to an initiation of vitellogenin synthesis. Treatment with 20-hydroxyecdysone and juvenile hormone doubles the response, but juvenile hormone alone had no effect.

The work of Borovsky and coworkers has filled in the above basic scheme by clarifying the participation of a number of peptide hormones or factors in the control of vitellogenesis. The following overall scheme emerges for regulation of mosquito yolk protein synthesis, involving a complex interaction between ecdysteroids, juvenile hormones, and peptide hormones. A blood meal, presumably via some neurosecretory signal, serves as a trigger on two levels. One is the activation of the corpora allata to produce juvenile hormone, which then acts at two sites: firstly, on the fat body to enhance the subsequent vitellogenic response (presumably in a manner analogous to that described for locusts, by increasing the efficiency of the protein synthetic and export machinery); and, secondly, on the ovary to facilitate yolk uptake. The other effect of the blood meal stimulus is at the ovaries, which secrete a corpus cardiacum stimulatory factor (CCSF) into the hemolymph. The production of this factor can also be stimulated by a male accessory gland factor acquired during mating (Borovsky 1985b). The CCSF causes the release of an egg developmental neurosecretory hormone (EDNH), a polypeptide of about 18.7 kD (Borovsky and Thomas 1985). EDNH in turn causes the ovary to secrete ecdysteroids, which then stimulate the juvenile-hormone-primed fat body to produce vitellogenins. An oostatic hormone (Borovsky 1985a) acts eventually to inhibit vitellogenin production.

The course of vitellogenesis in postmetamorphic molt *Drosophila* is illustrated in Fig. 22 (curve C). A low level of vitellogenin is detectable immediately posteclosion, with a tenfold increase by 6 h and a further fourfold increase by 24 h (Kambysellis 1977). Postlethwait and Shirk (1981) reported that juvenile hormone alone increases yolk protein synthesis in the fat body and in ovary, while 20-hydroxyecdysone alone stimulates yolk protein production in the fat body only. The apparent independent action of juvenile hormone on the fat body may be due to the presence of 20-hydroxyecdysone in post-ecdysial hemolymph (Kelly et al. 1987), since in vitro experiments have shown that 20-hydroxyecdysone stimulates fat body to produce vitellogenin in the absence of other endogenous factors that might either promote or interfere with vitellogenesis (Wu et al. 1987). Juvenile hormone does control yolk uptake into oocytes (Landers and Happ 1980). It seems likely, therefore, that in *Drosophila*, 20-hydroxyecdysone is the primary trigger of yolk protein synthesis in the fat body, while juvenile hormone is responsible for regulating vitellogenin synthesis by the follicle cells, as well as acting as a secondary factor in the fat body and as a regulator of yolk protein uptake by the oocyte.

An interesting and informative side line is the response to 20-hydroxyecdysone in male *Drosophila*. Under normal circumstances, fat bodies from females produce vitellogenins in response to ecdysteroids and those from males do not. In fact, immature ovaries transplanted into adult males develop normally and synthesize yolk proteins, but the fat bodies of the host males are not induced to synthesize vitellogenins (Bownes and Nothiger 1981). However, high doses of ecdysteroids do trigger vitellogenin synthesis in adult male fat body (Postlethwait et al. 1980a; Bownes 1982b; Shirk et al. 1983b; Kozma and Bownes 1986). Analysis of the response to 20-hydroxyecdysone at the level of specific tissues shows that vitellogenin transcript accumulation is greatly increased in fat body from both males and females, but not in other tissue. The capacity to respond to the hormone by the yolk protein genes is, therefore, tissue but not sex specific (Bownes et al. 1983b). In an interesting experiment using gynandromorphs by Postlethwait and Parker (1987) it was shown that in such mosaics, female cells had higher expression levels for vitellogenin than adjacent male cells, confirming an earlier prediction, based on the study of the *doublesex dominant* mutant, that the regulation of the expression of the yolk protein genes is intrinsic to the fat body (Bownes et al. 1983a). Clearly, vitellogenin gene expression in *Drosophila* is not solely regulated by circulating hormones. Normally, as demonstrated by Belote et al. (1985), sex determination genes regulate the sex specificity of vitellogenin gene expression, possibly by affecting hormone receptor levels. The key gene is the *transformer-2* (*tra-2*) gene. The products of this gene are required for the continuous transcription of the yolk protein genes. The sex specific availability of the *tra-2* product can be overridden by high doses of 20-hydroxyecdysone (Bownes et al. 1987). The situation in this regard is slightly different in *Sarcophaga*. Here 20-hydroxyecdysone stimulates yolk protein synthesis in males, while juvenile hormone does not (Cardoen et al. 1988); however, the level of stimulation depends on the amount of circulating hormone (Huybrechts and DeLoof 1977; Briers and Huybrechts 1984). Males produce less vitellogenin because of a lower ecdysone titer. So, while in *Drosophila* sexual genotype of each individual cell overrides circulating hormones in controlling yolk-protein gene expression, hormone level is the primary determinant of expression quantity in *S. bullata*.

3.5.3.3 Vitellogenin Genes

With the development of gene cloning and sequencing techniques, a large amount of information has been developed in the last decade on vitellogenin gene sequences. Most of this information, however, is on the genes of *Drosophila*, with some, but significantly less, data emerging on locust and mosquito yolk-protein genes.

In *Drosophila*, the cloning of the vitellogenin genes soon allowed the confirmation of the presence of three distinct genes coding for yolk proteins, namely YP1, YP2, and YP3. The genes were shown to be single copy, with the YP1 and YP2 closely spaced and YP3 approximately 1000 kb distant on the X chromosome (Barnett et al. 1980). The X-chromosome location has been confirmed by Riddell et al. (1981) by in situ hybridization; these investigators as well as Hung et al. (1982) also demonstrated that YP1 and YP2 are oriented in opposite directions on the chromosome. Barnett and Wensink (1981) have reported on transcript number and size. YP1 and YP3 each has a single species of transcript, of about 1.6 and 1.54 kb, respectively. YP2 produces transcripts of two distinct sizes, 1.59 and 1.67 kb. The complete base sequence for YP1 was published by Hovemann et al. (1981) and by Hung and Wensink (1981). The sequence for YP2 was reported by Hovemann and Galler (1982) and by Hung and Wensink (1981), and for YP3 by Yan et al. (1987). The technology has progressed so far that sequence data can now be used to characterize point mutations in the vitellogenin genes (Saunders and Bownes 1986).

Comparison of the projected amino acid compositions of the proteins shows 53% homology between YP1 and YP2, 53% homology between YP1 and YP3, and 48% homology between YP2 and YP3. The homologies in DNA and peptide sequences and in the intron locations and number suggest that the three yolk-protein genes are related. The possible precursor to the three genes probably had two introns, since generally intron loss can be documented in evolution, but there is no clear proof of intron addition (Gilbert et al. 1986). Gene duplication could then have created the precursors to YP3 and YP1/2; the latter must have then lost an intron and duplicated again (Yan et al. 1987). The predicted secondary structures have a much greater homology; for example, for YP1 and 2, amino acid arrangements at position numbers 21–166 and 258–400 are nearly identical (Hung and Wensink 1983), and it is possible that secondary structure is the most important component in the functional aspects (oligomerization or uptake by the oocyte) of these proteins. Another possible secondary structure, which can be configured as a stem-and-loop arrangement, near the 5'-end of the potential transcripts puts a number of consensus sequences (the TATA box, capping sequence, rRNA homology, and the translation initiation heptamer) in very similar positions. Each of the four consensus sequences is at one of the juctions between the duplex and single-stranded portions of the structure. Possibly, a specific spatial arrangement for the four consensus sequences may function in regulating expression.

A more detailed consideration of YP3 illustrates a number of interesting points. The +1 nucleotide at the ATCAAAC cap site, which shows a 5/7 match to the insect cap site consensus of ATCAG/TTC/T (Hultmark et al. 1986), marks the start of the transcript. Upstream from this is the Hogness-Goldberg TATA box, and, as in YP1 and YP2, a number of clustered -CGA- repeats at −85 to −117 nucleotides. Other repeated elements are located in the region −50 to −300, including three "H-boxes". Similarly, 13 nucleotide elements are found in YP1 and YP2:

YP1 5'-CTCAGCACAAGTC-3'   4 times between −100 and −450
YP2 5'-CTCATCA GAA GTG-3'   2 times between −150 and −190
YP3 5'-ATCAGCAGAACTA-3'   3 times between −50 and −300,

with a YP "H-box" consensus of 5'-ATCAGCAGAACTA-3'. A section of this consensus shows a reasonably strong homology (7/10; Yan et al. 1987) to part of a proposed ecdysone response element of the *hsp23* gene in *Drosophila* (Mestrill et al. 1986), and a somewhat weaker homology to the binding sites of the mammalian glucocorticoid receptor (Payvar et al. 1983). The *hsp23* gene is one of four small heat-shock genes which are activated by ecdysone as well as heat shock. Analyses of the promoter for *hsp27*, by binding and DNAse I footprinting assays, suggest that a 23-bp hyphenated dyad forms a protein binding site and is sufficient for ecdysone-inducibility (Riddihough and Pelham 1987). The *hsp27* element, however, shows little sequence homology to the promoter region of *hsp23* which has been implicated in ecdysone induction. A number of other ecdysone inducible genes have now been cloned and sequenced (Segraves and Richards 1990; Maschat et al. 1990). Comparisons of these promoter sequences, as well as results from more direct experiments (Cherbas et al. 1990) allow the derivation of a consensus sequence for ecdysone receptor binding: ggtcanTGA(A/C)C, (n, stands for any nucleotide; upper case letters indicate absolutely conserved nucleotides). The consensus is clearly a short imperfect palindrome, very closely related to the binding sequences for vertebrate steroid hormone receptors. Small DNA fragments containing this sequence can function as ecdysone elements. The YP "H-boxes" show a 4/5 match for the strongly conserved portion of the consensus ecdysone element, but with no clear, close-sequence stretch corresponding to the other half of the palindrome. It is clear that functional tests, rather than suggestions based on minor sequence similarities, will be necessary to decide if the "H-boxes" are involved in the response of the yolk protein genes to ecdysteroids. A number of other repeated elements are clustered at around −800 upstream from the cap site. Their functional significance is also not yet clear.

Downstream from the cap site is a 56-nucleotide, 5'-untranslated leader which precedes the first ATG triplet. The remaining, translated portion of the first exon includes triplets coding for a signal peptide of probably 19 amino acids, which is thought to direct the insertion of the protein into the lumen of the endoplasmic reticulum (Walter et al. 1984). Typical features of the signal peptide include the presence of positively charged amino acids near the amino terminus, a hydrophobic domain of about 15 amino acids, and an alanine at the probable cleavage site. The

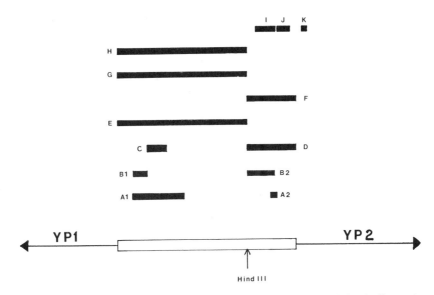

Fig. 23. Diagram illustrating P-element-mediated germ-line transformation analysis of yolk-protein gene regulatory elements. The *open box* represents the 1225 bp region between the divergently transcribed yolk protein 1 (*YP1*) and Yolk protein 2 (*YP2*) genes. *Hind III* Restriction nuclease Hind III site in the intergenic region. *A1, A2* Possible steroid response elements (Hung and Wensink 1983; Yan et al. 1987). *B1, B2* YP gene transcriptional enhancers (Voss and Pongs 1986). *C* Sex, stage, and tissue (fat body) specificity element (Garabedian et al. 1985). *D* Ovary specific element (Garabedian et al. 1985; Tamura et al. 1985). *E* Fat-body specific element (references as in *D*). *F, G* 20-Hydroxyecdysone specific element, functional in males only (Shirras and Bownes 1987). *H* Yolk-protein gene-specific, diet-enhanced transcriptional activity (Bownes et al. 1988a). *I, J, K* Ovary-specific enhancers (Logan and Wensink 1990)

first exon of 261 nucleotides is followed by an intron of 62 nucleotides. This intron is probably homologous to the single intron found in the YP1 and YP2 genes. The second exon is 383 nucleotides long, followed by the second intron of 72 nucleotides. The third exon is 844 nucleotides long. An in frame TAG stop codon appears at +1451. A stretch of 168 bases between this stop codon and the 3'-end of the transcript contains three other stop codons in phase, and five stop codons out of phase. S1 mapping data indicate that the G at +1622 is the polyadenylation site; this interpretation is strengthened by the fact that the G occurs in the context of a GAAAA consensus poly(A) addition site (Berget 1984). If the untranslated section and the introns are excluded, the coding section constitutes 1260 nucleotides, giving a protein of 420 amino acids. Comparing the sequencing data with the demonstration by gel electrophoresis that the initial transcript is approximately 1750 bases indicates that the poly(A) section is of about 80 nucleotides in length.

With the availability of base sequences for the yolk protein genes, more recent work has been concentrating on their regulation. Particular attention has been paid to YP1 and YP2; the intervening 1225 base pairs between these two divergently transcribed genes are likely to contain most, if not all, of the DNA elements which affect the expression of these genes. Using P-element mediated germ-line transformation (Spradling and Rubin 1982), a variety of gene constructs, including specific deletions, additions and fusions with reporter genes, have been tested for their effects on the expression of the YP1 and YP2 genes. The results from such experiments are illustrated in Fig. 23. In addition to the constitutive promoter elements, such as the TATA and CAAT boxes, the presence of a number of enhancer elements of various specificities has been demonstrated. Of particular interest is the occurrence of separate enhancers which determine the tissue specificity of yolk-protein gene expression. A region close to YP2, and another within the YP2 gene's first exon, mediate ovary-specific expression. Different segments of the first enhancer have different positive and negative effects on cell-type specificity of transcription (Logan and Wensink 1990). A region closer to the coding sequences of YP1 is concerned with specifying fat body expression (Garabedian et al. 1985; Wensink 1987). Later experiments have more closely defined the location of the fat body expression specific elements to a 125 bp region located between −196 and −321 upstream from YP1 (Garabedian et al. 1986). In fact, this element is involved in sex and developmental-stage specificity as well. It can direct a heterologous heat-shock gene promoter to be transcribed with YP1 specificity. Moreover, the specificity is retained when the region is in different orientations and at different distances from the coding region. It appears that both the fat body and ovary specifying regions are *cis*-acting bidirectional elements which act as positive enhancers for both the YP1 and YP2 genes (Tamura et al. 1985). Additional enhancer activities with different specificities include an element located in a 342 bp region proximal to YP2, which regulates the response to 20-hydroxyecdysone in males, but not in females (Shirras and Bownes 1987). The 883 bp region proximal to YP1 must contain regions which are concerned with sex determination gene effects on yolk protein expression, and a yolk-protein gene-specific, diet-enhanced transcription activity (Shirras and Bownes 1987; Bownes et al. 1988a).

Separate in vitro transcription studies indicate the presence of additional DNA motifs, between −86 and −159 upstream from YP1, and −161 and −341 upstream from YP2, which function as transcriptional enhancers (Voss and Pongs 1986). Preliminary studies indicate that at least some of the enhancer elements are regions of protein-DNA interactions (Voss et al. 1987). It has been shown for the *Bombyx mori* fibroin gene, that five distinct regions in the 5′-flanking sequence bind specific protein factors which are involved in enhancement of transcription and in developmental stage and tissue specificity. It will be interesting to see what sort of DNA-binding proteins are involved in the expression of the yolk protein genes.

Aedes and *Locusta* are two other insects in which the yolk protein genes have been cloned. In both the primary transcripts are very large, over 6000 nucleotides in length. This feature, and the fact that classical genetic information and techniques and the ability to manipulate the genes by procedures such as P-element mediated transformation are at a much less advanced stage, has meant that progress in the analysis of gene structure and function in these forms has been much slower than in *Drosophila*.

For *Aedes*, three clones containing different vitellogenin gene sequences have been isolated; two of these have been investigated in greater detail. Restriction maps suggest that the genes have substantial identity in the coding regions, but outside the coding sections, there is little if any homology. Intron number and size remain to be determined. A subcloned section of one of the sequences was used as a probe against southern transfers of whole genomic DNA digested with several different restriction enzymes. The results suggest that there may be a total of five different vitellogenin genes (Gemmill et al. 1986). Sequence information and analysis of any gene control regions are not yet available.

Clones making up two genes, VgA and VgB, have been isolated from genomic libraries of *Locusta* and shown to be the animal's only genes for vitellogenin (Locke et al. 1987). Both are on the X chromosome (Bradfield and Wyatt 1983) and both contain introns, although the precise number and location of the latter has not been determined. No cross-hybridization between the two genes could be obtained for most of the coding regions. However, sequence analysis shows that the N-terminal amino acid regions are very similar in the two genes. The availability of non-cross-hybridizing probes for the coding region of the two vitellogenin genes has allowed an assay of gene expression by means of dot hybridization (Dhadialla et al. 1987). A striking result from these assays was a precisely coordinate accumulation of transcripts from the two genes. The coordinate expression implies that the two genes possess at least some equivalent regulatory signals, possibly in their upstream flanking DNA. Sequencing of the region 500 bases upstream from the transcription initiation sites revealed that 11 regions, in blocks of 6–12 nucleotides, were similar between the 2 genes (Locke et al. 1987). On the basis of sequence similarity to two 12 bp regions in the *Periplaneta* oothecin gene 5′-flanking regions (Pau et al. 1987), which are also regulated by juvenile hormone, Wyatt (1988) has suggested that one or both of these elements in *Locusta* and the cockroach may represent juvenile hormone response elements. Further functional analysis of the locust vitellogenin gene regulatory elements will require the development of a homologous gene transfer system.

3.5.3.4 Vitellogenin Gene Expression

Studies specifically directed at the mechanisms of transcription, processing and transport of the mRNAs from the nucleus, translation, modification, and export of the vitellogenins have not been extensive. In part, this must be a reflection of the fact that fat body is a difficult tissue to work with for the preparation of subcellular fractions. Nevertheless, it is clear from the available data that the above processes follow in broad outline the mechanisms described for other systems (Kaulenas 1985). Messenger RNAs can be shown to accumulate in the cytoplasm (Izumi et al. 1980; Chinzei et al. 1982) and form appropriately-sized polysomes (Reid and Chen 1981). The mRNAs are associated with an extensive endoplasmic reticulum, which itself accumulates in response to hormone stimulation (della Cioppa and Engelmann 1984a,b). The products of translation are directed into the lumen of the rough endoplasmic reticulum by signal peptides, which are then cleaved from the proteins (Brennan et al. 1980). While in transit to the cell surface the vitellogenins are lipidated, glycosylated (Nordin et al. 1984), and in some cases, phosphorylated (Minoo and Postlethwait 1985a,b). Studies with tunicamycin indicate that the oligosaccharide attachment is necessary for the subsequent steps of vitellogenin maturation and export (Wojchowski et al. 1986). The final step is the secretion of the yolk proteins into the hemolymph.

3.5.3.5 Uptake of Vitellogenins by the Ovary

In many insects the onset of vitellogenic uptake is characterized by the formation of gaps and spaces between the cells of the follicular epithelium (Engelmann 1979). The gaps provide a means of access for the hemolymph proteins to the oocyte surface. Vitellogenins appear to concentrate in the perioocytic space and from there are later taken up by the oocyte by pinocytotic vesicles. The development of gaps between the follicle cells has been termed patency. In *Rhodnius*, this condition has been shown to be a development in response to juvenile hormone (Davey 1981). In this organism juvenile hormone brings about a (Na^+-K^+)-ATPase mediated shrinkage of the follicular cells. Follicle cells which have differentiated in the absence of juvenile hormone do not respond to the hormone by the development of patency. Juvenile hormone controls the development of a specialized endocytic core, consisting of coated vesicles and uncoated endosomes as well as microvilli, in *Aedes* oocytes (Raikhel and Lea 1985). In insects other than *Aedes* and *Rhodnius*, juvenile hormone also seems to be involved in yolk protein uptake (*Nauphoeta*, Kindle et al. 1988; *Periplaneta*, Sams and Bell 1977; *Locusta*, Minks 1967; *Drosophila*, Giorgi 1979; Kambysellis and Cradock 1976; Postlethwait and Weiser 1973), but in these cases the precise role of the hormone is not entirely clear.

While juvenile hormone appears to be involved in yolk protein uptake, its presence is not sufficient. For example, a number of nonvitellogenic female-sterile mutants have been described in *Drosophila* in which yolk proteins accumulate in the hemolymph, yet the phenotype is not rescued by juvenile hormone-treatment (Postlethwait and Jowett 1980). The characteristics of these mutants are most easily explained as a lesion in vitellogenin-specific receptors. Current evidence clearly points to yolk protein uptake being a receptor-mediated, process requiring energy (Roth et al. 1976; Röhrkasten and Ferenz 1985). The number of vitellogenin-binding sites per unit area of oocyte surface has been shown to vary with physiological state in *Rhodnius* (Oliveira et al. 1986). Similarly, incorporation per unit surface area increases fourfold during vitellogenesis in *Locusta*, while vitellogenin concentration in the hemolymph remains constant (Ferenz 1978).

Consistent with the presence of specific vitellogenin receptors are observations that yolk protein binding can occur at 4 °C, without the occurrence of internalization (Osir and Law 1986), and the facts that uptake is saturable (Röhrkasten and Ferenz 1985; Kindle et al. 1988), species specific (Kunkel and Pan 1976), Ca^{2+} (Osir and Law 1986) and energy dependent (Roth et al. 1976; Silverstein et al. 1977), and insensitive to protein synthesis inhibition (Kulakosky and Telfer 1987). The latter observation suggests that membrane components are recycled and most likely eliminates the theory that subsidiary proteins, such as paravitellogenins, are important in the yolk protein uptake mechanism. These proteins are synthesized by the follicular epithelium and secreted into the intercellular spaces around the oocyte. They are endocytosed and stored in the yolk along with vitellogenins (Anderson and Telfer

1969). Earlier speculations that paravitellogenins may serve as binding agents for vitellogenins and function as nonrecyclable entry mechanism into oocytes are inconsistent with the cycloheximide data.

In vitro studies have shown that vitellogenins bind to oocyte membranes with specificity (Ferenz and Lubzens 1981; Lange and Loughton 1981) and high affinity (Kd of about 5×10^{-7} M for *Locusta*; Röhrkasten and Ferenz 1986). In *Hyalophora* the vitellogenin receptor does appear to compete with high-density lipophorin for the same transporter, although vitellogenin is taken up more efficiently. Microvitellin seems to have a totally different transporter (Kulakosky and Telfer 1990). In a number of systems it has been shown that the rate of uptake is dependent on vitellogenin concentration (Röhrkasten and Ferenz 1985 in *Locusta*; Oliveira et al. 1986 in *Rhodnius*; Kindle et al. 1988 in *Nauphoeta*); a minimal vitellogenin concentration is necessary for the normal functioning of the endocytotic process. A possible interpretation of this observation is that multiple receptors may have to be filled before the internalization process is triggered. Currently, there is little information on the molecular characteristics of the receptors. Part of the recognition mechanism involves the high mannose oligosaccharides of vitellogenin (König et al. 1988), but the oligosaccharide signature by itself is not sufficient for binding and it is likely that specific signal sequences in the protein are also involved. The report by Yan and Postlethwait (1990) that in vitro fusion product between a protein of the vitellogenin polypeptide and a reporter catalase gene is sequestered into the oocyte, for *Drosophila*, holds substantial promise for a more detailed analysis of the molecular requirements for yolk protein uptake in the future.

Receptor-bound vitellogenins accumulate in specialized regions of the surface membrane, the coated pits, and are then internalized by the formation of coated vesicles. Vesicles of this type have been purified from *Locusta* oocytes by differential and sucrose density gradient centrifugation (Röhrkasten and Ferenz 1987). The major vesicular constituent, comprising about 50% of the total protein, is clathrin. Clathrin is an integral part of the molecular mechanism for internalizing receptor-bound material, and can be shown to exhibit the characteristic polygonal coat structure on the cytoplasmic surface of the locust vesicles. The subsequent fate of the coated vesicles is loss of the clathrin coat and fusion with endosomes, as demonstrated for mosquito oocytes (Raikhel and Lea 1986). Within the endosomal compartment a further processing step occurs in which the adsorbed yolk precursors dissociate from the membrane to become homogeneously distributed in the lumen (Roth and Porter 1964; Raikhel 1984). The dissociation step is promoted by the action of proton pumps in the vesicle membrane which acidify the lumen to a pH at which the receptors no longer bind the ligands. Without such dissociation, transfer of the endocyte contents to transitional yolk bodies is inhibited. In *Hyalophora*, the proton ionophores nigericin and monesin, which inhibit vesicle acidification, have been shown to stop transfer of vitellogenin from endosomes to growing yolk spheres (Stynen et al. 1988). It is of interest that endosomes filled with nonspecific internalized proteins fuse with lysosomes, while those containing vitellogenins follow the accumulative route and fuse with transitional yolk bodies (Raikhel and Lea 1986). As a final transformation, the transitional yolk body changes into a mature yolk body with the crystallization of the vitellogenins.

Chapter 4

Structure and Function of the Male Accessory Reproductive Systems

The development and relationships of the insect male reproductive system were reviewed in Chapter 2. In this Chapter the structure, function and regulation of the male accessory reproductive structures are discussed. As for the female system, the coverage will not consider the differentiation of the sex cells themselves, but concentrate on the role of the various adjunct cells and structures which contribute to the development, maintenance and transport of the sperm. The major emphasis will be on the male accessory glands.

A diagram of the generalized male reproductive system is illustrated in Fig. 24. The testis consists of a number of sperm tubes (testicular follicles), each of which contains germ cells at various stages of development, as well as other cells, and is surrounded by a double epithelial sheath. The sperm tubes may be totally distinct or fused to varying extents, depending on the species. The distal portion of the sperm tube contains spermatozoa and communicates with the vas deferens by a narrow tube, the vas efferens. The terminal portion of the vas deferens may be dilated to form the seminal vesicle, or the latter structure may be an independent invagination. Posteriorly, the vas deferens or seminal vesicles communicate with a single ejaculatory duct. Accessory glands may arise as outpouchings of the anterior duct system [(1) in Fig. 24A], or from the ejaculatory duct (2), or may exist as thickenings of a part of the ejaculatory duct [(3); Leopold 1976]. Variations in testicular structure and duct systems have been reviewed extensively by Snodgrass (1935) and Matsuda (1976), among others.

4.1 Accessory Systems Associated with the Testis

As illustrated in Fig. 24B, the generalized sperm tube may be divided into a number of regions. Apically, the germarium consists of the spermatogonia and, in many species, a prominent Versonian cell (Verson's cell; "apical cell"). The latter is particularly well developed in the Lepidoptera and the Diptera. The primary sperm cells divide to give a cytoplasmically interconnected spermatogonial group which becomes surrounded by cyst cells; together, this structure is known as the sperm cyst. The cyst cells are functionally, but probably not developmentally, equivalent to ovarian follicle cells. Trophic functions have been ascribed to the "apical cell", the cyst cells, and to various cells of the inner epithelial sheath which surrounds the sperm tube. For example, in some cockroaches, specialized epithelial cells of the vas deferens ("neck cells") produce lipoproteins, while other testicular follicle cells secrete mucopolysaccharides and/or mucoproteins (Lusis et al. 1970). Verson's cells (*Melanoplus*; Muck-

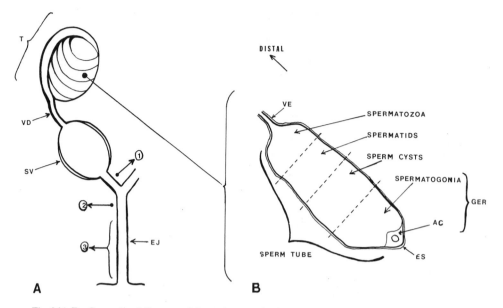

Fig. 24A,B. Generalized diagram of the male reproductive system. **A** Overall system, showing *1, 2, 3* possible derivations of the accessory glands (Leopold 1976). **B** Diagram of an individual sperm tube. *AC* Apical (Versonian) cell; *EJ* ejaculatory duct; *ES* epithelial sheath; *GER* germarium; *SV* seminal vesicle; *T* testis; *VD* vas deferens; *VE* vas efferens

enthaler 1964) and the cyst cells (*Chironomus*; Wensler and Rempel 1962) are said to have nutritive functions. In grasshoppers, a derivative of a cyst cell (the "nurse cell") forms a mucoprotein cap around the sperm heads, and may have an indirect nutritive role (Cantacuzène 1968). As a result of the cap, the sperm are arranged as bundles or spermatodesms, which travel down the vas deferens to the accessory gland complex, where they are stored in the seminal vesicle. Other functions of testicular cell secretions, such as the synthesis of "fecundity-enhancing substances" and "receptivity-inhibiting substances" are reviewed in detail by Gillott (1988).

4.2 Structures Associated with the Vasa Deferentia and the Seminal Vesicles

The basic arrangement for the vas deferens is as a one-cell-thick epithelial layer, encircled by a basement membrane, which is in turn surrounded by a muscle layer of variable thickness. Longitudinally, the upper (some Coleoptera; Poels 1972) or middle (some Lepidoptera; Riemann and Thorson 1979a) regions of the vas deferens can be used for sperm storage, in cases where a distinct seminal vesicle is absent, or, as storage sites in addition to the seminal vesicles. A specialized region of phagocytic cells is present in some cases (*Anagasta*, Riemann and Thorson 1979a; *Calpodes*, Lai-Fook 1982a). Lastly, there is often a region specialized for secretion. In such a case the cells are usually columnar, and exhibit an ultrastructure typical for secretory cells, rich in rough endoplasmic reticulum and Golgi complexes as well as export vesicles (e.g., *Locusta*, Cantocuzène 1971; *Samia*, Szolosi and Landureau 1977; *Calpodes*, Lai-Fook 1982). In *Samia*, these characteristics are established at metamorphosis in response to increasing ecdysterone titers. This type of terminal differentiation also requires an absence of juvenile hormone. In cases where juvenile hormone titer is artificially elevated during the critical differentiative period, abnormal development results (e.g., *Schistocerca*, Szollosi 1975).

No direct or detailed evidence on the function(s) of the secretory products is available, except in those cases where the secretion contributes to the formation of the spermatophore (e.g., *Lytta nuttalli*; Gerber et al. 1971b). Most of the speculations center on some nutritive contribution to the stored or transported sperm.

The major sites for sperm storage, before the sperm are packaged for donation to the female, are the seminal vesicles. These structures are of variable derivation (Matsuda 1976). In most cases, they are dilations of the terminal portions of the vasa differentia. In other cases they are dilations of the ejaculatory duct, or evaginations from the vasa differentia, or the ejaculatory duct, or some other arrangement, e.g., modified collateral glands. The typical structure is basically similar to that of other parts of the efferent duct system; consisting of a one-celled epithelium, a basement membrane and an outer muscle layer of variable thickness. There may or may not be a cuticular intima, depending on whether the structure is ectodermally or mesodermally derived.

The epithelium may (Cantacuzène 1972; Da Cruz-Landim and Ferreira 1977; Couche and Gillott 1988) or may not (Odhiambo 1969b) be secretory. In cases where it is, relatively little detailed information is available on the products or on the control of their synthesis. Juvenile hormone levels seem to have a minimal or no effect on the morphology or function (Cantacuzène 1967a; Odhiambo 1971; Lange et al. 1983; Gillott and Venkatesh 1985; Couche and Gillott 1988). This is somewhat curious, in view of the frequent examples of hormonal participation in the differentiation and function of many other parts of the male efferent reproductive system. Clearly, there is scope for additional work on this aspect.

4.3 Male Accessory Glands and Ejaculatory Duct-Associated Structures

The main function of the male accessory glands in many, if not all insects, is the formation of a spermatophore. This structure serves as a vehicle for the transfer of sperm from the male to the female. In species where a spermatophore is not formed, accessory gland function is generally related to the facilitation of sperm transfer or maintenance. The accessory glands also can have a number of subsidiary functions, such as influencing female behavior or providing nutrients to the female. The biochemical mechanisms by which such secondary functions are carried out are rather variable and idiosyncratic between species, and are best considered on an individual basis when specific examples are discussed.

Insect male accessory glands are morphologically extremely variable. They are often partially or totally of tubular form, with tubule numbers ranging from a single pair to many hundreds of tubules. Despite the variability in overall external morphology, a basic structural pattern often can be distinguished. The tubular components generally consist of an inner lumen surrounded by an epithelial layer, usually one cell in thickness, bounded by a basement membrane. The whole structure is surrounded by a muscular sheath of variable complexity. As indicated in Chapter 2, in most insects the embryological derivation of the accessory glands is mesodermal; such glands are classified as mesodenia. In other cases, they are of ectodermal origin and are termed ectadenia (Escherich 1894). In some insects, accessory glands are absent and their functions generally are taken over by specialized regions of the ejaculatory duct.

The functional morphology, biochemistry, and physiology of the male accessory gland have been reviewed reasonably recently by a number of authors, from different perspectives (Leopold 1976; Gillott and Friedel 1977; Chen 1984; Gillott 1988). The structure and synthesis of spermatophores has been discussed in a monograph by Mann (1984). For the present discussion, a "case history" approach will be used. The best understood examples will be discussed in detail; other cases will be used to highlight and contrast the main examples, which will be drawn from work on the Orthoptera, Coleoptera, Lepidoptera and Diptera.

4.3.1 Orthoptera

The use of a spermatophore for the delivery of sperm is widespread in the Orthoptera and related orders, such as Dictyoptera, and orthopteroid insect accessory glands will be considered as typical examples of the structures in exopterygotes.

4.3.1.1 The Acrididae

Accessory gland structure and function in the Acrididae (the grasshoppers and locusts) is probably the best understood among the orthopteroid insects. In particular, the work of Gillott's group on *Melanoplus sanguinipes* has built up a significant body of information (for references see the following account). However, even in this case information on the structure and control of the genes expressed in the accessory gland is largely lacking; as yet, no system is fully understood. Portions of the ejaculatory duct in some acridids also may be secretory, although the nature and function of such secretions are not entirely clear (Viscuso et al. 1985).

The acridid male accessory gland consists of two bilateral masses, each of which is composed of a number of intertwined tubules. The tubules are bound loosely together by trachae, and in some cases are associated with the paragonadal fat body. In the majority of cases examined, each mass consists of 16 tubules (*Locusta migratoria*, Gregory 1965; *Gomphocerus rufus, Schistocerca gregaria,* Cantocuzène 1967c, Odhiambo 1969a; *Camnula pellucida,* Ewen and Pickford 1975; *M. sanguinipes*, Gillott and Venkatesh 1985; Couche and Gillott 1990). Seventeen tubules have been found in *Taeniopoda eques* (Whitman and Loher 1984). The tubules can be subdivided into four main types, based on the appearance of their contents: (1) a single seminal vesicle; (2) a single opalescent or long hyaline gland; (3) four white glands; and (4) ten hyaline glands. In *T. eques*, two tubules, with a translucent-blue secretory product, probably correspond to the single opalescent tubule in other acridids. A schematic cross-section through a generalized acridid accessory gland tubule bundle is presented in Fig. 25. The figure presents the tubule nomenclature used in the various reports, as well as the approximate spatial relationships between different tubules.

The hyaline gland group and the white glands can be further subdivided on the basis of their secretory product appearance or the ultrastructural morphology of the tubule cells. For example, in *Gomphocerus*, there are three types of white gland; two tubules classified as WSI, one tubule as WS2 and one tubule as GSP, the latter with a speckled (*Gesprenkelte*) secretory product (Hartmann 1970). For the hyaline glands in *Locusta*, Gregory (1965) distinguished four large and six small tubules. On the basis of the secretion product color and tubule length, Lange and Loughton (1984) suggest that hyaline tubules 5/6, 7/8, and 9/10, as well as white glands 2/3, form identical pairs. This suggestion is strengthened by the demonstration that electrophoretic patterns of the products of these tubule pairs are identical. Even so, there may be as many as 12 different tubule types in *Locusta*. In *Gomphocerus*, Hartmann (1970) distinguishes eight different tubule types: the same number as are described for *Taeniopoda* (Whitman and Loher 1984). In fact, based on the occurrence of subtle differences in cellular ultrastructure and in the nature of their secretory products, Couche and Gillott (1990) suggest that there are 15 functionally specialized tubule types in the accessory gland of *Melanoplus*. This is a very substantial degree of regional specialization in an organ derived from a small subset of cells during the last larval stage. The way in which such specialization is brought about is a very interesting developmental question. Presumably, as in the case for imaginal disc differentiation, positional cues are important in the activation of appropriate genes in different stem cells. This developmental aspect has barely begun to be addressed with respect to accessory gland differentiation. The topic of the acquisition

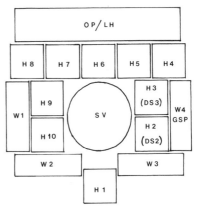

Fig. 25. Schematic cross-section through a generalized acridid male accessory-gland tubule bundle. *H 1–9 (DS2, DS3)* hyaline glands; *W 1–4 (GSP)* white glands; *OP/LH* opalescent or long hyaline gland; *SV* seminal vesicle

of regional specialization of differentiated function will be discussed in more detail in the consideration of the situation found in *Acheta*. Both the acridid and gryllid accessory glands provide distinctive material for the investigation of important questions in developmental biology.

The regional specialization in synthetic activity has important functional correlates in the formation of the spermatophore. Among acridids, two main modes of spermatophore formation are encountered. In *Locusta* (Gregory 1965), *Gomphocerus* (Hartmann 1970) and *Chorthippus* (Hartmann and Loher 1974), only one spermatophore is produced per mating. Once mating is completed, the empty spermatophore tube can remain in the spermathecal duct of the female, blocking the entry of other spermatophores, until it is partially dissolved, while the remainder is pushed out (Parker and Smith 1975). In other grasshoppers, such as *Schistocera* (Pickford and Padgham 1973), *Melanoplus* (Pickford and Gillott 1971) and *Taeniopoda* (Whitman and Loher 1984), several spermatophores are produced successively in a single mating. Empty spermatophores are removed from the genital tracts of the male and female before the next spermatophore is formed. As many as 14 spermatophores can be formed during a single mating in *Schistocerca* (Pickford and Padgham 1973). In both groups of grasshoppers, the spermatophore has a similar basic structure, with a hollow bulb from which extends a long tubular protrusion. Due to its gelatinous consistency, the spermatophore is molded by the combined genital tracts of the male and female, which act as a cast for the finished structure. Usually, the reservoir region is held in the spermatophore sac of the male, while the tubular extension reaches into the spermatheca of the female. In *Locusta*, the spermatophore is long (35–45 mm; Gregory 1965) and reaches the distal diverticulum of the spermatheca; in acridids, which form multiple spermatophores per mating, the structure is much shorter (1.5 mm in *Schistocerca*, Pickford and Padgham 1973; 4 mm in *Melanoplus*, Pickford and Gillott 1971), and reaches only a short distance into the spermatheca. In all grasshoppers the spermatoderms are pumped into the female through the spermatophore tube; they differ in how far the spermatoderms have to travel to reach the storage areas.

A series of ablation experiments have defined the function of the various regionally specific secretions in the formation of the spermatophore in *Gomphocerus* (Hartmann 1970). The structural components of the spermatophore are supplied by the secretions of the hyaline (translucent) tubules. The protrusion of the tubular portion of the spermatophore into the spermatheca of the female is produced by the seminal fluid, derived from the seminal vesicle, and by the secretion of one type of the white tubules. The formation of the spermatophore lumen is dependent on the secretion of another of the white tubule types (W2) and of the opalescent tubule. If either of these secretions are absent, the proximal portion of the spermatophore will not become hollow, although the spermatophore will continue to expand into the female seminal duct. In *Melanoplus*, the product of the long hyaline gland, an abundant glycoprotein of 72 kD (Cheeseman and Gillott 1988a), forms 65% of a viscous secretion that is discharged at the same time as the formation of the spermatophore. Bilateral ablation of this tubule type interferes with the uncoiling of the spermatophore, but not with its structural aspects (Cheeseman and Gillott 1989). These authors suggest that the product(s) of the long hyaline gland act as a lubricant and/or plasticiser, which facilitates the passage of the ejaculate into the spermatheca.

The ultrastructure of the epithelial cells of the accessory gland tubules, with the exception of the seminal vesicle, show features typically encountered in cells specialized for export protein synthesis; including abundant rough endoplasmic reticulum, Golgi complexes, and numerous lysosomes, mitochondria, and secretory vesicles (Odhiambo 1969b, 1971; Couche and Gillott 1990). The latter study, on *Melanoplus*, is the most detailed and may be used as a typical example. The white glands and the long hyaline gland are especially notable because of the extreme hypertrophy of the rough endoplasmic reticulum in the epithelial cells. These cells, along with the accessory gland cells of *Acheta* (Kaulenas et al. 1975, 1979) easily equal any other examples of rough endoplasmic reticulum in packing density. More moderate packing densities for the rough endoplasmic reticulum are encountered in the short hyaline glands 4,5,6,8, and 10. Glands 1,2,3,7, and 9, as well as the seminal vesicle, display a swollen endoplasmic reticulum with a much lower concentration of attached ribosomes, suggesting a much lower level of export protein synthetic activity.

Another interesting feature of the epithelial cell ultrastructure is the presence of complex lateral junctions, including apical belt desmosomes, pleated septate junctions, sclariform junctions, and linear and macular gap junctions. Such tight cell-to-cell sealing is not only useful in resisting stresses imposed on the epithelium by the luminal contents, but may also function to exclude free communication between the hemolymph and the lumena of all the tubules except the seminal vesicle. As Couche and Gillott (1990) indicate, this makes unlikely an earlier observation from this laboratory, namely that hemolymph proteins derived from the fat body contribute significantly to the accessory gland product (Friedel and Gillott 1976b). It is possible that these results suggest hemolymph protein uptake by the seminal vesicles. The epithelium of the seminal vesicles has intercellular spaces and pinocytotic activity has been described at the basal plasma membrane of individual cells. Alternatively, the result reported by Friedel and Gillott (1976b) could simply be an artifact. The antiserum used in these experiments was prepared against whole accessory gland homogenates (Friedel and Gillott 1976a), and the accessory gland tubules are very closely associated with paragonadal fat body in many grasshoppers, including *Melanoplus* (Odhiambo 1969a; Couche and Gillott 1990). Some of the antibodies could well have been against extra-glandular proteins, without such proteins having any functional significance in the accessory gland.

The protein biosynthetic capacities of the various tubule types have been characterized by SDS-polyacrylamide gel electrophoresis and/or isoelectric focusing in *Locusta* (Lange and Loughton 1984) and in much greater detail in *Melanoplus* (Gillott and Venkatesh 1985; Cheeseman and Gillott 1988a; Cheeseman et al. 1990). In *Melanoplus*, the long hyaline glands and the seminal vesicles each produce distinctive protein patterns on SDS-gels. In all cases, more than 20 prominent bands are resolved, including several glycoproteins. The long hyaline and the white glands also secrete lipoproteins (Gillott and Venkatesh 1985). The major product of the long hyaline gland has been characterized in greater detail (Cheeseman and Gillott 1988a). It is a glycoprotein (LHP1) with a native molecular weight of 72 kD. On SDS-gels a single 36 kD subunit is detectable, and presumably the native protein consists of a dimer. LHP1 is the single most abundant protein in the long hyaline gland, accumulating to about 1 mg in 17-day-old virgins. This quantity represents 37–51% of the total protein of the long hyaline gland. About 20% of the protein is lost from the gland during a single mating. LHP1 is not a structural protein of spermatophores, but constitutes a major component of a viscous secretion that may serve as a lubricant or a spermatophore plasticizer (Cheeseman and Gillott 1989).

Actual spermatophore structural proteins are much more difficult to analyze, since they are extensively modified and cross-linked in the finished spermatophore. Presumably, the rationale, if it can be classified as such, behind the evolution of multiple tubules with different synthetic repertoires is that bringing reactive components together too soon, as in the premature mixing of the separate constituents of a "binary bomb", could be disastrous. Once mixed, the products are largely intractable to most methods of analysis. In *Melanoplus* (Cheeseman et al. 1990), as in *Acheta* (Kaulenas, unpublished), once all reasonable protein solubilization procedures have been applied, a recognizable, structurally intact spermatophore remains. Nevertheless, a few structural spermatophore proteins are extractable without resort to heroic means. It is not clear that such proteins are necessarily the major, or representative, constituents of the spermatophore. However, they are analyzable. In *Melanoplus*, a number of soluble spermatophore proteins can be isolated (Cheeseman et al. 1990). One of them is SP62, a protein of 62 kD, which appears to be the product of the short hyaline gland three (SH3). Antiserum against SP62, however, recognizes proteins of 85 kD on Western blots of gels containing separated proteins from short hyaline glands, long hyaline glands and, in trace amounts, in white glands, as well as in the nonstructural viscous secretion. Whether the antibody recognizes precursors of SP62 or epitopes in related proteins is not clear. In either case the situation would be interesting. If the 85 kD protein is a precursor to SP62, different glands would be showing variable levels of expression of this gene, and analysis would be of great interest. If the immunological reactivity represents a common element among many accessory gland proteins, a common evolutionary origin or a highly constrained function for this region of the protein would be indicated. Currently, it is hard to decide which, if any, of these alternatives is correct. What seems clear is that SP62 is a major component of the spermatophore, and that it is a product of the SH3 tubules, generated from some precursor as a result of interaction with other soluble proteins from the remainder of the gland complex.

Cheeseman et al. (1990) have also identified a number of white gland products as spermatophore structural proteins. They have labeled them as A-group white gland proteins: WGPA. The major forms, of 22 and 21 kD, show intergland and between-individual male variation and decline substantially in concentration after mating. In the absence of SDS these proteins are largely insoluble, a characteristic which may be associated with the globular appearance of the white gland secretions, and may be responsible for the white appearance of these tubules. Antibodies raised against these proteins also recognized a larger (28 kD) form in white glands 1–3, and a small (9.6 kD) protein in white gland 4. Again, whether this represents a precursor-product relationship or the occurrence of common epitopes for some other reasons, is not currently clear.

The secretory cell phenotype and the full range of synthetic activity takes some time to develop in adult male acridids. In *Locusta*, for example, all of the accessory gland tubules, with the exception of the seminal vesicles, show little evidence of the protein secretory apparatus (rough endoplasmic reticulum, Golgi elements, etc.) immediately after adult emergence. It takes about 5 days to attain the adult cell ultrastructural morphology (Odhiambo 1971). Similarly, in the *Melanoplus* long hyaline gland, the epithelial cells in newly emerged adults contain almost no rough endoplasmic reticulum, have poorly developed Golgi complexes, and large numbers of free ribosomes. Within 24 h there is a rapid proliferation of the rough endoplasmic reticulum and the development of elaborate Golgi complexes, and by day 3 the full structural capacity for export protein synthesis is achieved (Couche and Gillott 1987).

Associated with these cytological changes are sequential changes in protein synthesis. Gillott and Venkatesh (1985) have documented the occurrence of age-specific protein patterns in the glandular secretion after the final molt. For example, a 27 kD protein appears on day 1 and continues to accumulate in increasing amounts later, while a 10 kD protein appears only between days 7 and 10. Similar variations can be documented for the short hyaline and white glands, with the final synthetic patterns being constructed by variation in the time of appearance of rates of synthesis of individual proteins. In *Locusta* some of the synthetic products begin to be synthesized in the final (fifth) larval instar; however, the full range of protein types is only achieved after the 15th day of imaginal life. Male accessory glands of young fifth instar larvae (0–1 day old) are not competent to produce the full range of secretion, even when transplanted into adult hosts. The competence to produce the full range of proteins is acquired during the second and third day of the last larval instar by the action of ecdysteroids in the absence of juvenile hormone (Gallois 1989).

While detailed experimental evidence for acridids is incomplete, from the available information and by analogy to related systems (e.g., *Periplaneta*; Dixon and Blaine 1972), it appears that the morphological differentiation of the gland, i.e., the formation of the various tubules, is triggered by the decrease of juvenile hormone titer to very low levels during the final instar, and the exposure of the cells to increasing ecdysterone levels. Elevated ecdysterone titer by itself, however, is insufficient to initiate the acquisition of the secretory cell phenotype. Some additional component associated with the final molt appears to be necessary to set this train of differentiation in motion. Whether there is such a component, and, if there is, what it may be, remains to be determined.

The older literature generally indicates that the hormonal regulation of accessory gland protein synthesis in adult exopterygotes is controlled by juvenile hormone; that is, even the acquisition of the morphology and the export protein synthetic phenotype is influenced not only by molt-related signals, but by juvenile hormone, and that, certainly, the synthesis of the specific specialized proteins is triggered by rising juvenile hormone titers in the adult (Cantacuzène 1967b; Hartmann 1971; Odhiambo 1966). This impression is probably fortified by analogies to the situation in endopterygotes. More recent results strongly indicate that the situation may be substantially more complex. For example, in *Melanoplus*, the differentiation and function of the seminal vesicles appear to be totally independent of juvenile hormone (Couche and Gillott 1988). Moreover, in this insect, over the first few days postemergence the corpora allata are practically inactive, at the time when the protein-export machinery is being established and the synthesis of at least some export proteins is being initiated (Couche et al. 1985; Gillott and Venkatesh 1985). A similar situation is found in *Schistocerca* (Avruch and Tobe 1978), where the corpora allata are not fully functional until ten days after the final molt. It seems very likely that juvenile hormone, in cases where it has any effect at all on accessory gland protein synthesis, may exert its major influence in regulating the quantity of expression, rather than controlling whether or not these genes are turned on (Lange et al. 1983; Cheeseman and Gillott 1988a,b). This situation may be equivalent to that found in *Periplaneta* (Blaine and Dixon 1973) and in *Rhodnius* (Barker and Davey 1981; Gold and Davey 1989), although the latter case is complicated by participation of the brain and the corpus cardiacum in regulatory activity (Barker and Davey 1983). Finer tools than assays for proteins are needed to settle these questions. The cloning and characterization of the genes involved will settle many of the extant questions in this area.

Currently, there is virtually no information on the genes active in accessory glands or the function of any possible regulatory elements. The investigation of the exopterygote systems presents somewhat of a dilemma, discussed in more detail in the consideration of the gryllid cases. The complex morphological and developmental features lead to many fascinating questions, but the large genome sizes and the virtual lack of genetics present serious impediments in their analysis.

In addition to the more obvious synthetic products, such as spermatophore structural proteins and lubricants, the acridid accessory gland produces a number of other substances, with a variety of functions. For example, crude accessory gland extracts from *Melanoplus* contain a trypsinlike activity (Cheeseman et al. 1990). Ablation of the short hyaline glands reduced the activity in extracts of the remaining gland by 78%, while ablation of the white glands produced a 59% decline. Ablation of the long hyaline glands or the seminal vesicles had no effect on the enzymatic activity of the remaining accessory gland. Some of the proteolytic activity could also be detected in spermatophores. Thus, limited proteolysis of spermatophore protein precursors may be necessary for spermatophore assembly. A similar suggestion has been made for spermatophore assembly in *Tenebrio* (Grimnes et al. 1986).

Using radioactively labeled male accessory-gland proteins, Friedel and Gillott (1977) have shown in *Melanoplus* that after copulation some of these proteins can enter the female's hemolymph and can even reach the ovary. They suggest that the transferred proteins, possibly derived from the fat body (Gillott and Friedel 1976), may be an important nutritional component for the developing oocytes. A trophic paternal contribution to the next generation is an appealing notion. Unfortunately, later calculations suggest that such a contribution may be rather meager. Cheeseman and Gillott (1989) show that if all of the radiolabeled protein transferred to the spermatheca was taken up by the ovary, the total gained would be 5 μg of protein. Since each egg represents about 6.5 mg of protein, and the female may lay between 1500 and 3000 eggs after a single copulation (Pickford and Gillott 1976), the male contribution to the protein budget is vanishingly small. Protein transfer from male to female, even at low doses, may be important, however. Pickford et al. (1969) have shown that male accessory glands contain an oviposition stimulant. This activity is absent from gland extracts of allatectomized males, and can be partially purified by ion-exchange chromatography (Friedel and Gillott 1976a). In *Locusta*, the oviposition stimulating factor is a protein of 13 kD produced by the opalescent gland (Lange and Loughton 1985). In fact, such fecundity-enhancing substances are present not only in *Melanoplus, Locusta,* and *Schistocerca* (Leahy 1973), but are of widespread occurrence in insects (see Gillott and Friedel 1977; Gillott 1988). The site of production is generally either the accessory glands or the testis; the site of action is unknown, although the cerebral neurosecretory cells, which produce an oviposition-inducing hormone, have been suggested as the likely target (Borovsky 1985a).

In addition, a more local or direct action of male accessory gland components on female fecundity has been demonstrated for *Locusta*. Extracts of whole glands or of the opalescent tubule alone have a direct effect on the oviduct, where they stimulate first the frequency and the amplitude, and then the tonus of contractions in a dose-dependent and reversible manner. They also stimulate the adenylate-cyclase activity of oviduct disrupted-cell preparations (Lafon-Cazal et al. 1987). These authors suggest that the tonus response is probably independent of the adenylate cyclase activity, because octopamine and forskolin did not mimic this effect. The frequency and amplitude responses can be induced through an adenylate cyclase-dependent receptor; in which case octopamine and forskolin and accessory gland extracts have a cumulative effect, suggesting that these compounds act on two discrete receptor types. Lafon-Cazal et al. (1987) suggest that their factor is distinct from the one described by Lange and Loughton (1985). The male accessory glands, therefore, can influence a number of female behaviors, probably by the action of independent factors.

Another component of the male acridid accessory glands which is passed to the female is a prostaglandin-synthesizing complex. In *Locusta* this complex, which stimulates the synthesis of prostaglandins from precursors, is produced by the opalescent gland and seminal vesicle (Lange 1984). The activity is associated with two high molecular weight fractions. This type of complex has been implicated in the control of egg laying in crickets (Destephano and Brady 1977), and will be discussed in greater detail later. In *Locusta*, however, prostaglandins do not induce oviposition, so the significance of transferring the synthetic machinery for their synthesis from male to female remains obscure.

4.3.1.2 The Gryllidae

The gryllid accessory gland is structurally the most complex gland yet described in insects, quite substantially more complex than those found for the Dictyoptera (Louis and Kumar 1971). The overall morphology of the gland has been described at various levels of detail in field and house crickets (Lespés 1885; Baumgartner 1910; Spann 1934; Kaulenas et al. 1975; Pustell 1979). Without question, the accessory gland of the house cricket, *Acheta domesticus*, has been investigated in the greatest detail, and the following account will concentrate largely on this system. The accessory gland is made up of a muscular central chamber, which receives the discharge from hundreds of delicate, blind-ended secretory tubules. The latter range in length from about 0.2–5 mm, and from 0.02–0.1 mm in diameter. The anterior central region is characterized by the smallest tubules (Fig. 26). Adjacent to them is an area of somewhat longer tubules which are filled with granular material, giving them a white appearance. The remainder of the tubules range from medium-length to long, and are also filled with secretory material (Kaulenas et al. 1975). Each of the tubules consists of a single layer of secretory epithelial cells surrounding a central cavity. Around the epithelial cells is a thin layer of circular muscle. A similar arrangement has been noted for *Gryllus bimaculatus*, where a single-fibrillar thin muscle surrounds each glandular

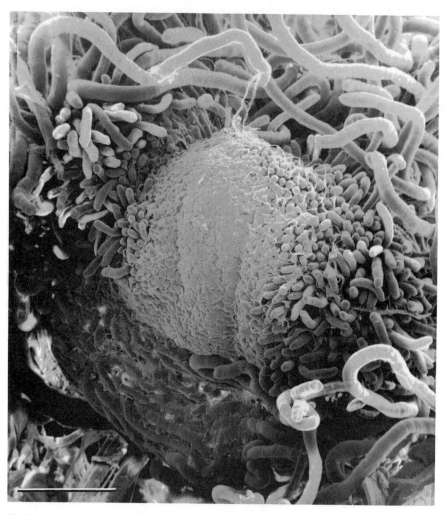

Fig. 26. Scanning electron micrograph of the anterior portion of the male *Acheta* accessory gland in situ. Note the large number of variously sized tubules. Glutaraldehyde-osmium fixation. *Marker bar* =300 μm (Micrograph by J. Pustell)

tubule, and multifibrillar muscle is located around the opening of each tubule in the anterior region of the ejaculatory duct (Yasuyama et al. 1988).

The central chamber of the gland, into which the tubules discharge, is about 2 mm long and 1.6 mm high. The internal wall consists of numerous ridges. The gland body endothelium is continuous with that of the tubules. The muscular walls of the gland body constrict the tubules at their point of entry, suggesting that the gland body serves as a valve controlling the entry of the secretory products into the central chamber. In fact, in both *Acheta* and *Gryllus bimaculatus* the secretory substances are probably squeezed from the tubules by the antagonistic action of two sets of muscles: the contraction of the circum-tubular muscle and the relaxation of the multifibrillar muscles. In *Gryllus*, sustained tubule contractions appear to be regulated by glutamate and by proctolin and are neurogenically evoked, while octopamine increased the frequency of myogenically evoked contractions (Kimura et al. 1989). These authors speculate that the use of proctolin at neuromuscular junctions may be related to the special requirements of the accessory gland muscles to develop and maintain sustained contractions over extended periods, when the tubules pour out their contents to form the spermatophore. The central chamber itself can be divided into five compartments, A through E; although all compartments are continuous, they are distinct morphologically and have distinct subsets of tubules discharging into them. The ejaculatory duct communicators with the gland body over most of its dorsal surface; at its posterior end it opens into the spermatophore mold, a region where the spermatophore ampulla is assembled. Although no tubules open into the ejaculatory duct, two small, hollow lateral vesicles project from the duct in the region where the duct enters the mold. A fine granular material is detectable in the lumena of the vesicles. Their outer surface is covered with muscle, which is continuous with that of the ejaculatory duct (Pustell 1979).

The dominant ultrastructural features of the tubules are specializations for extensive export protein synthesis, with the cells showing extensive rough endoplasmic reticulum and well-developed Golgi complexes. The apical cell regions have microvilli and secretory vesicles are found in the apical cytoplasm. The tubule lumen is filled with secretory product. The epithelial cells are extensively interdigitated laterally and joined by septate desmosomes (Kaulenas et al. 1975, 1979). Two exceptions to this ultrastructural phenotype have been noted by Pustell (1979). The first is a small tubule type, which discharges anteriorly in compartment A of the gland body. This type appears to be specialized for lipid export, as judged by the extensive myelin figures in the tubule lumena and apical cytoplasm, and the strong Sudan Black B staining in histological sections. Another set of small tubules has enlarged and particularly osmotically labile Golgi complexes, and seem to be involved in cyclic GMP synthesis and export.

The most striking feature of the secretory tubules is the very extensive regional specialization in the types of export proteins formed (Kaulenas 1976). Pustell (1979) has documented this regional specialization in detail by building up a three-dimensional reconstruction of the gland using histochemical, scanning and transmission electron-microscopic techniques, as well as SDS-polyacrylamide gel electrophoresis of the export products. The combined results indicate that about 30 tubule/gland types are distinguishable. The types of tubule involved, the position of discharge into the gland body and their histochemical characteristics are listed in Table 5. It is clear from this, as well as earlier studies (Kaulenas et al. 1975), that many of the products are glycoproteins. In addition, some tubule types specialize in lipid or lipoprotein synthesis, as well as more exotic products, such as cGMP.

The export proteins themselves constitute a very complex mixture, ranging in molecular weight from below 10 kD to well above 300 kD. One-dimensional SDS-polyacrylamide gel and two-dimensional isoelectric focusing and SDS-gel analyses are presented in Fig. 27A,B. Well over 200 distinct spots are detectable in the two-dimensional gels, with about 30 components making up the major products. To what extent all these are products of distinct genes or result from secondary cross-

Table 5. Tubule type characteristics

Type	Compartment	Diameter (mm)	Length (mm)	PAS[a]	AB	Mil	Sud	Appearance/comments[b]
1	A	29	360					No visible lumen
2	A	21	240	+++				Reddish, condensed in center of lumen
3	A	31	360					Light greenish, mesh or foamy
4	A	25	380				++	Greenish, condensed in center of lumen
5	A	27	380			+++		Reddish, compact with some bubbles
6	A	21	470	+++	+++			Dark greenish-blue, compact in center
7	A	43	1070	+++				Reddish compact; F-white[c]
8	A	25	400	+++	+++			Light greenish meshwork
9	A	40	1850		+			Greenish smooth compact; F-milky; cGMP
10	A	31	1000	++	+++	+		Greenish, very fine mesh work
11	A	27	400		++			Greenish, with some bubbles
12	A	44	850	++	++			Greenish, compact very grainy
13	A	43	1700	+	++	+		Greenish, compact light grain; F-white
14	A	27	400	++				Very dark purple, coarse mesh
15	A/B	20	460					Dark green, compact
16	A/B	40	1000			+		Blue, compact, grainy; F-milky
17	B	23	460					Reddish compact in center of lumen
18	B	42	670	+++				Reddish, compact
19	B	29	1000					Blue, compact with some grain
20	B	33	670				++	Dark blue mesh; mesh with Sudan also
21	B	33	680				+++	Appear empty (paraffin); compact by Sudan
22	B	27	1100	+++	+++			Red, compact
23	B	44	1100	++				Green, compact
24	B	93	5000					Loose green mesh with dark globules: F-clear
25	C	89	5000		+			Dark blue foamy, or coarse mesh: F-clear
26	C	77	4500	0			?	Blue-green, fine mesh
27	C	96	4000				++	Blue, smooth compact; F-white
28	E	76	4000	++				Purple, compact often on one tubule wall; F-white
29	D/E	33	900	N	NN			Reddish, fine mesh; F-clear
30	d	43	670	+++	+++			Blueish, smooth or coarse mesh; F-clear

[a]PAS, periodic acid-Schiff; AB, alcian blue 8GX, pH 2.6; Mil, Millon's reaction, Baker modification; Sud, Sudan Black B.
[b]Appearance of tissues fixed in situ with alcoholic glutaraldehyde and stained with hematoxyln and eosin.
[c]F, appearance of fresh tissue (if known).

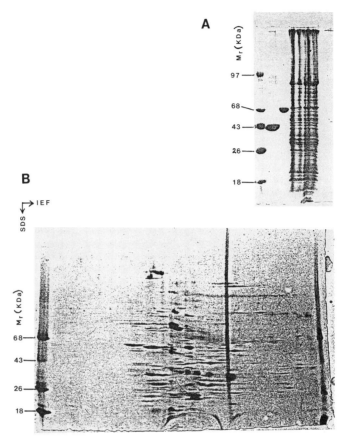

Fig. 27A,B. Electrophoretic analysis of *Acheta* male accessory gland proteins. **A** One-dimensional, SDS-polyacrylamide gel electrophoresis. **B** Two-dimensional separation, isoelectric focusing in the *horizontal* plane and SDS-polyacrylamide gel electrophoresis in the *vertical* plane of the picture. *Mr(kD)* molecular weight in kilodaltons

linking or modification (Kaulenas 1976), has not been definitively established, but it is clear that the gland produces a very complex mix of export proteins.

An even more interesting feature emerges when the synthetic capacity of individual tubules is examined. Figure 28 demonstrates the analysis of the proteins found in a row of adjacent large tubules on SDS-urea gels. Note that adjacent tubules may have quite substantial variation in protein concentration. To some extent this is due to some variation in the size of adjacent tubules; but it is also possible that there may be different discharge states in individual tubules of any group. More importantly, the product types of adjacent tubules, while having common elements may at the same time show differences in other protein bands. As shown in some portions of Fig. 28, it is common to find a specific band decreasing in concentration as a row of tubules is traversed, while other components remain constant. In fact, as pointed out originally by Pustell (1979), the gradientlike distribution of specific product types may explain the great heterogeneity encountered in any particular gland transect.

A

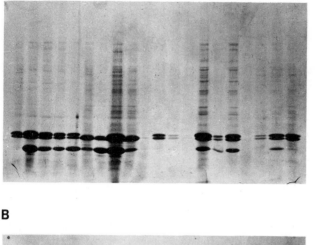

B

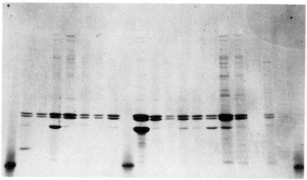

Fig. 28A,B. One-dimensional SDS-polyacrylamide gel electrophoretic analysis of *Acheta* accessory gland proteins. Each *lane* represents the total protein extracted from individual tubules. Adjacent lanes are from adjacent tubules. The *arrow* denotes the direction of migration

The relative amount of any given protein is distributed as a curve over the surface of the gland body. Many of the bands have an autonomous mode of distribution; that is, the distribution pattern of one band may be different from that of another band, even if both can be present in the same tubule. The pattern of expressed proteins in a particular tubule type appears to be a function of where the tubule is located in the distribution curves of its constituent, often independent, components. The concept of a specific tubule type may have to be refined, if individual genes have independent, though overlapping, domains of expression; although clearly there are dominant, position-related phenotypes for the tubules.

An interesting variant of such a dominant phenotype is the specialization of a small subset of tubules for the production of cGMP. Fallon and Wyatt (1975, 1977a,b) were the first to report on the impressive quantities of cGMP synthesized by cricket accessory glands. On a per gram basis this synthetic activity matched that reported for vertebrate outer rod segments, where this cyclic nucleotide plays a role in night vision by controlling sodium permeability in the rod plasma membrane (Miller 1983); the value for the rods was the highest specific activity for cGMP concentration reported up to that time. In fact, due to procedural details (Fallon and Wyatt prepared their tissue in aqueous media, in which cGMP is soluble) the values for cGMP concentrations in accessory gland tissues proved to be wild underestimates. Pustell (1979) has localized the production of cGMP to a set of anterior medium tubules, in which the level of this cyclic nucleotide is 330 000 pmol/mg protein, nearly three orders of magnitude greater than in bovine-rod outer segments. These values have been confirmed by Murtaugh et al. (1985). Moreover, these authors have demonstrated, using immunofluorescent localization, that cGMP accumulates in the lumina of the specialized tubules. The cGMP is secreted by the accessory gland and is incorporated into spermatophores. Interestingly, most of the spermatophore cGMP is located in the handle-capillary tube region of the spermatophore, a region which has little influence on the material transferred to the female. In fact, the concentration of cGMP in the seminal fluid is "only" 20 µM, and does not appear to be specifically associated with the sperm. Whatever cGMP is transferred to the female during insemination disappears rapidly. A physiological role for the cGMP is hard to imagine, especially since closely related crickets have much lower concentrations of the cyclic nucleotide. Possibly this is a rather convoluted adaptation to nitrogen excretion, or, as in the case of urate transfer in cockroach spermatophores (Schal and Bell 1982), a contribution to the female's nitrogen pool; assuming that she eats the remaining spermatophore after it serves its primary function.

Pustell's (1979) observations suggest that at least some of the tubules may be involved in lipoprotein or lipid biosynthesis. Among such lipids is probably arachidonic acid, which has been demonstrated as present in the male reproductive tract of *Acheta*; although the precise tubule origin has not been defined so far (Worthington et al. 1981). This long-chain, polyunsaturated fatty acid is of interest in that it is present in spermatophores and detectable at significant levels in spermathecae after mating (Stanley-Samuelson and Loher 1983). Arachidonic acid is the precursor of two prostaglandins (PGE_2 and $PGF_2\alpha$) in cricket tissues (*Teleogryllus commodus*, Tobe and Loher 1983; Stanley-Samuelson et al. 1987; *Acheta*, DeStephano and Brady 1977). Not only is the precursor for prostaglandins present in spermatophores, but prostaglandin-biosynthetic complex is also transferred to the female by the same route (Loher and Edson 1973). One of the main functions of the resulting prostaglandins is the stimulation of an intense bout of postcopulation egg-laying activity (DeStephano et al. 1982; Loher 1981). In *Acheta*, the prostaglandin synthetase is probably synthesized in the testes (DeStephano and Brady 1977), but then accumulates in the spermatophore for transfer to the female. Once in the spermatheca, the arachidonic acid is converted to the active prostaglandins by the donated prostaglandin synthetase (Tobe and Loher 1983). While the elevation of prostaglandin levels in female reproductive tissues is associated with a short-term ovipositional response, whether or not prostaglandins are involved in generating a sustained enhancement of oviposition is less clear. Murtaugh and Denlinger (1987) note that inactivation of the prostaglandin synthetase complex in males or females of *Acheta* failed to block the long-term mating-induced increase in oviposition. On the other hand, X-irradiated males, which retain high levels of prostaglandins in both testes and spermatophores but lack sperm, were unable to induce egg laying, even though they mated and transferred spermatophores. It appears that some sperm-associated factor or effect must also play a role, perhaps a dominant one, in the induction of egg-laying behavior in the female. In any event, the overall effect is one consistently found in insects; male-generated substances passed to the female during mating result in significant effects on female postcopulatory behavior.

Not all components synthesized at elevated amounts are necessarily passed to the female via the spermatophore. For example, the energy source for the massive protein synthesis is probably trehalose, and, at least in the related cockroaches, trehalases are an important component of the accessory glands (Ogisio et al. 1982, 1985; Ogisio and Takahashi 1984). While this synthetic activity has not been examined in *Acheta*, it is highly likely that similar results would be found for crickets.

As noted above, the secretory cell cytoplasm is dominated by a massive array of rough endoplasmic reticulum lamellae, packed at a very high density, which equals, if not surpasses that described for other systems heavily committed for export protein synthesis. The level to which these cells are specialized for extensive protein synthesis is underlined by considering data on ribosome and mRNA content. The average ribosome content of the male accessory gland cells in *Acheta* is 4.4×10^7 (Kaulenas et al. 1979), a value which compares to about 6×10^6 ribosomes per cell found for rat liver (Blobel and Potter 1967), although tubule cells are less than twice the volume of rat liver cells. In the accessory gland of *Acheta* approximately 70% of the ribosomes are found as polysomes (Kaulenas 1972; Yenofsky and Kaulenas 1975). Estimates of the number of polyA+ mRNA molecules per cell and their average length (the latter derived from direct measurements by electron microscopy), give values of 3×10^6/cell and 1300 nucleotides, respectively (Yenofsky 1977). Using these figures it is possible to calculate that, very approximately (allowing for a 5'-untranslated region and a poly A-tail), the average mRNA should be associated with six to ten ribosomes in a polysome and produce a protein of about 30 kD. These figures are close to those observed directly. The poly A+-mRNA population is composed of two classes of molecules. A complex class of some 3.5×10^4 different sequences, each present on an average of four copies of mRNA per gene per cell, and a prevalent class of a few hundred different sequences constituting the bulk (90%) of the mRNA population (Yenofsky 1977). The mRNAs belonging to the prevalent class have a long half-life (Kaulenas et al. 1975), as is typical for major mRNAs in terminally differentiated tissues (Buckingham et al. 1974). A partial cDNA library, corresponding to the prevalent accessory gland mRNAs, has been constructed in pUC18 plasmids (Kaulenas, unpubl.) and should permit additional characterization of the mRNAs and their genes. However, to fully explore the interesting developmental and structural possibilities inherent in this and the acridid systems, an Orthopteran equivalent of the P-element-mediated transformation system of *Drosophila* is desperately needed.

In crickets the morphology of the accessory gland is established over the last nymphal instar. The gland is derived from a medial, bilobed vesicle located in the posterior part of the ninth segment. The bilobed vesicle is formed from the fusion of two ampullae, derived from the ventral remnants of the coelomic sacs which are associated with the ends of the vas deferens rudiments (Snodgrass 1937). The accessory gland anlagen acquires the competence to differentiate tubules late in the pen-ultimate instar (Ranganathan 1977), but requires a rising ecdysterone titer in the absence of juvenile hormone to initiate differentiation. Once the tubules develop even in the last-stage nymph, they also acquire a limited capacity for export protein synthesis. The status of these proteins is not totally clear. Those proteins that are made are immunologically related to export proteins of the adult (Kaulenas et al. 1979), but it is clear that the full range and complexity of the gland's protein synthetic repertoire is not present in the nymph (Kaulenas et al. 1975). It is possible that the difference between nymph and adult is largely quantitative; that differentiation-specific genes are turned on in the late nymph but are expressed at a low level, the expression level being adjusted upward after the final molt. It has not been ruled out, however, that the relevant genes could be activated sequentially. The use of cloned transcripts as probes should settle this question.

Acquisition of the full synthetic capacity by the accessory gland requires the final molt (Kaulenas et al. 1975; Ranganathan 1977). Over the first few days post-molt, there is a rapid hypertrophy of the protein synthetic and export apparatus, and by about the fourth day the insect has the capacity to form spermatophores (McFarlane 1968a). In contrast to the situation found in many other insects, juvenile hormone appears to play no role in the adult development of the gland. In *Acheta* chemical allatectomy, by precocene treatment of early adults, results in the loss of the ability to synthesize vitellogenins in females, but has no detectable effect on the synthetic capacity of the male accessory gland (Kaulenas, unpubl.). These results confirm earlier reports in *Acheta* that allatectomy does not appear to affect accessory gland function (Beck, quoted by Loher 1974). A similar situation appears to exist in *Leucophaea* (Scharrer 1946). Apparently, whatever the final-molt associated signal may be, it entails a sequence of developmental events which occur autonomously from that point. In fact, the protein synthetic capacity of the accessory glands is a very stable character, since it continues unchanged even in senescent crickets (Burns and Kaulenas 1979).

The major function of the accessory gland is the formation of the spermatophore. In crickets the spermatophore is a rather complex structure, which may be correlated with the complexity of the accessory gland. The spermatophore is built up of multiple chambers, is equipped with an endogenous mechanism for moving the sperm into the female's spermatheca, provides a stable sealed environment for the sperm for extended periods, and is sufficiently strong and resistant to dessication to survive being "lumped" around by the female for what may be several hours (Khalifa 1949). On top of these qualities, it is capable of being formed rapidly from presynthesized material, using a fairly simple mold. As pointed out by Pustell (1979), many related insects have managed to avoid most of these problems; for instance, in the Acrididae the spermatophore functions essentially as an extension of the intromittent organ. It is formed during copulation and is retained almost entirely within the body, avoiding most of the problems of dessication, wear, sperm survival, and even propulsive force, which is either supplied by the sperm themselves or by the male musculature. The simple spermatophore of the Blattidae is protected by the enlarged subgenital plate of the female, and the sperm move under their own power (Khalifa 1950). By adopting a disposable packaging approach the crickets seem to have maximized some of their problems. Despite these problems the group is clearly successful, and the solution seems to have been an increased complexity of the cricket accessory gland.

4.3.2 Lepidoptera

The general arrangement for the Lepidopteran accessory gland/ejaculatory duct complex is illustrated in Fig. 29. The elongated duct system communicates with paired or single testes via paired vasa deferentia. The seminal vesicle(s) may be a dilation of the upper or lower vas deferens or the upper ejaculatory duct. The accessory glands may be fused over some portion of their length, while the ejaculatory duct is often divided into a single proximal region (simplex) and paired distal portions (duplex), which connect to the accessory glands.

In contrast to the Orthoptera, there are no multiple tubules in the accessory gland; however, both the accessory gland and the ejaculatory duct are longitudinally differentiated into distinct regions. Riemann and Thorson (1979b) describe five regions in the accessory glands of *Anagasta*, based on differences in cell morphology and the appearance of the secretory material in the lumen. Most of the epithelium is made up of two general cell types, although the most anterior region consists of a single cell type only. The cells in the anterior region and one class in each of the other four regions are typical exocrine cells with extensive rough endoplasmic reticulum.

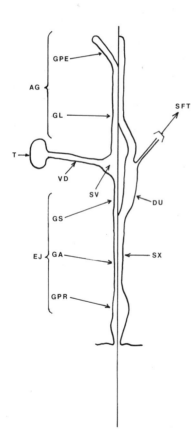

Fig. 29. Summary diagram of the lepidopteran accessory gland/ejaculatory duct complex. The condition in *Bombyx mori* is depicted on the *left*. The *right* portion of the figure summarizes the situation in *Anagasta kuhniella* (Riemann and Thorson 1979b) *Calpodes ethlius* (Lai-Fook 1982c); and *Lymantria dispar* (Giebultowicz et al. 1988). These moths differ largely in the location of the seminal vesicle, which is located in the upper ejaculatory duct in *Anagasta*, in the lower vas deferens in *Calpodes* and in the upper vas deferens in *Lymantria*. *AG* Accessory gland; *DU* duplex; *EJ* ejaculatory duct. *GPE, GL, GS, GA, GPR* Glands pellucida, lacteola, spermatophorae, alba and prostatica, respectively. *SFT* Leading to a single fused testis; *SV* seminal vesicle; *SX* simplex; *T* testis; *VD* vas deferens

Secretion is primarily via Golgi-derived vesicles. The second class of cells are foliate cells, which are found in the four posterior segments of the gland. These cells are characterized by long apical projections extending into the lumen. The projections contain large quantities of glycogen and much membranous material, which may form multilayered whorls. The apical portions of the foliate cells become detached during copulation and form a part of the ejaculate. Histochemical studies indicate that the proteins, especially basic proteins and carbohydrates, are the main secretory products (Hong 1977).

A very similar structural arrangement has been described for *Calpodes* (Lai-Fook 1982c). Six distinct regions are recognized in the accessory gland, and, as in *Anagasta*, two cell types are distinguishable. One type is a typical merocrine secretory cell, while the other type is an apocine secretory cell with highly modified mitochondria and an apical region filled with glycogen and organelles. The epithelium of the duplex portion of the ejaculatory duct is also secretory; the lumen contains not only its own secretions but also those from the vasa defferentia, as well as apyrene sperm and eupyrene sperm bundles. The long simplex in *Calpodes* is separated by distinct constrictions into seven segments; two of the segments can be further subdivided on the basis of cellular structure or secretory product appearance (Lai-Fook 1982b). Merocrine and apocrine secretory cells are again present. The membranous contribution of the apocrine cells, probably in both *Calpodes* and *Anagasta*, appear to make major contributions to the walls of the spermatophores. The merocrine secretory cells in all the segments have highly developed rough endoplasmic reticulum, numerous Golgi and mitochondria, and a microvillate apical surface. Nevertheless, cells of different segments are distinguishable either by some feature of their structure or their secretions. All of the segments are surrounded by two layers of muscle and are supplied with tracheoles and nerves.

A similar design pattern is found for the male duct systems in other Lepidoptera (*Bombyx*, Omura 1938; *Acroplepia*, Thibout 1971; *Lymantria*, Giebultowicz et al. 1988). It is clear that there is substantial regional specialization in the production of secretory products along the length of the duct complex. However, correlations between secretion types and regions have been largely histochemical and ultrastructural. There is scope for more detailed biochemical analysis, especially with regard to structural proteins of the spermatophore.

The lepidopteran spermatophore is generally formed in the bursa copulatrix of the female during mating. In *Bombyx* the various regional secretions and the seminal fluid are transferred to the female as partially mixed, viscous streams and are used to construct the spermatophore. The latter is made up of a four-layered wall, an inner and outer matrix, and a soft plug (Osanai et al. 1987). The glandular sources of some of these components have been identified. For example, the inner matrix contains seminal fluid (containing the apyrene and eupyrene sperm bundles) and the secretion from the prostatica region of the ejaculatory duct. The glycogen-rich outer matrix is derived from the secretion of the lacteal portion of the accessory gland as well as the prostatica region of the ejaculatory duct (Kasuga et al. 1985). In addition, at least in *Spodoptera*, the structural proteins of the spermatophore, possibly including collagen, are cross-linked after assembly (Naron et al. 1983).

Moth spermatophores are important sites for the terminal stages of sperm maturation. Two types of sperm are produced in the testis: (1) the nonnucleate, apyrene sperm; and (2) the nucleated eupyrene sperm. Both are formed as bundles or cysts of sperm, with 256 spermatozoa per cyst, each derived from a single spermatogonium. The apyrene sperm bundles break down as they leave the testis; the eupyrene bundles remain intact up to the spermatophore stage in the bursa copulatrix (Kasuga and Osanai 1984). Both apyrene and eupyrene sperm acquire motility in the spermatophore, as a result of the action of an activating factor, derived from the prostatica region of the ejaculatory duct (Shepherd 1974). The apyrenes in the spermatophore seem to act as "stirring bars" to promote the dissociation of the eupyrene bundles (Katsuno 1977). The liberated and activated eupyrene sperm then use a spermatophore-provided energy source to migrate to the receptaculum seminis of the female. This occurs after a portion of the inner matrix is digested, again by spermatophore-provided enzymes, to open a route for sperm migration.

Part of the energy source for sperm movement must be provided by the breakdown of the large amounts of glycogen derived from the accessory gland-ejaculatory duct complex of the male. An additional energy source is provided by the action of an unusual metabolic pathway which converts arginine to 2-oxoglutarate. The enzymes for the arginine degradation cascade are part of the materials supplied to the spermatophore by the male (Osanai et al. 1986a, 1987). In this pathway, free arginine is hydrolyzed by arginase to ornithine and urea (Aigaki and Osanai 1985). The ornithine is then metabolized to glutamate, which undergoes an amino transfer reaction with pyruvate (produced via glycolysis) to yield alanine and 2-oxyglutarate. This member of the Krebs cycle serves as the preferred energy source for sperm motility (Osanai et al. 1987). The various substrates and enzymes in this cascade are produced at separate portions of the male reproductive glands and mix only on the formation of the spermatophore. For example, high levels of arginase (Aigaki and Osanai 1985) and L-alanine-glutamate transferase are located in the vesicula seminalis (Osanai and Chen 1987). The free arginine is produced by the sequential action of an endopeptidase and an exopeptidase obtained from the accessory glands. An endopeptidase, which cleaves proteins on the carboxyl-side of arginine, has been located as a product of the prostatica portion of the ejaculatory duct (Aigaki et al. 1987). The endopeptidase has been named initiatorin. A carboxypeptidase, which is initially formed as an inactive zymogen, is produced by many regions of the male duct system (Aigaki et al. 1988). This enzyme, in its active form, liberates free arginine from peptides generated from basic proteins by initiatorin (Kasuga et al. 1987). The interplay of the various accessory gland and ejaculatory duct components which delivers functional sperm to the female in Lepidoptera is rather complex, and, moreover, very substantially different from the mechanisms adopted by the Orthoptera. A spermatophore component which does have its equivalent in Orthoptera is an oviposition stimulating factor described for *Bombyx* (Yamaoka and Hirao 1977). The chemical identity of this factor has not been characterized in detail.

A rather peculiar component of the accessory glands has been described for the giant silkmoth, *Hyalophora cecropia*. This product is juvenile hormone, initially described by Williams (1956) as a massive storage component in male abdomens. Juvenile hormone accumulation begins at about the time of eclosion (Gilbert and Schneiderman 1961). Shirk et al. (1976) later showed that almost all of the juvenile hormone is found in the accessory glands. It should be noted that in *H. cecropia*, juvenile hormone is not involved in the regulation of any aspect of spermatogenesis or accessory gland function (nor, in females, in the control of vitellogenesis or mating). The male corpora allata lack juvenile-hormone acid methyl transferase activity and secrete juvenile hormone acids (Shirk et al. 1983a). The methyltransferase activity is confined to the accessory glands. It is probable that male corpora allata secrete juvenile hormone acids, which are then methylated and stored by the accessory glands. The massive accessory gland storage of juvenile hormone is found only in *H. cecropia* and a few closely related species (Gilbert and Schneiderman 1961) and is as enigmatic as the massive accumulation of cGMP in *Acheta*, described above. It is of interest, however, that in *Manduca sexta*, and other moths, male corpora allata also lack juvenile hormone acid methyltransferase and produce juvenile hormone acid (Bhaskaran et al. 1988). Female corpora allata, however, can produce juvenile hormones. In such cases, male but not female reproductive tract tissue contain juvenile hormone acid methyltransferase activity. In the case of the *cecropia* moth, a characteristic feature of Lepidopteran males seems to have been amplified to levels way beyond normal bounds, producing a rather puzzling phenotype.

While juvenile hormone has no influence on the differentiation or function of the accessory gland complex in *H. cecropia* this is by no means the case in all Lepidoptera. In the monarch butterfly (*Danaus plexippus*; Herman 1975; Lessman et al. 1982) and other species (*Nymphalis antiopa*; Herman and Bennett 1975), juvenile hormone has at least quantitative effects on accessory gland function. Other hormonal effects influencing accessory gland development, include a necessary exposure to an ecdysteroid peak during the pupal period in *Bombyx* to ensure normal growth of the male reproductive organs (Shinbo and Happ 1989). In this regard, it is of interest that in the gypsy moth (*Lymantria dispar*), once the differentiation of the reproductive tract has been completed, a decline in ecdysterone titer is necessary for initiation of the rhythmic release of sperm from the testis in the adult male (Giebultowicz et al. 1990).

4.3.3 Coleoptera

Variations in the gross morphology of the Coleopteran accessory glands and efferent duct systems are illustrated in Fig. 30. The accessory gland may consist of a single pair of simple tubes (*Zygogramma*, Gerber et al. 1978; *Popillia*, Anderson 1950; *Leptinotrasa*, DeLoof and Lagasse 1972), two pairs of glands of different complexity (*Tenebrio*, Frenk and Happ 1976), three pairs of glands, which may be tubular (*Lytta*, Gerber et al. 1971a), or of more complex morphology (*Bruchidius*, Glitho and Huignard 1990), up to five pairs of glands of variable complexity (*Acanthoscelides*, Huignard 1975; Cassier and Huignard 1979).

All of the accessory glands have a similar basic organization: a thin connective envelope around the outside of the gland, muscle layer, an epithelium of varying thickness and a lumen, which, depending on physiological state, may be empty or filled with secretions. The epithelial cells generally display an ultrastructural morphology characteristic of protein/glycoprotein secretory cells, with abundant rough endoplasmic reticulum, Golgi complexes, and varying amounts of microvilli at their apical surfaces. They differ in the degree of intra- and interglandular specialization for the synthesis of different secretory products. These differences have been identi-

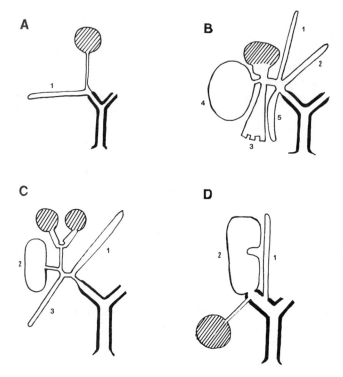

Fig. 30A-D. Diagrammatic representation of the range of morphological variation in coleopteran male accessory glands. Based on the descriptions of: **A** Gerber et al. (1978) for *Zygogramma. 1* A single unbranched accessory gland. **B** Huignard (1975) for *Acanthoscelides. 1* External median; *2* internal media; *3* tubular; *4* lateral; *5* inferior gland. **C** Glitho and Huignard (1990) for *Bruchidius. 1* Median; *2* ovoid lateral; *3* tubular lateral gland. **D** Dailey et al. (1980) for *Tenebrio.* 1 Tubular; 2 bean-shaped accessory glands. *Cross-hatched areas* testis

fied by a number of approaches, ranging from histochemical techniques to in situ immunochemistry using monoclonal antibodies for specific gland products.

The simplest case is that found in *Leptinotarsa*, where the secretory cells of the single pair of epithelial tubular glands all seem to be involved in the production of a neutral mucopolysaccharide-protein complex. No regional differentiation can be distinguished, either in the gland cell morphology or in the appearance of the luminal secretory products (DeLoof and Lagasse 1972). In other cases where a single pair of tubular accessory glands are found, there may be a differentiation of the gland into different zones, with distinctive cellular cytologies and different characteristics for the secretory products (*Popillia*, Anderson 1950).

This somewhat dissonant theme is played out further in *Tenebrio*, with two pairs of morphologically distinct glands. The tubular glands, which are composed of a secretory epithelium surrounded by a thin muscular sheath, do not appear to be regionally differentiated, either in cell structure or the appearance of the product. Each secretory cell has a distinct morphology, with a basal zone containing rough

146

endoplasmic reticulum and Golgi complexes, an intermediate zone in which secretory vesicles are the dominant components, and an apical region characterized by microvilli and other irregular protrusions of the plasma membrane (Gadzama et al. 1977). While there is no discernible regional differentiation in the tubular glands, their synthetic products are rather complex (Happ et al. 1977; Black et al. 1982; Grimnes and Happ 1985; Black and Happ 1985), and contribute to spermatophore contents rather than to structural components.

The bean-shaped gland products in *Tenebrio* form the spermatophore. All cells in the secretory epithelium are long and narrow and show the typical ultrastructures of protein-exporting cells. In this gland, seven to eight secretory cell types can be distinguished on the basis of variations in ultrastructure or the morphology of their secretory granules (Dailey et al. 1980; Dailey and Happ 1983). A three-dimensional map of the location of the various cell types in the bean-shaped gland has been constructed (Dailey et al. 1980). The secretions of these distinctive cell types form separate layers in a secretory plug. During mating, this plug is transferred into the ejaculatory duct by contractions of the muscular sheath. The products of the two bean-shaped glands fuse to give the walls of the spermatophore. The time course of spermatophore formation is very rapid in *Tenebrio*, on the order of minutes. This contrasts with a prolonged copulation period in many other Coleoptera; at least 3 h in the cockchafer (*Melolontha*; Landa 1960) and 8–10 h in *Lytta* (Gerber et al. 1971a).

The regional specificity in the synthetic repertoire of the bean-shaped gland of *Tenebrio* has been confirmed by the use of monoclonal antibodies against specific spermatophore proteins. For example, antibody produced by a hybridoma clone labeled as PL 3.4 recognized protein present in only one (type 3) of the eight cell types of the gland. This protein was also present in the secretory product and in discrete layers in the spermatophore. Two antigens are recognized by this antibody; they are of 29.4 and 27.6 kD in molecular weight in gland extracts, but are of 25.1 and 23.5 kD in the spermatophore, suggesting that processing of the proteins occurs during or after secretion (Grimnes and Happ 1986). Another monoclonal (PL 6.3) recognized a 9.6 kD protein, which was localized by immunohistochemistry in cell type 7 and at lower concentrations in cell type 5. The PL 6.3 antigen was concentrated in the secretory granules characteristic of these two cell types, but not detectable in any other cell type (Grimnes et al. 1986). Both PL 3.4 and PL 6.3 antigens remain as coherent, distinct masses on secretion, and appear to flow as part of an ordered array of secretions into the ejaculatory duct, and finally, give rise to specific layers in the spermatophore.

Using yet another monoclonal antibody (PL 21.1), against a different spermatophore protein, as an indicator of purification, Shinbo et al. (1987) have isolated and partially characterized a protein of 23 kD, which in the native state may exist as a 16-mer of 370 kD. The protein has a very high proline content (25.2%), as do other insect structural proteins, such as oothecins and some chorion proteins. Presumably, sequencing of this protein will permit more detailed inferences on its interactions with other components of the spermatophore.

The products of other complex accessory glands in beetles have not been characterized in any great detail to date. For example, the tripartite accessory gland of *Bruchidius* produces secretions made up of granules of variable shape and size, with electron-dense cortical regions. The two pairs of lateral glands secrete a fine granular material with several electron-dense globules (Glitho and Huignard 1990). No other information on the nature of these secretions is available; although gel electrophoretic separation of spermatophore proteins of another Bruchid beetle has been reported (Boucher and Huignard 1987). In *Acanthoscelides*, analysis of spermatophore proteins by one-dimensional gel electrophoresis shows that presence of about 12 major bands (Huignard and Lamy 1972). Substantial changes in the proteins of the spermatophore occur after its transfer to the female.

A number of aspects involved in the terminal differentiation of the accessory gland in *Tenebrio* have been investigated in some detail by Happ's group (see references below). The relevant time period is from pupal ecdysis, through the 9 days or so of the pupal stage, the imaginal ecdysis and up to about the sixth or seventh day of the adult stage. At pupal ecdysis, each pair of accessory glands, the BAG/TAG pair, "looks something like a pair of mittens, lying side by side with the thumbs inward" (Happ et al. 1982). Both types of gland are mesodermally derived, differentiating from a mesodermal pouch near the ninth sternite of the last instar larva (Huet 1966). Throughout the pupal stage and for the first week of adult life the glands grow in size, exponentially increasing their volume approximately tenfold over this period. The growth during the pupal stage is the result of cell division; cell numbers triple in the bean-shaped gland, while in the tubular glands the increase is 14-fold (Happ et al. 1985). Two mitotic maxima are detectable for each gland. The first occurs at days 1–2 of pupal development, and in vitro studies indicate that it is independent of concurrent hormonal influences (Szopa et al. 1985). The second mitotic "peak" occurs at day 4 and in vivo correspond to a major ecdysteroid peak (Delbecque et al. 1978). In-vitro experiments show that the second mitotic peak requires a physiological level of ecdysterone (Szopa et al. 1985). The hormone appears to act on some control point in the G_2 phase of the cell cycle, stimulating the transition of cells from G_2 and S to the G_1 phase (Yaginuma et al. 1988).

Other components increasing exponentially in the bean-shaped glands during the pupal-early adult period are RNA and protein. RNA increases about tenfold, before leveling off at about day 3 of the adult stage. Clearly, the bulk of this RNA must be ribosomal, and the increase is correlated with the expansion of the rough endoplasmic reticulum during this period as the secretory machinery of the epithelial cells matures (Grimes and Happ 1980). The protein changes have been analyzed in some detail by one- and two-dimensional gel electrophoresis (Happ et al. 1982), and by the use of monoclonal antibodies against spermatophore proteins (Grimnes and Happ 1986). The two-dimensional gel analysis shows over 40 proteins that appear to be differentiation-specific and are most probably secretory products. The appearance of these proteins is not totally synchronized; for example, the protein identified by the PL 6.3 monoclonal antibody appears first in the day-2 adult and reaches a maximum by day 8 (Grimnes et al. 1986). The protein identified by the PL 21.1 monoclonal antibody is first detectable in the day-8 pupa, reaches peak concentration in day-2 adult and then declines in later adult stages (Shinbo et al. 1987). The PL 3.4 antibody first detects a protein only at day 4 of adult development, with maximum levels at day 8 (Grimnes and Happ 1986).

The studies showing that different differentiation-specific proteins are produced by different types of secretory cells, also reveal an interesting adjustment of the cell phenotype (Dailey and Happ 1983). Secretory cells of each type occur in distinct

148

patches, and as the cells mature, unusual, short-lived cells appear in regions between different patches. These boundary cells can display secretory product morphologies that are mixtures of characteristics found in adjacent cell types. The transitional cell types disappear by three to four days after eclosion. Dailey and Happ (1983) suggest that a common synchronizing signal coordinates the maturation of all eight secretory cell types at or just after the imaginal molt. This signal is probably not ecdysone; whatever it is, it seems to trigger the final transition between the determined or committed state and the differentiated state. The presence of the intermediate, boundary cells suggests that cell-cell interactions may be required to stabilize a given differentiated phenotype.

The differentiated cell phenotype, including the secretory cell morphology and the synthesis of export proteins, appears to be dependent on the occurrence of the ecdysterone peak about halfway through pupal development. The hormone, therefore, controls not only the last wave of mitoses, but differentiation as well. Dependence of differentiation on 20-hydroxyecdysone can also be demonstrated in vitro. Organ cultures of young pupal accessory glands failed to differentiate in the absence of the hormone, but differentiated when 20-hydroxyecdysone was added to the culture medium (Grimnes and Happ 1987). Presumably, as in other systems of this sort, the ecdysterone stimulus must occur in the absence of juvenile hormone; although no definitive information on this is available for *Tenebrio*. In fact, the overall role of juvenile hormone in this system has not been defined. As discussed earlier, in some Orthoptera, juvenile hormone plays a role in the adult, at least on quantitative levels of differentiation-related protein expression. It appears that juvenile hormone does play some role in the regulation of protein secretory activity in some beetles. For example, in *Leptinotarsa*, allatectomy leads to the degeneration of some accessory gland cells, while others assume characteristics of diapausing cells (DeLoof and Lagasse 1972). Presumably, in this insect, the presence of juvenile hormone is necessary to maintain protein secretory activity.

Other work on *Leptinotarsa* strongly suggests that not all of the secretory polypeptides originate in the male accessory gland. Of the 50 or so proteins secreted by the gland, 2 appear to have their origin in the fat body. Neither of these proteins can be labeled during in-vitro incubation of accessory glands, although all of the other proteins can, and the immunostaining evidence for their extra-glandular origin is convincing (Peferoen and DeLoof 1984). There is some evidence that one of these proteins is a juvenile hormone-carrier protein (Kramer and DeKort 1978). Whether this means that the role played by this protein is related to juvenile hormone regulation of the gland or that it serves in the secretion or elimination of juvenile hormone, as in *Hyalophora cecropia* (Dahm et al. 1976), is unknown at present.

As discussed earlier with regard to the Acrididae (Friedel and Gillott 1977), there is some evidence that in some beetles a portion of the spermatophore contents end up in the female hemolymph. For example, in *Acanthoscelides*, both radioactivity from labeled spermatophores (Huignard 1978) and immunologically identifiable accessory gland proteins (Huignard 1983) reach the female hemolymph. Some of the radioactivity ends up in the oocytes, though no male antigens could be detected in ovaries. A similar situation has been described in *Caryedon* (Boucher and Huignard 1987), and the latter authors suggest that the male secretions constitute an important trophic contribution that increases female fecundity and vitellogenesis. The evidence for the transfer of male proteins to the female hemolymph is strong. However, the evidence for any trophic function is unconvincing. In *Acanthoscelides*, the radioactivity associated with one spermatophore is 7000 disintegration/min (Huignard 1983). At a specific activity of 45–60 mCi/mmol for the labeled arginine, this represents the transfer of about 0.01 µg of labeled arginine per spermatophore. Without the knowledge of the precursor pool specific activities, of course, it is impossible to translate this into protein weights. But by analogy to other systems (Bar-Zev 1973), if one were to assume that endogenous pools dilute the isotope by between 10^3 and 10^4, and that arginine constitutes 10% of the spermatophore proteins, an estimate for the quantity of protein per spermatophore would be in the range of 0.1–1 mg. If 20% of this is used to produce eggs, as suggested by Huignard's (1983) figures, then the distribution of 20–200 µg of protein among the several hundred eggs produced by the female after mating probably does not represent a serious contribution to the female's protein budget. It has been suggested by Boucher and Huignard (1987) and by Boggs and Watt (1981) that the trophic contribution from the male is only important in times of nutritional stress. However, it should be noted that the usual response of insects to such conditions is the resorption of the oocytes (Bell and Bohm 1975). Among the events which may be regulated or affected by the transferred substances are oogenesis and oviposition (Huignard 1969, 1974). It seems highly likely that "aphrodisiac" (Mann 1984) rather than gustatory properties of male accessory gland secretions may be of greater importance. The role of the transferred proteins may well be hormonal rather than subserving some bulk function.

4.3.4 Diptera

Most Diptera do not make definitive spermatophores, although these structures have been described in five families, including the Simuliidae (Linley and Simmons 1983), the Chironomidae (Nielsen 1959), and the Glossinidae, the tsetse flies (Pollock 1970). In other Diptera, mating plugs, which may represent modified spermatophores (Mann 1984), are often secreted, or, as in *Drosophila*, the sperm, at the time of ejaculation, may be enveloped in a membranous sac, formed by the accessory glands (Fowler 1973). With respect to accessory gland and ejaculatory duct structure and function in the Diptera, by far the most information is available on *Drosophila* and will be considered separately.

4.3.4.1 Drosophila

The morphology of the accessory glands and the ejaculatory duct in *Drosophila* varies slightly between different species (Chen 1984), but basically the system consist of paired, tubular accessory glands discharging into the ampullary portion of the ejaculatory duct, which in turn opens into a muscular ejaculatory bulb. The epithelia of the ejaculatory duct and the accessory glands are secretory, and are surrounded by a muscle sheath. In the accessory glands two main types of secretory cells are found: (1) hexagonal, binucleate "main" cells, which, as the name implies, comprise over 90% of the epithelium; and (2) larger, vacuolated "secondary" cells, containing

150

large, oblong, secretory granules. These cells are found mainly in the distal portion of the gland (Bairati 1968). About 70% of the volume of the secondary cells is occupied by the fused, filament-containing granules, with the filaments assuming a partially twisted shape. In the main cells, the rough endoplasmic reticulum has a labyrinth form; in the gland lumen there is a massive accumulation of a flocculent secretion (Federer and Chen 1982).

The accessory gland products include a mixture of proteins, some of them in aggregate or vesicular form, peptides, amino acids and carbohydrates. Together with the secretions of the ejaculatory duct and ejaculatory bulb, they form a part of the seminal fluid transferred to the female during mating. A large number of functions have been demonstrated or suggested for the male efferent duct products. These functions include the protection and stabilization of sperm and the provision of a suitable medium for sperm fertility and mobilization. The key role of accessory gland secretions in sperm transfer was clearly demonstrated by some early experiments of Lefevre and Jonsson (1962). Males become sterile after repeated matings despite the fact that large numbers of sperm are still available. The key variable is that the accessory gland products are exhausted. Fertility is restored when accessory gland secretions are replenished. In addition, the efferent duct secretions regulate female reproductive behavior, and possibly serve as a nutrient source.

The protein products have been characterized in some detail, although the function for most of them have not been defined. Two dimensional gel electrophoretic analysis of paragonial proteins after in vitro ^{35}S-methionine labeling, resolves about 1200 protein species. The in vitro labeling procedure detects all of the proteins labeled in vivo, but is more sensitive. Interestingly, none of these major protein species can be assigned to genes on the Y chromosome (Ingham-Baker and Candido 1980). While most of these proteins are of the nonexport variety, at least 85 types can be assigned to the secretory class and can be identified as components of the accessory gland lumen (Stumm-Zollinger and Chen 1985). There is a substantial amount of genetic polymorphism in the gland-specific proteins. Crossing between different strains has shown codominant expression of these variants, suggesting mutations in the structural genes (Coulthart and Singh 1988). Since the polymorphic loci have no detectable effect on sperm fertility within the same species, there must be substantial tolerance for genetic variation of the proteins involved in this aspect of the reproductive process (Whalen and Wilson 1986). Besides the accessory gland products, the secretion of the ejaculatory duct contains a distinct complement of proteins, although of much lesser complexity (Stumm-Zollinger and Chen 1985).

Possibly consistent with the high degree of intraspecific polymorphism for the accessory gland proteins, these secretory products have also been shown to be highly variable between species (Chen 1976; Chen et al. 1985), suggesting a very rapid evolutionary divergence for most of them. In fact, Fuyama (1983) has concluded from the results of mating experiments that the secretory proteins act as isolating factors in the interspecific cross of *D. pulchrella* female × *D. suzuki* male. It appears that the seminal fluid of *D. suzuki* is incapable of stimulating ovulation in *D. pulchrella* females; although, if such females are injected with a male extract from their own species following copulation with *D. suzuki* males, viable hybrid progeny are obtained. The following conclusions are reasonable: (1) there has been a rapid divergence between the species in the factor(s) which stimulates ovulation; (2) that, otherwise, the genetic incompatibility between these two species is probably small; and (3) the change in the specificity of the ovulation stimulating factor acts as an isolating mechanism in interspecific crosses. Similar observations have been made for crosses between the closely related species of *D. melanogaster, D. simulans,* and *D. mauritiana* (Stumm-Zollinger and Chen 1988).

A number of additional peptides, which were not resolved in the electrophoretic analyses of the accessory gland proteins discussed above, have been characterized in some detail. In *D. melanogaster,* Chen et al. (1988) have purified an accessory gland peptide which represses female sexual receptivity and stimulates oviposition. The purified peptide shows the same activity when injected into virgin females as it does on normal transfer during copulation (Chen et al. 1988); although its effect on sexual receptivity after injection is shorter than observed under normal conditions (Manning 1967). Analysis of the nucleotide sequence of the cDNA representing the mRNA for this peptide, as well as amino acid sequencing of the purified peptide, shows that it consists of 36 amino acids. The *D. melanogaster* peptide is also active in *D. simulans, D. mauritiana* and *D. sechellia,* where it also suppresses sexual receptivity and induces ovulation in virgin females. However, it has no effect in the more distantly related *D. funebris;* in this organism at least two peptides have been described, PS1 influences the receptivity of virgin females, while PS2 stimulates oviposition (Baumann 1974a,b). The amino acid sequence of PS1 has been determined and is unrelated to the *D. melanogaster* active material (Baumann et al. 1975). In comparison to the *D. melanogaster* peptide, the *D. funebris* material is of rather low activity, indicating that additional components may well be involved in generating the behavioral and physiological responses. In *D. melanogaster,* the single peptide appears to be involved in influencing both responses in the female, since, apart from the removal of the signal peptide, there seems to be no further proteolytic processing of the remaining material (Chen et al. 1988).

The female sexual receptivity response is rather complex and the peptide described by Chen et al. (1988) is unlikely to be the only active component. An enzyme secreted by the epithelium of the ejaculatory duct, esterase 6, also appears to play an important role (Richmond and Senior 1981). This enzyme is transferred to the female during copulation where it interacts with another component of the seminal fluid, *cis*-vaccenyl acetate [which is produced by the epithelium of the ejaculatory bulb (Brieger and Butterworth 1970)] to yield *cis*-vaccenyl alcohol (Mane et al. 1983). This alcohol, or some derivative, seems to act as an antiaphrodisiac, decreasing courtship behavior in the females. The courtship behavior can be further dissected into two components: (1) the female's attractiveness to males, which remains unaffected; and (2) female receptivity to further mating, which is inhibited (Burnett et al. 1973; Scott 1986). Esterase-6 itself may have multiple functions, since it has also been implicated in affecting sperm motility (Gilbert 1981). Similar β-esterases, produced by the ejaculatory bulb, have been described for *D. mulleri,* where the enzymes may be involved in supplying energy for sperm motility by metabolism of ejaculate lipids (Johnson and Beale 1968). Among other possible contributors to energy metabolism may be the high levels of glutamic acid produced by the accessory glands and transferred to the female in *D. nigromelanica* (Chen and Oechslin 1976). This component constitutes up to 70% of total free ninhydrin-positive material in the paragonia, and is associated with a high activity of accessory gland L-alanine aminotransferase (Chen and Baker 1976). While possible functions as a neurotransmitter cannot be ruled out, its vast accumulation in the seminal fluid of this, and not other species of *Drosophila*, indicate a more prosaic function in general intermediary metabolism.

Among other secretory components of the male accessory glands in *D. melanogaster* are the products of two tightly-linked genes which produce two proteins: msP 355a and msP 355b. The latter is a small, acidic, secreted protein, while the former has prohormonelike characteristics, with a region in which 11 or 17 amino acids are identical to the *Aplysia* egg-laying hormone (Monsma and Wolfner 1988). Sequence conservation between the molluscan and insect proteins may indicate common functions. The msP 355a sequence contains, in addition to a number of glycosylation signals, five pairs of basic amino acids. Paired basic residues of this type are commonly used as cleavage signals in the proteolytic processing of polyprotein precursors (Bond and Butler 1987). The msP 355a peptide undergoes a change in mobility by the end of mating, and it is possible that it is cleaved in the female genital tract to give physiologically active peptides. The relationship between this material and the peptide described by Chen et al. (1988) is unclear. The sequence of a small accessory gland export protein, msP 316, has been reported as well (DiBenedetto et al. 1990). The function of this basic, 52-amino acid protein has not been defined.

Other identified components of the seminal fluid include glucose oxidase, secreted by ejaculatory duct epithelium (Cavener 1980). There are a number of different types of this enzyme; one type yields H_2O_2 as a by-product of glucose oxidation. The initial suggestion was that the peroxide may be an important antibacterial or anti-fungal agent. However, later work suggests that the type of enzyme produced by the ejaculatory duct does not generate peroxide, and possibly the enzyme functions as a key link in general, energy-yielding metabolism (Cavener and MacIntyre 1983). Glucose oxidase is interesting from another perspective, since during the pupal stage it is expressed in both sexes, while in the adult it is limited to male ejaculatory duct. Such a switch from general to sex-limited expression is rare, and analysis of the regulatory regions of the gene would be of great interest.

Lastly, the transfer to the female via the ejaculate of methionine, in the form of the free amino acid, and in small peptides and proteins, has been documented in *D. melanogaster* and *D. pseudoobscura* by Bownes and Partridge (1987), who suggest that the transferred methionine may play a role in female nutrition. Clearly, this role cannot be a quantitative one, since the total protein of a pair of accessory glands is equivalent to that found in only five eggs, and only a small percentage of labeled methionine from the glands ends up in the female. However, when nutrient supply is low, it is possible that shortages in specific amino acids could affect female fecundity and fertility. Current experiments have not established decisively just how significant these effects may be.

A number of the genes for accessory gland male specific transcripts have been mapped, either by analysis of electrophoretic variants (Whalen and Wilson 1986), or by in situ hybridization, using genomic clones as probes (Schäfer 1986a). All of the genes mapped so far are autosomal; the loci are dispersed on the second and third chromosomes. The genes for the proteins msP 316 (DiBenedetto et al. 1990) and msP

355a and 355b (Monsma and Wolfner 1988) have been cloned and sequenced. The sequence of a cDNA complementary to the mRNA for a 36-amino-acid export peptide has also been published (Chen et al. 1988).

The genes coding for msP 355a and msP 355b show a rather unusual organization: the first nucleotide of the transcript mst 355b is located only 20 nucleotides downstream from the mst 355a polyadenylation site. The transcriptional control elements for mst 355b, therefore, are probably located in the coding region of mst 355a. The mst 355b transcription unit also does not appear to have a functional TATA element. All three genes (mst 316, mst 355a and mst 355b) have a similar exon-intron arrangement. A short, 5'-exon, composed of the 5'-untranslated region and a short section of the open reading frame, is followed by an intron of a similar length, which is followed by a long 3'-exon, consisting of the remaining open reading frame and a 3'-untranslated region. All three genes possess a 10 bp, A-rich motif upstream from the transcription initiation sites, while the two tandem genes also have very similar, 20-bp elements, at similar positions further upstream. A possible role for such elements as tissue specific enhancers is likely, but has not been demonstrated yet.

The expression of all three of these genes is under the control of the sex determination regulatory hierarchy (see Chap. 2), since these genes are expressed in chromosomal females carrying mutant alleles at the *doublesex, intersex* or the *transformer-2* loci (Chapman and Wolfner 1988). Temperature shift experiments using $X/X; tra-2^{ts2}$ homozygotes indicate that there is a critical period during which the tissue sets or determines the future expression of these genes. This critical period is during the third larval instar, and coincides with the morphological determination of the glands. Temperature shifts in the $tra-2^{ts2}$ homozygote at the adult stage have no effect on the expression of these genes, indicating that once determination has occurred, continuous action of *tra-2* is not essential (DiBenedetto et al. 1987). Actual transcription of these genes does not begin until the late pupal stage. Translation is initiated even later, at least for mst 316. Using an mst 316-*lacZ* fusion protein, DiBenedetto et al. (1990) have demonstrated that the translation product is first detectable only after eclosion, and is synthesized exclusively by the "main" cells of the accessory gland.

Since the transcription of the accessory gland specific genes precedes the translation of the messages by some margin, a measure of translational-level control is implied. Observations that the mRNAs for the tissue specific products are of long half-life (von Wyl and Steiner 1977; Schmidt et al. 1985b) add additional weight to this interpretation. The trigger for initiating or increasing levels of translation could be related to levels of juvenile hormone. The observation that juvenile hormone III titer peaks at eclosion in *D. melanogaster* lends support to this suggestion (Bownes and Rembold 1987). Moreover, juvenile hormone also affects the expression of an ejaculatory duct product, esterase 6. Precocene (an antiallatotropin) treatment of adult males decreases the levels of this enzyme to 37% of controls (Stein et al. 1984).

Further analysis of the initial observation that copulation leads to a rapid increase in protein synthesis by the accessory glands (Baumann 1974a) supports the interpretation that juvenile hormone is involved in the regulation of protein synthesis in this gland. Schmidt et al. (1985b) have shown that, while the synthesis of secretory protein messages is not enhanced by copulation, the level of translation is. In addition, synthesis of ribosomal proteins and ribosomal RNA is enhanced after mating, leading to increased ribosomal levels (Schmidt et al. 1985a). Using an in vitro system, Yamamoto et al. (1988) have shown that juvenile hormone III can induce the copulation-mediated responses. The effect is mediated by calcium and protein kinase C. Stimulation of protein synthesis by juvenile hormone did not occur in glands from mutants deficient in protein kinase C activity. Juvenile hormone may act via the diacylglycerol pathway to elevate intracellular levels of Ca^{2+}, which in turn affect the intensity at which the accessory gland messages are translated.

4.3.4.2 Other Diptera

In Diptera other than *Drosophila*, three approaches to the production of male accessory materials have been described:

1. Accessory glands are present, and, among other functions, produce the components necessary for the formation of a spermatophore (e.g., *Culicoides melleus*; Linley 1981a).
2. Accessory glands are present and generally produce secretions which contribute to the formation of a mating plug, as well as substances capable of affecting the physiology of the female. No definitive spermatophore is formed (*Aedes* sp., Dapples et al. 1974; Ramalingam and Craig 1978; Adlakha and Pillai 1975, 1976; *Culex*, Young and Downie 1987, 1989).
3. No accessory glands are present; secretory cells of the ejaculatory duct produce a variety of components whose main function is to influence the physiology of the female (*Musca*, Riemann 1973; Schlein and Galum 1984; *Sarcophaga*, Morrison et al. 1982).

The accessory glands of various species can show considerable variation in size and shape, in the appearance of their secretory granules and in the arrangement of different secretory areas (Lum 1961; Ramalingam and Craig 1978; Linley 1981a). Generally, substantial amounts of rough endoplasmic reticulum are found at the base of the secretory cells, with the apical regions packed with granular material. The mode of secretion can be by exocytosis of the vesicular material, but more often occurs by the pinching off of the apical portions of the columnar secretory cells (apocrine type: e.g., *Aedes*, Dapples et al. 1974); or the lysis of entire cells (holocrine type: *Musca*, Riemann 1973).

The physiological functions ascribed to the secretions of the accessory glands or the ejaculatory duct among various species is rather diverse, but largely analogous to those described for *Drosophila*. These include (1) stimulation of oviposition (Leahy and Craig 1965); (2) refractoriness to further insemination (Crag 1967; Riemann and Thorson 1969); (3) enhancement of egg fertility (Adlakha and Pillai 1975); (4) regulation of blood intake in mosquitos (Adlakha and Pillai 1976), and other functions.

In general, the biochemical nature of the various secretory components has not been well characterized. In *Musca*, 12 low-molecular-weight peptides (650–4150 daltons) have been resolved by gel electrophoresis (Terranova et al. 1972). In mature flies, export protein synthesis in the ejaculatory ducts cannot be inhibited by actinomycin D treatment, suggesting that the mRNAs are long-lived (Leopold et al. 1971).

155

The material responsible for monocoitic behavior in *Musca* is probably a low-molec-ular-weight peptide (Nelson et al. 1969), a situation similar to that found for *Dro-sophila*. In mosquitos, the accessory gland component, termed "matrone", which stimulated egg laying and induced female monogamy, was initially described as consisting of two protein fractions (Fuchs et al. 1969; Fuchs and Hiss 1970), of rather high molecular weight (Williams et al. 1978). Later studies suggest that the mosquito accessory gland proteins are subject to aggregation, and that at least the factor suppressing female receptivity is actually a low-molecular-weight peptide (Young and Downie 1987, 1989). The mechanisms by which these materials act in influencing female behavior are not really understood. Synthesis of the accessory factors are probably under the control of juvenile hormone (Ramalingam and Craig 1977).

Chapter 5

Concluding Remarks

The development of the efferent accessory reproductive structures is reasonably well understood at the structural or morphological level across a broad range of insect types. Details of the molecular mechanisms involved in the developmental processes, and especially of the genetic control of gene expression, have been explored in a much more limited range of insect species. In fact, the identities of some of the genes involved in the control of sexually related differentiation are known only in *Drosophila*. This observation serves to emphasize just how much work on *Drosophila* dominates the literature on the topics covered by this monograph. Nearly 30% of the references cited here involve work on this single genus. It is clear that over 80 years of intensive effort in the field of genetic analysis has built up a cumulative body of knowledge on this organism that now allows the total range of modern molecular and genetic techniques to be brought to bear fully on various aspects of development, physiology, and structure.

The power of the molecular-genetic technology is such that there is a tendency to transfer to *Drosophila* the study of interesting problems originally identified in other insects, or even other invertebrates. While this can sometimes be done usefully, it is by no means universally the case. For instance, there appears to be no obvious equivalent in *Drosophila* to the subtle spatial patterning of gene expression found for some orthopteran male accessory glands. Definition, at the molecular level, of how such patterning is achieved would yield important insights into the fine control of gene expression. The key element in the *Drosophila* system, which permits the analysis of such problems, is the availability of P-element-mediated gene transfer, which allows the functional analysis of genes or gene elements. Unfortunately, the *Drosophila* P-elements do not function outside the genus. What would be extremely useful in this field is the development of a more universally applicable gene transfer system. Work on other mobile elements found in insect genomes, or possibly the construction of artificial, chimeric plasmids containing centromeric elements, might be very rewarding.

An interesting variation in emphasis is discernible in the literature covered by this Volume. In most cases the impetus behind the approach is to define the specific adaptations or variations in biochemistry, physiology, or morphology displayed by the system under study, largely for its "own sake" or stressing comparative aspects. In other cases, the major motivation appears to be to use the systems as models for basic problems in cell, molecular, or evolutionary biology. Some of these latter approaches have been very successful. For instance, analysis of the sequential gene expression patterns in follicle cells and the regulation of transcription in fat body of *Drosophila* have made a substantial impact on our understanding of how genes are controlled in eukaryotes. Other contributions to basic problems in evolutionary, cell and molecular biology, by the use of insect systems can be documented. Overall, the study of insect accessory reproductive systems, in one way or another, have made large contributions to various aspects of modern biology. There is no reason to think that these contributions will diminish in significance in the future.

References

Abu-Hakima R (1981) Vitellogenin synthesis induced in locust fat body by juvenile hormone analog in vitro. Experientia 37:1309–1311

Abu-Hakima R, Davey KG (1977) The action of juvenile hormone on the follicle cells of *Rhodnius prolixus* in vitro: the effect of colchicine and cytochalasin B. Gen Comp Endocrinol 32:360–370

Adams TS (1970) Ovarian regulation of the corpus allatum in the housefly, *Musca domestica*. J Insect Physiol 14:349–360

Adams TS (1976) The ovaries, ring gland and neurosecretion during the second gonotrophic cycle in the housefly. Gen Comp Endocrinol 30:69–76

Adams TS, Filipi PA (1983) Vitellin and vitellogenin concentrations during oogenesis in the first gonotrophic cycle of the housefly, *Musca domestica*. J Insect Physiol 29:723–733

Adams TS, Filipi PA (1988) Interaction between juvenile hormone, 20-hydroxyecdysone, the corpus cardiacum-allatum complex, and the ovaries in regulating vitellogenin levels in the housefly, *Musca domestica*. J Insect Physiol 34:11–19

Adiyodi KG (1968) Left colleterial proteins in the viviparous cockroach *Nauphoeta cinerea*. J Insect Physiol 14:309–316

Adlakha V, Pillai MKK (1975) Involvement of male accessory gland substance in the fertility of mosquitoes. J Insect Physiol 21:1453–1455

Adlakha V, Pillai MKK (1976) Role of male accessory gland substance in the regulation of blood intake by mosquitoes. J Insect Physiol 22:1441–1442

Agui N, Takahashi M, Wada Y, Izumi S, Tomino S (1985) The relationship between nutrition, vitellogenin, vitellin and ovarian development in the housefly, *Musca domestica* L. J Insect Physiol 31:715–722

Ahmed I, Gillott C (1982a) The spermatheca of *Melanoplus sanguinipes* (Fabr.). I. Morphology, histology, and histochemistry. Int J Invertebr Reprod 4:281–295

Ahmed I, Gillott C (1982b) The spermatheca of *Melanoplus sanguinipes* (Fabr.). II. Ultrastructure Int J Invertebr Reprod 4:297–309

Ai N, Komatsu S, Kubo I, Loher W (1986) Manipulation of prostaglandin-mediated oviposition after mating in *Teleogryllus commodus*. Int J Invertebr Reprod 10:33–42

Aigaki T, Osanai M (1985) Arginase activity in the silkworm, *Bombyx mori*: developmental profiles, tissue distribution and physiological role. J Comp Physiol B 155:653–657

Aigaki T, Kasuga H, Osanai M (1987) A specific endopeptidase, BAEE esterase, in the glandula prostatica of the male reproductive system of the silkworm, *Bombyx mori*. Insect Biochem 17:323–328

Aigaki T, Osanai M, Kasuga H (1988) Arginine carboxypeptidase activity in the male reproductive glands of the silkworm, *Bombyx mori*. Insect Biochem 18:295–298

Alonso MC, Cabrera CV (1988) The *achaete-scute* gene complex of *Drosophila melanogaster* comprises four homologous genes. EMBO J 7:2585–2591

Ambrosio L, Schedl P (1984) Gene expression during Drosophila melanogaster oogenesis: Analysis by in situ hybridization to tissue sections. Dev Biol 105:80–92

Amrein H, Gorman M, Nöthiger R (1988) The sex-determining gene *tra-2* of Drosophila encodes a putative RNA binding protein. Cell 55:1025–1035

Amrein H, Maniatis T, Nöthiger R (1990) Alternatively spliced transcripts of the sex-determining gene *tra-2* of *Drosophila* encode functional proteins of different size. EMBO J 9:3619–3629

Andersen SO (1971) Phenolic compounds isolated from insect hard cuticle and their relationship to the sclerotization process. Insect Biochem 1:157–170

Andersen SO (1976) Cuticular enzymes and sclerotization in insects. In: Hepburd HR (ed) The insect integument. Elsevier, Amsterdam, pp 121–144

Anderson DT (1962) The embryology of *Dacus tryoni* (Frogg)(Diptera: Trypetidae = Tephritidae), the Queensland fruitfly. J Embryol Exp Morphol 10:248–292

Anderson E (1964) Oocyte differentiation and vitellogenesis in the roach *Periplaneta americana*. J Cell Biol 20:131–155

Anderson JM (1950) A cytological and cytochemical study of the male accessory reproductive glands in the japanese beetle *Popillia japonica*. Physiol Zool 23:308–316

Anderson KV (1987) Dorsal-ventral embryonic pattern genes of *Drosophila*. Trends Genet 3:91–97

Anderson KV, Lengyel JA (1980) Changing rates of histone mRNA synthesis and turnover in Drosophila embryos. Cell 21:717–727

Anderson KV, Nüsslein-Volhard C (1984) Information for the dorsal-ventral pattern is stored as maternal mRNA. Nature (Lond) 311:223–225

Anderson LM, Telfer WH (1969) A follicle cell contribution to the yolk spheres of moth oocytes. Tissue Cell 1:633–644

Anderson SO (1966) Covalent cross-links in a structural protein, resilin. Acta Physiol Scand 66:1–81

Arbogast RT, Byrd RV (1981) External morphology of the eggs of the meal moth, *Pyralis farinalis* (L.), and the murky meal moth, *Aglossa caprealis* (Hübner)(Lepidoptera: Pyralidae). Int J Insect Morphol Embryol 10:419–423

Auten M (1934) The early embryological development of *Phormia regina* (Diptera: Calliphoridae). Ann Entomol Soc Am 27:481–499

Awruch LI, Tobe SS (1978) Juvenile hormone biosynthesis by the corpora allata of the male desert locust, *Schistocerca gregaria*, during sexual matural. Can J Zool 56:2097–2102

Bachiller D, Sanchez L (1986) Mutations affecting dosage compensation in *Drosophila melanogaster*: effects in the germline. Dev Biol 118:379–384

Baeuerle PA, Lottspeich F, Huttner WB (1988) Purification of yolk protein 2 of *Drosophila melanogaster* and identification of its site of tyrosine sulfation. J Biol Chem 263:14925–14929

Bairati A (1968) Structure and ultrastructure of the male reproductive system in *Drosophila melanogaster*. Monit Zool Ital 2:105–182

Baker BS (1989) Sex in flies: the splice of life. Nature (Lond) 340:521–524

Baker BS, Belote JM (1983) Sex determination and dosage compensation in *Drosophila melanogaster*. Annu Rev Genet 17:345–393

Baker BS, Ridge KA (1980) Sex and the single cell: on the action of major loci affecting sex determination in *Drosophila melanogaster*. Genetics 94:383–423

Baker BS, Wolfner MF (1988) A molecular analysis of doublesex, a bifunctional gene that controls both male and female sexual differentiation in *Drosophila melanogaster*. Gen Dev 2:477–489

Baker BS, Nagoshi RN, Burtis KC (1987) Molecular genetic aspects of sex determination in *Drosophila*. Bioessays 6:66–70

Balbiani EG (1882) Sur la signification des cellules polaires des insectes. C R Acad Sci Paris 95:927–929

Bandziulis RJ, Swanson MS, Dreyfuss G (1989) RNA-binding proteins as developmental regulators. Gen Dev 3:431–437

Barker JF, Davey KG (1981) Neuroendocrine regulation of protein accumulation by the transparent accessory reproductive gland of male *Rhodnius prolixus*. Int J Invertebr Reprod 3:291–296

Barker JF, Davey KG (1983) A polypeptide from the brain and corpus cardiacum of male *Rhodnius prolixus* which stimulates in vitro protein synthesis in the transparent accessory reproductive gland. Insect Biochem 13:7–10

Barnett T, Wensink P (1981) Transcription and translation of yolk protein mRNA in the fat bodies of *Drosophila*. In: Brown DD (ed) Developmental biology using purified genes. Academic Press, New York, pp 97–106

Barnet T, Pachl C, Gergen JP, Wensink PC (1980) The isolation and characterization of *Drosophila* yolk protein genes. Cell 21:729–738

Bar-Zev A (1973) The effect of ecdysone on nucleic acid metabolism in tissues of *Gromphadorhina*. PhD Thesis, Univ Massachusetts, Amherst

Bassemir U (1977) Ultrastructural differentiations in the developing follicle cortex of *Locusta migratoria*, with special reference to vitelline membrane formation. Cell Tissue Res 185:247–262

Bast RE, Telfer WH (1976) Follicle cell protein synthesis and its contribution to the yolk of *Cecropia* moth oocytes. Dev Biol 52:83–97

Baudisch K (1956) Zytologische Beobachtungen an den Mycetocyten von *Periplaneta americana*. Naturwississenschaften 43:358

160

Bauer BJ, Waring GL (1987) 7C female-sterile mutants fail to accumulate early eggshell proteins necessary for later chorion morphogenesis in *Drosophila*. Dev Biol 121:349–358

Baumann H (1974a) The isolation, partial characterization, and biosynthesis of the paragonial substances, PS-1 and PS-2 of *Drosophila funebris*. J Insect Physiol 20:2181–2194

Baumann H (1974b) Biological effects of paragonial substances PS-1 and PS-2, in females of *Drosophila funebris*. J Insect Physiol 20:2347–2362

Baumann H, Wilson KJ, Chen PS, Humbel RE (1975) The amino acid sequence of a peptide (PS-1) from *Drosophila funebris*: a paragonial peptide from males which reduces the receptivity of the female. Eur J Biochem 52:521–529

Baumgartner WJ (1910) Observations on the Gryllidae. IV. Copulation. Kansas Univ Sci Bull 5:323–345

Beament JWL (1946) The waterproofing process in eggs of *Rhodnius prolixus*. Proc R Soc B 133:407–418

Beams HW, Kessel RG (1969) Synthesis and deposition of oocyte envelopes (vitelline membrane, chorion) and the uptake of yolk in the dragonfly (Odonata: Aeschnidae). J Cell Sci 4:241–264

Bean DW, Shirk PD, Brooks VJ (1988) Characterization of yolk proteins from the eggs of the Indian meal moth, *Plodia interpunctella*. Insect Biochem 18:199–210

Bell LR, Maine EM, Schedl P, Cline TW (1988) *Sex-lethal*, a *Drosophila* sex determination switch gene, exhibits sex-specific RNA splicing and sequence similarity to RNA binding proteins. Cell 55:1037–1046

Bell WJ (1969) Dual role of juvenile hormone in the control of yolk formation in *Periplaneta americana*. J Insect Physiol 15:1279–1290

Bell WJ, Bohm MK (1975) Oosorption in insects. Biol Rev 50:373–396

Belote JM (1983) Male-specific lethal mutations of *Drosophila melanogaster*. II. Parameters of gene action during male development. Genetics 105:881–896

Belote JM, Baker BS (1983) The dual functions of a sex determination gene in *Drosophila melanogaster*. Dev Biol 95:512–517

Belote JM, Lucchesi JC (1980) Control of X chromosome transcription by the maleless gene in *Drosophila*. Nature (Lond) 285:573–575

Belote JM, Handler AM, Wolfner MF, Livak KJ, Baker BS (1985) Sex-specific regulation of yolk protein gene expression in *Drosophila*. Cell 40:339–348

Benezra R, Davis RL, Lockshon D, Turner DL, Weintraub H (1990) The protein id:a negative regulator of helix-loop-helix DNA binding proteins. Cell 61:49–59

Benford HH, Bradley JT (1986) Early detection and juvenile hormone-dependence of cricket vitellogenin. J Insect Physiol 32:109–116

Berget SM (1984) Are U4 small nuclear ribonucleoproteins involved in polyadenylation? Nature (Lond) 309:179–182

Berk AJ, Schmidt MC (1990) How do transcription factors work? Gen Dev 4:151–155

Berleth T, Burri M, Thoma G et al. (1988) The role of localization of *bicoid* RNA in organizing the anterior pattern of the *Drosophila* embryo. EMBO J 7:1749–1756

Berry SJ (1985) RNA synthesis and storage during insect oogenesis. In: Browder LW (ed) Developmental biology. A comprehensive synthesis, vol 1. Oogenesis. Plenum Press, New York, pp 3251–384

Beyer A (1983) Ultrastructural analysis of the ribonucleoprotein structure of nascent hnRNA. Mol Biol Rep 9:49–58

Beyer AL, Miller OL Jr, McKnight SL (1980) Ribonucleoprotein structure in nascent hnRNA is non-random and sequence-dependent. Cell 20:75–84

Bhaskaran G, Sparagana SP, Dahm KH, Barrera P, Peck K (1988) Sexual dimorphism in juvenile hormone synthesis by corpora allata and in juvenile hormone acid methyltransferase activity in corpora allata and accessory sex glands of some Lepidoptera. Int J Invertebr Reprod 13:87–100

Bhide M, Sahai YN (1981) Cytological observations in the corpus luteum and resoptive bodies of *Periplaneta americana* Linn. Folia Morphol 29:353–358

Bier K (1963) Synthese, interzellulärer Transport und Abbau von Ribonukleinsäuren in Ovar der Stubenfliege *Musca domestica*. J Cell Biol 16:436–440

161

Bilinski S (1983) Oogenesis in *Campodea* sp. (Insecta, Diplura): chorion formation and the ultrastructure of follicle cells. Cell Tissue Res 228:167–170

Bilinski SM, Hage WJ, Bluemink JG (1985) Gap junctions between the follicle cells and the oocyte during oogenesis in an insect *Tribolium destructor*/Coleoptera. Wilhelm Roux's Arch Dev Biol 194:296–300

Billen J (1985) Ultrastructure of the worker ovarioles in *Formica* ants (Hymenoptera: Formicidae). Int J Insect Morphol Embryol 14:21–32

Bitsch J (1981a) Ultrastructure de l'epithelium du receptacle seminal chez *Thermobia domestica* (Packard)(Thysanura: Lepismatidae). Int J Insect Morphol Embryol 10:247–263

Bitsch J (1981b) Ultrastructural modifications of the glandular epithelium of the receptaculum seminis in *Thermobia domestica* (Insecta: Thysanura) during the moulting period. Cell Tissue Res 220:99–113

Black DL, Chabot B, Steitz JA (1985) U2 as well as U1 small nuclear ribonucleoproteins are involved in pre-messenger RNA splicing. Cell 42:737–750

Black PN, Happ GM (1985) Isolation, partial characterization, and localization of the A and B proteins from the tubular accessory gland of male *Tenebrio molitor*. Insect Biochem 15:639–650

Black PN, Landers MH, Happ GM (1982) Cytodifferentiation in the accessory glands of *Tenebrio molitor*. VIII. Crossed immuno-electrophoretic analysis of terminal differentiation in the postecdysial tubular accessory glands. Dev Biol 94:106–115

Blaine WD, Dixon SE (1973) The effect of juvenile hormone on the function of the accessory gland of the adult male cockroach *Periplaneta americana* (Orthoptera: Blattidae). Can Entomol 105:1275–1280

Blau HM, Kafatos FC (1979) Morphogenesis of the silkmoth chorion – patterns of distribution and insolubilization of the structural proteins. Dev Biol 72:211–225

Blobel G, Potter VR (1967) Ribosomes in rat liver: an estimate of the percentage of free and membrane-bound ribosomes interacting with messenger RNA in vivo. J Mol Biol 28:539–542

Blumenthal T, Zucker-Aprison E (1987) Evolution and regulation of vitellogenin genes. In: O'Connor JD (ed) Molecular biology of invertebrate development. Alan R Liss, New York, pp 3–19

Bock SC, Campo K, Goldsmith MR (1986) Specific protein synthesis in cellular differentiation. VI. Temporal expression of chorion gene families in *Bombyx mori* strain C108. Dev Biol 117:215–225

Bodenstein D, Shaaya E (1968) The function of the accessory sex gland in *Periplaneta americana* (L.). I. A quantitative assay for the juvenile hormone. Proc Natl Acad Sci USA 59:1223–1230

Bodenstein D, Sprague IB (1959) The developmental capacities of the sex glands in *Periplanata americana*. J Exp Zool 142:177–202

Boggs CL, Watt WB (1981) Population structure of pierid butterflies. IV. Genetical physiological investment in offspring by male *Colias*. Oecologia 50:320–324

Boggs RT, Gregor P, Idriss S, Belote JM, McKeown M (1987) Regulation of sexual differentiation in *D. melanogaster* via alternative splicing of RNA from the *transformer* gene. Cell 50:739–747

Bohrmann J, Gutzeit H (1987) Evidence against electrophoresis as the principal mode of protein transport in vitellogenic ovarian follicles of *Drosophila*. Development 101:279–288

Bohrmann J, Dorn A, Sander K, Gutzeit H (1986a) The extracellular electrical current pattern and its variability in vitellogenic *Drosophila* follicles. J Cell Sci 81:189–206

Bohrmann J, Huebner E, Sander K, Gutzeit H (1986b) Intracellular electrical potential measurements in *Drosophila* follicles. J Cell Sci 81:207–221

Bond JS, Butler PE (1987) Intracellular proteases. Annu Rev Biochem 56:333–364

Bonhag PF (1958) Ovarian structure and vitellogenesis in insects. Annu Rev Entomol 3:137–160

Bonhag PF, Wick JR (1953) The functional anatomy of the male and female reproductive systems of the milkweed bug, *Oncopeltus fasciatus* (Dallas)(Heteroptera; Lygaeidae). J Morphol 93:177–283

Borovsky D (1984) Control mechanisms for vitellogenin synthesis in mosquitoes. Bioessays 1:264–267

Borovsky D (1985a) Isolation and characterization of highly purified mosquito oostatic hormone. Arch Insect Biochem Physiol 2:333–349

Borovsky D (1985b) The role of the male accessory gland fluid in stimulating vitellogenesis in *Aedes taeniorhyncus*. Arch Insect Biochem Physiol 2:405–413

Borovsky D, Thomas BR (1985) Purification and partial characterization of mosquito egg development neurosecretory hormone: evidence for gonadotropic and steroidogenic effects. Arch Insect Biochem Physiol 2:265–291

Borovsky D, Whitney PL (1987) Biosynthesis, purification, and characterization of *Aedes aegypti* vitellin and vitellogenin. Arch Insect Biochem Physiol 4:81–99

Borovsky D, Thomas BR, Carlson DA, Whisenton LR, Fuchs MS (1985) Juvenile hormone and 20-hydroxyecdysone as primary and secondary stimuli of vitellogenesis in *Aedes aegypti*. Arch Insect Biochem Physiol 2:75–90

Boucher L, Huignard J (1987) Transfer of male secretions from the spermatophore to the female insect in *Caryedon serratus* (01.): analysis of the possible trophic role of these secretions. J Insect Physiol 33:949–957

Bownes M (1982a) Embryogenesis. In: Ranson R (ed) A handbook of *Drosophila* development. Elsevier, Amsterdam, pp 67–94

Bownes M (1982b) The role of 20-hydroxyecdysone in yolk-polypeptide synthesis by male and female fat bodies of *Drosophila melanogaster*. J Insect Physiol 28:317–328

Bownes M (1982c) Ovarian yolk-protein synthesis in *Drosophila melanogaster*. J Insect Physiol 28:953–960

Bownes M (1982d) Hormonal and genetic regulation of vitellogenesis in *Drosophila*. Q Rev Biol 57:247–274

Bownes M (1986) Expression of the genes coding for vitellogenin (yolk protein). Annu Rev Entomol 31:507–531

Bownes M (1990) Evidence that insect embryogenesis is regulated by ecdysteroids released from yolk protein. Invertebr Reprod Dev 18:106

Bownes M, Dale L (1982) Gametogenesis. In: Ransom R (ed) A handbook of *Drosophila* development. Elsevier, Amsterdam, pp 31–66

Bownes M, Hames BD (1978) Analysis of the yolk proteins in *Drosophila melanogaster*. Translation in a cell free system and peptide analysis. FEBS Lett 96:327–330

Bownes M, Nothiger R (1981) Sex determining genes and vitellogenin synthesis in *Drosophila melanogaster*. Mol Gen Genet 182:222–228

Bownes M, Partridge L (1987) Transfer of molecules from ejaculate to females in *Drosophila melanogaster* and *Drosophila pseudoobscura*. J Insect Physiol 33:941–947

Bownes M, Rembold H (1987) The titre of juvenile hormone during pupal and adult stages of the life cycle of *Drosophila melanogaster*. Eur J Biochem 164:709–712

Bownes M, Blair M, Kozma R, Dempster M (1983a) 20-hydroxyecdysone stimulates tissue-specific yolk-protein gene transcription in both male and female *Drosophila*. J Embryol Exp Morphol 78:249–268

Bownes M, Dempster M, Blair M (1983b) Expression of the yolk-protein genes in the mutant *doublesex dominant (dsx[D])* of *Drosophila melanogaster*. J Embryol Exp Morphol 75:241–257

Bownes M, Scott A, Blair M (1987) The use of an inhibitor of protein synthesis to investigate the roles of ecdysteroids and sex-determination genes on the expression of the genes encoding the *Drosophila* yolk proteins. Development 101:931–941

Bownes M, Scott A, Shirras A (1988a) Dietary components modulate yolk protein gene transcription in *Drosophila melanogaster*. Development 103:119–128

Bownes M, Shirras A, Blair M, Collins J, Coulson A (1988b) Evidence that insect embryogenesis is regulated by ecdysteroids released from yolk proteins. Proc Natl Acad Sci USA 85:1554–1557

Bradfield JY, Wyatt GR (1983) X-linkage of a vitellogenin gene in *Locusta migratoria*. Chromosoma 88:190–193

Bradley JT, Edwards JS (1978) Yolk proteins in the house cricket, *Acheta domesticus*: identification, characterization, and effect of ovariectomy upon their synthesis. J Exp Zool 204:239–248

Breitbart RE, Andreadis A, Nadal-Ginard B (1987) Alternative splicing: a ubiquitous mechanism for the generation of multiple protein isoforms from single genes. Annu Rev Biochem 56:467–495

163

Brennan MD, Mahowald AP (1982) Phosphorylation of the vitellogenin polypeptides of *Drosophila melanogaster*. Insect Biochem 12:669–673

Brennan MD, Warren TG, Mahowald AP (1980) Signal peptides and signal peptidase in *Drosophila melanogaster*. J Cell Biol 87:516–520

Brennan MD, Weiner AJ, Goralski TJ, Mahowald AP (1982) The follicle cells are a major site of vitellogenin synthesis in *Drosophila melanogaster*. Dev Biol 89:225–236

Brieger G, Butterworth FM (1970) *Drosophila melanogaster*: identity of male lipid in reproductive system. Science 167:1262

Briers T, Huybrechts R (1984) Control of vitellogenin synthesis by ecdysteroids in *Sarcophaga bullata*. Insect Biochem 14:121–126

Bronskill JF (1959) Embryology of *Pimpla turionellae* (L.)(Hymenoptera: Ichneumonidae). Can J Zool 37:655–688

Brookes VJ (1976) Protein synthesis in the fat body of *Leucophaea maderae* during vitellogenesis. J Insect Physiol 22:1649–1657

Brookes VJ (1986) The polypeptide structure of vitellogenin and vitellin from the cockroach, *Leucophaea maderae*. Arch Insect Biochem Physiol 3:577–591

Brun J, Chevassu D (1958) L'evolution des structures chromatiniennes dans les cellules nouricieres de ovocytes chez *Drosophila melanogaster* Meigen. Chromosoma 9:537–558

Brunet PCJ (1951) The formation of the ootheca by *Periplaneta americana*. I. The microanatomy and histology of the posterior part of the abdomen. Q J Microsc Sci 92:113–127

Brunet PCJ (1952) The formation of the ootheca by *Periplaneta americana* (L.). The structure and function of the left colleterial gland. Q J Microsc Sci 93:47–69

Brunet PCJ (1963) Synthesis of an aromatic ring in insects. Nature (Lond) 199:492–493

Brunet PCJ, Kent PW (1955) Observations on the mechanism of a tanning reaction in *Periplaneta* and *Blatta*. Proc R Soc B 144:259–274

Brunt AM (1970) Extensive system of microtubules in the ovariole of *Dysdercus fasciatus* Signoret (Heteroptera: Pyrrhocoridae). Nature (Lond) 228:80–81

Bryant PJ, Hsei BW (1977) Pattern formation in asymmetrical and symmetrical imaginal discs of *Drosophila melanogaster*. Am Zool 17:595–611

Buckingham ME, Caput D, Cohen A, Whalen RG, Gros F (1974) The synthesis and stability of cytoplasmic messenger RNA during myoblast differentiation in culture. Proc Natl Acad Sci USA 71:1466–1470

Büning J (1972) Untersuchungen an Ovar von *Bruchidius obtectus* Say (Coleoptera-Polyphaga). Zur Klärung des Oocytenwachstums in der Prävitellogenese. Z Zellforsch 128:421–282

Burke T, Waring GL, Popodi E, Minoo P (1987) Characterization and sequence of follicle cell genes selectively expressed during vitelline membrane formation in *Drosophila*. Dev Biol 124:441–450

Burke WD, Eickbush TH (1986) The silkmoth late chorion locus. I. Variation within two paired multigene families. J Mol Biol 190:343–356

Burnett B, Connolly K, Kearney M, Cook R (1973) Effects of male paragonial gland secretion on sexual receptivity and courtship behavior of female *Drosophila melanogaster*. J Insect Physiol 19:2421–2431

Burns AL, Kaulenas MS (1979) Analysis of the translational capacity of the male accessory gland during aging in *Acheta domesticus*. Mech Ageing Dev 11:153–169

Burtis KC, Baker BS (1989) Drosophila *doublesex* gene controls somatic sexual differentiation by producing alternatively spliced mRNAs encoding related sex-specific polypeptides. Cell 56:997–1010

Buschor J, Beycler P, Lanzrein B (1984) Factors responsible for the initiation of a second oocyte maturation cycle in the ovoviviparous cockroach *Nauphoeta cinerea*. J Insect Physiol 30:241–249

Butler B, Pirrotta V, Irminger-Finger I, Nothiger R (1986) The sex-determining gene *tra* of *Drosophila*: molecular cloning and transformation studies. EMBO J 5:3607–3613

Butt FH (1949) Embryology of the milkweed bug, *Oncopeltus fasciatus* (Hemiptera). Mem Cornell Univ Agric Exp Stn 283:1–43

Buys KS (1924) Adipose tissue in insects. J Morphol 38:485–527

Callahan PS, Cascio T (1963) Histology of the reproductive tract and transmission of sperm in the corn earworm, *Heliothis zea*. Ann Entomol Soc Am 56:535–556

Campuzano S, Carramolino L, Cabrera CV et al. (1985) Molecular genetics of the *achaete-scute* gene complex of *D. melanogaster*. Cell 40:327–338

Cantacuzène AM (1967a) Histologie des glandes annexes mâles de *Schistocerca gregaria* F. (Orthopteres). Effet de l'allatectomie sur leur structure et leur activité. C R Acad Sci Paris 264:93–96

Cantacuzène AM (1976b) Effets comparés de l'allatectomie sur l'activité des glandes annexes mâles et le comportement sexuel de deux Acridiens: *Schistocera gregaria* et *Locusta migratoria* (souches *migratorioides* et Kazalinsk). C R Acad Sci Paris 265:224–227

Cantacuzène AM (1967c) Recherches morphologiques et physiologiques sur les glandes annexes mâles des Orthoptères. I. Histophysiologie de l'appareil glandulaire des acridiens *Schistocerca gregaria* et *Locusta migratoria*. Bull Sox Zool Fr 92:725–738

Cantacuzène AM (1968) Recherches morphologiques et physiologiques sur les glandes annexes mâles des Orthoptères. III. Modes d'association des spermatzoides d'Orthoptères. Z Zellforsch 90:113–126

Cantacuzène AM (1971) Origine et caractères ultrastructuruax des cellules spermiophages du criquet migrateur *Locusta migratoria*. J Microsc Paris 10:179–190

Cantacuzène AM (1972) Recherches morphologiques et physiologiques sur les glandes annexes mâles des Orthoptères. IV. Ultrastructure de la vésicule séminal de *Locusta migratoria migratorioides* L. Ann Sci Nat Zool Paris 14:389–410

Capco D, Jeffery W (1979) Origin and spatial distribution of maternal messenger RNA during oogenesis of an insect, *Oncopeltus fasciatus*. J Cell Sci 39:63–76

Cardoen J, van Coillie C, Geysen J, DeLoof A (1988) Yolk polypeptide synthesis in the fat body of *Sarcophaga bullata*: localization, hormonal induction and cell-free translation. Insect Biochem 18:287–294

Carrière J, Bürger O (1897) Die Entwicklungsgeschichte der Mauerbiene (*Chalicodoma muraria* Fabr.) im Ei. Abk Kaisr Leopold-Carol Dtsch Akad Naturforsch 69:255–419

Cassier P, Huignard J (1979) Étude ultrastructurale des glandes annexes de l'appareil genital mâle chez *Acanthoscelides obtectus* Say (Coleoptera: Bruchidae). Int J Insect Morphol Embryol 8:183–201

Caudy M, Grell EH, Dambly-Chaudiere C, Ghysen A, Jan LY, Jan YN (1988a) The maternal sex determination gene *daughterless* has zygotic activity necessary for the formation of peripheral neurons in *Drosophila*. Gen Dev 2:843–852

Caudy M, Vasin H, Brand M, Tuma R, Jan LY, Jan YN (1988b) *daughterless*, a *Drosophila* gene essential for both neurogenesis and sex determination, has sequence similarities to *myc* and the *achaete-scute* complex. Cell 55:1061–1067

Cavener DR (1980) Genetics of male-specific glucose oxidase and the identification of other unusual hexose enzymes in *Drosophila melanogaster*. Biochem Genet 18:929–937

Cavener DR, MacIntyre RJ (1983) Biphasic expression and function of glucose dehydrogenase in *Drosophila melanogaster*. Proc Natl Acad Sci USA 80:6286–6288

Chalaye D (1979) Étude immunochimique des protéines hémolymphatiques et ovocytaires de *Rhodnius prolixus* (Stal). Can J Zool 57:329–336

Chaminade M, Laverdure A (1980) La vitellogenèse endogène chez *Tenebrio molitor* (Coleoptère). Bull Soc Zool 105:437–444

Chandra HS (1985) Sex determination: a hypothesis based on noncoding DNA. Proc Natl Acad Sci 82:1165–1169

Chapman KB, Wolfner MF (1988) Determination of male-specific expression in *Drosophila* accessory glands. Dev Biol 126:195–202

Chauvin G, Barbier R (1979) Morphogénèse de l'enveloppe vitelline, ultrastructure du chorion et de la cuticle serosale chez *Korscheltellus lupulinus* L. (Lepidoptera: Hepialidae). Int J Insect Morphol Embryol 8:375–386

Cheeseman MT, Gillott C (1988a) Identification and partial characterization of the major secretory protein of the long hyaline gland in the male grasshopper, *Melanoplus sanguinipes*. Insect Biochem 18:135–144

Cheeseman MT, Gillott C (1988b) Corpus allatum and corpus cardiacum regulation of long hyaline gland protein synthesis in the male grasshopper, *Melanoplus sanguinipes*. Gen Comp Endocrinol 72:416–423

Cheeseman MT, Gillott C (1989) Long hyaline gland discharge and multiple spermatophore formation by the male grasshopper, *Melanoplus sanguinipes*. Physiol Entomol 14:257–264

Cheeseman MT, Gillott C, Ahmed I (1990) Structural spermatophore proteins and a trypsin-like enzyme from the accessory reproductive glands of the male grasshopper, *Melanoplus sanguinipes*. J Exp Zool 255:193–204

Chen PS (1976) Species-specific protein patterns in *Drosophila* paragonial glands. Experientia 32:549–551

Chen PS (1984) The functional morphology and biochemistry of insect male accessory glands and their secretions. Annu Rev Entomol 29:233–255

Chen PS, Baker G (1976) L-Alanine aminotransferase in the paragonial gland of *Drosophila*. Insect Biochem 6:441–447

Chen PS, Oechslin A (1976) Accumulation of glutamic acid in the paragonial gland of *Drosophila nigromelanica*. J Insect Physiol 22:1237–1243

Chen PS, Stumm-Zollinger E, Caldelari M (1985) Protein metabolism of *Drosophila* male accessory glands. II. Species-specificity of secretion proteins. Insect Biochem 15:385–390

Chen PS, Stumm-Zollinger E, Aigaki T, Balmer J, Bienz M, Bohlen P (1988) A male accessory gland peptide that regulates reproductive behavior in female *D. melanogaster*. Cell 54:291–298

Chen TT (1980) Vitellogenin in locusts (*Locusta migratoria*): translation of vitellogenin mRNA in *Xenopus* oocytes and analysis of the polypeptide products. Arch Biochem Biophys 201:266–276

Chen TT, Strahlendorf W, Wyatt GR (1978) Vitellin and vitellogenin from locusts (*Locusta migratoria*). J Biol Chem 253:5325–5331

Chen TT, Couble P, Abu-Hakima R, Wyatt GR (1979) Juvenile hormone-controlled vitellogenin synthesis in *Locusta migratoria* fat body. Dev Biol 69:59–72

Cherbas L, Lee K, Cherbas P (1990) The induction of *Eip 28/29* by ecdysone in *Drosophila* cell lines. Invertebr Reprod Dev 18:108

Chia WK, Morrison PE (1972) Autoradiographic and ultrastructural studies on the origin of yolk protein in the housefly, *Musca domestica* L. Can J Zool 50:1569–1576

Chino H, Gilbert L (1965) Lipid release and transport in insects. Biochim Biophys Acta 98:94–110

Chino H, Downer RGH, Wyatt GR, Gilbert LI (1981) Lipophorins – a major class of lipoproteins of insect haemolymph. Insect Biochem 11:491

Chinzei Y, Chino H, Wyatt GR (1981) Purification and properties of vitellogenin and vitellin from *Locusta migratoria*. Insect Biochem 11:1–7

Chinzei Y, White BN, Wyatt GR (1982) Vitellogenin mRNA in locust fat body: identification, isolation, and quantitative changes induced by juvenile hormone. Can J Biochem 60:243–251

Choban RG, Gupta AP (1972) Meiosis and early embryology of *Blissus leucopterus hirtus* (Heteroptera: Lygaeidae). Int J Insect Morphol Embryol 1:301–314

Cholodkowsky H (1885) Über den Geschlechtsapparat von *Nematois metallicus* Pod. Z Wiss Zool 92:560–568

Chooi WY (1976) RNA transcription and ribosomal protein assembly in *Drosophila melanogaster*. In: King RC (ed) Handbook of genetics, vol 5. Plenum, New York, pp 219–265

Cline TW (1976) A sex-specific, temperature-sensitive maternal effect of the *daughterless* mutation of *Drosophila melanogaster*. Genetics 84:723–742

Cline TW (1978) Two closely linked mutations in *Drosophila melanogaster* that are lethal to opposite sexes and interact with *daughterless*. Genetics 90:683–698

Cline TW (1980) Maternal and zygotic sex-specific gene interactions in *Drosophila melanogaster*. Genetics 96:903–926

166

Cline TW (1984) Autoregulatory functioning of a *Drosophila* gene product that establishes and maintains the sexually determined state. Genetics 107:231–277

Cline TW (1985) Primary events in the determination of sex in *Drosophila melanogaster*. In: Halvorson HO, Monroy A (eds) The origin and evolution of sex. Alan R Liss, New York, pp 301–327

Cline TW (1986) A female-specific lethal lesion in an X-linked positive regulator of the *Drosophila* sex determination gene, *sex-lethal*. Genetics 113:641–663

Cline TW (1988) Evidence that *sisterless-a* and *sisterless-b* are two of several discrete "numerator elements" of the X/A sex determination signal in *Drosophila* that switch *Sxl* between two alternative stable expression states. Genetics 119:829–862

Cline TW (1989) The affairs of *daughterless* and the promiscuity of developmental regulators. Cell 59:231–234

Clore JN, Petrovitch E, Koeppe JK, Mills RR (1978) Vitellogenesis by the American cockroach: electrophoretic and antigenic characterization of haemolymph and oocyte proteins. J Insect Physiol 24:45–51

Cook BJ (1981) The action of proctolin and 5-hydroxytryptamine on the oviduct of the horsefly, *Tabanus proximus*. Int J Invertebr Reprod 3:209–212

Couble P, Chen TT, Wyatt GR (1979) Juvenile hormone-controlled vitellogenin synthesis in *Locusta migratoria* fat body: cytological development. J Insect Physiol 25:327–337

Couche GA, Gillott C (1987) Development of secretory activity in the long hyaline gland of the male migratory grasshopper, *Melanoplus sanguinipes* (Fabr.)(Orthoptera: Acrididae). Int J Insect Morphol Embryol 16:355–367

Couche GA, Gillott C (1988) Development of secretory activity in the seminal vesicle of the male migratory grasshopper, *Melanoplus sanguinipes* (Fabr.)(Orthoptera: Acrididae). Int J Insect Morphol Embryol 17:51–61

Couche GA, Gillott C (1990) Structure of the accessory reproductive glands of the male migratory grasshopper, *Melanoplus sanguinipes*. J Morphol 203:219–245

Couche GA, Gillott C, Tobe SS, Feyereisen R (1985) Juvenile hormone biosynthesis during sexual maturation and after mating in the adult male migratory grasshopper, *Melanoplus sanguinipes*. Can J Zool 63:2789–2792

Couchman JR, King PE (1979) Germarial structure and oogenesis in *Brevicoryne brassicae* (L.)(Hemiptera: Aphididae). Int J Insect Morphol Embryol 8:1–10

Coulthart MB, Singh RS (1988) Differing amounts of genetic polymorphism in testes and male accessory glands of *Drosophila melanogaster* and *Drosophila simulans*. Biochem Genet 26:153–164

Craig GB Jr (1967) Mosquitoes: female monogamy induced by male accessory gland substance. Science 156:1499–1501

Cronmiller C, Cline TW (1987) The *Drosophila* sex determinating gene *daughterless* has different functions in the germ line versus the soma. Cell 48:479–487

Cruickshank WJ (1971) Follicle cell protein synthesis in moth oocytes. J Insect Physiol 17:217–232

Cruickshank WJ (1972) Ultrastructural modifications in the follicle cells and egg membranes during development of the flour moth oocytes. J Insect Physiol 18:485–498

Cummings MR (1974) Ultrastructure of ovarian epithelial sheath in *Drosophila melanogaster* Meigen (Diptera: Drosophilidae). Int J Insect Morphol Embryol 3:137–145

Cummings MR, King RC (1969) The cytology of the vitellogenic stages of oogenesis in *Drosophila melanogaster*. I. General staging characteristics. J Morphol 128:427–442

Da Cruz-Landim C, Ferreira A (1977) Spermatophore formation in *Conocephalus saltator* (Sauss-ure). (Orthoptera: Conocephalidae). Int J Insect Morphol Embryol 6:97–104

Dahm KH, Bhaskaran G, Peter MG, Shirk PD, Seshan KR, Roller H (1976) On the identity of the juvenile hormone in insects. In: Gilbert LI (ed) The juvenile hormones. Plenum, New York, pp 19–48

Dailey PJ, Happ GM (1983) Cytodifferentiation in the accessory glands of *Tenebrio molitor*. XI. Transitional cell types during establishment of pattern. J Morphol 178:139–154

Dailey PJ, Gadzama NM, Happ GM (1980) Cytodifferentiation in the accessory glands of *Tenebrio molitor*. VI. A congruent map of cells and their secretions in the layered elastic product of the male bean-shaped gland. J Morphol 166:289–322

Dallai R (1975) Fine structure of the spermatheca of *Apis mellifera*. J Insect Physiol 21:89–109

Dambly-Chaudière C, Ghysen A (1987) Independent subpatterns of sense organs require independent genes of the *achaete-scuta* complex in *Drosophila* larvae. Gen Dev 1:297–306

Dambly-Chaudière C, Ghysen A, Jan LY, Jan YN (1988) The determination of sense organs in *Drosophila*: interaction of *scute* with *daughterless*. Wilhelm Roux's Arch Dev Biol 197:419–423

Dapples CC, Foster WA, Lea AO (1974) Ultrastructure of the accessory gland of the male mosquito, *Aedes aegypti* (L.)(Diptera: Culicidae). Int J Insect Morphol Embryol 3:279–291

Davenport R (1976) Transport of ribosomal RNA into the oocytes of the milkweed bug, *Oncopeltus fasciatus*. J Insect Physiol 22:925–926

Davenport R (1979) An outline of animal development. Addison-Wesley, Reading, Mass

Davey KG (1958) The migration of spermatozoa in the female of *Rhodnius prolixus* Stal. J Exp Biol 35:694–701

Davey KG (1981) Hormonal control of vitellogenin uptake in *Rhodnius prolixus* Stal. Am Zool 21:701–705

Davey KG (1985) The female reproductive tract. In: Kerkut GA, Gilbert LI (eds) Comprehensive insect physiology, biochemistry and pharmacology, vol 1. Pergamon Press, Oxford, pp 15–36

Davis CWC (1967) A comparative study of larval embryogenesis in the mosquito *Culex fatigens* Wiedermann (Diptera: Culicidae) and the sheepfly *Lucilia sericata* Meigen (Diptera: Calliphoridae). Aust J Zool 15:547–579

Davis RL, Cheng PF, Lassar AB, Weintraub H (1990) The MyoD binding domain contains a recognition code for muscle-specific gene activation. Cell 60:733–746

De Bianchi AG, Pereira SD (1987) The synthesis of *Musca domestica* vitellogenin during the first gonotrophic cycle. Comp Biochem Physiol 86B:697–700

De Bianchi AG, Winter CE, Terra WR (1982) Vitellogenins and other haemolymph proteins involved in the oogenesis of *Rhynchosciara americana*. Insect Biochem 12:177–184

De Bianchi AG, Coutinho M, Pereira SD, Marinotti O, Targa JH (1985) Vitellogenin and vitellin of *Musca domestica*. Quantification and synthesis by fat bodies and ovaries. Insect Biochem 15:77–84

De Cicco DV, Spradling AC (1984) Localization of *cis*-acting element responsible for the developmentally regulated amplification of *Drosophila* chorion genes. Cell 38:45–54

Degrugillier ME (1985) In vitro release of house fly, *Musca domestica* L. (Diptera: Muscidae), acrosomal material after treatment with secretion of female accessory gland and micropyle cap substance. Int J Insect Morphol Embryol 14:381–391

Delbecque JP, Hirn M, Delachambre J, Dereggi M (1978) Cuticular cycle and molting hormone levels during the metamorphosis of *Tenebrio molitor* (Insecta Coleoptera). Dev Biol 64:11–30

Delidakis C, Kafatos FC (1987) Amplification of a chorion gene cluster in *Drosophila* is subject to multiple *cis*-regulatory elements and to long-range position effects. J Mol Biol 197:11–26

Delidakis C, Kafatos FC (1989) Amplification enhancers and replication origin in the autosomal chorion gene cluster of *Drosophila*. EMBO J 8:891–901

Della Cioppa G, Engelmann F (1980) Juvenile hormone-stimulated proliferation of endoplasmic reticulum in fat body cells of a vitellogenic insect, *Leucophaea maderae* (Blattaria). Biochem Biophys Res Commun 93:825–832

Della Cioppa G, Engelmann F (1984a) Juvenile hormone regulation of phospholipid synthesis in the endoplasmic reticulum of vitellogenic fat body cells from *Leucophaea maderae*. Insect Biochem 14:27–36

Della Cioppa G, Engelmann F (1984b) Phospholipid synthesis in fat body endoplasmic reticulum during primary and secondary juvenile hormone stimulation of vitellogenesis in *Leucophaea madera*. Wilhelm Roux's Arch Dev Biol 193:78–85

Della Cioppa G, Engelmann F (1987) The vitellogenin of *Leucophaea maderae*. Synthesis as a large phosphorylated precursor. Insect Biochem 17:401–415

DeLoof A (1986) The electrical dimension of cells: the cell as a miniature electrophosis chamber. Int Rev Cytol 104:251–352

DeLoof A, Lagasse A (1970) Juvenile hormone and the ultrastructural properties of the fat body of the adult Colorado beetle, *Leptinotarsa decemlineata* Say. Z Zellforsch 106:439–450

DeLoof A, Lagasse A (1972) The ultrastructure of the male accessory reproductive glands of the Colorado Beetle. Z Zellforsch 130:545–552

DePamphilis M (1988) Transcriptional elements as components of eukaryotic origins of DNA replication. Cell 52:635–638

DeStephano DB, Brady UE (1977) Prostaglandin and prostaglandin synthetase in the cricket, *Acheta domesticus*. J Insect Physiol 23:905–911

DeStephano DB, Brady UE, Farr CA (1982) Factors influencing oviposition behavior in the cricket, *Acheta domesticus*. Ann Entomol Soc Am 75:111–114

Dewes E (1979) Über den Einfluß der Kulturdauer im larvalen Wirt auf die Entwicklungsleistungen implantierter mannlicher Genitalimaginalscheiben von *Ephestia kuehniella* Z Wilhelm Roux's Arch Dev Biol 186:309–331

De Wilde J (1964) Reproduction. In: Rockstein M (ed) The physiology of insecta, vol 1. Academic Press, New York, pp 10–58

Dhadialla TS, Wyatt GR (1983) Juvenile hormone-dependent vitellogenin synthesis in *Locusta migratoria* fat body: inducibility related to sex and stage. Dev Biol 96:436–444

Dhadialla TS, Cook KE, Wyatt GR (1987) Vitellogenin mRNA in locust fat body: coordinate induction of two genes by a juvenile hormone analog. Dev Biol 123:108–114

DiBenedetto AJ, Lakich DM, Kruger ND, Belote JM, Baker BS, Wolfner MF (1987) Sequences expressed sex-specifically in *D. melanogaster* adults. Dev Biol 119:242–251

DiBenedetto AJ, Harada HA, Wolfner MF (1990) Structure, cell-specific expression, and mating-induced regulation of a *Drosophila melanogaster* male accessory gland gene. Dev Biol 139:134–148

Diehl-Jones W, Huebner E (1989) Pattern and composition of ionic currents around ovarioles of the hemipteran, *Rhodnius prolixus* (Stahl). Biol Bull 176(S):86–90

Dittmann F, Maier E (1987) Developmental patterns of DNA-accumulation and nuclear division in the follicle epithelium of the red cotton bug, *Dysdercus intermedius* (Heteroptera). J Insect Physiol 33:191–200

Dittmann F, Ehni R, Engels W (1981) Bioelectric aspects of the Hemipteran teleotrophic ovariole (*Dysdercus intermedius*). Wilhelm Roux's Arch Dev Biol 190:221–225

Dittmann F, Hörner R, Engels W (1984) Endoploidization of tropharium nuclei during larval development and the first gonocycle in *Dysdercus intermedius* (Heteroptera). Int J Invertebr Reprod 7:279–290

Dittmann F, Trenczek T, Kleemann-Stumpf I (1985) Juvenile hormone-controlled vitellogenin cycles in *Dysdercus intermedius* (Heteroptera). J Insect Physiol 31:729–739

Dittmann F, Weiss DG, Munz A (1987) Movement of mitochondria in the ovarian trophic cord of *Dysdercus intermedius* (Heteroptera) resembles nerve axonal transport. Wilhelm Roux's Arch Dev Biol 196:407–413

Dittmann F, Steinbrück G, Münz A (1990) Amplification of tropharium rDNA in the teleotrophic ovariole of the bug, *Dysdercus intermedius*. Invertebr Reprod Dev 17:9–18

Dixon SE, Blaine WD (1972) Hormonal control of male accessory gland development in the cockroach, *Periplaneta americana* (L.). Proc Entomol Soc Ont 103:97–103

Donnelan JF, Kilby BA (1967) Uric acid metabolism by symbiotic bacteria from the fat body of *Periplaneta americana*. Comp Biochem Physiol 22:235–252

Dorn A (1977) Hormonal control of egg maturation and embryonic development in insects. In: Adiyodi KG, Adiyodi RG (eds) Advances in invertebrate reproduction, vol 1. Peralam-Kenoth, India, pp 451–481

Dorn A, Rademacher JM, Sehn E (1986) Ecdysteroid-dependent development of the oviduct in last-instar larvae of *Oncopeltus fasciatus*. J Insect Physiol 32:643–647

Dortland JF (1979) The hormonal control of vitellogenin synthesis in the fat body of the female Colorado potato beetle. Gen Comp Endocrinol 38:332–344

169

Dressler GR, Gruss P (1988) Do multigene families regulate vertebrate development? Trends Genet 4:214–219

Driever W, Nüsslein-Volhard C (1988a) A gradient of *bicoid* protein in *Drosophila* embryos. Cell 54:89–93

Driever W, Nüsslein-Volhard C (1988b) The *bicoid* protein determines position in the *Drosophila* embryo in a concentration-dependent manner. Cell 54:95–104

Dübendorfer A (1971) Untersuchungen zum Anlagenplan und Determination-zustand der weiblichen Genital- und Analprimordien von *Musca domestica* L. Wilhelm Roux's Arch Biol 168:142–168

Dübendorfer A, Eichenberger S (1985) In vitro metamorphosis of insect cells and tissues: development and function of fat body cells in embryonic cell cultures of *Drosophila*. In: Balls M, Bownes M (eds) Metamorphosis. Oxford Univ Press, Oxford, pp 145–161

Dübendorfer A, Nöthiger R (1982) A clonal analysis of cell lineage and growth in the male and female genital disc of *Drosophila melanogaster*. Wilhelm Roux's Arch Dev Biol 191:42–55

DuBois AM (1924) A contribution to the embryology of *Sciara* (Diptera). J Morphol 54:161–191

Duhamel RC, Kunkel JG (1978) A molting rhythm for serum proteins of the cockroach, *Blatta orientalis*. Comp Biochem Physiol 60B:333–337

DuPorte EM (1959) Manual of insect morphology. Reinholt Publ Corp, New York

Echard G (1968) Développement embryonnaire des gonads chez *Gryllus domesticus* (Orth.: Gryllidae). Ann Soc Entomol Fr 4:679–702

Edgar BA, O'Farrell PH (1989) Genetic control of cell division patterns in the *Drosophila* embryo. Cell 57:177–187

Edwards JP, Cerf DC, Staal GB (1985) Inhibition of ootheca production in *Periplaneta americana* (L) with the antijuvenile hormone fluoromevalonate. J Insect Physiol 31:723–728

Eickbush TH, Burke WD (1985) Silkmoth chorion gene families contain patchwork patterns of sequence homology. Proc Natl Acad Sci USA 82:2814–2818

Eickbush TH, Burke WD (1986) The silkmoth late chorion locus. II. Gradients of gene conversion in two paired multigene families. J Mol Biol 190:357–366

Eickbush TH, Kafatos FC (1982) A walk in the chorion locus of *Bombyx mori*. Cell 29:633–643

Eickbush TH, Rodakis GC, Lacanidou R, Kafatos FC (1985) A complex set of early chorion DNA sequences from *Bombyx mori*. Dev Biol 112:368–376

Elliott RH, Gillott C (1976) Histological changes in the ovary in relation to yolk deposition, allatectomy, and destruction of the median neuroscretory cells in *Melanoplus sanguinipes*. Can J Zool 54:185–192

Elliott RH, Gillott C (1979) An electrophoretic study of proteins of the ovary, fat body, and haemolymph in the migratory grasshopper, *Melanoplus sanguinipes*. J Insect Physiol 25:405–410

Ellis HM, Spann DR, Posakony JW (1990) *Extramacrochaetae*, a negative regulator of sensory organ development in *Drosophila*, defines a new class of helix-loop-helix proteins. Cell 61:27–38

Emmert W (1972a) Entwicklungsleitungen abdominaler Imaginalscheiben von *Calliphora erythrocephala* (Insecta, Diptera). Experimentelle Untersuchungen zur Morphologie des Abdomens. Wilhelm Roux's Arch Dev Biol 169:87–133

Emmert W (1972b) Experimente zur Bestimmung des Anlagenplans der männlichen und der weiblichen Genital-Imaginalscheibe von *Calliphora* (Insecta, Diptera). Wilhelm Roux's Arch Dev Biol 171:109–120

Engels W (1972) Quantitative untersuchungen zum Dotter-protein-Haushalt der Honigbiene (*Apis mellifica*). Wilhelm Roux's Arc Dev Biol 171:55–86

Engelmann F (1969) Female specific protein: biosynthesis controlled by corpus allatum in *Leucophaea madera*. Science 165:407–409

Engelmann F (1971) Juvenile-hormone-controlled synthesis of female-specific protein in the cockroach *Leucophaea maderae*. Arch Biochem Biophys 145:439–447

Engelmann F (1979) Insect vitellogenin: identification, biosynthesis and role in vitellogenesis. Adv Insect Physiol 14:49–108

170

Engelmann F (1983) Vitellogenin controlled by juvenile hormone. In: Downer RGH, Laufer H (eds) Endocrinology of insects. Alan R Liss, New York, pp 259–270

Engelmann F (1984) Regulation of vitellogenesis in insects: the pleiotropic role of juvenile hormones. In: Hoffmann J, Porchet M (eds) Biosynthesis, metabolism and mode of action of invertebrate hormones. Springer, Berlin Heidelberg New York, pp 444–453

Engelmann F, Mala J, Tobe SS (1987) Cytosolic and nuclear receptors for juvenile hormone in fat bodies of *Leucophaea maderae*. Insect Biochem 17:1045–1052

Epper F, Bryant PJ (1983) Sex-specific control of growth and differentiation in the *Drosophila* genital disc, studied using a temperature-sensitive *transformer-2* mutation. Dev Biol 100:294–307

Epper F, Nöthiger R (1982) Genetic and developmental evidence for a repressed genital primordium in *Drosophila melanogaster*. Dev Biol 94:163–175

Escherich K (1894) Anatomische Studien über das mäannliche Genitalsystem der Coleopteren. Z Wiss Zool 57:620–641

Ewen AB, Pickford R (1975) Morphology of the male sex organs, spermatophore formation and insemination in the clear-winged grasshopper *Camnula pellucida* (Scudder). Acrida 4:195–203

Fallon AM, Wyatt GR (1975) Cyclic guanosine 3′5′-monophosphate. High levels in the male accessory gland of *Acheta domesticus* and related crickets. Biochim Biophys Acta 411:173–185

Fallon AM, Wyatt GR (1977a) Guanylate cyclase in the accessory gland of the cricket, *Acheta domesticus*. J Insect Physiol 23:1037–1041

Fallon AM, Wyatt GR (1977b) Cyclic nucleotide phosphodiesterases in the cricket, *Acheta domesticus*. Biochim Biophys Acta 480:428–441

Fargnoli J, Waring GL (1982) Identification of vitelline membrane proteins in *Drosophila melanogaster*. Dev Biol 92:306–314

Fargnoli J, Waring GL (1984) Identification and cytogenetic localization of vitelline membrane messenger RNAs in *Drosophila*. Dev Biol 105:41–47

Favard-Sereno C (1971) Cycles sécrétoires successifs au cours de l'élaboration des envelopes de l'ovocyte chez le grillon (Insecte, Orthoptere). Rôle de l'appareil de Golgi. J Microsc 11:401–424

Favard-Sereno C (1973) Terminal differentiation of the adipose tissue in relation to vitellogenesis in the cricket. Mol Biol Rep 1:179–186

Federer H, Chen PS (1982) Ultrastructure and nature of secretory proteins in the male accessory gland of *Drosophila funebris*. J Insect Physiol 28:743–751

Fehrenbäch H, Dittrich V, Zissler D (1987) Eggshell fine structure of three lepidopteran pests: *Cydia pomonella* (L)(Tortricidae), *Heliothis virescens* (Fabr.), and *Spodoptera littoralis* (Boisd)(Noctuidae). Int J Insect Morphol Embryol 16:201–219

Feinsod FM, Spielman A (1980) Independently regulated juvenile hormone activity and vitellogenesis in mosquitoes. J Insect Physiol 26:829–832

Ferenz HJ (1978) Uptake of vitellogenin into developing oocytes of *Locusta migratoria*. J Insect Physiol 24:273–278

Ferenz HJ, Lubzens EW (1981) Vitellin and vitellogenin incorporation by isolated oocytes of *Locusta migratoria migratorioides* (R.F.). J Insect Physiol 27:869–875

Fiil A (1978) Follicle cell bridges in the mosquito ovary: syncitia formation and bridge morphology. J Cell Sci 31:137–143

Filosi M, Perotti ME (1975) Fine structure of the spermatheca of *Drosophila melanogaster* Meig. J Submicrosc Cytol 7:259–270

Fotaki ME, Iatrou K (1988) Identification of a transcriptionally active pseudogene in the chorion locus of the silkmoth *Bombyx mori*. Regional sequence conservation and biological function. J Mol Biol 203:849–860

Fourney RM, Pratt GF, Harnish DG, Wyatt GR, White BN (1982) Structure and synthesis of vitellogenin and vitellin from *Calliphora erythrocephala*. Insect Biochem 12:311–321

Fowler GL (1973) Some aspects of the reproductive biology of *Drosophila*: sperm transfer, sperm storage, and sperm utilization. Adv Genet 17:293–360

Fox AM, Reynolds SE (1990) Quantification of *Manduca* adipokinetic hormone in nervous and endocrine tissue by a specific radioimmunoassay. J Insect Physiol 36:683–689

Fragoulis EG, Traub P (1984) Inhibition of protein synthesis in a polyribosome-dependent cell-free system by a specific ribonuclease prepared from the follicles of two different stages of development of the silkmoth *Antherea pernyi*. Wilhelm Roux's Arch Dev Biol 194:25–31

Frenk E, Happ GM (1976) Spermatophore of the mealworm beetle: immunochemical characteristics suggest affinities with male accessory gland. J Insect Physiol 22:891–895

Frey A, Gutzeit H (1986) Follicle cells and germ line cells both affect polarity in *dicephalic* chimeric follicles of *Drosophila*. Wilhelm Roux's Arch Dev Biol 195:527–531

Frey A, Sander K, Gutzeit H (1984) The spatial arrangement of germ line cells in ovarian follicles of
· the mutant *dicephalic* in *Drosophila melanogaster*. Roux's Arch Dev Biol 193:388–393

Friedel T, Gillott C (1976a) Male accessory gland substance of *Melanoplus sanguinipes*. An oviposition stimulant under the control of the corpus allatum. J Insect Physiol 22:489–495

Friedel T, Gillott C (1976b) Extraglandular synthesis of accessory reproductive gland components in male *Melanoplus sanguinipes*. J Insect Physiol 22:1309–1314

Friedel T, Gillott C (1977) Contribution of male-produced proteins to vitellogenesis in *Melanoplus sanguinipes*. J Insect Physiol 23:145–151

Friedman S (1978) Trehalose regulation, one aspect of metabolic homeostasis. Ann Rev Entomol 23:389–407

Frohnhöfer HG, Nüsslein-Volhard C (1986) Organization of anterior pattern in the *Drosophila* embryo by the maternal gene *bicoid*. Nature (Lond) 324:120–125

Frohnhöfer HG, Nüsslein-Volhard C (1987) Maternal genes required for the anterior localization of *bicoid* activity in the embryo of *Drosophila*. Ge Dev 1:880–890

Fuchs MS, Hiss EA (1970) The partial purification and separation of the protein components of matrone from *Aedes aegypti*. J Insect Physiol 16:913–939

Fuchs MS, Craig GB Jr, Despommier DD (1969) The protein nature of the substance inducing female monogamy in *Aedes aegypti*. J Insect Physiol 15:701–709

Fujihara T, Kawabe M, Oishi K (1978) A sex transformation gene in *Drosophila melanogaster*. J Hered 69:229–285

Furneaux PJS, Mackay AL (1972) Crystalline protein in the chorion of insect eggshells. J Ultrastruct Res 38:343–359

Furneaux PJS, Mackay AL (1976) The conposition, structure and formation of the chorion and the vitelline membrane of the insect egg-shell. In: Hepburn HR (ed) The insect integument. Elsevier, Amsterdam, pp 157–176

Fuseini BA, Kumar R (1972) The accessory glands of some female mantids. Entomol Mon Mag 108:98–101

Fuyama Y (1983) Species-specificity of paragonial substances as an isolating mechanism in *Drosophila*. Experientia 39:190–192

Gade G, Beenakkers AMT (1977) Adipokinetic hormone-induced lipid mobilization and cyclic AMP accumulation in the fat body of *Locusta migratoria* during development. Gen Comp Endocrinol 32:401–487

Gadzama NM, Happ CM, Happ GM (1977) Cytodifferentiation in the accessory glands of *Tenebrio molitor*. I. Ultrastructure of the tubular gland in the post-ecdysial adult male. J Exp Zool 200:211–222

Gage G (1990) The adipokinetic hormone/red pigment concentrating hormone peptide family: structures, interrelationships and functions. J Insect Physiol 36:1–12

Gall JG, MacGregor HC, Kidston ME (1969) Gene amplification in the oocytes of Dytiscid water beetles. Chromosoma 26:169–187

Gallois D (1989) Control of cell differentiation in the male accessory reproductive glands of *Locusta migratoria*: acquisition and reversal of competence to imaginal secretion. J Insect Physiol 35:189–195

Galuszka H, Kubicz A (1970) Comparison of proteins from spermatheca fluid and hemolymph of the queen honey bee separated by polyacrylamide gel electrophoresis. Zool Pol 20:309–312

Garabedian MJ, Hung MC, Wensink PC (1985) Independent control elements that determine yolk protein gene expression in alternative *Drosophila* tissues. Proc Natl Acad Sci USA 82:1396–1400

Garabedian MJ, Shepherd BM, Wensink PC (1986) A tissue-specific transcription enhancer from the *Drosophila* yolk protein 1 gene. Cell 45:859–867

Garcia-Bellido A (1979) Genetic analysis of the *achaete-scute* system of *Drosophila melanogaster*. Genetics 91:491–520

Garcia-Bellido A, Ripoll P (1978) The number of genes in *Drosophila melanogaster*. Nature (Lond) 273:399–400

Garrell J, Modolell J (1990) The *Drosophila extramacrochaetae* locus, an antogonist of proneural genes that, like these genes, encodes a helix-loop-helix protein. Cell 61:39–48

Gartler SM, Riggs AD (1983) Mammalian X-chromosome inactivation. Annu Rev Genet 17:155–190

Geigy R (1931) Action de l'ultraviolet sur le pole germinal dans l'oeuf de *Drosophila melanogaster*. Rev Suisse Zool 38:187–288

Gelinas RE, Kafatos FC (1973) Purification of a family of specific messenger ribonucleic acids from moth follicular cells. Proc Natl Acad Sci USA 70:3764–3768

Gellisen G, Wyatt GR (1981) Production of lipophorin in the fat body of adult *Locusta migratoria*: comparison with vitellogenin. Can J Biochem 59:648–654

Gemmill RM, Hamblin M, Glaser RL et al. (1986) Isolation of mosquito vitellogenin genes and induction by 20-hydroxyecdysone. Insect Biochem 16:761–774

Gerber GH, Church NS, Rempel JG (1971a) The anatomy, histology, and physiology of the reproductive systems of *Lytta nuttali* Say (Coleoptera: Meloidae). I. The internal genitalia. Can J Zool 49:523–533

Gerber GH, Church NS, Rempel JG (1971b) The structure, formation, histochemistry, fate and functions of the spermatophore of *Lytta nuttalli* Say (Coleoptera: Meloidae). Can J Zool 49:1595–1610

Gerber GH, Neill GB, Westdal PH (1978) The anatomy and histology of the internal reproductive organs of the sunflower beetle, *Zygogramma exclamationis* (Coleoptera: Chrysomelidae). Can J Zool 56:2542–2553

Gergen JP (1987) Dosage compensation in Drosophila: evidence that *daughterless* and *sex-lethal* control X chromosome activity at the blastoderm stage of embryogenesis. Genetics 117:477–485

Gerling D, Rotary N (1974) Structure and function of the seminal vesicles and the spermatheca in *Bracan hebetor* Say (Hymenoptera: Braconidae). Int J Insect Morphol Embryol 3:159–162

Geysen J, Cardoen J, DeLoof A (1987) Distribution of yolk polypeptides in the follicle cells during the differentiation of the follicular epithelium in *Sarcophaga bullata* egg follicles. Development 101:33–43

Giebultowicz JM, Bell RA, Imberski RB (1988) Circadian rhythm of sperm movement in the male reproductive tract of the gypsy moth, *Lymantria dispar*. J Insect Physiol 34:527–532

Giebultowicz JM, Feldlaufer M, Gelman DB (1990) Role of ecdysteroids in the regulation of sperm release from the testis of the gypsy moth, *Lymantria dispar*. J Insect Physiol 36:567–571

Gigliotti S, Graziani F, DePonti L et al. (1989) Sex-, tissue-, and stage-specific expression of a vitelline membrane protein gene from region 32 of the second chromosome of *Drosophila melanogaster*. Dev Genet 10:33–41

Gilbert DG (1981) Ejaculate esterase 6 and initial sperm use by female *Drosophila melanogaster*. J Insect Physiol 27:641–650

Gilbert LI, Schneiderman HA (1961) The content of juvenile hormone and lipid in lepidoptera: sexual differences and developmental changes. Gen Comp Endocrinol 1:435–472

Gilbert W, Marchionni M, McKnight G (1986) On the antiquity of introns. Cell 46:151–154

Gillott C (1980) Entomology. Plenum, New York

Gillott C (1988) Arthropoda – Insecta. In: Adiyodi KG, Adiyodi RG (eds) Reproductive biology of invertebrates, vol III. Wiley, New York, pp 319–471

Gillott C, Elliott RH (1975) Reproductive growth in normal, allatectomized, median-nurosecretory-cell-cauterized, and ovariectomized females of *Melanoplus sanguinipes*. Can J Zool 54:162–171

Gillott C, Friedel T (1976) Development of accessory reproductive glands and its control by the corpus allatum in adult male *Melanoplus sanguinipes*. J Insect Physiol 22:365–372

Gillott C, Friedel T (1977) Fecundity enhancing and receptivity-inhibiting substances produced by male insects: a review. In: Adiyodi KG, Adiyodi RG (eds) Advances in invertebrate reproduction, vol 1. Peralam-Kenoth, India, pp 199–218

Gillott C, Venkatesh K (1985) Accumulation of secretory proteins in the accessory reproductive glands of the male migratory grasshopper, *Melanoplus sanguinipes*: a developmental study. J Insect Physiol 31:195–204

Giorgi F (1978) Intercellular bridges in ovarian follicle cells of *Drosophila melanogaster*. Cell Tissue Res 186:413–422

Giorgi F (1979) In vitro induced pinocytotic activity by a juvenile hormone analogue in oocytes of *Drosophila melanogaster*. Cell Tissue Res 203:241–247

Giorgi F, Deri P (1976) Cytochemistry of late ovarian chambers of *Drosophila melanogaster*. Histochem 48:325–334

Giorgi F, Postlethwait JH (1985) Development of gap junctions in normal and mutant ovaries of *Drosophila melanogaster*. J Morphol 185:115–129

Giorgi F, Baldini G, Simonini AL, Mengheri M (1982) Vitellogenesis in the stick insect *Carausius morosus*. II. Purification and biochemical characterization of two vitellins from eggs. Insect Biochem 12:553–562

Glass H, Emmerich H (1981a) Properties of two follicle proteins and their possible role for vitellogenesis in the African locust. Wilhelm Roux's Arch Dev Biol 190:22–26

Glass H, Emmerich H (1981b) Immunofluorescent localization of two SDS-soluble proteins in maturing terminal follicles of *Locusta migratoria*. Wilhelm Roux's Arch Dev Biol 190:27–32

Glass H, Emmerich H, Spindler KD (1978) Immunohistochemical localisation of ecdysteroids in the follicular epithelium of locust oocytes. Cell Tissue Res 194:237–244

Glitho IA, Huignard J (1990) A histological and ultrastructural comparison of the male accessory reproductive glands of diapausing and non-diapausing adults in *Bruchidius atrolineatus* (Pic)(Coleoptera: Bruchididae). Int J Insect Morphol Embryol 19:195–209

Gochoco CH, Kunkel JG, Nordin JH (1988) Experimental modifications of an insect vitellin affect its structure and its uptake by oocytes. Arch Insect Biochem Physiol 9:179–199

Gold SMW, Davey KG (1989) The effect of juvenile hormone on protein synthesis in the transparent accessory gland of male *Rhodnius prolixus*. Insect Biochem 19:139–143

Goldberg DA, Posakony JW, Maniatis T (1983) Correct developmental expression of a cloned alcohol dehydrogenase gene transduced into the *Drosophila* germ line. Cell 34:59–73

Goldsmith MR (1989) Organization and developmental timing of the *Bombyx mori* chorion gene clusters in strain C108. Dev Genet 10:16–23

Goldsmith MR, Clermont-Rattner E (1980) Organization of the chorion genes of *Bombyx mori*, a multigene family. III. Detailed marker composition of three gene clusters. Genetics 96:201–212

Goldsmith MR, Kafatos FC (1984) Developmentally regulated genes in silkmoths. Annu Rev Genet 18:443–487

Goltzene F, Porte A (1978) Endocrine control by neurosecretory cells of the pars intercerebralis and the corpora allata during the early phases of vitellogenesis in *Locusta migratoria migratorioides* R and F (Orthoptera). Gen Comp Endocrino 35:35–45

Goralski TJ, Edstrom JE, Baker BS (1989) The sex determination locus *transformer-2* of *Drosophila* encodes a polypeptide with similarity to RNA binding proteins. Cell 56:1011–1018

Görg I (1959) Untersuchungen am Keim von *Hierodula (Rhombodera) crassa* Caiglio Tos, ein Beitrag zur Embryologie der Mantiden (Mantodea). Dtsch Entomol Z 6:389–450

Graber V (1891) Beitrage zur vergleichenden Embryologie der Insekten. Denkschr Math Naturwiss Kais Akad Wiss Wien 58:803–866

Granadino B, Campuzano S, Sanchez L (1990) The *Drosophila melanogaster fl(2)d* gene is needed for the female-specific splicing of *sex-lethal* RNA. EMBO J 9:2597–2602

Grau V (1990) Asymmetrical distribution of an ecdysteroid-related antigen during late oogenesis and early embryogenesis in *Drosophila melanogaster*. Invertebr Reprod Dev 17:116

174

Grayson S, Berry SJ (1974) Synthesis and intracellular transport of protein by the colleterial gland of the cecropia silkmoth. Dev Biol 38:150–156

Gregory GE (1965) The formation and fate of the spermatophore in the African migratory locust, *Locusta migratoria migratorioides* Reiche and Fairmaire. Trans R Entomol Soc Lond 117:33–66

Griffin-Shea R, Thireos G, Kafatos FC, Petri WH, Villa-Kamaroff L (1980) Chorion cDNA clones of *D. melanogaster* and their use in studies of sequence homology and chromosomal location of chorion genes. Cell 19:915–922

Griffin-Shea R, Thireos G, Kafatos FC (1982) Organization of a cluster of four chorion genes in *Drosophila* and its relationship to developmental expression and amplification. Dev Biol 91:325–336

Griffith CM, Lai-Fook J (1986a) Structure and formation of the chorion in the butterfly, *Calpodes*. Tissue Cell 18:589–601

Griffith CM, Lai-Fook J (1986b) Corpus luteum formation and ovulation in the butterfly *Calpodes*. Tissue Cell 18:783–792

Grimes MJ, Happ GM (1980) Fine structure of the bean-shaped accessory gland in the male pupa of *Tenebrio molitor* L. (Coleoptera: Tenebrionidae). J Insect Morphol Embryol 9:281–296

Grimnes KA, Happ GM (1985) Partial characterization of the D group proteins of the tubular accessory glands of *Tenebrio molitor*. Insect Biochem 15:181–188

Grimnes KA, Happ GM (1986) A monoclonal antibody against a structural protein in the spermatophore of *Tenebrio molitor* (Coleoptera). Insect Biochem 16:635–643

Grimnes KA, Happ GM (1987) Ecdysteroids in vitro promote differentiation in the accessory glands of male mealworm beetles. Experientia 43:906–907

Grimnes KA, Bricker CS, Happ GM (1986) Ordered flow of secretion from accessory glands to specific layers of the spermatophore of mealworm beetles: demonstration with a monoclonal antibody. J Exp Zool 240:275–286

Grodner ML (1975) Aberrant spermatogenesis in hybrid progeny of subspecies of the boll weevil *Anthonomus grandis* Boheman (Coleoptera: Curculionidae). Int J Insect Morphol Embryol 4:107–114

Grodner ML, Steffens WL (1978) Evidence of a chemotactic substance in the spermathecal gland of the female boll weevil (Coleoptera: Curculionidae). Trans Am Microsc Soc 97:116–120

Gross J (1903) Untersuchungen über die Histologie des Insektenovariums. Zool Jahrb 18:71–186

Gupta BL, Smith DS (1969) The structural organization of the spermatheca in the cockroach, *Periplaneta americana*. Tissue Cell 1:295–324

Gupta PD (1948) On the structure, development and homology of the female reproductive organs in orthopteroid insects. Indian J Entomol 10:75–123

Guthrie C, Patterson B (1988) Spliceosomal snRNAs. Ann Rev Genet 22:387–419

Guthrie DM, Tindall AR (1968) The biology of the cockroach. Edward Arnold, London

Gutzeit HO (1980) Yolk synthesis in ovarian follicles of *Drosophila*. Wilhelm Roux's Arch Dev Biol 189:221–224

Gutzeit HO (1985) Oosome formation during in vitro oogenesis in *Bradysia tritici* (syn. *Sciara ocellaris*). Wilhelm Roux's Arch Dev Biol 194:404–410

Gutzeit HO (1986a) Transport of molecules and organelles in meroistic ovarioles of insects. Differentiation 31:155–165

Gutzeit HO (1986b) The role of microfilaments in cytoplasmic streaming in *Drosophila* follicles. J Cell Sci 80:159–169

Gutzeit HO (1986c) The role of microtubules in the differentiation of ovarian follicles during vitellogenesis in *Drosophila*. Wilhelm Roux's Arch Dev Biol 195:173–181

Gutzeit HO, Huebner E (1986) Comparison of microfilament patterns in nurse cells of different insects with polytrophic and telotrophic ovarioles. J Embryol Exp Morphol 93:291–301

Gutzeit HO, Koppa R (1982) Time-lapse film analysis of cytoplasmic streaming during late oogenesis of *Drosophila*. J Embryol Exp Morphol 67:101–111

Gutzeit HO, Strauβ A (1989) Follicle cell development is partly indpendent of germline cell differentiation in *Drosophila* oogenesis. Wilhelm Roux's Arch Dev Biol 198:185–190

Hagedorn HH (1985) Role of ecdysteroids in reproduction. In: Kerkut GA, Gilbert LI (eds) Comprehensive insect physiology, biochemistry and pharmacology, vol 8. Pergamon Press, Oxford, pp 205–261

Hallberg E (1984) The spermathecal complex in *Ips typographus* (L.): differentiation of the spermathecal gland related to age and reproductive state. J Insect Physiol 30:197–202

Hammond MP, Laird CD (1985) Chromosome structure and DNA replication in nurse and follicle cells of *Drosophila melanogaster*. Chromosoma 91:267–278

Hamodrakas SJ, Asher SA, Mazur GD, Regier JC, Kafatos FC (1982) Laser Raman studies of protein conformation in the silkmoth chorion. Biochim Biophys Acta 703:216–222

Hamodrakas SJ, Paulson JR, Rodakis GC, Kafatos FC (1983) X-ray diffraction studies of a silkmoth chorion. Int J Biol Macromol 5:583–589

Hamodrakas SJ, Etmektzoglou T, Kafatos FC (1985) Amino acid periodicities and their structural implications for the evolutionary conservative central domain of some silkmoth chorion proteins. J Mol Biol 186:583–589

Hansen-Delkeskamp E (1969) Synthese von RNS und Protein während der Oogene und früher Embryogenese von *Acheta domestica*. Wilhelm Roux's Arch Dev Biol 162:114–120

Happ GM, Happ CM (1970) Fine structure and histochemicatry of the spermathecal gland in the mealworm beetle, *Tenebrio molitor*. Tissue Cell 2:443–446

Happ GM, Happ CM (1975) Fine structure of the spermatheca of the mealworm beetle (*Tenebrio molitor* L.). Cell Tissue Res 162:253–269

Happ GM, Happ CM (1977) Cytodifferentiation in the accessory glands of *Tenebrio molitor*. III. Fine structure of the spermathecal accessory gland in the pupa. Tissue Cell 9:711–732

Happ GM, Yuncker C (1978) Patterns of leucine incorporation in the spermathecal accessory glands of the post-ecdysial adult female *Tenebrio molitor*. J Insect Physiol 24:417–421

Happ GM, Yuncker C, Huffmire SA (1977) Cytodifferentiation in the accessory glands of *Tenebrio molitor*. II. Patterns of leucine incorporation in the tubular glands of post-ecdysial adult males. J Exp Zool 200:223–236

Happ GM, Yuncker C, Dailey PJ (1982) Cytodifferentiation in the accessory glands of *Tenebrio molitor*. VII. Patterns of leucine incorporation by the bean-shaped glands of males. J Exp Zool 220:81–92

Happ GM, MacLeod BJ, Szopa TM et al. (1985) Cell cycles in the male accessory glands of mealworm pupae. Dev Biol 107:314–324

Harbecke R, Janning W (1989) The segmentation gene *Krüppel* of *Drosophila melanogaster* has homeotic properties. Gen Dev 3:114–122

Harnish DG, White BN (1982a) Insect vitellins: identification, purification, and characterization from eight orders. J Exp Zool 220:1–10

Harnish DG, White BN (1982b) An evolutionary model for the insect vitellins. J Mol Evol 18:405–413

Harnish DG, Wyatt GR, White BN (1982) Insect vitellins: identification of primary of translation. J Exp Zool 220:11–19

Harrison SC, Aggarwal AK (1990) DNA recognition by proteins with the helix-loop-helix motif. Ann Rev Biochem 59:937–969

Harry P, Pines M, Applebaum SW (1979) Changes in the pattern of secretion of locust female diglyceride-carrying lipoprotein and vittelogenin by the fat body in vitro during oocyte development. Comp Biochem Physiol 63B:287–293

Hartmann R (1970) Experimentelle und histologische Untersuchungen der Spermatophorenbildung bei der Feldheuschrecke *Gomphocerus rufus* L. (Orthoptera: Acrididae). Z Morphol Tiere 68:140–178

Hartmann R (1971) Der Einfluss endokriner Faktoren auf die männlichen akzessorischen Drüsen und die Ovarien bei der Keulenheuschrecke *Gomphocerus rufus* L. (Orthoptera: Acrididae). Z Vgl Physiol 74:190–216

Hartmann R (1978) The juvenile-hormone carrier in the haemolymph of the acridine grasshopper *Gomphocerus rufus* L.: blocking the juvenile hormone's action by means of repeated injections of an antibody to the carrier. Wilhelm Roux's Arch Dev Biol 184:300–324

Hartmann R, Loher W (1974) Control of sexual behavior pattern "secondary defense" in the female grasshopper *Chorthippus curtipennis*. J Insect Physiol 20:1713–1728

Hawley RJ, Waring GL (1988) Cloning and analysis of the dec-1 female-sterile locus, a gene required for proper assembly of the *Drosophila* eggshell. Gen Dev 2:341–349

Hay AR, Raikhel AS (1990) A novel protein produced by the vitellogenic fat body and accumulated in mosquito oocytes. Wilhelm Roux's Arch Dev Biol 199:114–121

Hazelrigg T, Wilkins WS, Marcey D, Tu C, Karow M, Lin X (1990) The *exuperentia* gene is required for *Drosophila* spermatogenesis as well as anteroposterior polarity of the developing oocyte, and encodes overlapping sex-specific transcripts. Genetics 126:607–617

Heck MMS, Spradling AC (1990) Multiple replication origins are used during *Drosophila* chorion gene amplification. J Cell Biol 110:903–914

Hecker H, Moloo SK (1983) Quantitative morphological changes of the uterine gland cells in relation to physiological events during a pregnancy cycle in *Glossina morsitans morsitans*. J Insect Physiol 29:651–658

Hegner RW (1909) The origin and early history of the germ cells in some chrysomelid beetles. J Morphol 20:231–297

Hegner RW (1912) The history of the germ cells in the paedogenetic larva of *Miastor*. Science 36:124–126

Heine U, Blumenthal T (1986) Characterization of cation-rich follicle cells in vitellogenic follicles of *Drosophila melanogaster*. Differentiation 28:237–243

Helfman DM, Roscigno RF, Mulligan GJ, Finn LA, Weber KS (1990) Identification of two distinct intron elements involved in alternative splicing of α-tropomyosin pre-mRNA. Gen Dev 4:98–110

Herman WS (1975) Juvenile hormone stimulation of tubular and accessory glands in male monarch butterflies. Comp Biochem Physiol 51A:507–510

Herman WS (1982) Endocrine regulation of the bursa copulatrix and receptacle gland of *Danaus plexippus* L (Lepidoptera: Danaidae). Experientia 38:631–632

Herman WS, Bennett DC (1975) Regulation of oogenesis, female specific protein production, and male and female reproductive gland development by juvenile hormone in the butterfly, *Nymphalis autiopa*. J Comp Physiol 99:331–338

Heymons R (1890) Über die hermaphroditische Anlage der Sexualdrüsen beim Männchen von *Phyllodromia (Blatta* L.) *germinica*. Zool Anz 13:451–458

Heymons R (1892) Die Entwicklung der weiblichen Geschlechtsorgane von *Phyllodromia (Blatta) germinica*. Z Wiss Zool 53:434–536

Heymons R (1895) Die Embryonalentwicklung von Dermapteren und Orthopteren. Fischer, Jena

Hibner BL, Burke WD, Lecanidou R, Rodakis GC, Eickbush TH (1988) Organization and expression of three genes from the silkmoth early chorion locus. Dev Biol 125:423–431

Higgins MJ, Walker VK, Holden JJA, White BN (1984) Isolation of two *Drosophila melanogaster* genes abundantly expressed in the ovary during vitelline membrane synthesis. Dev Biol 105:155–165

Hinton HE (1961) The structure and function of the egg-shell in the Nepidae (Hemiptera) J Insect Physiol 7:224–257

Hinton HE (1981) Biology of the insect egg, vol I-III. Pergamon Press, Oxford

Hirschler J (1909) Die Embryonalentwicklung von *Donacia crassipes* L. Z Wiss Zool 92:627–739

Hoch M, Schroder C, Seifert E, Jackle H (1990) Cis-acting control elements for *Krüppel* expression in the *Drosophila* embryo. EMBO J 9:2587–2595

Hodgkin J (1989) *Drosophila* sex determination: a cascade of regulated splicing. Cell 905–906

Hoffmann JA, Lagieux M (1985) Endocrine aspects of embryonic development in insects. In: Kerkut GA, Gilbert LI (eds) Comprehensive insect physiology, biochemistry and pharmacology, vol 1. Pergamon Press, New York, pp 435–460

Holman GM, Cook BJ (1985) Proctolin, its presence in and action on the oviduct of an insect. Comp Biochem Physiol 80C:61–64

Hong TK (1977) Histochemical and histological studies on male reproductive tract and neurosecretory cells in *Ephestia kuhniella* after hexamethylmelamine (Hemel) treatment. In: Adiyodi KG, Adiyodi RG (eds) Advances in invertebrate reproduction, vol 1. Peralan-Kenoth, India, pp 258–268

Hotchkin PG, Fallon AM (1987) Ribosome metabolism during the vitellogenic cycle of the mosquito, *Aedes aegypti*. Biochem Biophys Acta 924:352–359

Hough-Evans BR, Jacobs-Lorena M, Cummings MR, Britten RJ, Davidson EH (1980) Complexity of RNA in eggs of *Drosophila melanogaster* and *Musca domestica*. Genetics 95:81–94

Hovemann B, Galler R (1982) Vitellogenin in *Drosophila melanogaster*: a comparison of the YP1 and YP2 genes and their transcription products. Nucl Acids Res 10:2261–2274

Hovemann B, Galler R, Walldorf U, Bautz EKF (1981) Vitellogenin in *Drosophila melanogaster*: sequence of the yolk protein I gene and its flanking regions. Nucl Acids Res 9:4721–4734

Huebner E (1976) Experimental modulation of the follicular epithelium of *Rhodnius* oocytes by juvenile hormone and other agents. J Cell Biol 70:251a

Huebner E (1980) Spermathecal ultrastructure of the insect *Rhodnius prolixus* Stal. J Morphol 166:1–25

Huebner E (1981a) Oocyte-follicle cell interaction during normal oogenesis and atresia in an insect. J Ultrastruct Res 74:95–104

Huebner E (1981b) Nurse cell-oocyte interaction in the telotrophic ovarioles of an insect, *Rhodnius prolixus*. Tissue Cell 13:105–125

Huebner E (1984) The ultrastructure and development of the telotrophic ovary. In: King RC, Akai H (eds) Insect ultrastructure, vol 2. Plenum, New York, pp 3–48

Huebner E, Anderson E (1972) A cytological study of the ovary of *Rhodnius prolixus*. I. The ontogeny of the follicular epithelium. J Morphol 136:459–494

Huebner E, Davey KG (1973) An antigonadotropin from the ovaries of the insect *Rhodnius prolixus* Stal. Can J Zool 51:113–120

Huebner E, Gutzeit H (1986) Nurse cell-oocyte interaction: a new F-actin mesh associate with the microtubule-rich core of an insect ovariole. Tissue Cell 18:753–764

Huebner E, Injeyan HS (1980) Patency of the follicular epithelium in *Rhodnius prolixus* a re-examination of the hormone response and technique refinement. Can J Zool 58:1617–1625

Huebner E, Injeyan HS (1981) Follicular modulation during oocyte development in an insect: formation and modification of septate and gap junctions. Dev Biol 83:101–113

Huebner E, Tobe SS, Davey KG (1975) Structural and functional dynamics of oogenesis in *Glossina austeni*: vitellogenesis with special reference to the follicular epithelium. Tissue Cell 3:535–558

Huet C (1966) Étude expérimentale du développement de l'appareil génital mâle de *Tenebrio molitor* (Coléoptere: Ténébrionide). C R Soc Biol 160:2021–2025

Huettner AF (1923) The origin of the germ cells in *Drosophila melanogaster*. J Morphol 37:385–419

Hughes M, Berry SJ (1970) The synthesis and secretion of ribosomes by nurse cells of *Antheraea polyphemus*. Dev Biol 23:651–664

Hui C-C, Matsuno K, Suzuki Y (1990) Fibroin gene promoter contains a cluster of homeo-domain binding sites that interact with three silk gland factors. J Mol Biol 651–670

Huignard J (1969) Action stimulatrice du spermatophore sur l'ovogenèse chez *Acanthoscelides obtectus* Say. C R Acad Sci Paris 268:2938–2940

Huignard J (1974) Influence de la copulation sur la fonction reproductrice femelle chez *Acanthoscelides obtectus* (Coléoptère, Bruchidae). I. Copulation et spermatophore. Ann Sci Nat Zool 16:361–434

Huignard J (1975) Anatomie et histologie des glandes annexes mâles au cours de la vie imaginale chez *Acanthoscelides obtectus* Say (Coleoptera: Bruchidae). Int J Insect Morphol Embryol 4:77–88

Huignard J (1978) Transfert de sécrétions mâles du spermatophore vers l'hémolymphe chez *Acanthoscelides obtectus* Say (Coléoptère Bruchidae). C R Acad Sci Paris 287:1301–1304

Huignard J (1983) Transfer and fate of male secretions deposited in the spermatophore of females of *Acanthoscelides obtectus* Say (Coléoptère Bruchidae). J Insect Physiol 29:55–63

Huignard J, Lamy M (1972) Étude de l'évolution des protéins du spermatophore après l'accuplement chez *Acanthoscelides obtectus* (Coléoptère, Bruchidae). C R Acad Sci Paris 275D:1067–1070

Hultmark D, Klementz R, Gehring WJ (1986) Translational and transcriptional control elements in the untranslated leader of the heat-shock gene *hsp22*. Cell 44:429–438

Hung MC, Wensink PC (1981) The sequence of the *Drosophila melanogaster* gene for yolk protein 1. Nucl Acids Res 9:6407–6419

Hung MC, Wensink PC (1983) Sequence and structure conservation in yolk proteins and their genes. J Mol Biol 164:481–492

Hung MC, Barnett T, Woolford C, Wensink PC (1982) Transcript maps of *Drosophila* yolk protein genes. J Mol Biol 154:581–602

Huybrechts R, DeLoof A (1977) Induction of vitellogenin synthesis in male *Sacrophaga bullata* by exdysterone. J Insect Physiol 23:1359–1362

Huybrechts R, DeLoof A (1982) Similarities in vitellogenin and control of vittelogenin synthesis within the genera *Sarcophaga, Calliphora, Phormia* and *Lucilia* (Diptera). Comp Biochem Physiol 72B:339–344

Hyams JS, Stebbings H (1977) The distribution and function of microtubules in nutritive tubes. Tissue Cell 9:537–545

Hyams JS, Stebbings H (1979a) The formation and breakdown of nutritive tubes- massive microtubular organelles associated with cytoplasmic transport. J Ultrastruct Res 68:46–57

Hyams JS, Stebbings H (1979b) The mechanism of microtubule associated cytoplasmic transport. Isolation and preliminary characterization of a microtubule transport system. Cell Tissue Res 196:103–116

Hyatt AD, Marshall AT (1985) Ultrastructure and cytochemistry of the fat body of *Periplaneta americana* (Dictyoptera: Blattidae). Int J Insect Morphol Embryol 14:131–141

Iatrou K, Tsitilou SG (1983) Coordinately expressed chorion genes of *Bombyx mori*: is developmental specificity determined by secondary structure recognition? EMBO J 2:1431–1440

Iatrou K, Tsitilou SG, Goldsmith MR, Kafatos FC (1980) Molecular analysis of the GR^B mutation in *Bombyx mori* through the use of a chorion cDNA library. Cell 20:659–669

Iatrou K, Tsitilou SG, Kafatos FC (1984) DNA sequence transfer between two high-cysteine chorion gene families in the silkmoth *Bombyx mori*. Proc Natl Acad Sci USA 81:4452–4456

Ibrahim MM (1958) Grundzuge der Organbildung im Embryo von *Tachycines* (Insecta: Saltatoria). Zool Jahrb Anat 76:541–594

Idris BEM (1960) Die Entwicklung im normalen Ei von *Culex pipiens* L. (Diptera). Z Morphol Okol Tiere 49:387–429

Ilenchuk TT, Davey KG (1987a) The development of responsiveness to juvenile hormone in the follicle cells of *Rhodnius prolixus*. Insect Biochem 17:525–529

Ilenchuk TT, Davey KG (1987b) Effects of various compounds on Na/K-ATPase activity. JH I binding capacity and patency response in follicles of *Rhodnius prolixus*. Insect Biochem 17:1085–1088

Illmensee K (1973) The potentialities of transplanted early gastrula nuclei of *Drosophila melanogaster*. Production of their imago descendants by germ-line transplantation. Wilhelm Roux's Arch Dev Biol 171:331–343

Illmensee K, Mahowald AP (1974) Transplantation of posterior pole plasm in *Drosophila*. Induction of germ cells at the anterior pole of the egg. Proc Natl Acad Sci USA 71:1016–1020

Illmensee K, Mahowald AP (1976) The autonomous function of germ plasm in somatic region of the *Drosophila* egg. Exp Cell Res 97:127–140

Illmensee K, Mahowald AP, Loomis MR (1976) The ontogeny of germ plasm during oogenesis in *Drosophila*. Dev Biol 49:40–65

Imaizumi T (1958) Recherches sur l'expression des facteurs létaux héreditaires chez l'embryon de la drosophile. V. Sue l'embryo cours de développement embryonniare. Cytologia (Tokyo) 23:270–283

Imboden H, Konig R, Ott P, Lustig A, Kampfer U, Lanzrein B (1987) Characterization of the native vittelogenin, and vitellin of the cockroach, *Nauphoeta cinerea*, and comparison with other species. Insect Biochem 17:353–365

Imboden H, Law JH (1983) Heterogeneity of vitellins and vittelogenins of the tobacco hornworm, *Manduca sexta* L. Time course of vitellogenin appearance in the haemolymph of the adult female. Insect Biochem 13:151–162

Imms AD (1957) A general textbook of entomology. Methuen, London

Ingham PW (1988) The molecular genetics of embryonic pattern formation in *Drosophila*. Nature (Lond) 335:25–33

Ingham-Baker J, Candido EPM (1980) Proteins of the *Drosophila melanogaster* male reproductive system: two-dimensional gel pattern of protein synthesis in the XO, XY, and XYY testis and paragonial gland and evidence that the Y chromosome does not code for structural sperm proteins. Biochem Genet 18:809–828

Inoue K, Hoshijima K, Sakamoto H, Shimura Y (1990) Binding of the *Drosophila sex-lethal* gene product to the alternative splice site of *transformer* primary transcript Nature (Lond) 344:461–463

Irvine DD, Brasch K (1981) The influence of juvenile hormone on polyploidy and vitellogenesis in the fat body of *Locusta migratoria*. Gen Comp Endocrinol 45:91–99

Isaac PG, Bownes M (1982) Ovarian and fat body vitellogenin synthesis in *Drosophila melanogaster*. Eur J Biochem 123:527–534

Ivanova-Kazas OM (1949) Embryonalnoe razvitie *Anopheles muculipennis* Mg. Izv Akad Nauk SSSR Ser Biol 2:140–176

Izumi S, Tomino S (1983) Vitellogenin synthesis in the silkworm, *Bombyx mori*: separate mRNAs encode two subunits of vittelogenin. Insect Biochem 13:81–85

Izumi S, Toto S, Tomino S (1980) Translation of fat body mRNA from the silkworm, *Bombyx mori*. Insect Biochem 10:429–434

Jacob J, Sirlin JL (1959) Cell function in the ovary of *Drosophila*. I. DNA classes in nurse cell nuclei as determined by autoradiography. Chromosoma 10:210–228

Jaffe E, Laird C (1986) Dosage compensation in *Drosophila*. Trends Genet 2:316–321

Jensen PV, Hansen BL, Hansen GN, Thomsen E (1981) Vitellogenin and vitellin from the blowfly *Calliphora vicina*: occurrence, purification and antigenic characterization. Insect Biochem 11:129–135

Johnson FM, Beale S (1968) Isozyme variability in species of the genus *Drosophila*. V. Ejaculatory bulb esterases in *Drosophila* phylogeny. Biochem Genet 2:1–18

Johnson MS, Turner JRG (1979) Absence of dosage compensation for a sex-linked enzyme in butterflies (*Heliconius*). Heredity 43:71–77

Joly L, Goltzene F, Porte L (1978) L'action excercee par l'appareil endocrine sur les phases tardives de l'ovogénèse chez *Locusta migratoria*. J Insect Physiol 24:187–193

Jones CW, Kafatos FC (1980a) Coordinately expressed members of two chorion multigene families are clustered, alternating, and divergently oriented. Nature (Lond) 284:635–638

Jones CW, Kafatos FC (1980b) Structure, organization and evolution of developmentally regulated chorion genes in a silkmoth. Cell 22:855–867

Jones CW, Rosenthal N, Rodakis GC, Kafatos FC (1979) Evolution of two major chorion multigene families as inferred from cloned cDNA and protein sequences. Cell 18:1317–1332

Jones JC, Fischman DA (1970) An electron microscopic study of the spermathecal complex of virgin *Aedes aegypti* mosquitoes. J Morphol 132:293–312

Jones N (1990) Transcriptional regulation by dimerization: two sides to an incestuous relationship. Cell 61:9–11

Juberthie-Jupeau L, Cazals M (1985) Ultrastructure et maturation de la glande accessoire de la spermatheque chez *Speonomus delarouzeei* Fairm. (Coleoptera: Cotopidae) du milieu souterrain. Int J Insect Morphol Embryol 14:75–86

Kafatos FC (1972) The cocoonase zymogen cells of silkmoth. Curr Topics Dev Biol 7:125–191

Kafatos FC (1981) Structure, evolution and developmental expression of the silkmoth chorion multigene families. Am Zool 21:707–714

Kafatos FC, Regier JC, Mazur GD et al. (1977) The eggshell of insects: differentiation-specific proteins and the control of their synthesis and accumulation during development. In: Beermann N (ed) Results and problems in cell differentiation, vol 8. Springer, Berlin Heidelberg New York, pp 45–145

Kafatos FC, Mitsialis SA, Spoerel N, Mariani B, Lingappa JR, Delidakis C (1985) Studies on the developmentally regulated expression and amplification of insect chorion genes. Cold Spr Harb Symp Quant Biol 50:537–547

Kafatos FC, Mitsialis SA, Nguyen HT, Spoerel N, Tsitilou SG, Mazur GD (1987) Evolution of structural genes and regulatory elements for the insect chorion. In: Raff RA, Raff EC (eds) Development as an evolutionary process. Alan R Liss, New York, pp 161–178

Kalfayan L, Levine J, Orr-Weaver T et al. (1985) Localization of sequences regulating *Drosophila* chorion gene amplification and expression. Cold Spring Harbor Symp Quant Biol 50:527–535

Kambysellis M (1977) Genetic and hormonal regulation of vitellogenesis in *Drosophila*. Am Zool 17:535–549

Kambysellis MP, Cradock EM (1976) Genetic analysis of vitellogenesis in *Drosophila*. Genetics 83:538

Kappler C, Goltzene F, Lagueux M, Hetru C, Hoffmann JA (1986) Role of the follicle cells and the oocytes in ecdysone biosynthesis and esterification in vitellogenic females of *Locusta migratoria*. Int J Invertebr Reprod 9:17–34

Kasuga H, Osanai M (1984) Migration mode of two types of spermatozoa of *Bombyx mori* from testis to receptaculum seminis. Zool Sci 1:942

Kasuga H, Osanai M, Aigaki T (1985) Post-testicular maturation of spermatozoa of the silkworm, *Bombyx mori*. Zool Sci 2:953

Kasuga H, Aigaki T, Osanai M (1987) System for supply of free arginine in the spermatophore of *Bombyx mori*. Arginine-liberating activities of contents of male reproductive glands. Insect Biochem 17:317–322

Katsuno S (1977) Studies on eupyrene and apyrene spermatozoa in the silkworm, *Bombyx mori* L. (Lepidoptera: Bombycidae). IV. The behaviour of the spermatozoa in the internal reproductive organs of female adults. Appl Entomol Zool 12:352–359

Kauleneas MS (1964) General and experimental embryology of *Acheta domesticus* (L.). PhD Thesis, London Univ London, England

Kaulenas MS (1972) The stability of subunit association in *Acheta* ribosomes. J Insect Physiol 18:649–673

Kaulenas MS (1976) Regional specialization for export protein synthesis in the male cricket accessory gland. J Exp Zool 195:81–96

Kaulenas MS (1985) Molecular biology: protein synthesis. In: Kerkut GA, Gilbert LI (eds) Comprehensive insect physiology, biochemistry and pharmacology, vol 10. Pergamon Press, Oxford, pp 255–305

Kaulenas MS, Yenofsky RL, Potswald HE, Burns AL (1975) Protein synthesis by the accessory gland of the male house cricket, *Acheta domesticus*. J Exp Zool 193:21–36

Kaulenas MS, Potswald HE, Burns AL, Yenofsky RL (1979) Development of structural and functional specializations for export protein synthesis by the accessory gland of the male cricket, *Acheta domesticus*. Int J Insect Morphol Embryol 8:33–49

Kawasaki H, Yago M (1983) The identification of two N-acyldopamine glucosides in the left collelterial gland of the praying mantid, *Tenodera aridifolia sinensis* Saussure, and their role in the oothecal sclerotization. Insect Biochem 13:267–271

Kawasaki H, Sato H, Suzuki M (1971a) Structural proteins in the silkworm eggshells. Insect Biochem 1:130–148

Kawasaki H, Sato H, Suzuki M (1971b) Structural proteins in the eggshell of the oriental garden cricket, *Gryllus mitratus*. Biochem J 125:495–505

Kawasaki H, Sato H, Suzuki M (1974) Structural proteins in the egg envelopes of dragonflies, *Sympetrum infuscatum* and *S. frequens*. Insect Biochem 4:99–111

Kawasaki H, Sato H, Suzuki M (1975) Structural proteins in the egg envelopes of the mealworm beetle, *Tenebrio molitor*. Insect Biochem 5:25–34

Kawasaki H, Sato H, Yago M (1976) Structural proteins in the eggshell of the horned beetle, *Xylotrupes dichotomus*. Insect Biochem 6:43–52

Kawooya JK, Law JH (1983) Purification and properties of microvitellogenin of *Manduca sexta*. Role of juvenile hormone in appearance and uptake. Biochem Biophys Res Commun 117:643–650

Keeley LL (1978) Endocrine regulation of fat body development and function. Annu Rev Entomol 23:329–352

Keller W (1984) The RNA lariat: a new ring to the splicing of mRNA precursors. Cell 39:423–425

Kelly TJ, Hunt LM (1982) Endocrine influence upon the development of vitellogenic competency in *Oncopeltus fasciatus*. J Insect Physiol 28:935–941

Kelly TJ, Adams TS, Schwartz MB, Birnbaum MJ, Rubenstein EC, Imberski RB (1987) Juvenile hormone and ovarian maturation in the Diptera: a review of recent results. Insect Biochem 17:1089–1093

Kempa-Tomm S, Hoffmann KH, Engelmann F (1990) Vitellogenins and vitellins of the Mediterranean field cricket, *Gryllus bimaculatus*: isolation, characterization and quantification. Physiol Entomol 15:167–178

Kent PW, Brunet PCJ (1959) The occurrence of protocatechuic acid and its 4-O-β-D-glucoside in *Blatta* and *Periplaneta*. Tetrahedron 7:252–256

Khalifa A (1949) The mechanism of insemination and the mode of action of the spermatophore in *Gryllus domesticus*. Q J Microsc Sci 90:281–292

Khalifa A (1950) Spermatophore production in *Galleria mellonella* L. (Lepidoptera). Proc R Entomol Soc Lond 25A:33–42

Kilby BA (1963) The biochemistry of the insect fat body. Adv Insect Physiol 1:112–174

Kim HR, Ko YG, Mayer RT (1988) Purification, characterization, and synthesis of vitellin from the cabbage butterfly *Pieris rapae* L. Arch Insect Biochem Physiol 9:67–79

Kimber SJ (1980) The secretion of the eggshell of *Schistocerca gregaria*. Ultrastructure of the follicle cells during the termination of vitellogenesis and eggshell secretion. J Cell Sci 46:455–477

Kimber SJ (1981) The secretion of the eggshell of *Schistocerca gregaria*. Analysis of the kinetics of secretion in vitro by light and electron microscope autoradiography. J Cell Sci 50:225–243

Kimura T, Yasuyana K, Yanaguchi T (1989) Proctolinergic innervation of the accessory gland in male crickets (*Gryllus bimaculatus*): detection of proctolin and some pharmacological properties of myogenically and neurogenically evoked contractions. J Insect Physiol 35:251–264

Kindle H, König R, Lanzrein B (1988) In vitro uptake of vittelogenin by follicles of the cockroach *Nauphoeta cinerea*: comparison of artificial media with haemolymph media and role of vittelogenin concentration and juvenile hormone. J Insect Physiol 34:541–548

King RC (1970) Ovarian development in *Drosophila melanogaster*. Academic Press, Lond New York

King RC, Büning J (1985) The origin and functioning of insect oocytes and nurse cells. In: Kerkut GA, Gilbert LI (eds) Comprehensive insect physiology, biochemistry and pharmacology, vol 1. Pergamon Press, Oxford, pp 37–82

King RC, Koch EA (1963) Studies on ovarian follicle cells of *Drosophila*. Q J Microsc Sci 104:297–320

King RC, Vanoucek EG (1960) Oogenesis in adult *Drosophila melanogaster*. X. Studies on the behavior of the follicle cells. Growth 24:333–338

King RC, Aggarwal SK, Aggarwal V (1968) The development of the female *Drosophila* reproductive system. J Morphol 124:143–166

Klaembt C, Knust E, Tietze K, Campos-Ortega JA (1989) Closely related transcripts encoded by the neurogenic gene complex *Enhancer of split* of *Drosophila melanogaster* EMBO J 8:203–211

Kloc M, Matuszewski B (1977) Extrachromosomal DNA and the origin of oocytes in the telotrophic-meroistic ovary of *Creophilus maxillosus* (L.)(Staphylinidae, Coleoptera-Polyphage). Wilhelm Roux's Arch Dev Biol 183:351–368

Klowden MJ (1990) The endogenous regulation of mosquito reproductive behavior. Experientia 46:660–670

Koch EA, Spitzer RH (1983) Multiple effects of colchicine on oogenesis *Drosophila*: induced sterility and switch of potential oocyte to nurse-cell developmental pathway. Cell Tissue Res 228:21–32

Koeppe JK, Wellman SE (1980) Ovarian maturation in *Leucophaea maderae*: juvenile hormone regulation of thymidine uptake into follicle cell DNA. J Insect Physiol 26:219–228

Koeppe JK, Hobson K, Wellman SE (1980) Juvenile hormone regulation of structural changes and DNA synthesis in the follicular epithelium of *Leuocophaea maderae*. J Insect Physiol 26:229–240

Koeppe JK, Kovalick GE, Prestwich GD (1984) A specific photoaffinity label for hemolymph and ovarian juvenile hormone-binding proteins in *Leuocophaea maderae*. J Biol Chem 259:3219–3223

Komitopoulou K, Gans M, Margaritis LH, Kafatos FC, Masson M (1983) Isolation and characterization of sex-linked female sterile mutants in *Drosophila melanogaster* with special attention to eggshell mutants. Genetics 105:897–920

Komitopoulou K, Margaritis LH, Kafatos FC (1988) Structural and biochemical studies on four sex-linked chorion mutants of *Drosophila melanogaster*. Dev Genet 9:37–48

König R, Lanzrein B (1985) Binding of vitellogenin to specific receptors in oocyte membrane preparations of the ovoviviparous cockroach, *Nauphoeta cinerea*. Insect Biochem 15:735–747

König R, Nordin JH, Gochoco CH, Kunkel JG (1988) Studies on ligand recognition by vitellogenin receptors in follicle membrane preparations of the German cockroach, *Blatella germanica*. Insect Biochem 18:395–404

Korschelt E (1887) Zur Bildung der Eihüllen, der Mikropylen und Chorionanhange bei den Insekten. Nova Acta Ksl Leop-Carol Dtsch Akad Naturforsch 51:185–252

Korschelt E, Heider K (1890) Entwicklungsgeschichte der wirbellosen Thiere. Fischer, Jena

Kovalick GE, Koeppe JK (1983) Assay and identification of juvenile hormone binding proteins in *Leucophaea maderae*. Mol Cell Endocrinol 31:271–286

Kozma R, Bownes M (1986) Yolk protein induction in males of several *Drosophila* species. Insect Biochem 16:263–271

Kramer SJ, DeKort CAD (1978) Juvenile hormone carrier lipoproteins in the haemolymph of the Colorado potato beetle, *Leptinotarsa decemlineata*. Insect Biochem 8:87–92

Kramer SJ, Ong J, Law JH (1973) Oothecal proteins of the oriental praying mantid *Tenodera sinensis*. Insect Biochem 3:297–306

Kramer SJ, Mundall EC, Law JH (1980) Purification and properties of manducin, an amino acid storage protein of the haemolymph of larval and pupal *Manduca sexta*. Insect Biochem 10:279–288

Krause G (1934) Analyse erster Differenzierungsprozesse im Keim der Gewächshausschrecke durch künstlich erzeugte Zwillings-, Doppel- und Mehrfachbildungen. Wilhelm Roux's Arch Dev Biol 132:115–205

Krause G (1938) Die Ausbildung der Korpergrundgestalt im Ei der Gewachshausschrecke, *Tachycines asynamorus*. Z Morphol Okol Tiere 34:499–564

Kroeger H (1959a) Determinationsmosaike aus kombiniert im plantierten Imaginalscheiben von *Ephestia kühniella* Z. Wilhelm Roux's Arch Dev Biol 151:113–135

Kroeger H (1959b) The genetic control of genital morphology in *Drosophila*. Wilhelm Roux's Arch Dev Biol 151:301–322

Kuhl D, dela Fuente J, Chaturvedi M et al. (1987) Reversible silencing of enhancers by sequences derived from the human IFN-α-promoter. Cell 50:1057–1069

Kulakosky PC, Telfer WH (1987) Selective endocytosis, in vitro, by ovarian follicles from *Hyalophora cecropia*. Insect Biochem 17:845–858

Kulakosky PC, Telfer WH (1990) Lipoprotein as a yolk precursor in *Hyalophora cecropia*: uptake kinetics and competition with vittelogenin. Arch Insect Biochem Physiol 14:269–285

Kulshrestha SK (1969) Observations on the ovulation and oviposition with reference to corpus luteum formation in *Musca domestica neubolo* Fabr. (Muscidae: Diptera). J Nat Hist 3:561–570

Kunkel JG (1979) Stages of vitellogenic competence in the cockroach. Am Zool 19:747

Kunkel JG, Nordin JH (1985) Yolk proteins. In: Kerkut GA, Gilbert LI (eds) Comprehensive insect physiology, biochemistry and pharmacology, vol 1. Pergamon Press, Oxford, pp 83–11

Kunkel JG, Pan ML (1976) Selectivity of yolk protein uptake: comparison of vitellogenins of two insects. J Insect Physiol 22:809–818

Kuster JE, Davey KG (1983) The effect of allatectomy or neurosecretory cell ablation on protein synthesis in the spermathecae of *Rhodnius prolixus*. Int J Invertebr Reprod 6:189–195

Lafon-Cazal M, Gallois D, Lehouelleur J, Bockaert J (1987) Stimulatory effects of male accessory-gland extracts on the myogenicity and the adenylate cyclase activity of the oviduct of *Locusta migratoria*. J Insect Physiol 33:909–915

Lai-Fook J (1982a) The vasa deferentia of the male reproductive system of *Calpodes ethlius* (Hesperiidae, Lepidoptera). Can J Zool 60:1172–1183

Lai-Fook J (1982b) Structure of the noncuticular simplex of the internal male reproductive tract of *Calpodes ethlius* (Hesperiidae, Lepidoptera). Can J Zool 60:1184–1201

Lai-Fook J (1982c) Structure of the accessory glands and duplex of the internal male reproductive system of *Calpodes ethlius* (Hesperiidae, Lepidoptera). Can J Zool 60:1202–1215

Lai-Fook J (1986) The virgin bursa copulatrix of the butterfly, *Calpodes*. Tissue Cell 18:545–558

Lakhotia SC, Mukherjee AS (1969) Chromosomal basis of dosage compensation in *Drosophila*. I. Cellular autonomy of hyperactivity of the male X-chromosome in salivary glands and sex differentiation. Genet Res 14:137–150

Landa V (1960) Origin, development, and function of the spermatophore in cockchafer (*Melolontha melolontha* L.). Acta Soc Entomol Cechosloveniae 57:297–316

Landers MH, Happ GM (1980) Precocene inhibition of vitellogenesis in *Drosophila melanogaster*. Experientia 36:619–620

Lange AB (1984) The transfer of prostaglandin-synthesizing activity during mating in *Locusta migratoria*. Insect Biochem 14:551–556

Lange AB (1987) Hormonal control of locust oviducts. Arch Insect Biochem Physiol 4:47–56

Lange AB (1990) The presence of proctolin in the reproductive system of *Rhodnius prolixus*. J Insect Physiol 36:345–351

Lange AB, Loughton BG (1981) The selective accumulation of vittelogenin in the locust oocyte. Experientia 37:273–274

Lange AB, Loughton BG (1984) An analysis of the secretions of the male accessory reproductive gland of the African migratory locust. Int J Invertebr Reprod 7:73–81

Lange AB, Loughton BG (1985) An oviposition-stimulating factor in the male accessory reproductive gland of the locust, *Locusta migratoria*. Gen Comp Endocrinol 57:208–215

Lange AB, Phillips DR, Loughton BG (1983) The effects of precocene II on early adult development in male *Locusta*. J Insect Physiol 29:73–81

Lange AB, Orchard I, Adams ME (1986) Peptidergic innervation of insect reproductive tissue: the association of proctolin with oviduct visceral musculature. J Comp Neurol 254:279–286

Lanot R, Thiebold J, Lagueux M, Goltzene F, Hoffmann JA (1987) Involvement of ecdysone in the control of meiotic reinitiation in oocytes of *Locusta migratoria* (Insecta, Orthoptera). Dev Biol 121:174–181

LaPointe MC, Koeppe JK (1984) Thymidine kinase from ovaries of the cockroach *Leucophaea maderae*: regulation by juvenile hormone. Insect Biochem 14:53–63

LaPointe MC, Koeppe JK, Nair KK (1985) Follicle cell polyploidy in *Leucophaea maderae*: regulation by juvenile hormone. J Insect Physiol 31:187–193

Laufer H, Vafopoulou-Mandalos X, Deak P (1986) Ecdysteroid titres in *Chironomus* and their relation to haemoglobins and vittelogenins. Insect Biochem 16:281–285

Laugé G (1975) Mise en place d'éléments mésodermiques dans le disque génital de *Drosophila melanogaster* Meig. C R Acad Sci Paris 280:339–342

Laugé G (1982) Development of the genitalia and analia. In: Ransom R (ed) A handbook of *Drosophila* development. Elsevier Amsterdam, pp 237–263

Laurence BR, Simpson MG (1974) Cell replication in the follicular epithelium of the adult mosquito. J Insect Physiol 20:703–715

Lautenschlager F (1932) Die Embryonalentwicklung der weiblichen Keimdrüse bei der Psychide *Solenobia triquetrella*. Zool Jahrb Anat 56:121–162

Lauverjat S (1969) Effects de l'allatectomie sur le développement imaginal des voies génitales femelles de *Locusta migratoria migratorioides* (Insecte Orthoptère). C R Acad Sci Paris 268:2109–2112

Lauverjat S (1977) L'évolution post-imaginale du tissu adipeux femelle de *Locusta migratoria* et son contrôle endocrine. Gen Comp Endocrinol 33:13–34

Lauverjat S, Girardie A (1974) Les voies génitales femelles (oviductes et glandes pseudocollétériques) de *Locusta migratoria*. I. Étude ultrastructurale du développement imaginal. Rôle des corps allataes. Gen Comp Endocrinol 23:325–339

Leahy MG (1973) Oviposition of virgin *Schistocerca gregaria* (Forskal)(Orthoptera: Acrididae) after implant of the male accessory gland complex. J Entomol 48A:69–78

Leahy MG, Craig GB Jr (1965) Male accessory gland substance as a stimulant for oviposition in *Aedes aegypti* and *A. albopictus*. Mosquito News 25:448–452

Lecanidou R, Tsitilou SG, Kafatos FC (1980) Isolation of transcriptionally active nuclei from developing follicles of the silkmoth, *Antheraea polyphemus*, and optimization of ionic conditions for in vitro transcription. Insect Biochem 10:367–374

Lecanidou R, Eickbush TH, Rodakis GC, Kafatos FC (1983) Novel B family sequence from an early chorion cDNA library of *Bombyx mori*. Proc Natl Acad Sci USA 80:1955–1959

Lecanidou R, Rodakis GC, Eickbush TH, Kafatos FC (1986) Evolution of the silkmoth chorion gene superfamily: gene families CA and CB. Proc Natl Acad Sci USA 83:6514–6518

Lehmann R, Nüsslein-Volhard C (1986) Abdominal segmentation, pole cell formation and embryonic polarity require the localized activity of *oskar*, a maternal gene in *Drosophila*. Cell 47:141–152

Lehmann R, Nüsslein-Volhard C (1987) Involvement of the *pumilio* gene in the transport of an abdominal signal in the *Drosophila* embryo. Nature (Lond) 329:167–170

Lefevre G, Johnsson UB (1962) Sperm transfer, storage, displacement and utilization in *Drosophila melanogaster*. Genetics 47:1719

Lensky Y, Alumot E (1969) Proteins in the spermathecae and haemolymph of the queen bee (*Apis mellifera* L. var *ligustica* Spin). Comp Biochem Physiol 30:569–575

Leopold RA (1976) The role of male accessory glands in insect reproduction. Annu Rev Entomol 21:199–221

Leopold RA, Degrugillier ME (1973) Sperm penetration of house fly eggs: evidence for involvement of a female accessory secretion. Science 181:555–557

Leopold RA, Terranova AC, Thorson BJ, Degrugillier ME (1971) The biosynthesis of the male housefly accessory secretion and its fate in the mated female. J Insect Physiol 17:987–1003

Lespés C (1885) Memoire sur les spermatophores des grillons. Ann Sci Nat Zool 3:366–377

Lessman CA, Rollins L, Herman WS (1982) Effects of juvenile hormones I, II, and III on reproductive tract growth in male and female monarch butterflies. Comp Biochem Physiol 71A:141–144

Leuckart R (1855) Über die Micropyle und den feineren Bau der Schalenhaut bei den Insekteneiern. Zugleich ein Beitrag zur Lehre von der Befruchtung. Arch Anal Physiol Wiss Median 1855:90–264

Leuzinger H, Weismann R, Lehman FE (1926) Zur Kentness der Anatomie und Entwicklungsgeschickte der Stabheuschrecke *Carausius morosus*. Zool Vergl Anat Zurich, 414 pp

Levedakou EN, Sekeris CE (1987) Isolation and characterization of vitellin from the fruitfly, *Dacus oleae*. Arch Insect Biochem Physiol 4:297–311

Levine J, Spradling A (1985) DNA sequence of a 3.8 kilobase pair region controlling *Drosophila* chorion gene amplification. Chromosoma 92:136–142

Levis R, Hazelrigg T, Rubin GM (1985a) Effects of genomic position on the expression of transduced copies of the *white* gene of *Drosophila*. Science 229:558–561

Levis R, Hazelrigg T, Rubin GM (1985b) Separable *cis*-acting control elements for expression of the *white* gene of *Drosophila*. EMBO J 4:3489–3499

Lew A, Ball JH (1980) Effect of copulation time on spermatozoan transfer of *Diabrotica virgifera* (Coleoptera, Chrysomelidae). Ann Entomol Soc Am 73:360–361

Lima-de-Faria A (1962) Metabolic DNA in *Tipula oleracea*. Chromosoma 12:47–59

Lineruth K, Lambertsson A (1985) Stage specific synthesis of some follicle cell proteins in *Drosophila melanogaster*. Wilhelm Roux's Arch Dev Biol 194:436–439

Lineruth K, Lambertsson A (1986) Correlation between a female sterile mutation and a set of follicle cell proteins in *Drosophila melanogaster*. Mol Gen Genet 205:213–216

Lineruth K, Lambertsson A, Lindberg M (1985) Genetic localization of a follicle cell protein locus in *Drosophila melanogaster*. Mol Gen Genet 201:375–378

Linley JR (1981a) Ejaculation and spermatophore formation in *Culicoides melleus* (Coq.)(Diptera: Ceratopogonidae). Can J Zool 59:332–346

Linley JR (1981b) Emptying of the spermatophore and spermathecal filling in *Culicoides melleus* (Coq.)(Diptera: Ceratopogonidae). Can J Zool 59:347–356

Linley JR, Simmons KR (1981) Sperm motility and spermathecal filling in lower Diptera. Int J Invertebr Reprod 4:137–145

Linley JR, Simmons KR (1983) Quantitative aspects of sperm transfer in *Simulium decorum* (Diptera: Simuliidae). J Insect Physiol 29:581–584

Littlefield CL, Bryant PJ (1979) Prospective fates and regulative capacities of fragments of the female genital disc of *Drosophila melanogaster*. Dev Biol 70:127–148

Liu TP, Darley JJ, Davies DM (1975) Differentiation of ovariolar follicular cells and formation of previtelline-membrane substance in *Simulium vittatum* Zetterstedt (Diptera: Simuliidae). Int J Insect Morphol Embryol 4:331–340

Locke J, White BN, Wyatt GR (1987) Cloning and 5′ end nucleotide sequences of two juvenile hormone-inducible vitellogenin genes of the African migratory locust. DNA 6:331–342

Logan SK, Wensink (1990) Ovarian follicle cell enhancers from the *Drosophila* yolk protein genes: different segments of one enhancer have different cell-type specificities that interact to give normal expression. Gen Dev 4:613–623

Loher W (1974) Circadian control of spermatophore formation in the cricket *Teleogryllus* commodus Walker. J Insect Physiol 20:1155–1172

Loher W (1979) Circadian rhythmicity of locomotor behavior and oviposition in female *Teleogryllus commodus*. Behav Ecol Sociobiol 5:253–262

Loher W (1981) The effect of mating on female sexual behavior of *Teleogryllus commodus* Walker. Behav Ecol Sociobiol 9:219–225

Loher W, Edson K (1973) The effect of mating on egg production and release in the cricket *Teleogryllus commodus*. Entomol Exp Appl 16:483–490

Loher W, Ganjian I, Kubo I, Stanly-Samuelson D, Tobe SS (1981) Prostaglandins: their role in egg-laying of the cricket *Teleogryllus commodus*. Proc Natl Acad Sci USA 78:7835–7838

Lohs-Schardin M (1982) *Dicephalic* – a *Drosophila* mutant affecting polarity in follicle organization and embryonic patterning. Wilhelm Roux's Arch Dev Biol 191:28–36

Lohs-Schardin M, Sander K (1976) A dicephalic monster embryo of *Drosophila melanogaster* Roux Arch 179:159–162

Louis D, Kumar R (1971) Morphology and histology of the mushroom-shaped gland in some Dictyoptera. Ann Entomol Soc Am 64:977–982

Lubbock J (1859) On the ova and pseudova of insects. Phil Trans R Soc Lond 149:341–369

Lucchesi JC (1983) The relationship between gene dosage, gene expression, and sex in *Drosophila*. Dev Genet 3:275–282

Lucchesi JC, Manning JE (1987) Gene dosage compensation in *Drosophila melanogaster*. Adv Genet 24:371–429

Lum PTM (1961) Studies on the reproductive system of some Florida mosquitoes. II. The male accessory glands and their role. Ann Entomol Soc Am 54:430–433

Lusis O, Sandor T, Lehoux JC (1970) Histological and histochemical observations on the testes of *Byrsothria fugimata* Guer. and *Gromphadorhina portentosa* Schaum. Can J Zool 48:25–30

Lynn DE, Oberlander H (1981) The effect of cytoskeletal disrupting agents on the morphological response of a cloned *Manduca sexta* cell line to 20-hydroxyecdysone. Wilhelm Roux's Arch Dev Biol 190:150–155

Ma M, Gong H, Zhang JZ, Gwadz R (1987) Response of cultured *Aedes aegypti* fat bodies to 20-hydroxyecdysone. J Insect Physiol 33:89–93

Maa WCJ, Bell WJ (1977) An endogenous component of the mechanism controlling the vitellogenic cycle in the American cockroach. J Insect Physiol 23:895–897

MacGregor HC, Stebbings H (1970) A massive system of microtubules associated with cytoplasmic movement in telotrophic ovarioles. J Cell Sci 6:431–449

Madhavan MM, Schneiderman HA (1977) Histological analysis of the dynamics of growth of imaginal discs and histoblast nests during the larval development of *Drosophila melanogaster*. Wilhelm Roux's Arch Dev Biol 183:269–305

Mahowald AP (1962) Fine structure of pole cells and polar granules in *Drosophila melanogaster*. J Exp Zool 151:201–216

Mahowald AP (1971) Polar granules of *Drosophila*. IV. Cytochemical studies showing loss of RNA from polar granules during early stages of embryogenesis. J Exp Zool 176:345–352

Mahowald AP (1972a) Ultrastructural observations on oogenesis in *Drosophila*. J Morphol 137:29–48

Mahowald AP (1972b) Oogenesis. In: Counce SJ, Waddington CH (eds) Developmental systems, vol 1, insects. Academic Press Lond New York, pp 1–47

Mahowald AP, Strassheim JM (1970) Intercellular migration of centrioles in the germarium of *Drosophila melanogaster*. An electron microscopic study. J Cell Biol 45:306–320

Mahowald AP, Caulton JH, Edwards MK, Floyd AD (1979) Loss of centrioles and polyploidization in follicle cells of *Drosophila melanogaster*. Exp Cell Res 118:404–410

Maine EM, Salz HK, Cline TW, Schedl P (1985) The *sex-lethal* gene of Drosophila: DNA alterations associated with sex-specific lethal mutations. Cell 43:521–529

Malcolm DB, Sommerville J (1974) The structure of chromosome-derived ribonucleoprotein in oocytes of *Triturus cristatus carnifax*. Chromosoma 48:137–158

Mane SD, Tompkins L, Richmond RC (1983) Male esterase 6 catalyzes the synthesis of a sex pheromone in *Drosophila melanogaster* females. Science 222:419–421

Mann T (1984) Spermatophores. Development, structure, biochemical attributes and role in the transfer of spermatozoa. Springer, Berlin Heidelberg New York

Manning A (1967) The control of sexual receptivity in female *Drosophila*. Anim Behav 15:239–250

Mardon G, Mosher D, Disteche CM, Nishioka Y, McLaren A, Page DC (1989) Duplication, deletion, and polymorphism in the sex-determining region of the mouse Y chromosome. Science 243:78–83

Mardon G, Page DC (1989) The sex-determining region of the mouse Y chromosome encodes a protein with a highly acidic domain and 13 zinc fingers. Cell 56:765–770

Margaritis LH (1985a) Structure and physiology of the eggshell. In: Kerkut GA, Gilbert LI (eds) Comprehensive insect physiology, biochemistry and pharmacology, vol 1. Pergamon Press, Oxford, pp 153–230

Margaritis LH (1985b) The egg-shell of *Drosophila melanogaster*. III. Covalent cross-linking of the chorion proteins involves endogenous hydrogen peroxide. Tissue Cell 17:553–559

Margaritis LH, Kafatos FC, Petri WH (1980) The eggshell of *Drosophila melanogaster*. I. Fine structure of the layers and regions of the wild-type eggshell. J Cell Sci 43:1–35

Mariani BD, Langappa JR, Kafatos FC (1988) Temporal regulation in development: negative and positive *cis* regulators dictate the precise timing of expression of a *Drosophila* chorion gene. Proc Natl Acad Sci USA 85:3029–3033

Marks EP, Holman M (1979) Ecdysone action on insect cell lines. In vitro 15:300–307

Marsh JL, Wieschaus E (1978) Is sex determination in germline and soma controlled by separate genetic mechanisms? Nature (Lond) 272:249–251

Martinez T, Hagedorn HH (1987) Development of responsiveness to hormones after a blood meal in the mosquito *Aedes aegypti*. Insect Biochem 17:1095–1098

Martinez-Cruzado JC, Swimmer C, Fenerjian MG, Kafatos FC (1988) Evolution of the autosomal chorion locus in *Drosophila*. I. General organization of the locus and sequence comparisons of genes s15 and s19 in evolutionarily distant species. Genetics 119:663–677

Maruo F, Okada M (1987) Monoclonal antibodies against *Drosophila* ovaries: their reaction with ovarian and embryonic antigens. Cell Differ 20:45–54

Maschat F, Dubertret ML, Thérond P, Claverie JM, Lepesant JA (1990) Structure of the ecdysone-inducible P1 gene of *Drosophila melanogaster*. J Mol Biol 214:359–372

Masler EP, Ofengand J (1982) Biochemical properties of the two forms of *Laucophaea maderae* vitellin and their subunits. Insect Biochem 12:441–453

Masuda H, Oliveira PL (1985) Characterization of vitellin and vittelogenin from *Rhodnius prolixus*. Insect Biochem 15:543–550

Mathew G, Rai KS (1975) Structure and formation of egg membranes in *Aedes aegypti* (L.)(Diptera: Culicidae). Int J Insect Morphol Embryol 4:369–380

Matsuda R (1976) Morphology and evolution of the insect abdomen. Pergamon Press, Oxford

Matsuzaki M (1971) Electron microscopic studies on the oogenesis of dragonfly and cricket with special reference to the panoistic ovaries. Dev Growth Differ 13:379–398

Matsuzaki M, Ando H, Neumann Visscher S (1979) Fine structure of oocyte and follicular cells during oogenesis in *Galloisiana nipponensis* (Casdell and King)(Grylloblattodea: Grylloblattidae). Int J Insect Morphol Embryol 8:257–263

Mattaj IW (1989) A binding consensus: RNA-protein interactions in splicing, snRNPs, and sex. Cell 57:1–3

Matuszewski B, Ciechomski K, Nurkowska J, Kloc M (1985) The linear clusters of oogonial cells in the development of telotrophic ovarioles in polyphage Coleoptera. Wilhelm Roux's Arch Dev Biol 194:462–469

Mays M (1972) Autoradiographische Untersuchungen zum Stofftransport von den Nährzellen zur Oocyte der Feuerwanze *Pyrrhocoris apterus* L. (Heteroptera). Z Zellforsch 123:395–410

Mazur GD, Regier JC, Kafatos FC (1982) Order and defects in the silkmoth chorion. A biological analogue of a cholesteric liquid crystal. In: King RC, Akai H (eds) Insect ultrastructure, vol 1. Plenum Press, New York, pp 150–185

Mazzini M, Gaino E (1985) Fine structure of the egg shells of *Habrophlebia fusca* (Curtis) and *H. consiglioi* Biancheri (Ephemeroptera: Leptophlebiidae). Int J Insect Morphol Embryol 14:327–334

Mazzini M, Giorgi F (1985) The follicle cell-oocyte interaction in ovarian follicles of the stick insect *Bacillus rossius* (Rossi):(Insecta: Phasmatodea). J Morphol 185:37–49

McCaffery AR, McCaffery VA (1983) Corpus allatum activity during overlapping cycles of oocyte growth in adult female *Melanoplus sanguinipes*. J Insect Physiol 29:259–266

McCoubrey WK, Nordstrom KD, Meneely PM (1988) Microinjected DNA from the X chromosome affects sex determination in *Caenorhabditis elegans*. Science 242:1146–1151

McFarlane JE (1962) The action of pepsin and trypsin on the egg shell of *Acheta domesticus*. Can J Zool 40:553–557

McFarlane JE (1968a) Diel periodicity in spermatophore formation in the house cricket, *Acheta domesticus* (L.). Can J Zool 46:695–698

McFarlane JE (1968b) Cation antagonism and a model for the cell membrane. Can J Zool 46:943–945

McKeown M, Belote JM, Andrew DJ, Scott TN, Wolfner MF, Baker BS (1986) Molecular genetics of sex determination in *Drosophila*. Symp Soc Dev Biol 44:3–17

McKeown M, Belote JM, Boggs RT (1988) Ectopic expression of the female transformer gene product leads to female differentiation of chromosomally male *Drosophila*. Cell 53:887–895

Mellanby H (1936) The later embryology of *Rhodnius prolixus*. Q J Microsc Sci 79:1–42

Meola SM, Mollenhauer HH, Thompson JM (1977) Cytoplasmic bridges within the follicular epithelium of the ovarioles of two Diptera, *Aedes aegypti* and *Stomoxys calcitrans*. J Morphol 153:81–86

Mercer EH, Brunet PCJ (1959) The electron microscopy of the left colleterial gland of the cockroach. J Biophys Biochem Cytol 5:257–261

Mesnier M (1980) Study of oocyte growth within the ovariole in a stick-insect, *Clitumnus extradentatus*. J Insect Physiol 26:59–65

Mestril R, Schiller P, Amin J, Klapper H, Ananthan J, Voellmy R (1986) Heat shock and ecdysterone activation of the *Drosophila melanogaster* hsp23 gene; a sequence element implied in developmental regulation. EMBO J 5:1667–1673

Metschnikow E (1866) Embryologische Studien an Insekten. Z Wiss Zool 16:389–493

Miller WH (1983) Physiological effects of cyclic GMP in the vertebrate retinal rod outer segment. Adv Cyclic Nucl Res 15:405–511

Mindrinos MN, Petri WH, Galanopoulos VK, Lombard MF, Margaritis LH (1980) Crosslinking of the *Drosophila* chorion involves a peroxidase. Wilhelm Roux's Arch Dev Biol 189:187–196

Mindrinos MN, Scherer LJ, Garcini FJ, Kwan H, Jacobs KA, Petri WH (1985) Isolation and chromosomal location of putative vitelline membrane genes in *Drosophila melanogaster*. EMBO J 4:147–153

Mine E, Izumi S, Katsuki M, Tomino S (1983) Developmental and sex-dependent regulation of storage protein synthesis in the silkworm, *Bombyx mori*. Dev Biol 97:329–337

Minks AK (1967) Biochemical aspects of juvenile hormone action in the adult *Locusta migratoria*. Arch Neerl Zool 17:175–257

Minoo P, Postlethwait J (1985a) Biosynthesis of *Drosophila* yolk polypeptide. Arch Insect Biochem Physiol 2:7–27

Minoo P, Postlethwait JH (1985b) Processing and secretion of a mutant yolk polypeptide in *Drosophila*. Biochem Genet 23:913–932

Mintzas AC, Chrysanthis G, Christodoulou C, Marmaras VJ (1983) Translation of the mRNAs coding for the major hemolymph proteins of *Ceratitis capitata* in cell-free system: comparison of the translatable mRNA levels to the respective biosynthetic levels of the proteins in the fat body during development. Dev Biol 95:492–496

Mintzas AC, Kambysellis MP (1982) The yolk proteins of *Drosophila melanogaster*: isolation and characterization. Insect Biochem 12:25–33

Mitsialis SA, Kafatos FC (1985) Regulatory elements controlling chorion gene expression are conserved between flies and moths. Nature (Lond) 317:453–456

Mitsialis SA, Spoerel N, Leviten M, Kafatos FC (1987) A short 5'-flanking DNA region is sufficient for developmentally correct expression of moth chorion genes in *Drosophila*. Proc Natl Acad Sci USA 84:7987–7991

Miya K (1958) Studies on the embryonic development of the gonad in the silkworm, *Bombyx mori* L. I. Differentiation of germ cells. J Fac Agric Iwate Univ 3:36–67

Miyake T, Mae N, Shiba T, Kondo S (1987) Production of virus-like particles by the transposable genetic element, *copia*, by *Drosophila melanogaster*. Mol Gen Genet 207:29–37

Monsma SA, Wolfner MF (1988) Structure and expression of a *Drosophila* male accessory gland gene whose product resembles a peptide pheromone precursor. Gen Dev 2:1063–1073

Morrison PE, Venkatesh K, Thompson B (1982) The role of male accessory gland substance on female reproduction with some observations on spermatogenesis in the stable fly. J Insect Physiol 28:607–614

Morrow CS, Hunsley JR, Liszewski MK, Munns TW (1981) Developmental changes in the methylation of silkmoth follicular epithelial messenger ribonucleic acid. Biochemistry 20:2086–2091

Moshitzky P, Applebaum SW (1990) The role of adipokinetic hormone in the control of vitellogenesis in locusts. Insect Biochem 20:319–323

Muckenthaler FA (1964) Autoradiographic study of nucleic acid synthesis during spermatogenesis in the grasshopper, *Melanoplus differentialis*. Exp Cell Res 35:531–547

Müller HP, Schaffner W (1990) Transcriptional enhancers can act in *trans*. Trends Genet 6:300–304

Mundall E, Engelmann F (1977) Endocrine control of vitellogenin synthesis and vitellogenesis in *Triatoma protracta*. J Insect Physiol 23:825–836

Mundall EC, Law JH (1979) Physical and chemical characterization of vitellogenin from the hemolymph and eggs of the tobacco hornworm, *Manduca sexta*. Comp Biochem Physiol 63B:459–468

Mundall EC, Szibbo CM, Tobe SS (1983) Vitellogenin induced in adult male *Diploptera punctata* by juvenile hormone and juvenile hormone analogue: identification and quantitative aspects. J Insect Physiol 29:201–207

Müntz A, Dittmann F (1987) Voltage gradients and microtubules both involved in intercellular protein and mitochondria transport in the telotrophic ovariole of *Dysdercus intermedius*. Wilhelm Roux's Arch Dev Biol 196:391–396

Murre C, McCann PS, Baltimore D (1989a) A new DNA binding and dimerization motif in immunoglobulin enhancer binding, *daughterless, MyoD,* and *myc* proteins. Cell 56:777–783

Murre C, Schonleber McCaw P, Vaessin H et al. (1989b) Interactions between heterologous helix-loop-helix proteins generate complexes that bind specifically to a common DNA sequence. Cell 58:537–544

Murtaugh MP, Denlinger DL (1985) Physiological regulation of long-term oviposition in the house cricket, *Acheta domesticus*. J Insect Physiol 31:611–617

Murtaugh MP, Denlinger DL (1987) Regulation of long-term oviposition in the house cricket, *Acheta domesticus*: roles of prostaglandin and factors associated with sperm. Arch Insect Biochem Physiol 6:59–72

Murtaugh MP, Kapoor CL, Denlinger DL (1985) Extracellular localization of cyclic GMP in the house cricket male accessory reproductive gland and its fate in mating. J Exp Zool 233:413–423

Nadel MR, Goldsmith MR, Goplerud J, Kafatos FC (1980) Specific protein synthesis in cellular differentiation. V. A secretory defect of chorion formation in the Gr^{col} mutant of *Bombyx mori*. Dev Biol 75:41–58

Nagoshi RN, Baker BS (1990) Regulation of sex-specific RNA splicing at the *Drosophila doublesex* gene: *cis*-acting mutations in exon sequences alter sex-specific splicing patterns. Gen Dev 4:89–97

Nagoshi RN, McKeown M, Burtis KC, Belote JM, Baker BS (1988) The control of alternative splicing at genes regulating sexual differentiation in *D. melanogaster*. Cell 53:229–236

Nair KK, Chen TT, Wyatt GR (1981) Juvenile hormone-stimulated polyploidy in adult locust fat body. Dev Biol 81:356–360

Naron A, Nesbitt J, Henzel W, Mulligan K, Mullen JA, Sugumaran M, Lipke H (1983) The effect of D-isoascorbic acid on spermatophore composition in *Spodoptera littoralis*. Insect Biochem 13:247–250

Nel RI (1929) Studies on the development of the genitalia and the genital ducts in insects. I. Female of Orthoptera and Dermaptera. Q J Microsc Sci 73:25–85

Nelsen OE (1934) The segregation of the germ cells in the grasshopper, *Melanoplus differentialis* (Acrididae: Orthoptera). J Morphol 55:545–575

Nelson DR, Adams TS, Pomonis JG (1969) Initial studies in the extraction of the active substance inducing monocoitic behavior in houseflies, black blowflies and screwworm flies. J Econ Entomol 62:634–639

Nicklas JA, Cline TW (1983) Vital genes that flank *sexlethal*, an X-linked sex-determining gene of *Drosophila melanogaster*. Genetics 103:617–631

Nicolaro ML, Bradley JT (1980) Yolk proteins in developing follicles of the house cricket *Acheta domesticus*. J Exp Zool 212:225–232

Nielsen ET (1959) Copulation of *Glyptotendipes (Phytotendipes) paripes* Edwards. Nature (Lond) 184:1252–1253

Nijhout MM, Riddiford LM (1974) The control of egg maturation by juvenile hormone in the tobacco hornworm moth, *Manduca sexta*. Biol Bull 146:377–392

Nordin JH, Gochoko CH, Wojchowski DM, Kunkel JG (1984) A comparative study of the size-heterogeneous high-mannose oligosaccharides of some insect vitellins. Comp Biochem Physiol 79B:379–391

Nöthiger R, Steinmann-Zwicky M (1985) Sex determination in *Drosophila*. Trends Genet 1:209–215

Nöthiger R, Dübendorfer A, Epper F (1977) Gynandromorphs reveal two separate primordia for male and female genitalia in *Drosophila melanogaster*. Wilhelm Roux's Arch Dev Biol 181:367–373

Nöthiger R, Leuthold M, Andersen N et al. (1987) Genetic and developmental analysis of the sex-determining gene 'double sex' of *Drosophila melanogaster*. Genet Res 50:113–123

Nüsslein-Volhard C, Wieschaus E (1980) Mutations affecting segment number and polarity in *Drosophila*. Nature (Lond) 287:795–801

Odhiambo TR (1966) Growth and the hormonal control of sexual maturation in the male desert locust, *Schistocerca gregaria* (Forskal). Trans R Entomol Soc Lond 118:393–412

Odhiambo TR (1969a) The architecture of the accessory reproductive glands of the male desert locust. I. Types of glands and their secretions. Tissue Cell 1:155–182

Odhiambo TR (1969b) The architecture of the accessory reproductive glands of the male desert locust. IV. Fine structure of the glandular epithelium. Phil Trans R Soc Lond 256B:85–114

Odhiambo TR (1971) The architecture of the accessory reproductive glands of the male desert locust. 5. Ultrastructure during maturation. Tissue Cell 3:309–324

Ogiso M, Takahashi SY (1984) Trehalases from the male accessory glands of the American cockroach: developmental changes and the hormonal regulation of the enzymes. Gen Comp Endocronol 55:387–392

Ogiso M, Shinohara Y, Hanaoka K, Takahashi SY (1982) Purification of trehalases from the male accessory glands of the American cockroach, *Periplaneta americana*. Comp Biochem Physiol 72B:511–515

Ogiso M, Shinohara Y, Hanaoka K, Kageyama T, Takahashi SY (1985) Further purification and characterization of trehalases from the American cockroach, *Periplaneta americana*. J Comp Physiol B 155:553–560

Okelo O (1979) Mechanisms of sperm release form the receptaculum seminis of *Schistocerca vaga* Scudder (Orthoptera: Acrididae). Int J Invertebr Reprod 1:121–131

Oliveira PL, Gondim KC, Guedes DM, Masuda H (1986) Uptake of yolk proteins in *Rhodnius prolixus*. J Insect Physiol 32:859–866

Oliver B, Perrimon N, Mahowald AP (1988) Genetic evidence that the sans fille locus is involved in *Drosophila* sex determination. Genetics 120:159–171

Omura S (1938) Studies on the reproductive system of the male of *Bombyx mori*. II. Post-testicular organs and post-testicular behaviour of the spermatozoa. J Fac Agric Hokkaido Univ 40:129–170

Orchard I, Lange AB (1987) Cockroach oviducts: the presence and release of octopamine and proctolin. J Insect Physiol 33:265–268

Orchard I, Belanger JH, Lange A (1989) Proctolin: a review with emphasis on insects. J Neurobiol 20:470–496

Orr W, Komitopoulou K, Kafatos FC (1984) Mutants suppressing in *trans* chorion gene amplification in *Drosophila*. Proc Natl Acad Sci USA 81:3772–3777

Orr-Weaver TL, Johnston CG, Spradling AC (1989) The role of ACE 3 in *Drosophila* chorion gene amplification. EMBO J 8:4153–4162

Osanai M, Chen PS (1987) Comparative biochemistry of the ejaculated substances between silkworm and fruit fly. Zool Sci 4:1017

Osanai M, Aigaki T, Kasuga H (1986a) Energy metabolism in the spermatophore of the silkmoth, *Bombyx mori*, associated with accumulation of alanine derived from arginine. Insect Biochem 17:71–75

Osanai M, Aigaki T, Kasuga H, Yonezawa Y (1986b) Role of arginase transferred from the vesicula seminalis during mating and changes in amino acid pools of the spermatophore after ejaculation in the silkworm, *Bombyx mori*. Insect Biochem 16:879–885

Osanai M, Kasuga H, Aigaki T (1987) Spermatophore and its structural changes related to the sperm maturation of the silkworm, *Bombyx mori*. J Morphol 193:1–11

Osheim YN, Miller OL Jr (1983) Novel amplification and transcriptional activity of chorion genes in *Drosophila melanogaster* follicle cells. Cell 33:543–553

Osheim YN, Miller OL Jr, Beyer AL (1985) RNP particles at splice junction sequences on *Drosophila* chorion transcripts. Cell 43:143–151

Osheim YN, Miller OL Jr, Beyer AL (1986) Two *Drosophila* chorion genes terminate transcription in discrete regions near their poly(A) sites. EMBO J 5:3591–3596

Osheim YN, Miller OL Jr, Beyer AL (1988) Visualization of *Drosophila melanogaster* chorion genes undergoing amplification. Mol Cell Biol 8:2811–2821

Osir EO, Law JH (1986) Studies on binding and uptake of vitellogenin by follicles of the tobacco hornworm, *Manduca sexta*. Arch Insect Biochem Physiol 3:513–528

Osir EO, Anderson DR, Grimes WJ, Law JH (1986a) Studies on the carbohydrate moiety of vittelogenin from the tobacco hornworm, *Manduca sexta*. Insect Biochem 16:471–478

Osir EO, Wells MA, Law JH (1986b) Studies on vittelogenin from the tobacco hornworm, *Manduca sexta*. Arch Insect Biochem Physiol 3:217–233

Overall R, Jaffe LF (1985) Patterns of ionic current through *Drosophila* follicles and eggs. Dev Biol 108:102–119

Padgett RA, Mount SM, Steitz JA, Sharp PA (1983) Splicing of messenger RNA precursors is inhibited by antisera to small nuclear ribonucleoprotein. Cell 35:101–107

Padgett RA, Grabowski PJ, Konarska MM, Seiler S, Sharp PA (1986) Splicing of messenger precursors. Annu Rev Biochem 55:1119–1150

Paglia LM, Berry SJ, Kastern WH (1976) Messenger RNA synthesis, transport, and storage in silkmoth ovarian follicles. Dev Biol 51:173–181

Pan ML, Wyatt GR (1971) Juvenile hormone induces vittelogenin synthesis in the Monarch butterfly. Science 174:503–505

Parker GA, Smith JL (1975) Sperm competition and the evolution of the precopulatory passive phase behavior in *Locusta migratoria migratorioides*. J Entomol Lond 49:155–171

Parks S, Spradling A (1987) Spatially regulated expression of chorion genes during *Drosophila* oogenesis. Gen Dev 1:497–509

Parks S, Wakimoto B, Spradling A (1986) Replication and expression of an X-linked cluster of *Drosophila chorion* genes. Dev Biol 117:294–305

Paterson NF (1935) Observations on the embryology of *Corynodes pusis* (Coleoptera: Chrysomelidae). Q J Microsc Sci 78:91–131

Pau RN (1984) Cloning of cDNA for a juvenile hormone-regulated oothecin mRNA. Biochim Biophys Acta 782:422–428

Pau RN (1987) Characterization of juvenile hormone-regulated cockroach oothecin genes. Insect Biochem 17:1075–1078

Pau RN, Brunet PCJ, Williams MJ (1971) The isolation and characterization of proteins from the left colleterial gland of the cockroach, *Periplaneta americana* (L.). Proc R Soc Lond 177B:565–579

Pau RN, Weaver RJ, Edwards-Jones K (1986) The regulation of cockroach oothecin synthesis by juvenile hormone. Arch Insect Biochem Physiol (Suppl) 1:59–73

Pau RN, Birnstingl S, Edwards-Jones K, Gillen CU, Matsakis E (1987) The structure and organization of genes coding for juvenile hormone-regulated 16 Kdalton oothecins in the cockroach *Periplaneta americana*. In: O'Connor JD (ed) Molecular biology of invertebrate development. Alan R Liss, New York, pp 265–277

Payre F, Yanicostas C, Vincent A (1988) Expression of *serendipity delta*, a gene coding for a DNA binding finger protein in *Drosophila melanogaster*. Genome 30 (Suppl) 1:32

Payvar F, DeFranco D, Firestone GL et al. (1983) Sequence-specific binding of glucocorticoid receptor to MTV DNA at sites within the upstream of the transcribed region. Cell 35:381–392

Peferoen M, DeLoof A (1984) Intraglandular and extraglandular synthesis of proteins secreted by the accessory reproductive glands of the Colorado potato beetle, *Leptinotarsa decemlineata*. Insect Biochem 14:407–416

Peferoen M, Stynen D, DeLoof A (1982) A re-examination of the protein pattern of the hemolymph of *Leptinotarsa decemlineatea*, with special reference to vitellogenins and diapause proteins. Comp Biochem Physiol 72B:345–351

Pereira SD, DeBianchi AG (1983) Vitellogenin and vitellin of *Rhynchosciara americana*: further characterization and time of synthesis. Insect Biochem 13:323–332

Petersen W (1900) Beiträge zur Morphologie der Lepidopteren. Mem Acad Imp Sci St Petersbourg 8, 9:1–144

Petri WH, Wyman AR, Kafatos FC (1976) Specific protein synthesis in cellular differentiation. III. The eggshell proteins of *Drosophila melanogaster* and their program of synthesis. Dev Biol 49:185–199

Petri WH, Mindrinos MN, Lombard MF (1979a) Independence of vitelline membrane and chorion cross-linking in the *Drosophila melanogaster* eggshell. J Cell Biol 83:23a

Petri WH, Mindrinos MH, Lombard MF, Margaritis LH (1979b) In vitro development of the *Drosophila* chorion in a chemically defined agar culture medium. Wilhelm Roux's Arch Dev Biol 186:351–362

Petri WH, Scherer LS, Harris DH, White MK (1987) Sequence analysis of two *Drosophila* vitelline membrane genes and an unidentified ovarian cDNA. Genetics 116:s7

Philippe C (1982) Culture of fat body of *Periplaneta americana*: tissue development and establishment of cell lines. J Insect Physiol 28:257–265

Phipps J (1950) The maturation of ovaries and the relation between weight and maturity in *Locusta migratoria migratorioides* (R & F). Bull Entomol Res 40:539–557

Phipps J (1960) The ovaries of some Sierra Leone Acridoidea (Orthoptera) with some comparisons between east and west African forms. Proc R Entomol Soc 37:13–21

Pickford R, Gillott C (1971) Insemination in the migratory grasshopper, *Melanoplus sanguinipes* (Fabr). Can J Zool 49:1583–1588

Pickford R, Gillott C (1976) Effect of varied copulatory periods of *Melanoplus sanguinipes* (Orthoptera: Acrididae) females on egg hatchability and hatching sex ratios. Can Entomol 108:331–335

Pickford R, Padgham DE (1973) Spermatophore formation and sperm transfer in the desert locust, *Schistocerca gregaria* (Orthoptera: Acrididae). Can Entomol 105:613–618

Pickford R, Ewen AB, Gillott C (1969) Male accessory gland substance: an egg-laying stimulant in *Melanoplus sanguinipes* (F). Can J Zool 47:1199–1203

Pijnacker LP, Godeke J (1984) Development of ovarian follicle cells of the stick insect, *Carausius morosus* Br (Phasmatodea), in relation to their function. Int J Insect Morphol Embryol 13:21–28

Pines M, Lubzens E, Harry P, Applebaum SW (1980) Disparity between in vivo and in vitro synthesis of yolk protein by fat bodies of vitellogenic *Locusta migratoria* after allotectomy. Gen Comp Endocrinol 41:417–420

Pipa R (1986) Disinhibition of oocyte growth in adult, virgin *Periplaneta americana* by corpus allatum denervation: age dependency and relatedness to mating. Arch Insect Biochem Physiol 3:471–483

Plachter H (1981) Chorionic structures of the eggshells of 15 fungus- and root-gnat species (Diptera: Mycetophiloidea). Int J Insect Morphol Embryol 10:43–63

Poels A (1972) Histophysiologie des voies genitales males de *Tenebrio molitor* L. (Coleoptera: Tenebrionidae). Ann Soc R Zool Belg 102:199–234

Pollock JN (1970) Sperm transfer by spermatophores in *Glossina austeni* Newstread. Nature (Lond) 225:1063–1064

Popodi E, Minoo P, Burke T, Waring GL (1988) Organization and expression of a second chromosome follicle cell gene cluster in *Drosophila*. Dev Biol 127:248–256

Postlethwait JH, Giorgi F (1985) Vitellogenesis in insects. In: Browder LW (ed) Developmental biology. A comprehensive synthesis. Plenum Press, New York, 1:85–126

Postlethwait JH, Jones GT (1978) Endocrine control of larval fat body histolysis in normal and mutant *Drosophila melanogaster*. J Exp Zool 203:207–214

Postlethwait JH, Jowett T (1980) Genetic analysis of the hormonally regulated yolk polypeptide genes in *D. melanogaster*. Cell 20:671–678

Postlethwait JH, Parker J (1987) Regulation of vitellogenesis in *Drosophila*. In: O'Connor JD (ed) Molecular biology of invertebrate development. Alan R Liss, New York, pp 29–42

Postlethwait JH, Shirk PD (1981) Genetic and endocrine regulation of vitellogenesis in *Drosophila*. Am Zool 21:687–700

Postlethwait JH, Weiser K (1973) Vitellogenesis induced by juvenile hormone in female sterile mutant apterous-four in *Drosophila melanogaster*. Nature (Lond) 244:284–285

Postlethwait JH, Bownes M, Jowett T (1980a) Sexual phenotype and vittelogenin synthesis in *Drosophila melanogaster*. Dev Biol 79:379–387

Postlethwait JH, Laugé G, Handler AM (1980b) Yolk protein synthesis in ovariectomized and genetically agametic [X^{87}] *Drosophila melanogaster*. Gen Comp Endocrinol 40:385–390

Powell JR, Hollander AL, Fuchs MS (1988) Development of the *Aedes aegypti* chorion: proteins and ultrastructure. Int J Invertebr Reprod 13:39–54

Price JV, Clifford RJ, Schüpbach T (1989) The maternal ventralizing locus *torpedo* is allelic to *faint little ball*, an embryonic lethal, and encodes the *Drosophila melanogaster* EGF receptor homolog. Cell 56:1085–1092

Proshold FI, Karpenpo CP, Graham CK (1982) Egg production and oviposition in the tobacco budworm: effect of age at mating. Ann Entomol Soc 75:51–55

Pryor MGM (1940) On the hardening of the cuticle of insects. Pro R Soc Lond 128B:393–407

Pustell JM (1979) The accessory gland of the cricket, *Acheta domesticus*: a multifaceted study. MS Thesis, Univ Massachusetts, Amherst

Quadri MAH (1940) On the development of the genitalia and their ducts of orthopteroid insects. Trans R Entomol Soc Lond 90:121–175

Raabe M (1986) Insect reproduction: regulation of successive steps. In: Evans PD, Wigglesworth VB (eds) Advances in insect physiology. Academic Press, Lond New York, 19:29–154

Racioppi JV, Gemmill RM, Kogan PH, Calvo JM, Hagedorn HH (1986) Expression and regulation of vitellogenin messenger RNA in the mosquito, *Aedes aegypti*. Insect Biochem 16:255–262

Raikhel AS (1984) The accumulative pathway of vitellogenin in the mosquito oocyte: a high resolution immuno- and cytochemical study. J Ultrastruct Res 87:285–302

Raikhel AS (1986) Role of lysosomes in regulating of vitellogenin secretion in the mosquito fat body. J Insect Physiol 32:597–604

Raikhel AS, Leo AO (1983) Previtellogenic development and vitellogenin synthesis in the fat body of a mosquito: an ultrastructural and immunocytochemical study. Tissue Cell 15:281–300

Raikhel AS, Lea AO (1985) Hormone-mediated formation of the endocytic complex in mosquito oocytes. Gen Comp Endocrinol 57:422–433

Raikhel AS, Lea AO (1986) Internalized proteins directed into accumulative compartment of mosquito oocytes by the specific ligand, vitellogenin. Tissue Cell 18:559–574

Raikhel AS, Pratt LH, Lea AO (1986) Monoclonal antibodies as probes for processing of yolk protein in the mosquito; production and characterization. J Insect Physiol 32:879–890

Rakshpal R (1961) Structure and development of the reproductive organs of *Gryllus veletis* (Alexander and Bigelow) and *G. pennsylvanicus* Burmeister. Indian J Entomol 23:23–39

Ramalingam S, Craig GB Jr (1977) The effects of a JH mimic and cauterization of the corpus allatum complex on the male accessory glands of *Aedes aegypti* (Diptera: Culicidae). Can Entomol 109:897–906

Ramalingam S, Craig GB Jr (1978) Fine structure of the male accessory glands in *Aedes triseriatus*. J Insect Physiol 24:251–259

Ramamurty PS, Engels W (1977) Occurrence of intercellular bridges between follicle epithelial cells in the ovary of *Apis mellifica* queens. J Cell Sci 24:195–202

Ramaswamy SB, Mbata GN, Cohen NE (1990) Necessity of juvenile hormone for choriogenesis in the moth, *Heliothis virescens* (Noctuidae). Invertebr Reprod Dev 17:57–63

Ranganthan LS (1977) Endocrine regulation of development and differentiation of the accessory reproductive gland of male *Plebeiogryllus guttiventris*. In: Adiyodi KG, Adiyodi RG (eds) Advances in invertebrate reproduction, vol 1. Peralam-Kenoth, India, pp 252–257

Rankin MA, Jäckle H (1980) Hormonal control of vitellogenin synthesis in *Oncopeltus fasciatus*. J Insect Physiol 26:671–684

Rasch EH, Cassidy JD, King RC (1977) Evidence for dosage compensation in parthenogenetic Hymenoptera. Chromosoma 59:323–340

Ray A, Ramamurty PS (1979) Sources of RNA supply to the oocytes in *Crynodes peregrinus* Fuessly (Coleoptera: Chrysomelidae). Int J Insect Morphol Embryol 8:113–122

Readio J, Meola R (1985) Two stages of juvenile hormone-mediated growth of secondary follicles in *Culex pipiens*. J Insect Physiol 31:559–562

Regier JC (1986) Evolution and higher-order structure of architectural proteins in silkmoth chorion. EMBO J 5:1981–1989

Regier JC, Kafatos FC (1985) Molecular aspects of chorion formation. In: Kerkut GA, Gilbert LI (eds) Comprehensive insect physiology, biochemistry and pharmacology, vol 1. Pergamon Press, Oxford, pp 113–151

Regier JC, Pacholski P (1985) Nucleotide sequences of an unusual regionally expressed silkmoth chorion RNA: predicted primary and secondary structures of an architectural protein. Proc Natl Acad Sci USA 82:6035–6039

Regier JC, Wong JR (1988) Assembly of silkmoth chorion proteins: in vivo patterns of disulfide bond formation. Insect Biochem 18:471–482

Regier JC, Mazur GD, Kafatos FC (1980) The silkmoth chorion: morphological and biochemical characterization of four surface regions. Dev Biol 76:286–304

Regier JC, Mazur GD, Kafatos FC, Paul M (1982) Morphogenesis of silkmoth chorion: initial framework formation and its relation to synthesis of specific proteins. Dev Biol 92:159–174

Regier JC, Kafatos FC, Hamodrakas SJ (1983) Silkmoth chorion multigene families constitute a superfamily: comparison of C and B family sequences. Proc Natl Acad Sci USA 80:1043–1047

Regier JC, Hatzopoulos AK, Durot AC (1986) Patterns of region-specific chorion gene expression in the silkmoth and identification of shared 5′ flanking genomic elements. Dev Biol 118:432–441

Reid PC, Chen TT (1981) Juvenile hormone-controlled vitellogenin synthesis in the fat body of the locust (Locusta migratoria): Isolation and characterization of vitellogenin polysomes and their induction in vivo. Insect Biochem 11:297–305

Renkawitz R, Kunz W (1975) Independent replication of the ribosomal RNA genes in the polytrophic-meroistic ovaries of Calliphora erythrocephala, Drosophila hydei, and Sarcophaga barbata. Chromosoma 53:131–140

Renkawitz-Pohl R (1975) Unterreplikation der Satelliten-DNA von Drosophila virilis in polyploiden Kernen, die keine Polytänchromosomen enthalten. Verh Dtsch Zool Ges 68:1–2

Renucci M, Strambi C (1983) Juvenile hormone levels, vitellogenin and ovarian development in Acheta domesticus. Experientia 39:618–620

Ribbert D, Buddendick M (1984) Synthesis and processing of ribosomal RNA in the growing oocytes of Calliphora erythrocephala. Insect Biochem 14:569–586

Richmond RC, Senior A (1981) Esterase 6 of Drosophila melanogaster: kinetics of transfer to females, decay in females and male recovery. J Insect Physiol 27:849–853

Riddell DC, Higgins MJ, McMillan BJ, White BN (1981) Structural analysis of the three vitellogenin genes in Drosophila melanogaster. Nucl Acids Res 9:1323–1338

Riddihough G, Pelham HRB (1987) An ecdysone response element in the Drosophila hsp27 promoter. EMBO J 6:3729–3734

Riemann JG (1973) Ultrastructure of the ejaculatory duct region producing the male housefly accessory material. J Insect Physiol 19:213–223

Riemann JG, Thorson BJ (1969) Effect of male accessory material on oviposition and mating by female house flies. Ann Entomol Soc Am 62:828–834

Riemann JG, Thorson BJ (1979a) Foliate and granule-secreting cells in the ejaculatory duct (simplex) of the Mediterranean flour moth. J Ultrastruct Res 66:1–10

Riemann JB, Thorson BJ (1979b) Ultrastructure of the accessory glands of the Mediterranean flour moth. J Morphol 159:355–393

Rina MD, Mintzas AC (1987) Two vitellins-vitellogenins of the Mediterranean fruit fly Ceratitis capitata: a comparative biochemical and immunological study. Comp Biochem Physiol 86B:801–808

Rina MD, Mintzas AC (1988) Biosynthesis and regulation of two vitellogenins in the fat body and ovaries of Ceratitis capitata (Diptera). Wilhelm Roux's Arch Dev Biol 197:167–174

Ritter R (1890) Die Entwicklung des Geschlechtsorgane und des Darmes bei Chironomus. Z Wiss Zool 70:408–427

Roberts PE, Wyatt GR (1983) Juvenile hormone binding by components of fat body cytosol from vitellogenic locusts. Mol Cell Endocrinol 31:53–69

Robertson M (1990) More to muscle than MyoD. Nature (Lond) 344:378–379

Rodakis GC, Kafatos FC (1982) Origin of evolutionary novelty in proteins: how a high-cysteine chorion protein has evolved. Proc Natl Acad Sci USA 79:3551–3555

Rodakis GC, Laconidou R, Eickbush TH (1984) Diversity in a chorion multigene family created by tandem duplications and a putative gene-conversion event. J Mol Evol 20:265–273

Roehrdanz RL, Kitchens JM, Lucchesi JC (1977) Lack of dosage compensation for an autosomal gene relocated to the X-chromosome in *Drosophila melanogaster*. Genetics 85:489–496

Röhrkasten A, Ferenz HJ (1985) In vitro study of selective endocytosis of vitellogenin by locust oocytes. Wilhelm Roux's Arch Dev Biol 194:411–416

Röhrkasten A, Ferenz HJ (1986) Properties of the vitellogenin receptor of isolated locust oocyte membranes. Int J Invertebr Reprod 10:133–142

Röhrkasten A, Ferenz JH (1987) Coated vesicles from locust oocytes: isolation and characterization. Int J Invertebr Reprod 12:341–346

Rogers SH, Wells H (1984) The structure and function of the bursa copulatrix of the monarch butterfly (*Danaus plexippus*). J Morphol 180:213–221

Romani S, Campuzano S, Modolell J (1987) The *achaete-scute* complex is expressed in neurogenic regions of *Drosophila* embryos. EMBO J 6:2085–2092

Romano CP, Bienz-Tadmor B, Mariani BD, Kafatos FC (1988) Both early and late *Drosophila* chorion gene promoters confer correct temporal, tissue and sex specificity on a reporter *Adh* gene. EMBO J 7:783–790

Roonwal ML (1937) Studies on the embryology of the African migratory locust, *Locusta migratoria migratorioides* II. Philos Trans R Soc Lond B 227:175–244

Roth TF, Cutting JA, Atlas SB (1976) Protein transport: a selective membrane mechanism. J Supramol Struct 4:527–585

Roth TF, Porter KR (1964) Yolk protein uptake in the oocyte of the mosquito. J Cell Biol 20:313–322

Rothe M, Nauber U, Jäckle H (1989) Three hormone receptor-like *Drosophila* genes encode an identical DNA-binding finger. EMBO J 8:3087–3094

Rubacha A, Tucker MA, DeValoir T, Belikoff EJ, Beckingham K (1988) Genes with specific functions in the ovarian follicles of *Calliphora erythrocephala* (Diptera). Dev Biol 129:449–463

Rubenstein EC (1979) The role of an epithelial occlusion zone in the termination of vitellogenesis in *Hyalophora cecropia* ovarian follicles. Dev Biol 71:115–127

Rubin GM, Spradling AC (1982) Genetic transformation of *Drosophila* with transposable element vectors. Science 218:348–353

Rubin GM, Spradling AC (1983) Vectors for P element-mediated transformation in *Drosophila*. Nucl Acids Res 11:6341–6351

Rubtzov IA (1934) Fertility and climatic adaptations in Siberian grasshoppers. Bull Entomol Res 25:339–348

Sael L, Young MW (1988) In situ localization of the *per* clock protein during development of *Drosophila melanogaster*. Mol Cell Biol 8:5378–5385

Sahota TS (1977) Hormonal regulation of vitellogenesis in insects. In: Adiyodi KG, Adiyodi RG (eds) Advances in invertebrate reproduction, vol 1. Peralam-Kenoth, India, pp 432–450

Saito S (1937) On the development of the tusser, *Antheraea pernyi* Guerin-Meneville, with special reference to the comparative embryology of insects. J Fac Agric Hokkaido Univ 40:35–109

Salz HK, Cline W, Schedl P (1987) Functional changes associated with structural alterations induced by mobilization of a P element inserted in the *sex-lethal* gene of *Drosophila*. Genetics 117:221–231

Salz HK, Maine EM, Keyes LN, Samuels ME, Cline TW, Schedl P (1989) The *Drosophila* female-specific sex-determination gene, *sex-lethal,* has stage-, tissue-, and sex-specific RNAs suggesting multiple modes of regulation. Gen Dev 3:708–719

Sams GR, Bell WJ (1977) Juvenile hormone initiation of yolk deposition in vitro in the ovary of the cockroach, *Periplaneta americana*. In: Adiyodi KG, Adiyodi RG (eds) Advances in invertebrate reproduction, vol 1. Peralam-Kenoth, India, pp 404–413

Sánchez L, Nöthiger R (1982) Clonal analysis of *sex-lethal*, a gene needed for female sexual development in *Drosophila melanogaster*. Wilhelm Roux's Arch Dev Biol 191:211–214

Sánchez L, Nöthiger R (1983) Sex determination and dosage compensation in *Drosophila melanogaster*: production of male clones in XX females. EMBO J 2:485–491

Sander KL (1959) Analyse des ooplasmatischen Reaktionsystems von *Euscelis plebejus* Fall (Cicadina) durch Isolieren und Kombinieren von Keimteilen. I. Die Differenzierungsleistungen vorderer und hintere Eiteile. Wilhelm Roux's Arch Dev Biol 151:430–497

Sander KL (1960) II. Die Differenzierungsleistungen nach Verlagern von Hinterpolmaterial. Wilhelm Roux's Arch Dev Biol 151:660–707

Sander KL (1961) Umkehr der Keimstreifpolaritat in Eifragmenten von *Euscelis* (Cicadina). Experientia 17:179–180

Sander KL (1976) Specification of the basic body pattern in insect embryogenesis. Adv Insect Physiol 12:125–238

Saunders RDC, Bownes M (1986) Sequence analysis of a yolk protein secretion mutant of *Drosophila melanogaster*. Mol Gen Genet 205:557–560

Schäfer U (1986a) Genes for male-specific transcripts in *Drosophila melanogaster*. Mol Gen Genet 202:219–225

Schäfer U (1986b) The regulation of male-specific transcripts by sex determining genes in *Drosophila melanogaster*. EMBO J 5:3579–3582

Schal C, Bell WJ (1982) Ecological correlates of paternal investment of urates in a tropical cockroach. Science 218:170–173

Scharrer B (1946) The relationship between corpora allata and reproductive organs in adult *Leucophaea maderae* (Orthoptera). Endocrinology 38:46–55

Schlein Y, Galun R (1984) Male housefly (*Musca domestica* L.) genital system as a source of mating pheromone. J Insect Physiol 30:175–177

Schmidt T, Chen PS, Pellegrini M (1985a) The induction of ribosomal biosynthesis in a nonmitotic secretory tissue. J Biol Chem 260:7645–7650

Schmidt T, Stumm-Zollinger E, Chen PS (1985b) Protein metabolism of *Drosophila melanogaster* male accessory glands. III. Stimulation of protein synthesis following copulation. Insect Biochem 15:391–401

Schooneveld H, Tesser GJ, Veenstra JA, Romberg-Privee HM (1983) Adipokinetic hormone and AKH-like peptide demonstrated in the corpora cardiaca and nervous system of *Locusta migratoria* by immunocytochemistry. Cell Tissue Res 230:67–76

Schubiger JL, Wahli W (1986) Linkage arrangement in the vitellogenin gene family of *Xenopus laevis* as revealed by segregation analysis. Nucl Acids Res 14:8723–8734

Schüpbach T (1982) Autosomal mutations that interfere with sex determination in somatic cells of *Drosophila* have no direct effect on the germline. Dev Biol 89:117–127

Schüpbach T (1987) Germ line and some cooperate during oogenesis to establish the dorsoventral pattern of egg shell and embryo in *Drosophila melanogaster*. Cell 49:699–707

Schüpbach T, Wieschaus E (1986) Maternal-effect mutations altering the anterior-posterior pattern of the *Drosophila* embryo. Wilhelm Roux's Arch Dev Biol 195:302–317

Schüpbach T, Wieschaus E, Nothiger R (1978) The embryonic organization of the genital disc studied in genetic mosaics of *Drosophila melanogaster*. Wilhelm Roux's Arch Dev Biol 185:249–270

Scott D (1986) Inhibition of female *Drosophila melanogaster* remating by a seminal fluid protein (esterase 6). Evolution 40:1084–1091

Sefiani M (1987) Regulation of egg laying on in vitro oviductal contractions in *Gryllus bimaculatus*. J Insect Physiol 33:215–222

Segraves WA, Richards G (1990) Regulatory and developmental aspects of ecdysone-regulated gene expression. Invertebr Reprod Dev 18:67–76

Sehl A (1931) Furchung und Bildung der Keimanlage bei der Mehlmotte *Ephestia kühniella* Zell., nebst einer allgemeinen Übersicht über den Verlauf der Embryonalentwicklung. Z Morphol Okol Tiere 20:533–598

Seidel F (1924) Die Geschlechtsorgane in der embryonalen Entwicklung von *Pyrrhocoris apterus*. Z Morphol Okol Tiere 1:429–506

Seidel F (1926) Die Determination der Keimanlage bei Insekten. I. Biol Zentralbl 46:321–343

Seidel F (1934) Das Differenzierungszentrum im Libellenkeim. I. Die dynamischen Voraussetzungen der Determination und Regulation. Wilhelm Roux's Arch Dev Biol 131:135–187

Shaaya E, Sekeris CE (1970) The formation of protocatechuic acid-4-O-β-glucoside in *Periplaneta americana* and the possible role of the juvenile hormone. J Insect Physiol 16:323–330

Shafiq SA (1954) A study of the embryonic development of the gooseberry sawfly, *Pteronidea ribesii*. Q J Microsc Sci 95:93–114

Shea MJ, Mariani BD, Kafatos FC (1989) Cis- and trans-regulation of a chorion gene. Biol Bull 176:65

Shepherd B, Garabedian MJ, Hung MC, Wensink PC (1985) Developmental control of *Drosophila* yolk protein 1 gene by cis-acting DNA elements. Cold Spring Harbor Symp Quant Biol 50:521–526

Shepherd JG (1974) Sperm activation in saturniid moths: some aspects of the mechanism of activation. J Insect Physiol 20:2321–2328

Shinbo H, Happ GM (1989) Effects of ecdysteroids on the growth of the post-testicular reproductive organs in the silkworm, *Bombyx mori*. J Insect Physiol 35:855–864

Shinbo H, Yaginuma T, Happ GM (1987) Purification and characterization of a proline-rich secretory protein that is a precursor to a structural protein of an insect spermatophore. J Biol Chem 262:4794–4799

Shirk PD, Dahm KH, Roller H (1976) The accessory sex glands as the repository for juvenile hormone in male cecropia moths. Z Naturforsch 31c:199–200

Shirk PD, Bhaskaran G, Roller H (1983a) Developmental physiology of corpora allata and accessory sex glands in the cecropia silkmoth. J Exp Zool 227:69–79

Shirk PD, Minoo P, Postlethwait JH (1983b) 20-Hydroxyecdysone stimulates the accumulation of translatable yolk polypeptide gene transcript in adult male *Drosophila melanogaster*. Proc Natl Acad Sci USA 80:186–190

Shirk PD, Bean D, Millemann AM, Brookes VJ (1984) Identification, synthesis and characterization of the yolk polypeptides of *Plodia interpunctella*. J Exp Zool 232:87–98

Shirras A, Bownes M (1987) Separate DNA sequences are required for normal female and ecdysone-induced male expression of *Drosophila melanogaster* yolk protein 1. Mol Gen Genet 210:153–155

Siebel CW, Rio DC (1990) Regulated splicing of the *Drosophila* P transposable element third intron in vitro: somatic repression. Science 248:1200–1208

Silverstein SC, Steinmann RM, Cohn ZA (1977) Endocytosis. Ann Rev Biochem 46:669–722

Sim GK, Kafatos FC, Jones CW, Koehler MD, Efstratiadis A, Maniatis T (1979) Use of a cDNA library for studies on evolution and developmental expression of the chorion multigene families. Cell 18:1303–1316

Singh T (1958) Ovulation and corpus luteum formation in *Locusta migratoria migratorioides* Reiche and Fairmaire and *Schistocerca gregaria* (Forskal). Trans R Entomol Soc 110:1–20

Siva-Jothy MT (1987) The structure and function of the female sperm-storage organs in Libellulid dragonflies. J Insect Physiol 33:559–567

Slifer EH (1938) The formation and structure of a special water-absorbing area in the membrane covering the grasshopper egg. Q J Microsc Sci 80:437–457

Smith DS, Telfer WH, Neville AC (1971) Fine structure of the chorion of a moth, *Hyalophora cecropia*. Tissue Cell 3:477–498

Smith GR, Kunes SM, Schultz DW, Taylor A, Trinman KL (1981) Structure of chi hotspots of generalized recombination. Cell 24:429–436

Smith PH, Barton Browne L, van Gerwen ACM (1988) Sperm storage and utilization and egg fertility in the sheep blowfly, *Lucilia cuprina*. J Insect Physiol 34:125–129

Snodgrass RE (1935) Principles of insect morphology. McGraw-Hill, New York

Snodgrass RE (1937) The male genitalia of Orthopteroid insects. Smithson Misc Collect 96:1–107

Snyder PB, Galanopoulos VK, Kafatos FC (1986) *Trans*-acting amplification mutants and other eggshell mutants of the third chromosome in *Drosophila melanogaster*. Proc Natl Acad Sci USA 83:3341–3345

Soltani-Mazouni N, Bordereau C (1987) Changes in the cuticle, ovaries and colleterial glands during the pseudergate and neotenic molt in *Kalotermes flavicollis* (Fabr)(Isoptera: Kalotermitidae). Int J Insect Morphol Embryol 16:221–235

Sonnenblick BP (1941) Germ cell movements and sex differentiation of the gonad in the *Drosophila* embryo. Proc Natl Acad Sci USA 27:484–489

Sosnowski BA, Belote JM, McKeown M (1989) Sex-specific alternative splicing of RNA from the *transformer* gene results from sequence-dependent splice site blockage. Cell 58:449–459

Spann L (1934) Studies on the reproductive systems of *Gryllus assimilis* Fabr. Trans Kansas Acad Sci 37:299–340

Spoerel N, Nguyen HT, Kafatos FC (1986) Gene regulation and evolution in the chorion locus of *Bombyx mori*. Structural and developmental characterization of four eggshell genes and their flanking DNA regions. J Mol Biol 190:23–35

Spoerel NA, Nguyen HT, Eickbush TH, Kafatos FC (1989) Gene evolution and regulation in the chorion complex of *Bombyx mori*. Hybridization and sequence analysis of multiple developmentally middle A/B chorion gene pairs. J Mol Biol 209:1–19

Spradling AC (1981) A chromosome inversion alters the pattern of specific DNA replication in *Drosophila* follicle cells. Cell 27:203–209

Spradling AC, Mahowald AP (1979) Identification and genetic localization of mRNAs from ovarian follicle cells of *Drosophila melanogaster*. Cell 16:589–598

Spradling AC, Mahowald AP (1980) Amplification of genes for chorion proteins during oogenesis in *Drosophila melanogaster*. Proc Natl Acad Sci USA 77:1096–1100

Spradling AC, Mahowald AP (1981) The organization and amplification of two chromosomal domains containing *Drosophila* chorion genes. Cell 27:193–201

Spradling A, Rubin GM (1982) Transposition of cloned P elements in *Drosophila* germ line chromosomes. Science 218:34–37

Spradling AC, Waring GL, Mahowald AP (1979) *Drosophila* bearing the *ocelliless* mutation underproduce two major chorion proteins both of which map near this gene. Cell 16:609–616

Spradling AC, Digan ME, Mahowald AP, Scott M, Craig EA (1980) Two clusters of genes for major chorion proteins of *Drosophila melanogaster*. Cell 19:905–914

Spradling AC, DeCicco DV, Wakimoto BT, Levine JF, Kalfayan LJ, Cooley L (1987) Amplification of the X-linked *Drosophila* chorion gene cluster requires a region upstream from the s38 chorion gene. EMBO J 6:1045–1053

Srdic Z, Beck H, Gloor H (1978) Yolk protein differences between species of *Drosophila*. Experientia 34:1572–1574

Srdic Z, Reinhardt C, Beck H, Gloor H (1979) Autonomous yolk protein synthesis in ovaries of *Drosophila* cultured in vivo. Wilhelm Roux's Arch Dev Biol 187:255–266

Stanley-Samuelson DW, Loher W (1983) Arachidonic and other long-chain polyunsaturated fatty acids in spermatophores and spermathecae of *Teleogryllus commodus*: significance in prostaglandin-mediated reproductive behavior. J Insect Physiol 29:41–45

Stanley-Samuelson DW, Jurenka RA, Blomquist GJ, Loher W (1987) Sexual transfer of prostaglandin precursor in the field cricket, *Teleogryllus commodus*. Physiol Entomol 12:347–354

Stay B, King A, Roth LM (1960) Calcium oxalate in the oothecae of cockroaches. Ann Entomol Soc Am 53:79–86

Stebbings H (1981) Observations on cytoplasmic transport along ovarian nutritive tubes of polyphagous coleopterans. Cell Tissue Res 220:153–161

Stebbings H, Bennett CE (1976) The effect of colchicine on the sleeve element of microtubules. Exp Cell Res 100:419–423

Stebbings H, Hunt C (1985) Binding of axonemal dynein to microtubules comprising the cytoplasmic transport system in insect ovarioles. Cell Biol Int Rep 9:245–252

Stebbings H, Sharma KK, Hunt C (1986) Microtubule-associated proteins in the ovaries of hemipteran insects and their association with the microtubule transport system linking nutritive cells and oocytes. Eur J Cell Biol 42:135–139

Steele JE (1964) The activation of phosphorylase in an insect by adenosine 3′,5′-phosphate and other agents. Am Zool 4:328

Stein SP, Tepper CS, Able ND, Richmond RC (1984) Studies of esterase 6 in *Drosophila melanogaster*. XVI. Synthesis occurs in the male reproductive tract (anterior ejaculatory duct) and is modulated by juvenile hormone. Insect Biochem 14:527–532

Steinmann-Zwicky M (1988) Sex determination in *Drosophila*: the X-chromosome gene *liz* is required for *Sxl* activity. EMBO J 7:3889–3898

Steinmann-Zwicky M, Schmid H, Nöthiger R (1989) Cell-autonomous and inductive signals can determine the sex of the germ line of *Drosophila* by regulating the gene *Sxl*. Cell 57:157–166

Stern C, Hadorn E (1939) The relation between the color of testes and vasa efferentia in *Drosophila*. Genetics 24:162–179

Stinchcomb DT, Struhl K, Davis RW (1979) Isolation and characterization of a yeast chromosomal replicator. Nature (Lond) 282:39

Stoppie P, Briers T, Huybrechts R, DeLoof A (1981) Moulting hormone, juvenile hormone and the ultrastructure of the fat body of adult *Sarcophaga bullata* (Diptera). Cell Tissue Res 221:233–244

Storella JR, Wojchowski DM, Kunkel JG (1985) Structure and embryonic degradation of two native vitellins in the cockroach, *Periplaneta americana*. Insect Biochem 15:259–275

Storto PD, King RC (1989) The role of polyfusomes in generating branched chains of cystocytes during *Drosophila* oogenesis. Dev Genet 10:70–86

Strong L (1981) Glandular pouches of the genital chamber of female *Schistocerca gregaria* (Forskal)(Orthoptera: Acrididae). Int J Insect Morphol Embryol 10:377–385

Stumm-Zollinger E, Chen PS (1985) Protein metabolism of *Drosophila melanogaster* male accessory glands. I. Characterization of secretory proteins. Insect Biochem 15:375–382

Stumm-Zollinger E, Chen PS (1988) Gene expression in male accessory glands of interspecific hybrids of *Drosophila*. J Insect Physiol 34:59–74

Stynen D, Woodruff RI, Telfer WH (1988) Effects of ionophores on vitellogenin uptake by *Hyalophora* oocytes. Arch Insect Biochem Physiol 8:261–276

Sun YA, Syman RJ (1987) Lack of an oocyte to nurse cell voltage difference in *Drosophila*. Neuroscience 13:1139

Sun YA, Wyman RJ (1989) The *Drosophila* egg chamber: external ionic currents and the hypothesis of electrophoretic transport. Biol Bull 176(S):79–85

Szabad J, Hoffmann G (1989) Analysis of follicle-cell functions in *Drosophila*: the *Fs(3)Apc* mutation and the development of chorionic appendages. Dev Biol 131:1–10

Szollosi A (1975) Imaginal differentiation of the spermiduct in acridids: effect of JH. Acrida 4:205–216

Szollosi A, Landureau JC (1977) Imaginal cell differentiation in the spermiduct of *Samia cynthia* (Lepidoptera). Responses in vitro to ecdysone and ecdysterone. Biol Cell 28:23–36

Szopa TM (1981a) The role of the accessory reproductive glands and genital ducts in egg pod formation in female *Schistocerca gregaria*. J Insect Physiol 27:23–29

Szopa TM (1981b) The hormonal control of accessory reproductive gland development in female *Schistocerca gregaria*. J Insect Physiol 27:441–446

Szopa TM (1982) Development of the accessory reproductive glands and genital ducts in female *Schistocerca gregaria*. J Insect Physiol 28:475–483

Szopa TM, Happ GM (1982) Cytodifferentiation of the accessory glands of *Tenebrio molitor*. IX. Differentiation of the spermathecal accessory gland in vitro. Cell Tissue Res 222:269–281

Szopa TM, Lenoir Rousseaux JJ, Yuncker C, Happ GM (1985) Ecdysteroids accelerate mitoses in accessory glands of beetle pupae. Dev Biol 107:325–336

Tadkowski TM, Jones JC (1979) Changes in the fat body and oocysts during starvation and vitellogenesis in a mosquito, *Aedes aegypti* (L.). J Morphol 159:185–204

Takahashi SY (1984) Ovarian protein kinases and endogenous substrates from the silkworm, *Bombyx mori*. Insect Biochem 14:219–229

Takeichi M (1990) Cadhedrins: a molecular family important in selective cell-cell adhesion. Annu Rev Biochem 59:237–252

Tamura T, Kunert C, Postlethwait J (1985) Sex- and cell-specific regulation of yolk polypeptide genes introduced into *Drosophila* by P-element-mediated gene transfer. Proc Natl Acad Sci USA 82:7000–7004

Tautz D, Lehman R, Schnurch H et al. (1987) Finger protein of novel structure encoded by *hunchback*, a second member of the gap class of *Drosophila* segmentation genes. Nature (Lond) 327:383–389

Telfer WH (1975) Development and physiology of the oocyte-nurse cell syncytium. Adv Insect Physiol 11:223–319

Telfer WH, Kunkel JG (1991) The function and evolution of insect storage hexamers. Annu Rev Entomol 36:205–228

Telfer WH, Smith DS (1970) Aspects of egg formation. In: Neville AC (ed) Insect ultrastructure. Blackwell, Oxford, pp 117–134

Telfer WH, Woodruff RI, Huebner E (1981) Electrical polarity and cellular differentiation in meroistic ovaries. Am Zool 21:675–686

Telfer WH, Keim PS, Law JH (1983) Arylphorin, a new protein from *Hyalophora cecropia*: comparisons with calliphorin and manducin. Insect Biochem 13:601–613

Terranova AC, Leopold RA, Degrugillier ME, Johnson JR (1972) Electrophoresis of the male accessory secretion and its fate in the mated female. J Insect Physiol 18:1573–1591

Thibout E (1971) Description de l'appareil génital mâle et formation du spermatophore chez *Acroplepia assectella* (Lepidoptere: Plutellidae). C R Acad Sci Paris 273:2546–2549

Thireos G, Kafatos FC (1980) Cell-free translation of silkmoth chorion mRNAs: identification of protein precursors and characterization of cloned DNAs by hybrid-selected translation. Dev Biol 78:36–46

Thireos G, Griffin Shea R, Kafatos FC (1979) Identification of chorion protein precursors and the mRNAs that encode them in *Drosophila melanogaster*. Proc Natl Acad Sci USA 76:6279–6283

Thireos G, Griffin-Shea R, Kafatos FC (1980) Untranslated mRNA for a chorion protein of *Drosophila melanogaster* accumulates transiently at the onset of specific gene amplification. Proc Natl Acad Sci USA 77:5789–5793

Thomas A (1979) Nervous control of egg progression into the common oviduct and genital chamber of the stick-insect *Carausius morosus*. J Insect Physiol 25:811–823

Thomas TL, Posakony JW, Anderson DM, Britten RJ, Davidson EH (1981) Molecular structure of maternal RNA. Chromosoma 84:319–335

Thomsen E, Thomsen M (1974) Fine structure of the fat body of female *Calliphora erythrocephala* during the first egg-maturation cycle. Cell Tissue Res 152:193–217

Tobe SS (1977) Inhibition of growth in developing oocytes of the desert locust. Experientia 33:343–345

Tobe SS, Davey KG (1974) Nucleic acid synthesis during the reproductive cycle of *Glossina austeni*. Insect Biochem 4:215–223

Tobe SS, Langley PA (1978) Reproductive physiology of *Glossina*. Annu Rev Entomol 23:283–307

Tobe SS, Loher W (1983) Properties of the prostaglandin synthetase complex in the cricket *Teleogryllus commodus*. Insect Biochem 13:137–141

Tobe SS, Davey KG, Huebner E (1973) Nutrient transfer during the reproductive cycle in *Glossina austeni* Newst.:histology and histochemistry of the milk gland, fat body, and oenocytes. Tissue Cell 5:633–650

Tobler J, Bowman JT, Simmons JR (1971) Gene modification in *Drosophila*: dosage compensation and relocated w^+-genes. Biochem Genet 5:111–117

Tolias PP, Kafatos FC (1990) Functional dissection of an early *Drosophila* chorion gene promoter: expression throughout the follicular epithelium is under spatially composite regulation. EMBO J 9:1457–1464

Tomino S (1985) Major plasma proteins of *Bombyx mori*. Zool Sci 2:293–303

Torres M, Sánchez L (1989) The *scute* (T4) gene acts as a numerator element of the X:A signal that determines the state of activity of *sex-lethal* in *Drosophila*. EMBO J 8:3079–3086

Tourmente S, Savre-Train I, Berthier F, Renaud M (1990) Expression of six mitochondrial genes during *Drosophila* oogenesis: analysis by in situ hybridization. Cell Differ Dev 31:137–149

Trenczek T, Engels W (1986) Occurrence of vitellogenin in drone honeybees (*Apis mellifica*). Int J Invertebr Reprod 10:307–311

Trenczek T, Faye I (1988) Synthesis of immune proteins in primary cultures of fat body from *Hyalophora cecropia*. Insect Biochem 18:299–312

Ueno K, Natori S (1984) Identification of storage protein receptor and its precursor in the fat body of *Sarcophaga peregrina*. J Biol Chem 259:12107–12111

Ueno K, Ohsawa F, Natori S (1983) Identification and activation of storage protein receptor of *Sarcophaga peregrina* fat body by 20-hydroxyecdysone. J Biol Chem 258:12210–12214

Ullmann SL (1973) Oogenesis in *Tenebrio molitor*: histological and autoradiographical observations on pupal and adult ovaries. J Embryol Exp Morphol 30:179–217

Underwood EM, Caulton JH, Allis CD, Mahowald AP (1980) Developmental fate of pole cells in *Drosophila melanogaster*. Dev Biol 77:303–314

Vafopoulou-Mandalos X, Laufer H (1984) Tissue-specificity of hemoglobin synthesis: localization of heme synthesis in the subepidermal fat body of *Chironomus thummi* (Diptera). Arch Insect Biochem Physiol 1:191–197

Vale RD, Schnapp BJ, Reese TS, Sheetz MP (1985) Organelle, bead, and microtubule translocations promoted by soluble factors from the squid giant axon. Cell 40:559–569

Valle D, Lima Gomes JEP, Goldenberg S, Garcia ES (1987) *Rhodnius prolixus* vitellogenesis: dependence upon the blood source. J Insect Physiol 33:249–254

Van Breugel FMA, Huizing M (1985) Partial hyperploidy of the X-chromosome in *Drosophila hydei* leading to duplication of male gonadal and genital structures. Wilhelm Roux's Arch Dev Biol 194:491–494

Van der Starre-van der Molen LG (1972) Embryogenesis of *Calliphora erythrocephala* Meigen. I, Morphology. Neth J Zool 22:119–182

Van Handel E, Lea AO (1984) Vitellogenin synthesis in blood-fed *Aedes aegypti* in the absence of the head, thorax and ovaries. J Insect Physiol 30:871–875

Van het Schip FD, Samallo J, Broos J et al. (1987) Nucleotide sequence of a chicken vitellogenin gene and derived amino acid sequence of the encoded yolk precursor protein. J Mol Biol 196:245–260

Venkatesh K, Chippendale GM (1986) Synthesis and release of proteins from cultured larval fat body of the south-western corn borer, *Diatraea grandiosella*. Insect Biochem 16:917–927

Verachtert B, DeLoof A (1989) Intra- and extracellular electrical fields of vitellogenic polytrophic insect follicles. Biol Bull 176(S):91–95

Villares R, Cabrera CV (1987) The *achaete-scute* gene complex of *D. melanogaster*: conserved domains in a subset of genes required for neurogenesis and their homology to *myc*. Cell 50:415–424

Villavaso EJ (1974) Artificial insemination of the boll weevil, *Anthonomus grandis* Boheman. Ann Entomol Soc Am 67:825–827

Villavaso EJ (1975) The role of the spermathecal gland of the boll weevil, *Anthonomus grandis*. J Insect Physiol 21:1457–1462

Viscuso R, Longo G, Sottile L (1985) Ultrastructural modifications in the ejaculatory duct epithelium of *Eyprepocnemis plorans* (Charp.)(Orthoptera: Acrididae) during sexual maturation. Int J Insect Morphol Embryol 14:163–177

Von Wyl E, Steiner E (1977) Paragonial proteins of *Drosophila melanogaster* adult male: in vitro biosynthesis. Insect Biochem 7:15–20

Voss D, Pongs O (1986) Upstream sequences modulate in vitro transcription from *Drosophila* yolk protein genes I and II. Eur J Biochem 158:25–32

Voss D, Holzer T, Wefels E, Katzenmeyer B, Janknecht R, Pongs O (1987) Regulation of *Drosophila melanogaster* yolk protein genes in vitro and in vivo. Biol Chem Hoppe-Seyler 368:577–578

Vournakis JN, Efstradiadis A, Kafatos FC (1975) Electrophoretic patterns of deadnenylated chorion and globin mRNAs. Proc Natl Acad Sci USA 72:2959–2963

Voy A (1949) Contribution à l'étude anatomique et histologique des organes accessoires de l'appareil génital femelle chez quelques éspèces d'Orthopteroides. Ann Sci Nat Zool 11:269–345

Wahli W (1988) Evolution and expression of vitellogenin genes. Trends Genet 4:227–232

Wakimoto BT, Kalfayan LJ, Levine JF, Spradling AC (1986) Localization of regions controlling *Drosophila* chorin gene expression. Symp Soc Dev Biol 44:43–54

Waloff N (1954) The number and development of ovarioles of some Acridoidea (Orthoptera) in relation to climate. Physiol Comp Ecol 3:370–390

Walter P, Gilmore R, Blobel G (1984) Protein translocation across the endoplasmic reticulum. Cell 38:5–8

Waring GL, Mahowald AP (1979) Identification and time of synthesis of chorion proteins in *Drosophila melanogaster*. Cell 16:599–607

Waring GL, Pollack JC (1987) Cloning and characterization of a dispersed, multicopy, X chromosome sequence in *Drosophila melanogaster*. Proc Natl Acad Sci USA 84:2843–2847

Waring GL, Allis CD, Mahowald AP (1978) Isolation of polar granules and the identification of polar granule-specific protein. Dev Biol 66:197–206

Waring GL, Diorio JP, Hennen S (1983) Isolation of germ line-dependent female-sterile mutation that affects yolk specific sequestration and chorion formation in *Drosophila*. Dev Biol 100:452–463

Warn R (1975) Restoration of the capacity to form pole cells in UV-irradiated *Drosophila* embryos. J Embryol Exp Morphol 33:1003–1011

Warn RM, Gutzeit HO, Smith L, Warn A (1985) F-Actin rings are associated with the ring canals of the *Drosophila* egg chamber. Exp Cell Res 157:355–363

Watson AJ, Huebner E (1986) Modulation of cytoskeletal organization during insect follicle cell morphogenesis. Tissue Cell 18:741–752

Weaver RJ, Pau RN (1987) Absence of sequential or cyclic synthesis of oothecal isoproteins during the reproductive cycle of female *Periplaneta americana*. Insect Biochem 17:673–684

Weaver RJ, Pratt GE (1977) The effect of enforced virginity and subsequent mating on the activity of the corpus allatum of *Periplaneta americana* measured in vitro as related to changes in the rate of ovarian maturation. Physiol Entomol 2:59–76

Weaver RJ, Pratt GE (1981) Effects of starvation and feeding upon corpus allatum activity and oocyte growth in adult female *Periplaneta americana*. J Insect Physiol 27:75–83

Weaver RJ, Pratt GE, Finney JR (1975) Cyclic activity of the corpus allatum related to gonotrophic cycles in adult female *Periplaneta americana*. Experientia 31:597–598

Wensink PC (1987) DNA elements that control *Drosophila* yolk protein gene expression. In: O'Connor JD (ed) Molecular biology of invertebrate development. Alan R Liss, New York, pp 21–28

Wensler RJD, Rempel JG (1962) The morphology of the male and female reproductive systems of the midge, *Chironomus plumosus* L. Can J Zool 40:199–229

Whalen M, Wilson T (1986) Variation and genomic localization of genes encoding *Drosophila melanogaster* male accessory gland proteins separated by sodium dodecyl sulfate polyacrylamide gel electrophoresis. Genetics 114:77–92

Wheeler DE, Kawooya JK (1990) Purification and characterization of honey been vitellogenin. Arch Insect Biochem Physiol 14:253–267

Wheeler WM (1893) A contribution to insect embryology. J Morphol 8:1–160

Whitehead DL (1970) The role of haemocytes in the biosynthesis of protocatechuate in the cockroach colleterial system. Biochem J 119:65P–66P

Whitman DW, Lohwer W (1984) Morphology of male sex organs and insemination in the grasshopper *Taeniopoda eques* (Burmeister). J Morphol 179:1–12

Wieschaus E, Nöthiger R (1982) The role of the transformer genes in the development of genitalia and analia of *Drosophila melanogaster*. Dev Biol 90:320–334

Wieschaus E, Szabad J (1979) The development and function of the female germline in *Drosophila melanogaster* and cell lineage study. Dev Biol 68:29–46

Wieschaus E, March JL, Gehring WJ (1978) *fs(1)K10*, a germline-dependent female sterile mutation causing abnormal chorion morphology in *Drosophila melanogaster*. Wilhelm Roux's Arch Dev Biol 184:75–82

Wigglesworth VB (1953) The principles of insect physiology. Methuen, London

Wigglesworth VB, Beament JWL (1950) The respiratory mechanism of some insect eggs. Q J Microsc Sci 91:429–452

Wigglesworth VB, Salpeter MM (1962) The aeroscopic chorion of the egg of *Calliphora erythrocephala* Meig. (Diptera) studied with the electron microscope. J Insect Physiol 8:635–641

Williams CM (1956) The juvenile hormone of insects. Nature (Lond) 178:212–213

Williams JL, Bownes M (1986) Reduced stability of RNA coding for yolk polypeptide 3 in *Drosophila melanogaster* ovary. Eur J Biochem 161:95–101

Williams RW, Hagan NKB, Berger A, Despommier DD (1978) An improved assay technique for matrone, a mosquito pheromone, and its application in ultrafiltration experiments. J Insect Physiol 24:127–132

Willis JH, Brunet PCJ (1966) The hormonal control of colleterial gland secretion. J Exp Biol 44:363–478

Winter H (1974) Ribonucleoprotein-partikel aus dem telotroph-meroistischen Ovar von *Dysdercus intermedius* Dis. (Heteroptera, Pyrrhoc.) und ihr Verhalten im zellfreien Proteinsynthesesystem. Wilhelm Roux's Arch Dev Biol 175:102–127

Wojchowski DM, Kunkel JG (1987) Purification of two distinct oocyte vitellins and identification of their corresponding vitellogenins in fat body and hemolymph of *Blaberus discoidalis*. Insect Biochem 17:189–198

Wojchowski DM, Parsons PP, Nordin JH, Kunkel JG (1986) Processing of provitellogenin in insect fat body: a role for high-mannose oligosaccharide. Dev Biol 116:422–430

Wollberg Z, Cohen E, Kalina M (1976) Electrical properties of developing oocytes of the migratory locust, *Locusta migratoria*. J Insect Physiol 88:145–158

Wong YC, Pustell J, Spoerel N, Kafatos FC (1985) Coding and potential regulatory sequences of a cluster of chorion genes in *Drosophila melanogaster*. Chromosoma 92:124–135

Woodruff RI (1989) Charge-dependent molecular movement through intercellular bridges in *Drosophila* follicles. Biol Bull 176(S): 71–78

Woodruff RI, Anderson KL (1984) Nutritive cord connection and dye-coupling of the follicular epithelium to the growing oocytes in the telotrophic ovarioles in *Oncopeltus fasciatus*, the milkweed bug. Wilhelm Roux's Arch Dev Biol 193:158–163

Woodruff RI, Telfer WH (1973) Polarized intercellular bridges in ovarian follicles of the *Cecropia* moth. J Cell Biol 58:172–188

Woodruff RI, Telfer WH (1980) Electrophoresis of proteins in intercellular bridges. Nature (Lond) 286:84–86

Woodruff RI, Huebner E, Telfer WH (1986) Ion currents in *Hyalophora* ovaries: the role of the epithelium and the intercellular spaces of the trophic cap. Dev Biol 117:405–416

Woodruff RI, Kulp JH, Lagaccia ED (1988) Electrically mediated protein movement in *Drosophila* follicles. Wilhelm Roux's Arch Dev Biol 197:231–238

Worthington RE, Brady RU, Thean NE, Wilson DM (1981) Arachidonic acid: occurrence in the reproductive tract of the male house cricket (*Acheta domesticus*) and field cricket (*Gryllus* spp.). Lipids 16:79–81

Wu SJ, Ma M (1986) Hybridoma antibodies as specific probes to *Drosophila melanogaster* yolk polypeptides. Insect Biochem 16:789–795

Wu SJ, Zhang JZ, Ma M (1987) Monitoring the effects of juvenile hormones and 20-hydroxyecdysone on yolk polypeptide production of *Drosophila melanogaster* with enzyme immunoassay. Physiol Entomol 12:355–361

Wyatt GR (1988) Vitellogenin synthesis and the analysis of juvenile hormone action in locust fat body. Can J Zool 66:2600–2610

Wyatt GR, Dhadialla TS, Roberts PE (1984) Vitellogenin synthesis in locust fat body: juvenile hormone-stimulated gene expression. In: Hoffmann J, Porchet M (eds) Biosynthesis, metabolism and mode of action of invertebrate hormones. Springer, Berlin Heidelberg New York, pp 475–484

Wyatt GR, Kanost MR, Locke J, Walker VK (1986) Juvenile hormone-regulated locust vitellogenin genes: lack of expression after transfer into *Drosophila*. Arch Insect Biochem Physiol (Suppl) 1:35–46

Wyatt GR, Cook KE, Firko H, Dhadialla TS (1987) Juvenile hormone action on locust fat body. Insect Biochem 17:1071–1073

Xiong Y, Sakaguchi B, Eickbush TH (1988) Gene conversions can generate sequence variants in the late chorion multigene families of *Bombyx mori*. Genetics 120:221–231

Yaginuma T, Kai H, Happ GM (1988) 20-Hydroxyecdysone accelerates the flow of cells into the G_1 phase and the S phase in a male accessory gland of the mealworm pupa (*Tenebrio molitor*). Dev Biol 126:173–181

204

Yago M, Kawasaki H (1984) The identification of five N-acyldopamine glucosides in the left colleterial gland of the praying mantid, *Hierodula patellifera* Serville. Insect Biochem 14:487–489

Yago M, Sato H, Kawasaki H (1984) The identification of N-acyldopamine glucosides in the left colleterial gland of the praying mantids, *Mantis religiosa* L., *Statilia maculate* Thunberg and *Tenodera angustipennis* Saussure. Insect Biochem 14:7–9

Yajima H (1960) Studies on embryonic determinations of the harlequin-fly, *Chironomus dorsalis*. I. Effects of centrifugation and of its combination with constriction and puncturing. J Embryol Exp Morphol 8:198–215

Yamaja Setty BN, Ramaiah TR (1980) Effect of prostaglandin and inhibitors of prostaglandin biosynthesis on oviposition in the silkmoth *Bombyx mori*. Ind J Exp Biol 18:539–541

Yamamoto K, Chadarevian A, Pellegrini M (1988) Juvenile hormone action mediated in male accessory glands of *Drosophila* by calcium and kinase C. Science 239:916–919

Yamaoka K, Hirao T (1977) Stimulation of virginal oviposition by male factor and its effect on spontaneous nervous activity in *Bombyx mori*. J Insect Physiol 23:57–63

Yamashita O (1986) Yolk protein system in *Bombyx* eggs: synthesis and degradation of egg-specific protein. In: Porchet M, Andries JC (eds) Invertebrate reproduction, vol IV. Elsevier, Amsterdam, pp 79–84

Yamashita O, Irie K (1980) Larval hatching from vitellogenin-deficient eggs developed in male hosts of the silkworm. Nature (Lond) 283:385–386

Yan YL, Postlethwait JH (1990) Vitellogenesis in *Drosophila*: sequestration of a yolk polypeptide/invertase fusion protein into developing oocytes. Dev Biol 140:281–290

Yan YL, Kunert CJ, Postlethwait JH (1987) Sequence homologies among the three yolk polypeptide (Yp) genes in *Drosophila melanogaster*. Nucl Acids Res 15:67–85

Yang JT, Laymon RA, Goldstein LSB (1989) A three-domain structure of kinesin heavy chain revealed by DNA sequence and microtubule binding analyses. Cell 56:879–889

Yannoni CZ, Petri WH (1980) Characterization by isoelectric focusing of chorion protein variants in *Drosophila melanogaster* and their use in developmental and linkage analysis. Wilhelm Roux's Arch Dev Biol 189:17–24

Yannoni CZ, Petri WH (1984) Localization of a gene for a minor chorion protein in *Drosophila melanogaster*: a new chorion structural locus. Dev Biol 102:504–508

Yarden Y, Ullrich A (1988) Growth factor receptor tyrosine kinases. Annu Rev Biochem 57:443–478

Yasuyama K, Kimura T, Yamaguchi T (1988) Musculature and innervation of the internal reproductive organs in the male cricket, with special reference to the projection of unpaired median neurons of the terminal abdominal ganglion. Zool Sci 5:767–780

Yenofsky RL (1977) Structure and complexity of *Acheta* male accessory gland polysomes and partial characterization of the *Acheta* genome. PhD Thesis, Univ Massachusetts, Amherst

Yenofsky RL, Kaulenas MS (1975) Isolation and properties of *Acheta* accessory gland polysomes. J Insect Physiol 21:889–901

Yin CM, Zou BX, Stoffolano JG Jr (1989a) Dietary induced hormonal control of terminal oocyte development in *Phormia regina* Meigen. In: Borovsky D, Spielman A (eds) Host regulated developmental mechanisms in vector arthropods. pp 81–88

Yin CM, Zou BX, Stoffolano JG Jr (1989b) Precocene II treatment inhibits terminal oocyte development but not vitellogenin synthesis and release in the black blowfly, *Phormia regina* Meigen. J Insect Physiol 35:465–474

Yin CM, Zou BX, Yi X, Stoffolano JG Jr (1990) Ecdysteroid activity during oogenesis in the black blowfly, *Phormia regina* (Meigen). J Insect Physiol 36:375–382

Young ADM, Downie AER (1987) Male accessory gland substances and the control of sexual receptivity in female *Culex tarsalis*. Physiol Entomol 12:233–239

Young ADM, Downie AER (1989) The action of male accessory gland fluids in the control of sexual receptivity in *Culex tarsalis* Coq. In: Borovsky D, Spielman A (eds) Host regulated developmental mechanisms in vector arthropods. pp 206–211

Zalokar M (1968) Effect of corpora allata on protein and RNA synthesis in colleterial glands of *Blatella germanica*. J Insect Physiol 14:1177–1184

Zalokar M (1971) Transplantation of nuclei in *Drosophila melanogaster*. Proc Natl Acad Sci USA 68:1539–1541

Zalokar M (1973) Transplantation of nuclei into the polar plasm of *Drosophila* eggs. Dev Biol 32:189–193

Zhai QH, Postlethwait JH, Bodley JW (1984) Vitellogenin synthesis in the lady beetle *Coccinella septempunctata*. Insect Biochem 14:299–305

Zhai QH, Zhang JZ, Gong H (1987) Regulation of vitellogenin synthesis by juvenile hormone analogue in *Coccinella septempunctata*. Insect Biochem 17:1059–1064

Zhu J, Indrasith LS, Yamashita O (1986) Characterization of vitellin, egg-specific protein and 30kDa protein from *Bombyx* eggs, and their fates during oogenesis and embryogenesis. Biochim Biophys Acta 882:427–436

Ziegler R, Hoff R, Rohde M (1988) Site of storage of glycogen phosphorylase activating hormone in larvae of *Manduca sexta*. J Insect Physiol 34:143–150

Zieve G, Penman S (1981) Subnuclear particles containing a small nuclear RNA and heterogeneous nuclear RNA. J Mol Biol 145:501–523

Subject and Species Index

207

clathrin 121
cleavage
− furrow 35
− nuclei 6, 7, 8
Clitumnus extradentatus 35
clonal analysis 11, 15
clone/cloning 19, 22, 25, 26, 28, 30, 44, 46,
 48, 49, 50, 57, 58, 62, 65, 71, 72, 78, 93,
 94, 102, 113, 115, 116, 118, 119, 132, 141,
 147, 153, 154
coated pit(s) 40
coated vesicles 48, 120, 121
Coccinella 108
C. septempunctata 104
cockchafer, see *Melolontha*
cockroach(es) 5, 6, 35, 90, 91, 93, 94, 95,
 99, 119, 123, 139, 140
− ovoviviparous 35
coding region(s) 154
codon 23, 25, 117
− stop 23, 25, 117
coelomic cavities 5, 8, 9, 13, 100, 101
− sacs 140
colchicine 40, 41, 45, 81
Coleoptera 8, 10, 12, 14, 34, 38, 43, 89, 90,
 102, 104, 108, 112, 124, 126, 145, 147
− polyphagous 34, 38, 76
coleopteran 46, 76, 81, 146
collagen 143
colleterial
− glands 2, 3, 90, 91, 92, 93, 94, 95, 125
− protein 94
− tubules 91
competence 111, 112, 131
contractile ring 35
copia 25, 26, 27
copulation 132, 141, 143, 151, 152, 154,
 155
Corixa 81
corpus allatum/corpora allata 82, 95, 100,
 112, 113, 131, 145
corpus cardiacum/corpora cardiaca 83, 96,
 132
corpus cardiacum stimulatory factor
 (CCSF) 109, 114
corpus luteum 43
cortex 47, 48
Corynodes 8
Creophilus 38
cricket(s) 5, 53, 54, 88, 89, 133, 138, 139,
 140, 141
− field 133
− house, see also *A. domesticus* 53, 133
critical period 154
Crynodes 77
Culex 8, 39, 84, 155
C. pipiens 41

Culicoides melleus 155
Current(s) 42, 80, 81
− electrical 42
− electrophoretic 80
− ionic 81
cuticle 82, 83, 84, 85, 87, 91, 92, 93
cuticular
− intima 82, 83, 91, 125
− lining 82
− pores 86
− sclerotization 92
cuticulogenesis 87
cyclic GMP (cGMP) 135, 138, 139, 145
cycloheximide 121
Cyclorapha 6, 8
cyst cells 123, 124
cysteine 55−59, 73
cystine 55, 56, 59
cystoblast 16, 35
cystocyte(s) 16, 37
cytochalasin B 40, 80
cytokinesis 35, 38, 39
cytolysis 101
cytoplasmic streaming 80
cytoskeleton 8, 40, 41, 45, 78, 81
cytosol 110

Dacus 8
D. oleae 105
Danaus 83, 108
D. plexippus 145
daughter cell 16, 35
daughterless (da) 17, 18, 19, 20, 22
− DNA sequence 19
− protein 20
dec-1 61
Delarouzeei 86
deletion(s) 19, 73, 93, 118
− mapping 60
denominator elements 17, 18, 21
Dermaptera 12, 13, 34, 90, 103
Dermestes 38
desmosome(s) 39, 129
− belt 129
− septate 39, 135
determination 1, 6, 17, 154
− germ cell 6
− sex 17
development 1, 2, 7, 12, 17, 19, 23, 25, 34,
 37, 38, 40, 41, 57, 77, 78, 82, 84, 86, 87,
 91, 95, 96, 100, 101, 111, 114, 123, 125,
 127, 140, 141
− accessory gland 12, 145
− embryonic 2, 100
− female 17
− imaginal 84
− previtellogenic 37

217

molt(ing) 82, 86, 87, 95, 100, 108, 110, 111, 112, 131, 141
– imaginal 82, 87, 108, 110, 111, 112, 149
– metamorphic 112
monoamine oxidase 92
morphogenetic materials 8
morphogens 8
mosaic(s) 114
mosquito 41, 108, 113, 115, 121, 155,156
moth(s) 46, 51, 73, 74, 79, 142, 145
– bombycid 51
– *cecropia* 145
– gypsy 145
– saturniid 51
msP316 gene 153, 154
nsP355a,b genes 153, 154
mucopolysaccharides 88, 123
– neutral 146
mucoprotein 53, 88, 123
– cap 124
mucus 52
multivesiculate bodies 39
Musca 12, 37, 43, 77, 78, 90, 113, 155, 156
M. domestica 45, 106
muscle 37, 83, 85, 96, 124, 125, 133, 135, 143
– cells 37
muscular layer 145
muscular sheath 126, 146, 147, 150
musculature 82, 141
mutagenesis 19
mutant(s) 16, 19, 28, 41, 49, 61, 67, 78, 114, 120, 154, 155
– phenotype 16
mutations 19, 21, 22, 24, 26, 29, 30, 61, 62, 73, 78, 79, 93, 115, 151
– point 115
mycetocytes 98, 99
Myo D1 19, 20
– protein 20
myoblast 19
myogenically 135
myosin 81

N-acetyl-dopamine 92
(Na^+-K^+)-ATPase 40, 43, 120
Nauphoeta 35, 120, 121
N. cinerea 93, 103
neck cells 123
Nematocera 6, 8
Nematois metallicus 37
Nemophora 37
nerves 143
nervous system 19, 29
– central 89
– embryonic 19
– peripheral 19

neurogenesis 21
neurogenically 135
Neuroptera 34, 89
neurosecretion 74, 109
neurosecretory 113
– cells 82, 109, 133
– – brain 74
– – peptide 109
neurotransmitter 153
non-coding sequences 21
Northern blots 65
Notonecta 77, 81
nuclear division 6
nuclear oncogenes 19
nucleic acid(s) 57
– sequencing 57
nucleus/nuclei 6, 33, 37, 38, 41, 42, 59, 63, 76, 77, 85, 98, 99, 110, 119
numerator elements 17, 18, 20
nurse cell(s) 2, 3, 16, 33, 36 – 38, 41, 45, 71, 75 – 81, 124
– degenerating 36
nutrients 125
nutrition 109, 153
nutritional
– component 132
– status 109
nutritive
– contribution 125
– function 124
– role 124
nymph 9, 10, 13, 140, 141
nymphal stage 32
Nymphalis antiopa 145

ocelliless 61, 62, 63, 65
octopamine 83, 133, 135
Odonata 12, 13, 33
oenocytes 98, 100
oligosaccharide(s) 120, 121
– high mannose 121
Oncopeltus 6, 37, 77, 81, 84, 86, 112
O. fasciatus 104
oocytes 1, 2, 13, 16, 33 – 49, 51, 52, 71, 75, 77 – 81, 96, 97, 102, 108, 114, 115, 120, 121, 132, 149, 150
– penultimate 34, 35
– previtellogenic 34, 36
– subterminal 35
– surface 120
– terminal 13, 34, 35
– vitellogenic 35 – 38, 41
oogenesis 7, 24, 33, 48, 56, 58, 61, 67, 68, 75, 76, 77, 79, 150
– stages 7, 48, 56
oogonia 15, 34, 35, 37, 38
oogonial cells 38

oolemma 38, 40
ooplasm 7, 8, 80
oosome 8
oostatic hormone (OoH) 37, 109, 114
ootheca 82, 90−93
oothecal coverings 82
oothecal proteins 92, 93, 95
oothecin(s) 50, 91−94, 147
− gene(s) 50, 94, 95, 119
− iso- 93, 94
opercular cells 53, 54
organ cultures 149
organizing centers 78
organules 87
ornithine 144
Orthoptera 12, 13, 34, 87, 103, 108, 126, 140, 142, 144, 149
orthopteran 157
orthopteroid insects 5, 7, 9, 13, 82, 95, 126
Oryctes 51
Oscar (osk) 78, 79
ovarian sheath 15, 34
ovariectomy 100
ovariole 7, 15, 34, 35, 37, 38, 43, 75, 81
ovary 2, 3, 7, 13, 15, 24, 33, 34, 35, 36, 37, 38, 42−46, 63, 67, 70, 75, 76, 77, 78, 79, 80, 81, 82, 95, 99, 100, 109, 113, 114, 117, 118, 120, 123, 132, 149
− meroistic 2, 33−37, 42, 75, 77, 79
− − polytrophic 2, 33−38, 75−77, 80
− − telotrophic 2, 33−38, 75, 77, 80−82
− panoistic 2, 33, 34, 36, 37, 42
− specific element 117
− specific expression 118
oviduct 2, 3, 7, 13, 14, 15, 34, 82, 83, 84, 89, 133
− cells 83
− common 13, 14, 15, 82, 83, 89
− contractions 133
− lateral 7, 13, 14, 15, 82, 83
− median 14, 82
oviposition 49, 53, 56, 83, 89, 133, 139, 150, 152, 155
− inducing hormone 133
− stimulant 132, 144, 152, 155
ovipositor 14, 34, 82
ovoviviparous 92, 95, 107
ovulation 35, 53, 59, 151
− stimulating factor 152
2-oxyglutarate 144

palindrome 116
paragonia 11, 153
Paraneoptera 34
paravitellogenins 46, 120, 121
patency 38, 40, 41, 43, 120
paternal 132

pattern formation 1, 79
pedicel(s) 13, 14
P-element 22, 30, 65, 66, 70, 71, 74, 108
− mediated transformation 30, 65, 66, 71, 74, 116, 118, 140, 157
− transposon tagging 22
peptide(s) 83, 144, 151−156
− hormone(s) 113
per clock gene 79
perioocytic space 120
Periplaneta 5, 35, 38, 39, 43, 83, 86, 91, 93, 95, 98, 99, 108, 119, 120, 131, 132
P. americana 91, 104
peroxidase 49, 56
peroxide (H_2O_2) 153
Phaedon 51
phages 22, 65
phagocytic cells 124
phallic lobes 9, 10
Phasmida 12, 103
phenol oxidase 91, 92
phenylalanine 97
Philonthus 38
Phormia 8, 108, 113
P. terrae-novae 106
phosphoglycolipoprotein(s) 105
phospholipase 88
phospholipid 99
phospholipoglycoprotein(s) 102, 104, 105
phosphoprotein(s) 104
phosphorylated 102, 119
Pieris rapae 105
Pimpla 8, 80
pinocytosis 129
plasmid 25, 27, 65, 140, 157
plasticiser 128, 130
plastron 51
Plecoptera 12, 90
pleiotropic 111
Plodia interpunctella 46
polar disc 8
polar granules 6, 79
polar plasm 8, 78
polarity 16, 78
− antero-posterior 78
− axial 16
pole cells 6, 8, 78
− cytoplasm 6
− formation 8
poly(a)/polyadenylation 49, 59, 60, 77, 79, 117
− site 60, 117, 154
polyfusome 35, 38
Polyneoptera 34
polyploidization 37, 42, 43
polyploidy 37, 42, 43, 76, 77, 98, 99
polyprotein 153